THE ENTERPRISE YEARS

THE ENTERPRISE YEARS

A Businessman in the Cabinet

Lord Young

HEADLINE

First published in 1990
by HEADLINE BOOK PUBLISHING PLC

10 9 8 7 6 5 4 3 2 1

British Library Cataloguing in Publication Data

Young, David Young, Baron *1932–*
   The enterprise years.
   1. Great Britain. Politics – Biographies
   I. Title
   320.092

   ISBN 0-7472-0275-3

Typeset in 11/11½ pt English Times
by Colset Private Limited, Singapore

Printed and bound in Great Britain by
Richard Clay Ltd, Bungay, Suffolk

HEADLINE BOOK PUBLISHING PLC
Headline House
79 Great Titchfield Street
London W1P 7FN

To Stuart

for the tales and the years we were denied

and to my grandchildren
that they should someday know
that their Papa was once young at heart

Contents

Acknowledgements ix

Introduction 1

1. Emigration 3

2. Return to Reality 19

3. On the Job Training 35

4. Why Not Me? 49

5. Waiting 63

6. Chairman 73

7. Dawn Raid on Education 89

8. Problems and Solutions 103

9. Cabinet 115

10. Beveridge and Beijing 127

11. Back to Employment 141

12. Restart 153

13. Triumph and Tragedy 169

14. Manifesto Time 191

15. Election Campaign 205

16. The Special Adviser Returns 233

17. The Enterprise Initiative 247

18. The Rigours of Regulation 265

19. Rover's Return 285

20. Opportunities 303

21. Epilogue 323

Index 331

Acknowledgements

There are many to whom I owe thanks: to Keith Joseph for taking me on and for being my guide, mentor and above all friend, to Norman Tebbit for giving me my first chance and for the sheer fun of the early days and to Margaret Thatcher for the confidence and trust she always gave me; to my wife Lita and all my family for standing by me during the dark days and keeping me in touch with reality during the golden hours; to Sir Geoffrey Holland and Sir Brian Hayes for their friendship and support and to the countless civil servants who supported and befriended me over the decade; to all the colleagues who were ministers with me in all our departments and who had to put up with my many enthusiasms; to Margaret Bell and Norman Dodds for following me in my odyssey without complaint over all the years; to William Wellesley for checking the facts; to Jeffrey Archer for introducing me to my literary consultant, George Greenfield; to George for all his encouragement and advice; and finally to Peter Luff, my last Special Adviser, who enthused me with the idea of writing this book on the very first morning after leaving office.

Introduction

I grew up with two unspoken yet unshakeable assumptions about the future.

The first was the irresistible rise of socialism. Socialism had been spreading around the world since Karl Marx wrote *Das Kapital*. Indeed some argued that it had always existed and traced it back to Judeo-Christian sources. The only area of uncertainty left was how long this would take and whether socialism led to communism or vice versa. We even believed that it was a more efficient way of conducting the economy, despite all the evidence to the contrary.

I can remember during the sixties thinking that the United States would be the last refuge of an entrepreneurial society and that I might well have to end my days there. That was still my belief in those depressing, but happily now distant days during the mid-seventies when all did appear lost.

The other certainty was the inevitable decline of the United Kingdom. When I first went to school it seemed only right that London should be the largest city in the world, that our Empire should be the greatest the world had ever seen and that any map of the world should have the UK in the centre.

As I grew up and the war ended, I lost my certainty that God was an Englishman. As I entered college, I realised that we were poorer than the Americans, largely because we suffered more in the war, but at least we were far richer and more efficient than the continentals. After I left college and started work, country after country passed us by.

In the autumn of 1974, just after the last Arab-Israel war ended but before the first oil price rise, I went to the Hudson Institute in upper New York State, the home of the futurologist Hermann Kahn. One of his forecasts was that by the mid-nineties the prize for the lowest per capita income standard of living in the whole of Europe might well be shared by Albania and the United Kingdom.

What was so depressing (although I did not appreciate it at the time) was that when he produced this forecast, it caused no outcry, no letters of protest to *The Times* signed by 364 economists, no complaints at all. Perhaps we thought it a little exaggerated but in our hearts we knew that it was right.

The corporatism that started in the sixties and flourished during the seventies, encouraged by both political parties, seemed less and less relevant to my experience of life. Eventually even this failed and, in the view of many, the country became ungovernable. All this has changed. Socialism is seen to be a failed creed. Maybe something new will one day emerge and challenge our system but socialist parties around the world today are socialist in name only – unless they are in opposition.

We now accept that there is no inevitability about our decline. The future may be different, but for the last decade we have been making up some of the lost ground. Our progress should continue, but whether it does or not is today in our hands. It is our responsibility and if we fail it will be our fault.

I was there whilst these changes took place. I was part spectator, part bit player, and, on occasion, was given a speaking role. This is the story of those days.

Chapter 1
EMIGRATION

I woke with a start from a disturbed sleep. My wife Lita slept on but in the distance I could hear the wail of police sirens. We were in the Ritz Carlton, one of the better hotels in Boston. The night before we had gone to sleep in a sombre mood having arrived on the afternoon flight from London.

This was to be the first day of my new life in the States. I was no stranger to the East Coast; for many years I had had business interests there. This was to be a visit with a difference. This time we had come over to see if we should stay. It was still early in the morning, so I thought back over the last few years and the events that had made me, at forty-two, decide that the time had come to emigrate.

My paternal grandfather, Rehosh Yankalovich, had a similar idea about seventy years before. He was a shadowy figure to me for he died before I was eight years old. My father's eldest sister dictated a journal in her last years which paints an evocative picture of another world so far distant from our own. They lived around the turn of the century in a village called Yurevitch, near Mariapol in the county of Minsk in what is now Lithuania.

My aunt told of a single-storey house built in wood. She remembered a big hall with many doors, each leading to a separate apartment. The one they lived in had two rooms, one of which was almost filled by a huge stove on which the two children – for my father was now born – could climb up and sleep when the snow was high against the window.

My grandfather had a *Zavort*, or factory, just off the village square which made lemonade and other drinks. He was a very educated man and, as with most men of his learning in his community, he spent far more time studying than working. It was always my grandmother who had to work in the business. From what I have been told it was not a prosperous affair. These were troubled times, and my aunt recollected one occasion when they had to flee

3

in the middle of the night and watch many of the wooden houses in their village burning from afar. She suspected that there was some malevolent cause, but the reasons are now long lost. Life was not easy in this very rural community. My grandfather suffered greatly from bronchitis in the winter; it was long before houses in these areas would have baths and all the villagers would wash in the River Yemen, one place for the men and another for the women.

By 1905, when my father was still under five years old, they decided that the climate was too harsh for my grandfather's health. My great-grandfather had settled in London and in time, aware of their plight, he invited them to stay and even sent tickets for the ship. By then my father's younger brother was born so it was a family of six, including a niece they picked up on the way, that set out on their journey. My aunt recounts that, with no permit to leave, they had to smuggle themselves over the border. She does not remember how, but they enlisted the help of a friendly border soldier. In the middle of the night they slipped out of their lodgings, met the soldier, and crept quietly towards the border. They then had to cross a stream that marked the border under the very eyes of the border patrol. The soldier even carried the children across. The children, excited by the great adventure and soaked through, finally arrived safely in Germany. After this the journey to Hamburg was an anticlimax. There they boarded the ship to England.

I doubt whether ships of this type were ever inspected for either hygiene or safety. After an uncomfortable journey lasting two long nights and a day they sailed up the Thames into London under a bridge that actually opened to receive them. Their entire journey from Yurevitch had taken about a month. All my grandfather had when he arrived was a piece of paper with the address of his father. He must have been amazed at how many Englishmen spoke Yiddish, for he had come to the heart of the East End. That was the period when it was home for countless Jewish immigrants finding a haven of peace and safety from the turmoil and persecution of the Pale of Settlement in Russia.

My great-grandfather lived in Morgan Street in two rooms with his wife and three children. It was a market street, lined with stalls and very busy during the day. There they had a small shop with a bakery at the back. For the next three months they all lived together and my grandfather started work in the family bakery.

In time, with the aid of his family, he was able to start his own bakery. He found similar premises in Old Montague Street with a shop in front and a bakery behind. The life was hard. My grandmother used to open the shop at 4 o'clock every morning and not

4

close it until 2 o'clock the following morning six days a week. The Sabbath was of course a day of rest, for all the family were strictly orthodox Jews and life then centred around the synagogue.

The bakery business prospered and in time they would employ two bakers. Long hours were quite common. At one time there was a strike of all Jewish workers to reduce their working day to sixteen hours! The strike lasted some six weeks and was finally won by the workers.

Over the next few years their family expanded with my father having two more brothers and two more sisters. The business continued to prosper and my grandfather found that he could buy flour surplus to his own requirements and sell it at a profit to other bakeries. He gradually gained a reputation as a flour factor and soon found that he did better from this than the bakery.

By now it was 1914 and the war brought changes. Until then there was a pub on the corner of almost every street. They would open at 8 o'clock each morning and not close until the early hours of the next day. Drunkenness was endemic, and in an endeavour to help the war effort the Government introduced licensing. As if by magic much of the obvious drunkenness disappeared and many pubs closed.

One of these closed pubs was in Hanbury Street, also in the East End. About a year later my grandfather leased it, moved in with his family and opened an office on the ground floor as a flour factor. The bakery was given to another member of the family and this was the business that my father, as the eldest son, came into as soon as he was allowed to leave school. As soon as he was twenty-one he became naturalised and took the name Young.

My grandfather never shook off the bronchitis that would return each winter and gradually my father took over more and more of the business. Before long they had moved out of the East End altogether and bought a house in Stamford Hill. By the mid-twenties my father had taken up golf and gained an enthusiasm that never left him. He told me once how he bought his first car. He had never driven, and the salesman met him in Hyde Park with his new car and took him on one circuit of the park. Once completed, he left him to make his own way home through all the traffic. A far cry from the driving tests of today!

My parents met in the mid-twenties. My maternal grandfather came from Tilsit and established a leather business in Osborn Street in the East End where my mother worked after she left school. My parents married and set up home in Lingwood Road in Clapton Common.

5

I came along in the February of 1932. My early memories are few and the earliest I recall is playing ball in our garden and being told to hush as my mother had just given me a brother to play with. I remember that at the time I would have preferred to play ball!

I grew up with my brother Stuart in a close and warm family atmosphere. We had many cousins, for both our parents' families were large. We went to a local primary school and lived a typical lower-middle-class life. Eventually it became apparent even to us that something disturbing was going on. My parents would sometimes hold conversations that excluded us and seemed very worried, often by events in the newspapers. Distant cousins from the Continent began to appear on their way to the United States. Those who did not get out in time were never heard of again. Within a few years the very village my father came from was to be razed to the ground and all the inhabitants disappear.

A day or two before war was declared our school was evacuated. My brother and I, our gas masks in their regulation brown cardboard box slung over our shoulders, marched, with all our friends, two by two across Clapton Common to board a bus to an unknown destination. My mother walked by our side trying her hardest not to cry. We were too excited by this great adventure to even notice.

Our name ensured that it was always myself and my brother's fate to be at the end of the class. This occasion was to be no exception. When we reached our destination they found that they were two places short. As we were the last two in alphabetical order in our entire school we were taken off to another place and we never saw our school friends again.

But we were back in time for the Blitz and we spent the war mainly in London. My father's business disappeared in a plethora of wartime controls and he ended up making children's coats. We all moved to Finchley where we both went to school, but to different schools. Our father managed to ensure that, as often as possible, we rarely competed. Perhaps large families (my father was one of seven and my mother likewise) brought home lessons about sibling rivalries.

My father continued with his golf at Potters Bar Golf Club and from time to time we would walk around with him. On one occasion the sky was darkened for nearly an hour with aircraft towing gliders on their way to Arnhem. We celebrated the end of the war in Europe in a fitting manner: on VE day, having the day off from school, we played our first round of golf. Someone, I now forget who, gave us a set of old hickory shafted clubs. We shared the clubs and from that moment onwards we were hooked on the game.

After a while our habit of throwing clubs at each other came to my father's notice and we soon had a set each. Whilst my brother Stuart was still fourteen he shot two seventy-sevens round Moor Park in the Carris Trophy (the English Boys' Championship) and came third. I used to tease him ever after that it is given to few to peak at fourteen!

In my early teens I knew what I wanted to do, with a certainty that I was never to achieve again. I had become a keen photographer with my own primitive darkroom and I wanted to become a film director. As it happened my father had a very good friend who was high up in the Rank Film organisation. He arranged for me to have an interview with the union before starting a seven year apprenticeship. One day I came back from school to find my father waiting for me. His friend had telephoned. The Government had just abolished film quotas and allowed unrestricted admission of Hollywood films. As a result there was yet another crisis in our film industry. The interview had been cancelled.

I was at a loss for words. My father said to me that I had an uncle who was a solicitor; he would speak to him and see if I could become articled to him. In those days and in our circle sons tended to listen to their fathers. Not knowing what else to do I agreed. In time my father decided that my brother would become an accountant.

I left school with matriculation exemption. Not even my mother could claim that I had been a good pupil and it was with some surprise that the school noted that I managed to pass to a standard sufficient for the Law Society.

I now entered the mysterious world of a solicitor's office. School left me totally unprepared for the world of work which was all very exciting and more than a little worrying. My uncle Sol Teff was the senior partner in a medium sized firm of solicitors, Teff & Teff, in Bishopsgate. I soon found that I needed Latin and had to disappear to a crammer for three months. In a few months I had sufficient command of Latin only to forget it all just as efficiently after the exam. On my return I entered into articles for five long years. In those days we were not paid, but for the last year or so of my articles I was receiving no less than £1 per week.

By then my parents had left Finchley and moved to Brondesbury Park in Willesden. One morning in September 1951 I woke up with a great idea. I had just finished Law School and had no further examinations for three years. If I could take a law degree at University College I might be able to play golf for them. That morning, on the way to the office, I got off the Underground at Euston Square and called in, without an appointment, to the Law Faculty.

To my slight amazement the Dean of the Law Faculty saw me and told me that my matriculation exemption was sufficient. I was accepted for the next term.

That set the pattern for the next few years. I would work during the day as an articled clerk, leave the office at 5.30 for my evening lecture between 6 to 7.30 and then on to the library to study. This was four nights a week, and sometimes coming home I would run into Stuart who also studied late. My two weeks' annual holiday went each year in study leave before each exam. In the end I gained a law degree, and, far more important to me, I played golf for my university. I went through the agonies of being Secretary in my second year and the sinecure of captaincy in my last. I learned far more about life and people out of playing golf for my university than ever I learned reading law.

Some memories come back. I was once playing top game against a London club. My opponent was a rather good player. In the bar after the game he poured his heart out to me. When he had applied to join the club he put his occupation down as civil servant. As he had a low handicap there was no difficulty in joining. After a while it came out that he was the local tax inspector. From that day on he was shunned. 'When I come into the bar all conversation stops,' he complained to me. In my innocence I could not understand why.

In my last year I was taking a team to play the Scottish Universities. My problem was to find two cars – that is, two players of a sufficient standard with cars. This was 1954 when even fathers with cars were scarce, let alone students. I found the two and then there was another hitch. One of my drivers confessed that he was only taking the driving test on the very morning of our departure. We met with all our gear in Portland Place at 10 o'clock in the morning. Such is the sublime optimism of the young that I do not recall even contemplating what would happen if he failed. Finally he drove up grinning broadly. Then we set off to drive uncertainly to Scotland!

I passed my solicitors' finals. During my last year at London there had been much friendly rivalry between the army and the RAF. They both wanted to strengthen their golf teams and used to scour all the university golf teams for likely recruits. In the end I succumbed to the lures of the RAF. Ten weeks squarebashing as a maximum, I was promised, and then off to Germany to spend the remainder of the next two years on a golf course. It sounded heaven to me. When my call up papers came I gave notice to my employer and said goodbye to my friends.

I took the medical at West Drayton. The first culture shock was the intelligence test. It seemed simple enough; then the Instructor asked for all those who had difficulty writing their own name to put their hands up. To my horror four or five out of thirty did. I suddenly realised that I had been brought up in a tight, very narrow world. Everyone I knew took reading and writing as abilities you were born with. I had been an indifferent scholar – my degree was only a lower second – but I had finished the intelligence test in a few minutes and some of the others were still there forty minutes later. I went to my medical in a thoughtful mood.

I went from room to room to be prodded and poked to their evident satisfaction. I entered one room and a doctor, examining some records, asked in a very quiet worried voice, 'When were you last with a woman?' 'What?' I shrieked. 'Nothing wrong with your hearing then,' he said with a grin, 'next please.' I got to the end and went before a panel. 'I am sorry to tell you that you have failed,' I was told. My heart froze in panic. Had I some incurable illness? I asked myself. Is this the end? I plucked up courage and asked why. 'Flat feet' was the surprising answer. The more I protested that I played golf, that the RAF were expecting me, that they should telephone my contact, the more they remained adamant. I took my paper and went slowly home. All dreams of golf in Germany evaporated.

I went to work for a firm of solicitors in Piccadilly. I met Lita and we married. Lita had thought that she was marrying a solicitor, and so she was – but not for long. My cousin Ruth had married Leonard Wolfson (now Lord Wolfson of Marylebone) and at our wedding reception he asked me to see him on our return. As a result I gave up the law and entered The Great Universal Stores. I can still remember the great culture shock that I suffered during the first weeks of my new job.

I was put to work in a subsidiary company called Rego Clothiers on the North Circular Road. My entire training as an articled clerk and as a young solicitor had taught me to say no, to point out the drawbacks to any action. Now I was expected just to get on with it. I had not been there very long before I realised how much happier I was in a commercial environment than in the professional world. All those years I had been cramping my more entrepreneurial nature into a professional strait jacket.

I learned a great deal during the five years I spent with GUS. One day I received the call to come into the group head office in Tottenham Court Road. After a few months I found myself as an assistant to the Chairman, Isaac Wolfson (now Sir Isaac Wolfson Bt) known throughout the group, and in the popular press as well, as IW.

9

He was a formidable man. At that time approaching his sixtieth birthday, he was of medium height with a florid complexion and a full head of snow white hair. Indeed, in many ways he reminded me physically of my father but there the resemblance ended. As much as my father was a success as a man, business success always eluded him. IW had started his business in his native Glasgow, still kept his Scots accent and had built up in his lifetime the greatest mail order, departmental stores and retail group that the country had ever seen. At that time our profits were almost double those of Marks & Spencer. He had a magnetic personality and seemed to part charm, part hypnotise people into accepting his terms for almost anything he wanted.

My day would start just after 7 o'clock for IW would be in each day at exactly 7.15. We would first look at the post, and I would record the desired action, then at a quarter to eight the first appointment arrived. Every twenty minutes or so another suppliant (for he had extensive charitable interests), business rival, or senior executive of the group would arrive. I would make notes of what was required and this would carry on until 2 o'clock when to my great relief he would go home for a sleep. Then I would frantically carry out all my instructions until just after 4.00 p.m. when I would go round to his flat in Portland Place when it would start all over again. Some time after 8.00 p.m. his wife Edith would say 'Isaac, remember David has a wife and a home' and I would be let off with a broad grin.

He had a great capacity to inspire loyalty. If I ever did anything well he would put his arm around me and tell me how much the group owed to me. He had this great knack of always knowing exactly when I would want to speak to him about my salary, for then the praise would be the greatest and I would go home floating on air – until I realised that I had not raised the subject. I never managed to.

He taught me a great deal. At odd moments he would call me in and explain the inner workings and interpretations of balance sheets, often going through past triumphs and explaining what he first saw in the company and how it worked out in practice. At that time we were buying about two companies a week. These were always by agreement but this gave me a marvellous grounding in commerce.

I gained a great deal out of this experience. Firstly, the capacity to deal with many different problems one after the other. I would be dealing one moment with mail order, the next with Scotch whisky, then charity, then property. All had to be dealt with and soon I began to see the thread that runs through all commerce. Then he infected me with the excitement and the challenge of commercial life. It was exciting and held a fascination that has never left me. Finally I learned to dissociate personal money and business money. At a time when I did not possess £1,000 myself I was regularly dealing in hundreds of thousands or even millions for the group.

During this period I became friendly with one of our principal solicitors, Stanley Berwin. Stanley was a young partner in the City firm of Herbert Oppenheimer Nathan & Vandyk. Lord Nathan, the senior partner, would appear on occasion but all of the commercial work would fall to Stanley. He was a workaholic, an inveterate cigarette smoker, except in the company of IW, and a solicitor of immense ability and energy. He would often come in for instructions on a new acquisitions late one evening and then reappear at 7.30 p.m. the following morning with a thirty-page purchase and sale agreement. This was decades before copying machines, let alone word processors came into use. We became friends although I never quite aspired to his habit of getting the first train, just before five thirty each morning, from Hampstead station to the City.

We would meet socially and one evening over dinner I confided in him. My father-in-law was a property developer and like all developers required further funds for expansion. I asked Stanley if he knew of any possible investors who would be prepared to put up funds for expansion and take a share in the equity. He spoke to clients of his and found one who said that they would be interested. They were the trustees of the Gestetner family settlements and we arranged to meet. At their request I prepared a detailed proposal and they agreed to invest. A few days before the completion the trustees added one further condition: me. They would expect me to leave GUS and join the company.

Although it came as a bolt out of the blue I had been thinking of leaving for some considerable time. It was not that the work was not enjoyable – it was, but it was more than that. I was becoming increasingly irritated with colleagues of mine at work who would hesitate before taking decisions. They seemed to me to be more concerned not to be in a position where they could be blamed for anything than to take a decision. Time after time I would find simple decisions wait until confirmed by their superior. And then he would wait until his superior confirmed what to me was still a simple decision. I had this great desire to get out and take the consequences of my own mistakes. I knew nothing about property but here was the chance to get out into business for myself. I thought about it overnight and the next day I went to see Leonard

11

Wolfson. Once he heard that I was going to work for myself he did not stand in my way.

It was in March 1961 that I decided to accept and leave GUS. I had greatly enjoyed my time with them but I was now twenty-nine and it was time that I took the plunge. I had learned my lessons well and still thought in the scale of my previous job. But there was more culture shock. For years I had had at my command all the facilities of a large organisation. By the time I left I was used to pushing buttons and giving orders. Now my brother (for by now Stuart had qualified and started his own practice) let me share a room with his partner. I could use it when he was out. I had no one to give orders to since I was all by myself. The first time I persuaded Stuart's secretary to type a few letters for me I had to go down to the Post Office to buy the stamps. Yet I was happy. There was an exhilaration in working for yourself, in creating a company, in the sheer challenge of business that was far more than anything else that I had known.

It was not the money. Indeed I was far worse off, and remained that way for some years since I agreed not to draw a salary until the company was profitable. But in the end there is something very creative about building up an organisation, about doing something that has not been done before, at least not in that way.

There is a gap between generations that creates a different perspective that each generation has to relearn. After some months my father-in-law and I decided to part, at least in terms of business. He had been concerned with building new blocks of flats and I preferred to look in the commercial field. I looked for some time until one day my brother spoke to me. A client of his had acquired a recently defunct ironfoundry with a four-acre site on High Street Stratford. I went to see him and I persuaded him to give me a three months option to purchase the site, which was zoned purely for industrial uses.

I had some vague idea that it might be suitable for warehouse use and I instructed an architect friend to prepare plans. He suggested that it might help if we submitted an application for office use as well, since a rejection there might help to get the warehouse application through. I agreed and it was done. In due course we arranged to go down to West Ham to see the Planning Officer.

The council offices were rather derelict since, I was told, the authority was due to disappear in a few weeks in a local government reorganisation. The Chief Planning Officer had a resigned, 'seen-it-all-before' air. As soon as we sat down he tossed the application for office planning permission to one side and said, 'This should be all right, although I cannot think who on earth would want to build offices there.' We then carried on with a rather desultory discussion about the minutiae of the warehouse application. I paid scant attention. All I could think was, had I heard correctly? I did not want to reopen the subject and could scarcely wait until we were finished and out of the meeting. Yes, I had heard correctly.

For some reason our application missed the next meeting of the planning committee but we did make the one after. We had our planning permission for a large office block with just seven days to spare before my option expired. Then I found that my new partners were unpersuaded of the value of an office permission to the east of the City. Nor were their valuers. Finally, with just twenty four hours to go I managed to persuade both.

I advertised the building as being less than four miles from the Bank and at a rent well under half of City rents. In the end I never built the building, but another developer did and he arranged for the Prudential to take a 125-year building lease at a very substantial ground rent as part of a financing package. I was able to mortgage the freehold for over half a million pounds. This gave me enough capital to build up the business.

One day another friend came to me. He had just bought a small public company called The Ashton Vale Iron Company. Its only asset was a seventeen-acre site just outside Bristol and it was for sale. I went down to look with Gerry Hirst, a surveyor who was now my first employee. Those were the days before the M4 and the drive to Bristol took many hours, not helped by Gerry driving in his new Triumph. By the time we got there we were both tired and fed up. We went on to a derelict site with a pit four acres in area, another four acres covered by a shale heap, some derelict buildings with broken windows and missing roofs and two mine shafts over 700 feet deep. At one point I took one end of a surveyor's tape and Gerry climbed down into the pit. The tape ran out before he got to the bottom. In disgust I asked to be taken to the station. Later that evening a tired Gerry rang me at home and said that there may be more to the pit than appeared at first sight.

Ashton Vale told the story of the industrial revolution. The great pit bore mute testimony to the one time workings for iron ore and the shale heap was all that was left of the coal mine workings. The ore and the coal had been mined and an iron works flourished. When the deposits ran out they all closed. All that was left was zoning for industrial use, and whilst the land was not expensive the engineering problems were formidable. Over the years we were to tip the shale into the pit, cap the mine shafts, clear the site and

13

create a modern trading estate of over sixty factories of varying sizes.

But as a result I did find my niche. At that time the old warehouses, built at the time of the expansion of the railways in city centres near rail termini, were rapidly becoming inefficient through traffic congestion. Now the new motorways were being constructed and I reasoned that it would be far more efficient for the warehouses to be there. We built standard units and concentrated on building the new estates near the motorway intersections. We even advertised 'Most Motorways lead to Eldonwall' and could claim to be the first to launch a proper advertising campaign in my industry.

I branched out into construction, plant hire, retail and manufacturing as well. Some did well, and some did not, but I learned from them all. By 1970 I had probably expanded further than I should on my existing capital base. It was anyway time for a change. I commenced negotiations to sell my company to Town & City Properties Ltd, in those days one of the leading property companies.

At the crucial meetings my brother Stuart would appear. He had become a consummate negotiator, with an ability to bluff that was part genius part ham. Given a rather weak hand he inferred that I was awarding an enormous benefit by parting with the company for what they offered. They agreed, I conferred that benefit and became part of a large group. Within a few months I joined their board.

But even during that exciting period I had been busy with other things. We had been brought up in a fairly conventional Jewish household. Our parents impressed two things on both of us. One was that we must study. Our mother used to tell us time after time that if we did not we would not have the money for a hawker's licence. I never did find out what a hawker's licence was, but the spur was sufficient to ensure that we both ended up with professional qualifications. The other was to put something back – not just to take but to give. Both Stuart (whilst he was busy building up a very successful accountancy firm) and I gradually came to spend more and more of our time in voluntary activities.

But politics was not one of them. My interest in politics had been scant. I was an uncommitted Labour supporter during the fifties because in my innocence I still believed that planning worked. Later, when I realised that it did not none of the parties seemed to talk of the world I lived in. Their world was one in which wealth creation was a dirty word and somehow people thought that the wealth that our society needed to look after the less fortunate was created by Government. I felt by instinct that it was not.

14

When Ted Heath paraded Selsdon man, I perked up: Here, at long last, was the realisation that the wealth of a nation has to be created by its citizens and not by its government. That the role of that government is to create conditions in which people, call them entrepreneurs or what you will, can flourish. There was even an acceptance that the power of the state had a limit: that the state was not there to create wealth, but only to create the climate for wealth creation. The 1970 election seemed to bring a ray of hope to us all. Here was a chance to get going again, for my business travels had made me realise just how far we were beginning to slip behind all our competitors.

Alas, at the first sign of trouble it all evaporated. Gone went the idea of an entrepreneurial society and in came the corporate state with a vengeance. There was no one that I knew on the CBI and few if any of our employees were ever members of unions. What had they to do with my world? Worse still was the mad dash for growth created by the new policies. Instead of the creation of real wealth for our society we had manipulation and asset stripping. It all ended in tears with the secondary banking crisis and the stock exchange crash.

But long before then I had left the active management of the company. Because of considerable policy differences (I was being uncharacteristically cautious) I agreed with Barry East, the Chairman, that I should go non-executive. That was at Christmas 1972 and then followed the most depressing year of my life. I was comfortably off and I thought that any more money would be bad for my children. Was there more challenge to life than money making? What else should I do?

I had flirted with the idea of undertaking some public service, and I had been approached with the suggestion that I become the Chairman of British Rail Property Board. I had a number of meetings with Sir Richard (now Lord) Marsh. I decided to accept and arranged to meet him to tell him. The weekend before one of the Sunday papers led with an exposé of alleged corruption. Although I was in no way involved, indeed I had never met any of the parties mentioned, I suddenly realised that, such was the atmosphere of the times, I would stand no chance as a former property developer. I thought about it overnight and then refused.

Over the years Jeffrey Sterling had become a good friend. We had met many years before when he was a blue button on the stock exchange. A few months after I left GUS he came to see me and asked if he should join IW. At the time I said no, but he did, and like me, learned a great deal. Years later when he started his own

15

company, Sterling Guarantee Trust, I worked with him. I looked at the property content of the first few acquisitions that he made. That was at the end of the sixties and when I went to Town & City Properties we continued our association.

One day he came to me and told me that they were considering making a bid for Gamages, the department store in Holborn. When he did I agreed terms on behalf of Town & City to acquire the site in a new joint venture company to carry out the redevelopment. The original scheme that Col Seifert, the architect, submitted had great architectural merit – and was promptly turned down by the planners. As the site straddled both the City and Camden what pleased one set of planners annoyed the other. It took many years, and no less than seventeen different schemes, before the planners were satisfied. I for one thought that each scheme submitted was inferior in architectural merit. What did increase each time was the eventual cost.

This first venture was speedily followed by a number more. Earls Court, Olympia, Buck & Hickman; the pattern was set and it was an exciting time. At the end of this series of deals we both thought that, as Earls Court and Olympia were going to be redeveloped, we should go on a tour of the conference centres of the Far East. We arranged to leave in November.

We were due to fly on a Monday to Singapore. I went into the office first and my stock broker telephoned me. Town & City were at 116p he said, and they will be 125p before Christmas. 'Good,' I said, 'let me sell some', and I gave a selling order at 125p. After I put the phone down I said to my secretary that I was being greedy and if I wanted to sell I should sell now. 'Get him back,' I asked. His line was engaged. I left for the airport and tried to telephone him from the lounge. His line was still engaged.

The long flight out was tedious so Jeffrey Sterling and I played chess. Before long we had a small crowd watching us. By the third game the crowd included the Chinese cabin staff and some Chinese passengers. One of the spectators asked us what we were playing for! Our chess is not up to a high standard, certainly not worth watching and we both realised what was going on at the identical moment – our spectators were gambling on the result and assumed that we were. We put away the chess board.

Running out of reading material I calculated a list of my assets and liabilities. My liabilities were only about 8 per cent of my assets. As soon as I arrived in my hotel in Singapore I telephoned London. We had flown through Black Tuesday and the market had broken. Town & City were about 90p. In Hong Kong, Tokyo and Manila I would telephone London. The slide continued.

16

Within a few months of my return my liabilities actually exceeded my assets. One day I woke up with renewed purpose and vigour. I knew what I had to do. I had to get back to work. My depression evaporated.

Then we had the two elections of 1974 and now had a Labour Government back again. This time it seemed even more doctrinaire. Shirley Williams embarked on a gigantic experiment in social engineering and restructured the school system into comprehensive. Hardly anyone noticed that all the technical schools were being eliminated.

That was not all. Michael Foot, as Employment Secretary, was talking about introducing legislation to bring all employment within five miles of the River Thames under the control of the Transport & General Workers' Union. My new joint venture with Manufacturers Hanover, the American bank, was held up by bureaucracy in Washington and I could see no future for any of us at home. So we had decided to try Boston where I had some friends. And now we were at the Ritz Carlton. We got up and went down for breakfast. I thought the waiters acted rather nervously and in the background there was still the sound of police sirens.

After breakfast we went to walk across the common. The sun was shining, it looked a nice day and my first appointment was not until later. As soon as we went outside the racket became very apparent. There was the acrid smell of tear gas in the air. It was the first Monday of the school bussing riots and it seemed as if the whole city was at war. As we walked across the common Lita said that she could not see us leaving all the family for this. Nor could I.

We returned by the night flight. It is only a few hours back from Boston and in September the nights are still short. I could not sleep and watched the sun come up. If I could not leave I had to make the best of it. 'Don't moan,' I thought to myself, 'do something.'

But what?

Chapter 2
RETURN TO REALITY

We returned to London. I went back to the rather luxurious offices that Manufacturers Hanover Trust, the American Bank, had provided for me in Brook Street, overlooking Grosvenor Square. Our discussions to create a joint company to undertake real estate financing ran deeper and deeper into the morass of the regulations of the Federal Reserve Board in Washington. We seemed to make no progress and the few loans we made were on a provisional basis. Progress eventually stopped and in the end we gave ourselves until the end of 1975. If we did not get the consent through we would unscramble the few loans we had made. I would then have to find something else to do. In early November I was in Dallas when I received a phone call. With only a few weeks in hand, the Federal Reserve Board came through with their consent. I took the next flight back to London and we very quickly agreed the legal formalities. I sat back and waited for the board meeting of the bank to ratify the arrangement.

A day or two later Harry Taylor, the head of the bank in London, telephoned me. He told me that the Chairman of the board of Manufacturers Hanover, Gabe Hauge, was in China. Following the visit of President Nixon to Beijing, China was just beginning to open up as the Cultural Revolution gradually faded from the scene. Chairman Mao was in decline although he was still to be seen from time to time swimming in the Yangtzee. As part of this new policy Gabe Hauge had been invited as part of a small group on a tour of China. Harry told me that he would be coming out through Hong Kong and he thought that it would help if, by any chance, I happened to be there and we met.

I required no further encouragement and I took an early flight out, arriving in Hong Kong the morning before Hauge was due. After I checked in to the Mandarin Hotel I asked the concierge for a car and a driver who could show me around. Within the hour I went out on a tour of Hong Kong and the New Territories desperately

19

memorising all that I was told. The following day we met. Gabe Hauge turned out to be a rather piratical looking figure with a black eye patch but who was, in reality, a charming and cultured man. He was accompanied by his wife and I took them both on the full tour. I would say 'around the next bend you will see . . .' and crossed my fingers that we would. We ended up at the Repulse Bay Hotel, now long since gone, for tea. Afterwards he presented me with a copy of Mao's little red book. For years to come I would show this to my friends and say solemnly that it was presented to me by the Chairman himself!

About ten days later Harry rang and told me that it had gone through without a hitch. I was told that when my name came up Hauge merely said that he did not know what I knew about real estate but I was certainly an expert on Hong Kong! I then settled down and found again all the old excitement of creating a new business. This time it was to be something entirely new.

It had started some years earlier when I was still with Town & City Properties. The bank had wanted to start lending on property but decided not to do so until they had a partner. Discussion started with Town & City Properties but when I became non-executive Barry East discontinued the negotiations. In the middle of 1973 Harry Taylor of the bank rang me up and asked me if I would join with them in the venture in my personal capacity. I would become an equity partner with the bank and would guarantee my proportion of the loans. I agreed all the terms within a few weeks, but I was then to find out all about the delays involved with American bureaucracy.

I was keen to start because I could put into practice the very matter on which I fell out with Barry East. I argued that commercial property had no intrinsic value and it was only worth the value of its secure income. Therefore we would lend a multiple of the secure income and not bother with any valuations. On that basis we started our joint venture and over many years there was never a need to write off one penny of any loan.

All that would take time to prove. Now I had one large embarrassment. When I had originally discussed the arrangements with Harry Taylor of Manufacturers Hanover I had been in a very different financial position. To show my confidence in the new business I had offered to take no salary, at least until the new company had proved itself. Although the market had collapsed, and taken with it all my assets, I did not feel that I could reopen our discussions. I had substantial financial liabilities to meet (at least these days they now seemed very substantial), a growing family to keep, and no income to do it all with. My arrangement with the bank would allow me to do other things so I looked around to see what I could find.

There was nothing to do in the United Kingdom. The market was shell shocked and we had a government that was rapidly showing its incompetence to even understand what was going on. I took a chance and on impulse went over to the United States. New York was also in trouble and was going through a very bad period. It hovered on the brink of bankruptcy for month after month and business activity was also depressed. But there was a whole world of difference between a depressed market in the United States and in the United Kingdom. There were opportunities and I started to look around.

My old company, Town & City Properties, was now in considerable financial trouble. They had assets in Boston and I negotiated a sale for them. I found other situations and before long would spend five to ten days a month on the other side of the Atlantic. I actually visited over forty states during that period and discovered middle America and began to appreciate the great strengths of the people.

On one occasion I was interested in an industrial estate in one of the cities in the Gulf of Mexico. I flew to Miami on the Sunday to meet my associates. They left a message for me telling me that they would meet me the following day on the site. Very early on the Monday morning I caught a flight that landed at every small airport en route. I was too sleepy to pay much attention but eventually appreciated that as passengers would come on board they would be eagerly questioned about a hurricane. Hurricane?, I thought. Now, one of the benefits of having been brought up in Britain is that you never consider the elements dangerous. I was now finding otherwise and questioning on my part revealed that Mobile, Alabama, was right in the path of the storm.

We landed at about 11 o'clock. The airport was packed with people clamouring for a flight out. The arrivals side was deserted and there were no taxis and all the buses had stopped. I stopped a truck and for $20 hitched a ride in to town. The clouds were low and sullen. It had started to rain heavily and there was the ominous calm that is supposed to precede the storm. I went to my hotel and found that I was now the only guest left. Everyone else had left town, including my friends. There was a message waiting for me. If you get this we am very sorry, it said, but we assume that you know about the hurricane and cancelled the trip. We have left town and will be back when it is all over.

I sat in the deserted bar and ordered a large drink. All the staff

21

were busy taping brown paper strips over the windows, reminding me of wartime London. The announcer on television spoke in a funereal voice and seemed to be enjoying every moment of it. The storm was heading our way and would strike in another three hours. When announcing the speed of the winds he would bring in another expert who would become technical and only confuse me all the more. I ordered a second drink when the phone went, and it was for me. It was my business associates and before I could complain they told me that they had not yet left town and would pick me up in twenty minutes. They had their own plane. By the time we took off, on what was probably the last flight out, the eerie calm had gone and gusting winds were reaching sixty miles an hour. I never went back, for the hurricane largely demolished the industrial estate we had come to see.

During that rather nerve-racking period I found enough to do in the States to cover all my mortgage obligations and pay for my family until the new company with the bank had prospered sufficiently to pay me a salary. Then I stopped travelling hopefully. In future I would only go when I knew that there was something to do for my joint venture with the bank. It was a difficult period and one I would rather not go through again, but it had its challenge. I learned something about myself, and also about the importance of persistence in commercial life.

But despite all my travels I still had outside interests. I had become interested in an organisation called ORT – the Organisation for Rehabilitation through Training. It had been started nearly a hundred years before in St Petersburg by a number of wealthy Jews to help their distressed coreligionists learn a trade to enable them escape from the Pale of Settlement in Russia where they were confined. Over the following nine decades it had expanded all over the world and at that time operated in some twenty two countries. In addition it ran technical assistance programmes all over the Third World at the behest of the World Bank and the various national aid organisations. But my interest was confined to helping them raise funds in the UK and I had recently become Chairman of the UK organisation.

Max Braude was the Director-General of the World ORT Union. He was a onetime American Rabbi who served with the American forces in Europe and was amongst the first to enter the camps. What he saw there kept him in Europe for the rest of his life, and he was one of those instrumental in helping countless displaced persons start a new life in the months after the war, in either Palestine or the USA.

He was a charismatic personality with a deep, barely intelligible voice. One day he rang me up and grunted in his inimitable manner that no one in the world is too important not to be able to take a week off. I replied that I was certainly not too important and I could always take a week off. On the spot I agreed to come with him to Israel to, as he put it, 'see the schools'.

That week changed my life. We stayed in Tel Aviv and would start at about 7 o'clock each morning and not return until 8 or 9 each evening. We went up to the Lebanon border and down deep into the Negev desert. I saw established schools up to the best modern standards and I saw new schools in huts in settlements. I saw schools in slums, schools in good areas, Arab schools and religious schools. Some were apprenticeship centres and some were adult training institutes. There were schools for the deaf and for the disabled. They all had one factor in common – they concentrated on vocational education.

Now I remembered my own education. I went to Christ's College in Finchley, a grant maintained school in the state system. There were Hendon Grammar, Woodhouse (where Stuart went) and other schools. There was also Hendon Tech. No one went there. We looked down on the technical school and knew that most, if not all, left at fifteen, at least until the leaving age was raised.

What technical education they provided was reserved for carpentry and elementary metal bashing. The schools I was now seeing considered themselves as good as any. They included a general education but the technical element included electronics and not a few of the graduates went on to further study. Many of the pupils were considered drop-outs by their previous schools – now they walked tall.

Far more important than even this was the clear indication that many young people, who just did not benefit from academic schools, came alive in these establishments. I began to realise that academic education was not for all; that the human condition is that many of us are pragmatic beings and will learn when we know the reason why or what for.

I returned to the UK with much to think about. From that moment on I spent rather more time on the affairs of ORT, eventually heading the Administrative Committee of the World ORT Union. But at the same time I was also painfully aware that at home we were going in exactly the opposite direction. The reforms being pushed through by Shirley Williams were trying to transform the entire school system into an academic one. The secondary modern schools and the technical schools were all disappearing and being merged with the grammar schools into the new monster comprehensive. It simply did not tie up with what I now knew, but I could do little about it.

My job kept me travelling the world. I would be in the United States every month, the Far East almost quarterly and, on occasion, the Gulf states. The Gulf was a particularly interesting area: at that time it was enjoying the first flush of the oil price rise boom and resembled nothing more than an enormous building site. Such was the demand that rented accommodation for expatriates had reached impossible heights.

One of my clients came to an arrangement with a relation of one of the ruling families to develop a parcel of his land for rented accommodation. He did all the work and just when all the houses were finished the local partner sent a message that he would buy the property back. My client thought the deal was a good one until he saw the price – it was just under cost. When my client protested and said that their agreement provided for any sale at a far higher price, his local partner said nothing. The next day my client's most important director had his work permit cancelled, and he was on the plane back to the UK. The following day the same happened to his site agent. My client went to his partner and sold out at cost. I learnt one great lesson which stood me in good stead in the months to come, the importance of only dealing in countries where the rule of law prevails.

Wherever I went I noticed that, all too often, the companies were being run by entrepreneurial Britons. That applied all over the Gulf, often even in the States, and especially in Hong Kong. Whenever I discussed matters with them I would find that they simply wanted to better themselves and their families but the confiscatory tax system in the UK would not let them. How could you save out of earnings if taxes shot up to 83 per cent – and to 98 per cent on dividends? People could still make money at home, and I had found a way – but not to earn it.

There seemed to be a myopia that blurred successive governments' vision. I used to argue that we needed a system common to the majority of industrialised nations that would allow a person to save out of his earnings, that would give the incentive for people to better themselves and their families. Instead, the prevailing attitude of the Labour Government was to stop people earning. We were caught up with notions about the redistribution of wealth, forgetting the need to create it in the first place. Even the last Conservative Government had been little better.

I took my family that year to Florida on holiday. One day we went through Fort Lauderdale and we stopped to explore. There were boat cruises being advertised, inviting people to see the houses of the rich. And they went, not in a spirit of envy but almost saying there, next year if I do better I will be there. I thought of the differences at home. Anybody who did well would hide it, for unless you won the pools or were a pop star money was almost theft.

My travels also made me painfully aware that our reputation was going down in the world. This was hard to notice at home for living standards had undoubtedly improved over the last twenty years – but not at the pace of the Continent, the United States or Japan. We, once so proud of being world leaders, began to subside into a kind of genteel poverty. We deluded ourselves for years that America might be richer, that the Germans might work harder but we had the better quality of life. Alas, what became very apparent as time went on was that this was no longer so.

In schools on both sides of the Atlantic the date of 1776 is remembered, but for very different reasons. Every American pupil celebrates the date of the Declaration of Independence as their liberation from colonial rule. Over here, for obvious reasons, it is less well known. After all, the loss of our Empire in the West is not really a cause for celebration. However, I believe that the date and the decade should be one to be remembered and celebrated, not only on our side of the Atlantic, but all over the entire developed world. This was the decade that started off the Age of Enterprise. What happened on our side of the Atlantic had far more effect on the world than the efforts of the early colonists in the Americas in throwing off the colonial yoke.

Whilst all London was absorbed in the loss of our Empire in the West changes were taking place, unnoticed by King and Ministers, all over the new United Kingdom. The industrial revolution was beginning to stir in the land and the advance guard of the new revolution – the entrepreneurs – were there in plenty. They came from all social classes and from all parts of the country – from the Duke of Bridgewater to the carpenters and blacksmiths who were our first engineers and machine builders. The Quakers were especially well represented: Lloyds, Barclays and Cadbury's remain household names to this very day. Why that should be is a matter of conjecture but legal restrictions on their other activities, their practical education and their religious convictions may explain their enterprise. We see parallels today in some of the newer minority groups.

Many entrepreneurs started, as they do today, from home.

Samuel Unwin, a large mill owner from Nottingham, built himself a new mansion in 1788. He left 'the best rooms to be occupied as a warehouse for his cotton manufactory'.

Of course there were many factors that came together. Newly discovered resources, a rising population and a developing middle class all played a crucial role, but it was the entrepreneurs that brought all these advantages together. Peter Mathias, the historian, said that they were the 'shock troops of historical change'. Innovators and inventors such as Brunel and Stevenson illustrated that they had to be organisers and managers as well as risk-takers.

Today we forget the sheer speed of growth in the century after 1776. Between 1815 and 1850 our yearly output of iron increased eightfold to two million tons and coal production tripled to fifty million tons. In just eighteen years over 5,000 miles of railways were laid. Britain produced half of the world's cotton, one third of its energy and dominated world trade. Our income and product per capita was double that of western Europe.

All this was achieved by the small firm. The great corporations were yet to evolve. The average textile firm employed less than one hundred employees. Progress was spontaneous and happened all over. There was no push from public spending, no drive from imported capital, above all no planners and precious little government. But we did have the entrepreneurs.

As we expanded at home, so did we overseas. We consolidated our position in Africa, we controlled Australia, New Zealand and Canada. In India we took province after province. Finally Disraeli made Queen Victoria Empress of India in 1876. Just a hundred years after we lost our Empire in the West we acquired an even greater Empire.

A new empire requires new skills. Administrators are anything but entrepreneurs. Gradually, but surely, the antithesis of enterprise – a strong contempt for trade – was growing. The children of industrialists and inventors were painlessly absorbed into the land-owning gentry. Even Isambard Kingdom Brunel sent his two sons to Harrow. The urge for enterprise was submerged in a search for stability. The numbers engaged in the main professions increased sharply and their very spirit was antagonistic to enterprise. They claimed expertise and integrity in an attempt to rise above the market place, to regulate and limit competition.

In education, public schools resisted teaching science which was seen as inferior to classics. If it was taught at all it was pure rather than applied, for science was seen as having the great disadvantage of some association with vulgar industry and, even worse,

commercial utility. Vocational preparation carried with it the stigma
of industry. The world of business was openly disparaged in the
new public schools. *Tom Brown's Schooldays* describes business as
'mere money making'. Some careers were exalted – the military,
politics, the civil service, the church and the professions. These
beliefs and prejudices became crucial, not just because the public
schools took a central place in the lives of the establishment but
because the new state system was being modelled on them and
absorbed their values.

It was not just the schools; Oxbridge reflected a similar set of
values. It might not have mattered so much if these attitudes were
universal. The United States and Germany, unlike Britain, did not
rely on the brilliant amateur or gifted mechanic. In Germany a
systematic education in science and technology met the needs of the
chemicals, dyestuffs and electrical industries. The new technology
of electric power and the key industry it created was a good
example. Initially demand was stronger in Britain than in the
United States. Not only were we soon overtaken but by 1914 we
actually had a deficit with the poorer Germany. Siemens, the largest
German giant, now had eight times as many employees as our
largest company.

The industrial world was spreading. When Birmingham University decided to establish a degree in Commerce to train the sons of
local manufacturers it attracted more Japanese and other foreign-
ers than local students. By the twenties, when Birmingham firms
were far wealthier than their Japanese equivalents, the largest
donor to the new Chair of Commerce was Mitsui. The proportion
of graduates in Japanese senior management was already higher
then than it was in British management until very recently.

All this affected our industrial structures. Our industry was based
on the family firm but prevailing attitudes often ensured that they
were milked as cash cows by third or fourth generation owners who
often had little connection with the business. Even where this was
not the case it was easier to avoid innovation and re-equipment.
Trade associations sought to close down competition by agreeing
prices and segmenting markets. Amalgamations often maintained
the status quo at the expense of efficiency.

Such behaviour did not merely reflect narrow self interest. Successive governments encouraged market sharing and increased
regulation of the market as human guarantees of regular employment at higher wages, despite their disastrous long term effect on
income and wealth creation. These attitudes were encouraged by
the new perception that the Industrial Revolution was the period in

27

which humanity was sacrificed for profit. The very word 'Victorian' became pejorative. In fact living standards improved considerably during the second half of the nineteenth century but later perceptions would have it otherwise. Finally it was seen that the cruder instincts of capitalism had been tamed and replaced by patrician attitudes.

All this had a price and we paid it. Before long we had lost our dominant industrial position. Our share of world production fell from 32 per cent in 1870 to 14 per cent at the outbreak of the First World War. During this entire period our average yearly growth of output was a mere 0.9 per cent p.a. with Germany a third more and the United States double ours. We started that period top in the ranking of productivity. We were overtaken by the United States in 1880, by Sweden between the wars, by France and Germany by 1960, Italy around 1970 and Japan in the late seventies.

A slowdown in comparison with our principal competitors was, perhaps, inevitable. The UK economy did experience growth but, taken as a whole, there was a failure of innovation and development. We simply did not rise to the new challenges. Our traditional industries, faced with German and American competition, merely switched to less competitive Empire markets. Our lack of innovation came through in our failure to develop new industries in the emerging chemicals and electrical sectors as fast as our competitors.

All these failures continued well into the twentieth century. Few noticed the problems immediately after the Second World War. I remembered going to a lunch in the early seventies and feeling a chill run down my spine as I heard C. P. Snow describe the fifties and the sixties as 'the Golden Age for upper middle class Western man'. The growth of the world economy carried all along. The United Kingdom continued on its slow relative decline, sliding gently, or perhaps more appropriately 'genteelly', towards the bottom of the income per head tables of our European neighbours.

By the middle of the seventies inflation had risen so that money was halving in value every three years. Some forecasters were beginning to compare us to Albania by the beginning of the next century. Our Chancellor of the Exchequer had to return home from Heathrow and call the International Monetary Fund to London. We had achieved Third World status and it was exactly one hundred years since Disraeli made Queen Victoria Empress of India.

The Conservative party had elected a new leader a year or so before. I had taken very little interest in the outcome and even less when Keith Joseph had withdrawn and Margaret Thatcher won. I shed no tears for Ted Heath after the way his last government had gone, but I did think that in selecting a woman their chances would be even slimmer.

One day I read a speech of Margaret Thatcher's and began to look out for what she was saying and for Keith Joseph as well. Here at last, I began to think, was something I could understand. Here was the realisation of the limitations of government and a disavowal of the corporate state. Here was the acceptance that wealth has to be created before it can be spent, that it was people that matter not institutions.

I remembered my journey back from Boston and wondered how I could meet either of them. As part of my fundraising for ORT* I had instituted some years before an Annual Business Lunch where a prominent personage would address the company. Jeffrey Sterling offered to get Keith Joseph and in due course we met. The lunch went very well and certainly Keith pleased his audience. He spoke of the need for entrepreneurs, for the creation of new businesses, for the need to end dependence on the state. After lunch I said to him that I would like to volunteer to help him. 'Why?' he replied, 'you don't believe.'

I was quite taken aback, and not knowing how to reply I merely mumbled, 'Why not try me?' A week or two later I went to meet Keith Joseph at his office at the Centre for Policy Studies. The CPS was at 8 Wilfred Street, just behind Victoria Street. It is an old, rather rickety building, and a far cry from my rather lush office off Grosvenor Square. Keith had a fairly small office on the first floor. We talked about my experience with the planning system and we spent some time discussing ways in which it could be improved. Keith was thoughtful, intense, and had a rather disconcerting habit of often saying 'Why?' to any statement I might make. Over the years he certainly taught me to think before making any provocative statements. We parted agreeing to meet soon and over the months and years to come I became a frequent caller at the CPS.

Keith had embarked on a programme of speaking to universities and schools about the need for wealth creation. He put it simply. Britain needed more millionaires. At the time that was a heretical belief. The creation of wealth was still not socially acceptable, thought divisive and represented greed. Keith brought home the simple truth. The state creates nothing but the climate for enterprise; the rest was up to them. He was howled down at meeting after meeting but gradually the message came home.

* The Organisation for Rehabilitation through Training, an international network of vocational schools.

29

The presiding genius of the Centre for Policy Studies was Alfred Sherman. Alfred had been a communist in his youth, and one who had put his beliefs into action by fighting in the Spanish Civil War. He had since seen the light and was now very free market orientated. It was alleged that he had written the speech that Keith delivered that was responsible for Keith's withdrawal from the leadership campaign. He would come out, from time to time, with the most outrageous statements that always had more than a kernel of truth. He had a great gift for a telling phrase, but, like many very clever people, never knew where to draw the line between the principle and the practice.

After a while Keith Joseph put me on a party policy committee considering future policy for town planning. It was chaired first by Tim Raison and later by Hugh Rossi. We met very often and drafted some recommendations that were, I thought, rather splendid. However I suspect that they were more radical than the party was yet prepared to contemplate at the time, for they went into a pigeon hole and were never acted on or even heard of again.

In the meantime my business affairs prospered. I no longer needed to live from hand to mouth and had given up travelling monthly to the States. I even established a housebuilding company that did quite well. I bought a subsidiary company from Cubitts whose chairman was Tony Greenwood (Lord Greenwood of Rossendale). I asked him to continue and he agreed. I found him a delightful person and through him I gained an insight into some of the rivalries of political life. The name of the company was changed to Greenwood Homes and he continued until his death a few years later. One day I was with him in his room at the Lords. He was the Chairman of the Scrutiny Committee on Common Market legislation. I little thought what impact that would have one day on my life.

The affairs of the Government of the day did not prosper, and they began to look less and less likely to last. Pacts with the Liberals gave them a little more time but it did begin to appear that there was a good chance of a change.

One day a former business partner of mine, Martin Barber, came into the bank with what seemed to me at first to be a crazy idea. He had the concept of using small prefabricated buildings, Portacabins, that when put together would create small workshops. These would not be more than about 500 square feet or so, more like a double garage. Now I had been building factories for years and I thought that I knew the market and I thought that it was nonsense. He thought that local authorities would grant licences for say seven years and we could create small industrial estates consisting of temporary workshops. The figures made sense but in the end it did not work because it was possibly more difficult to persuade a local authority to grant a licence for seven years than to purchase the site outright. In any event he would still have to obtain planning permission.

One fact amazed me: the demand for the units was remarkable. He put a box number advertisement in a paper and was overwhelmed with the response. Finally we estimated that there was a demand for as many as 20,000 workshops in Kent alone. It took me some time to work out the reason. I had been building factories for about fifteen years. I was not untypical but I had never built any building smaller than 5,000 feet. I had nothing against them but none of the pension funds and insurance companies, who were the only source of our funds, would ever contemplate financing anything that small. It was just too much trouble, even as part of a larger estate. In all the town centre developments since the war all the 'under-the-arches' workshops had been destroyed by the planners but no more had been built. Little did I realise at the time what that was doing to our economy.

But something good did come out of it. I went to Hugh Jenkins who ran the Coal Board pension fund. They also had a need to invest part of their funds on a community basis. We dreamt up a method of funding these small units on a partnership basis and for the first time institutional funds helped them to be built. And they let.

The ORT Businessmen's Lunch of 1978 came round and this time I was determined that we would ask Margaret Thatcher. David Wolfson was a very old friend and sometime business partner of mine and he had recently gone to help to organise Margaret Thatcher's private office. I did not go through him but through another contact in the office and before long I received confirmation that she had accepted.

The tickets went quickly and soon we had a full house. About two weeks before the lunch I received a phone call from David Wolfson. I had told him the night before about the lunch and he had looked in her appointment book and it was not there. At that, panic broke out and I went immediately to the man who had made the arrangements. He still insisted that it was all right but, of course, it was not. I then wrote to Margaret Thatcher explaining the circumstances and sending copies of the confirmation I had received. After a few days of doubt I finally heard that as the tickets had already been sold she would honour the commitment. I suspect that in any other

31

circumstances she would not have accepted the invitation.

The Prime Minister arrived in good time and went round the room meeting all the guests. I noticed that when she spoke to anyone she gave them all her attention. Not for her was the politician's disconcerting trait of looking around the room for the next victim whilst still speaking to the last. She appeared interested in what she heard and asked question after question. I noticed that she also had Keith's habit of not accepting statements at face value. She also had the great knack of giving everybody just the right amount of time. Not too short, so that they might feel slighted, nor too long so that she could not get round to meet the entire company.

Her speech went very well and the audience had value for money. Afterwards she answered questions in a very forthright manner which was quite untypical of the vast majority of political figures that I had met. Over lunch I had told her of my work with Keith Joseph. As we parted she said, 'I have no doubt we will meet again.' 'If only she could deliver,' one member of the audience said to me rather wistfully after lunch, 'If only.'

I began to wonder what I should do with myself. On the one hand it seemed to me that at last there might be a government that was dedicated to bring back an entrepreneurial, wealth creating society. One that just might roll back the limits of state involvement. On the other my work with the bank was already established. I liked innovating, introducing new methods and building up new companies. Our joint venture was well and truly established, creating a very profitable subsidiary for the bank, and I had no desire to spend the rest of my days there. Perhaps it was time for me to seek other things to do.

In the autumn Keith Joseph came to dinner to discuss future policy. He was the shadow spokesman on industry and we discussed what had to be done. Rather nervously I suggested that I might be able to help and he accepted my offer. I made up my mind there and then that I should shed my business commitments and take two years out of my working life. After all, I justified, I had missed National Service and this would promise to be far more fun than squarebashing.

The year went on and conditions deteriorated. James Callaghan reaped the harvest he had sewn a decade before with his opposition to Harold Wilson and Barbara Castle's attempt to reform the unions with their White Paper 'In case of strife'.

That winter, which entered our political mythology as the 'winter of discontent', was one of the more shameful periods in our long history. Overseas friends would telephone their concern and almost offer to send food parcels. Not only were the unions uncontrollable but so were their members. We were descending rapidly into a state of anarchy. But I did not have a good winter either. I was not well and before Christmas had to undergo surgery and was away from the office for some time. By the time I came back the Government was on its last legs and an election was imminent.

Chapter 3
ON THE JOB TRAINING

The 1979 election was an anxious, nail-biting time for me. I had so much riding on it, yet I had never played a part in practical politics and was scarcely a member of my local Conservative association. Our own MP, Kenneth Baker, was unknown to me as were all the local members of the party. At the time I thought that my interest in government was at the administrative rather than at the political level. In later years I was to regret my absence from the campaign. I little guessed that by the following election I would be a civil servant and isolated from all the action. By the one after I would find myself right in the heart of the storm.

My negotiations with the bank had been concluded before Easter in anticipation of a change of government. I had put all my other affairs in order so I had no real business obligations left. Keith Joseph was expecting to go to the Department of Industry and assuming that I would come with him.

I played no part in the campaign but remained a very concerned spectator. The mood changed during the last two days and I went to our usual election evening party in a very confident mood. That weekend, once Keith was safely returned for Leeds North-East and appointed Secretary of State for Industry, I telephoned. We arranged to meet at 10 o'clock on his first morning in office.

Ashdown House, the main office of the Department of Industry, is halfway down Victoria Street. I went there for the very first time on the Tuesday morning and asked to see the Secretary of State. I had to fill in a form and was taken to a waiting room on the eighth floor. So far it appeared little different from my dentist, for the magazines were just as old. After a few minutes his Private Secretary came in and introduced himself. I went with him through the adjoining Private Office. The Private Office is an institution peculiar to the Civil Service. I know of no better mechanism for packing more into a hard-pressed minister's day, and of course, his ministerial boxes at night. Of course whether this contributes to better government is quite another matter.

It was a very large room with about ten people working away on what seemed an enormous mass of paper. This is where the Principal Private Secretary lived together with a further two Assistant Private Secretaries who were each responsible for different areas of the Department. There were also two or three officials whose sole job was to arrange the diary and others whose precise functions always remained a mystery to me. Somewhere else was the typing pool where all the letters were produced.

I entered Keith's room. It was rather large with a good view of Westminster looking west. It contained a desk (which always appeared unused), a large mahogany conference table laden with papers and books, a settee and two armchairs arranged around a coffee table. It was a room that I was to get very used to in the years to come but my first meeting was quite short.

After I congratulated Keith he told me that I was his first appointment in his new job. He then asked me to become his Industrial Adviser on a part-time basis which I suggested should be unpaid. At the beginning he said he would like me to concentrate on the property affairs of the Department and their many nationalised industries and agencies.

I was then formally introduced to his Private Secretary and told that an Assistant Secretary (which I could not make out was important or not!) by the name of Jeffrey Walmsley would shortly contact me. Keith also wanted me to meet Sir Peter Carey, his Permanent Secretary. I left and went back to my office in Grosvenor Square wondering what the new world would hold for me.

Within a few days I received a phone call from Jeffrey Walmsley and I was asked out to lunch. We met in the Kundam – an Indian restaurant not very far from the Department – where I was obviously being sounded out to see whether it would be safe to introduce me into the system. However, Jeffrey sounded enthusiastic and said that he would be in touch soon. He was as good as his word. Over the next few weeks he initiated me into the mysteries of the Civil Service. I plagued him with questions. What was the difference between an Under Secretary and a Deputy Secretary? Where did an Assistant Secretary come in this hierarchy? How did it all work?

He led me gently through the structure of civil service departments. The Permanent Secretary, who was the Civil Service head of department, sat on the right hand of God. Then under him there would be a number of Deputy Secretaries. That I could follow, but then under them came the Under Secretary. After them came the Assistant Secretary. I asked, 'What comes under an Assistant

Secretary?' and I was told 'a Principal'. Then there were other grades but by then I was really lost. It took me quite a time before I was at home with the very extensive hierarchies that make up a department.

I was told that all jobs were graded and that you could only hold a job if you were of the right grade. 'How did you go up the grades?' I asked. By a board, I was told, which was a review panel consisting of at least three people, with higher grades. You were only eligible for your board after differing time intervals, but boards did not apply above the grade of Principal. Thereafter it was all a mysterious process that depended in some way on your annual report.

I was not really there at the beginning when Keith Joseph first handed down his reading list of about a dozen books. They went from Adam Smith and De Tocqueville to Sam Brittan and Keith himself – even Peter Jay was included. In years to come I was to be told that Frank Broadway's *Upper Clyde Shipbuilders*, which chronicled a disaster created by the Department, was the most salutary. 'If you read that you knew exactly what he wanted' I was told many years later. Many of them were read, but I doubt if anyone read them all.

That was the method that Keith chose to ensure that his civil servants made policy suggestion along lines that were likely to be acceptable to him and his colleagues. Our new policies would mean changing the entire approach of the Department to the private sector and that way he made sure that the Department would understand what it was that he expected of them. In fact I ended up with an additional job, as for many months afterwards I acted as a sort of unofficial interpreter. I was always being asked what would be the monetarist line on this, or where should the line be drawn between the state and the private sector (almost invariably those in the Department wanted to do too much) or how should we express this or that in a minute to the Secretary of State.

This was evident in my first meeting with Sir Peter Carey, the Permanent Secretary, a few weeks later. Peter struck me as a quiet urbane man who gave the appearance of being quite unflappable. I was to find out over the years that he had unparalleled contacts throughout British industry and commerce. There are those who claim that Peter was the original model for Sir Humphrey in *Yes, Minister*. I should doubt that, for he went on to create a most distinguished career in both the City and in Industry after he retired from the Service. Nevertheless I suspect that he was capable of giving a good impression of Sir Humphrey during those frenetic days when Tony Benn was Secretary of State. As our meeting wore on I began to feel for him. In a few short years he had moved from being the Permanent Secretary to Tony Benn to Keith Joseph. That should have put the famed flexibility of the Civil Service to the test.

Peter Carey's office, it seemed to me, was larger and rather better furnished than Keith's. I was to find out that was the case in most departments but it simply demonstrated that ministers may come and go but officials go on for ever. I sat down and after a few pleasantries Peter asked me what I thought the Department should do to help the Government in its new role. I think that I surprised the life out of him. Here was a Department used to 'running' the nationalised industries, to contemplating Planning Agreements and other horrors with major companies during the last Labour Government and often thinking and taking a so called strategic view of industry. My reply was simple, one word, and I believe entirely unexpected. 'Workshops.'

I went on to explain how I thought that we were short of the under-the-arches workshops that were required to start up new businesses. I explained how I had become aware of this a few years before when one of my banking clients had come to me with a scheme for temporary workshops erected under licence on local authority land. In the event the project came to nothing but I was amazed at the demand from possible tenants. We also went on to discuss the need for more small firms and what we could do to encourage their growth.

It seemed to me, I expounded, that all businesses were organic. They all had to be born, and there was not a company in the land that did not start off as a small firm. Some of them fail in the early years, or remain small, others grow and become medium-size businesses; a very few become large. But they all, after a period of growth, reach a size and then, if they are not careful, start to decay. There were exceptions, of course, but it was always necessary to have a good supply of new companies to renew the stock. Today I thought that we showed all the signs of an economy that depended on too many ageing and decaying companies.

I am sure that Peter Carey ended our first meeting realising that his world had changed. Indeed, throughout my whole time in the Department of Industry I always concentrated on the micro level not the macro. There were always people who concentrated on the macro but I believed then, and my belief is even stronger today, that the economy is only the sum of many small parts and if we get conditions right for them the whole will prosper.

At about this time I went into No. 10 for the first time. As I entered through the famous door I could scarce believe it myself. In time I would get used to it and come to regard it as another office, but I never lost the faint sense of disbelief. Of course, at that time I had no great affairs of state to attend to. David Wolfson had taken up the post of Chief of Staff and had an office on the ground floor in No. 10. I would go to see him from time to time for little more than a chat over a sandwich lunch. Over the next few months I would get to meet and work with the Policy Unit people (who also were located in No. 10) on many matters connected with privatisation.

In the Department I concentrated on small units. Our Department had the responsibility for small firms and I worked with the relevant officials. First I thought we should get the facts so we commissioned a report from Drivers Jonas. I was becoming sure that my hunch was correct and that the supply of small units had been reducing over the years as comprehensive redevelopments had eliminated all the small workshops in the city centres without any small units replacing them in the new estates in the city fringes. But we still had to find out the facts.

By the autumn I found that I was spending more and more time in the Department and one day I agreed with Keith that I would take an office and become full time. I was given a small office on the third floor of Kingsgate House, which was just opposite Ashdown House where Ministers and most senior officials worked.

My office was the standard accommodation for a Principal. One desk, three chairs, a carpet square, a coat rack and a dictating machine. My secretary, Margaret Bell, had to stay behind in the rather more luxurious offices I still had in Grosvenor Square. Not only did I have the accommodation of a principal but once I was in the Department I started to work as a principal. I reported to an Assistant Secretary, never saw the Under Secretary who was always away on mysterious errands in Brussels and occasionally – once every six weeks or so – met with a very remote figure: the Deputy Secretary.

Not that Anne Müller, the Deputy Secretary responsible for regional policy in the Department at that time, was remote. She is today a Permanent Secretary and during my time showed me every consideration, but such was my position within the Department that for many months my work rarely brought me to Deputy Secretaries let alone ministers. Of course, that was because I started doing a specialist job, but also due to Keith who, I began to suspect, wanted me to sink or swim by myself.

I was the beneficiary. It was only some years later that I realised how different my introduction to the Civil Service was compared to those other half-a-dozen or so special advisers who started with

39

me in 1979. Over the months I learned how the Department really operated; how policy was thrashed out gradually with decisions going upwards until a submission was made to the Minister; how departmental budgets were finally agreed and as a result who had influence and who did not; how, whilst the spending round was being negotiated, to go into Treasury and persuade, badger and even plead with minor Treasury officials to get our expenditure line agreed. In the years ahead this experience was to be invaluable, but at the time it was all rather painful.

I was asked to take a look at the way the Post Office was dealing with its property. Sir William Barlow had been given the task of dividing up the Post Office into British Telecom, the telephone half, and the Post Office, which included the Giro.

I went into both organisations. At the time they had barely separated and employed about a quarter of a million people each. They were spending hundreds of millions of pounds a year on property developments. Yet only ten years before, the Post Office had been part of Government and in many ways it was still run as if it was still there. I found that the person in charge of the property development in the Post Office had just come from spending three years being responsible for parcels. He would go on to another part of the organisation in two or three years' time. It was a hangover from the Civil Service system of job rotation. It might be all right in the Service (and I was not too sure about that) but it would never do in commerce. The newcomer would have to have explained to him almost every time the difference between a freehold and a leasehold, or what a planning permission does. Yet he would be responsible for spending hundreds of millions of pounds a year.

I found only one valuation surveyor in the entire organisation. It was my job to introduce private sector finance and before too long it started to happen. However the more time I spent in the nationalised industries the more I became convinced of the real need for privatisation. All those working in the organisations had many concerns, pensions, salaries and working conditions – but never, it seemed to me, the customer.

The unemployment figures for August 1980 came out and they were a great shock. The headline figure now exceeded two million: two million! Yet it was only four months since it had first breached one and a half million. Where would it stop? I asked myself. These figures certainly added to the general feeling of gloom.

By now I had started to spend more of my time with ministers. I worked with David Mitchell, who was the Parliamentary Under Secretary of State (a junior minister) responsible for small firms, and with the Department's other ministers as well. One day Keith decided that I was too far away across the road in Kingsgate House so I was given an office on the third floor of Ashdown House. I had come in from the cold and now Margaret Bell, my secretary who had stayed in my old offices at Grosvenor Square, could move in next door to me. The office opposite was occupied by Colette Bowe, who was to achieve a certain amount of recognition one day in the Westland affair.

Soon the report on small units by Coopers & Lybrand Associates and Drivers Jonas was in its final draft. It brought out a number of conclusions: it confirmed that past demolition policies and rigid regimes created a shortage of small business premises; there was clear evidence that the shortage of premises constrained the establishment and development of new firms. It went on to give powerful support to my arguments. We already knew that the number of new businesses was at an all time low. We also found that the seed corn of new businesses, the self-employed, had been falling steadily during the last decade. But it was the birth rate of new businesses that was so worrying. I knew by then that if we wanted to deal in any way with the rising burden of unemployment then it could only be by starting new businesses.

Of course, the taxation policies of the last few decades could take much of the blame for this; but so could the shortage in the supply of premises. Our conclusions were that many small businesses did not start because there was simply nowhere for them to go.

As a result of all of this I was determined that we should put in a suggestion in our Budget proposals to the Chancellor for a new tax allowance to encourage people to invest in these small workshops. My reasoning was simple: if we were to allow investors to write off the cost of these units against their taxes then the net cost to them would be much less. That way they would not mind if the capital value when they were completed was less than they originally cost them. For this reason I was convinced that the tax allowance must be set at 100 per cent. I put up a submission to Keith Joseph.

Shortly after I went off on a day trip to Cwmbran. This was a New Town north of Newport and I was helping them with the introduction of private sector finance. Once again I spoke to them about small units. They were not really interested and they were keeping their undeveloped land available for new projects of over 100,000 square feet. No matter how often I would point out how few tenants existed in the world for properties of this size, it seemed to make no impression. However, I did manage to help them with the disposal of some of their completed properties and promised to introduce

41

some of the institutions to help to finance their future projects.

The next day my secretary, Margaret Bell, showed me a minute without any comment. Whilst I had been away there had been a gap in Keith Joseph's diary and a meeting had been called where, amongst other matters, they had agreed that the Workshop Building Allowance should allow a tax allowance at only 50 per cent. When I protested and enquired further I found that they had rushed the submission off to the Chancellor that very day.

I was furious. I knew that at a 50 per cent tax allowance it would not work. We had to attract sufficient investors since we were trying to persuade successful individuals who wanted to shield their tax liabilities. What they would end up with would not necessarily make a good investment and they needed the maximum possible incentive. I paced up and down my office. I knew that on this basis the scheme would not work. But there was more to it than that. If I was going to let myself be out manoeuvred then I really would be wasting my time. Either I had to stand up for myself or get out.

I went to Keith Joseph and told him of my concern. He agreed to reconsider the matter. The following day there assembled what seemed like all the senior officials in the Department. We had a good long argument with me against the rest. I was sure that many officials were against me only on grounds of solidarity and to my great joy and relief, Keith came down on my side. The following day he said another letter would go to the Chancellor. As I left the meeting one official, a friend of mine, said to me that it would not do me any good. When I asked why he just gave me a knowing wink and said it would get lost in the Treasury. However, to the great surprise of everyone in the Department, it did end up in the 1980 Budget as the Small Industrial Buildings Allowance – and at 100 per cent. Geoffrey Howe liked the idea and that was that. Our report was published and that added to the interest.

The scheme took off like lightning. Within a few months on my travels around the country I would see new small workshop estates being erected. All I could think was: that's my idea! For the very first time it came home to me that what I was doing could make a difference. It was a thought both sobering and exciting.

Whilst I was fighting my corner in the bowels of the Department, momentous events were occurring outside. The haemorrhage of losses of the British Steel Corporation had to be first contained and then reduced. These losses alone for the first half of 1979 were 140 million and could not be sustained. By December of that year a reduction of capacity from 21.6 million tons to 15 million was sought which would involve some 50,000 redundancies. The Unions first threatened then, after Christmas, came out on strike. The advice to Keith Joseph was clear and unequivocal. The unions could not be defeated. The line taken by most officials I spoke to was that the Corporation could never win and this view certainly only increased when the Transport and General Workers' Union threatened and then brought out the railways and the docks.

Although British Steel could not win, we could not afford to lose either. If we were to make any real difference in the economy then we had to increase our productivity. The last decade had seen wages increase by 316 per cent and output by only 16 per cent. The unions were not striking about saving a large number of jobs – they were actually destroying all the jobs in the Corporation. If they won the strike, then there would be a good chance that in time we would lose the entire Corporation. There were good compensation terms for those employees who would unfortunately become redundant and we were looking at new schemes for job creation in the steel areas. The sooner we diversified into other jobs the better and more secure the employment prospects would be in the steel areas.

I would see Keith Joseph from time to time over the thirteen weeks of the strike. He would listen to the advice of officials in his usual courteous manner and then just carry on. The CBI and almost everyone else came in and echoed the defeatist advice of the Department. By early February even *The Times* was saying that the Government should move, or at least appoint a Court of Enquiry.

On the 12 February, Keith was pelted with missiles on a visit to South Wales. There were angry scenes as Sheerness and then Sheffield were picketed. The stocks of steel in the country dropped and dropped – until about week eight. Then, surprisingly, they stabilised and to everyone's amazement, began to increase. Despite the blockade on all main ports around the country there still existed a sufficient number of smaller ports through which, for almost the first time in their existence, steel came into the country.

By March it was clear that the unions would not win and Charles Villiers agreed to a Committee of Enquiry limited to pay. The Committee reported on 1 April and its report was accepted. The strike was over after thirteen weeks and for the first time we had demonstrated that the country was governable. *The Times* described it as 'the most significant success the Government has had in the domestic field since it took office . . . achieved by the resolute refusal to act.' I doubt if any other Secretary of State would have been so resolute at that time.

But the strike harmed BSC grievously. Customers found out that they could import steel at prices lower than the British Steel

Corporation. Many did not go back and preferred to remain with their new suppliers. In addition, the price of steel was now much lower as a result of the new competition from Europe. This not only hastened the restructuring but it also greatly harmed the small private sector which used to shelter behind the umbrella of the high BSC prices. For the next year or two we saw the private sector shrink faster than the public sector. This was not what we were about, and a great deal of time and effort went into helping them survive.

Keith would hold a 'state of the union' meeting once a month. At that time all senior officials and ministers would congregate in his office and discuss the outlook for industry. Hans Liesner, his Chief Economic Adviser, would give both the Treasury forecast and then his own assessment. The discussion would then start. It was not a meeting I looked forward to, for it always had a great air of pessimism. Tom Trenchard (Lord Trenchard, the Minister of State on the industry side) would rail on in his deep booming voice that the pound was too high. It was, but what could we do about it? The officials would long to say that we should spend more on this, decide more on that – but they knew that it was forbidden.

I now spent a great deal of my time travelling around the country. In April I had been made a member of the board of English Industrial Estates Corporation, and they would hold monthly board meetings in different parts of the country. English Estates had the responsibility to build industrial buildings in parts of the North East, North West and South West. Until the change of government it only built factories but now we were encouraging them to build whatever the market wanted. That change, small in itself, represented a minor revolution. There was a feeling that only factories were respectable, that somehow jobs in warehouses were not real jobs. The greatest obstacle we had to overcome, especially in the North, was to gain acceptance for the idea that jobs could be real and wealth could be created even if things were not manufactured. The concept of added value is still not fully accepted today.

It was my responsibility to introduce private sector capital for the first time and it was not long before the Legal and General were financing developments which, a year or two before, would have been down to the taxpayer. After Tony Pender came as the Chief Executive we began to see a great variety of different developments including a very active subsidiary, Beehive Investments, that concentrated on small units.

One day we had a meeting in Keith Joseph's office when we realised that we did not have enough money in English Estates for the construction of these workshop units in the North East and

North West. The shortfall was about £20 million. We broke up just before lunch.

Just by chance, I had fixed lunch that day with Hugh Jenkins, the man responsible for running the Coal Board Pension Fund. We had worked together a year or two before to devise methods to start funding workshop units. I explained our need for finance and before coffee was served we agreed a line of credit of £20 million for English Estates. I went back to the office and asked to see Keith. When I told him of my discussion and that as a result of the new arrangement the programme could go ahead without being a cost to the public sector (and thus no need to ask the Treasury for the money) he opened the door to his private office and said to all and sundry but to no one in particular, 'From now on I have an open door for David Young.' I thought that rather eccentric at the time, but it was only later that I realised what he meant.

As the year went on unemployment started to move relentlessly upwards. The West Midlands, for the last hundred years the centre of wealth creation in the country, went into steep decline following the slump in the car industry. British Leyland, that misbegotten child of the 'economies of scale' generation, started to deteriorate so fast that few would have given much for its chance of survival. By the end of the year unemployment was increasing by 100,000 a month and there seemed to be no reason why it should ever slow down.

One day Keith asked me to come in. He said that I had now been working for him in the Department for over a year and that he would now like me to take a wider interest in the work of the Department. I would in future be concerned with privatisation as well, and he would like me to see all the papers that came before him. He told me that he had written to the P.M. to obtain permission that I be appointed his Special Adviser. Today every Cabinet Minister, and many ministers outside Cabinet, have a Special Adviser but at that time there were only about five or six throughout the whole of Government. Within a few days the confirmation came through and was announced. It caused a small flurry of publicity. I now began to take an interest in the forthcoming privatisation of British Aerospace and Cable & Wireless.

I was asked to join on a committee as the representative of the Department investigating the feasibility of privatising the Royal Ordinance Factories. There were some seventeen factories working almost exclusively for the Ministry of Defence. This provided me with a great education into the working of committees. The secretariat was provided by the Royal Ordinance Factories (ROF) and

45

we would meet under the chairmanship of Lord Strathcona, the Minister of State at the Ministry of Defence.

I would go into the cavernous Ministry of Defence building and we would meet in one of their meeting rooms. There were under a dozen on the committee, some from the outside, some half in, half out like me, and some from the Service. I suspect that the majority on the committee, like me, were all in favour of privatisation. I felt certain that the secretariat were not. I was never quite sure where the sympathies of the Chairman lay.

The first point to decide was whether it would be one company or seventeen separate companies. Those of us who wanted privatisation preferred to keep the companies as individual units for then there would be a good chance that some of them at least could be sold off. Those who were against privatisation wanted all to be held by just one company, for that way it would be more difficult to sell the whole. So the more cynical of us thought.

We would hold long, fraught meetings and eventually agree on a few points and then adjourn. The minutes of the previous meeting arrived almost invariably late, bearing little or no resemblance to what actually had happened. So we would start again and would spend half the next meeting rewriting the minutes of the last one. Exactly the same would happen the next time: three steps forward and two back. It was not the most fruitful period, and it was hardly surprising that the eventual privatisation took many years.

As we started to slump in the opinion polls I began to notice that the enthusiasm for our policies in the Department started to diminish. Not all civil servants changed, but a significant number did. Before long the problems became more difficult and I quickly began to realise that for some who worked in the Department we represented a temporary interruption in their normal way of life. The outlook was so bleak that they assumed that we would be swept away in the next election. This was not for any political reasons, but life for some civil servants was much more fun under a Labour government when they had more money to spend and more decisions to take.

Keith Joseph sent for me one day and asked me to go and help Jim Prior. His constituency included Lowestoft and the Philips factory employing over 1,000 people was closing. This factory had been producing televisions but obviously could not compete with imports at the current exchange rates. Unfortunately, they had had a poor labour relations record and the plant had been losing money for years. I went there and began work to see if I could divide the buildings up and create some sort of small workshop estate to enable some jobs at least to be created.

Towards the end of the year I visited Consett, a steel town some fifteen miles from Newcastle. Originally it had been built on a hill of iron ore to service a steel works. It had become uneconomic and its closure had been announced in June 1980. Strenuous efforts had been made to keep it open and there was even a consortium formed to try to run it as a separate company. Everything had failed and in the end it closed in September. When I went there it was by far the most depressing day that I had ever had. There seemed to be no reason why anybody in the town would ever work again. Apart from a few corner shops there had been no other employers; yet no one wanted to leave. How could we bring jobs to such an isolated location? Other than starting new companies there seemed to be no other option.

Christmas came and I went away on a short holiday. On my return there were to be changes in the Department that would transform my future.

Chapter 4
WHY NOT ME?

On my flight back from our Christmas break I read of the reshuffle that had taken place whilst I was away. Most of our ministers had changed. Tom Trenchard moved over to become Minister of State at Defence. I would still come across him as he was to take over the chair of our committee on the Royal Ordinance Factories. He had little patience with the secretariat, believed in privatisation and from that moment onwards we made good progress.

He was succeeded by Norman Tebbit, who came from the Department of Trade where he had been Parliamentary Under Secretary of State. From the very first we hit it off. Norman had a quiet, almost withdrawn manner, but suddenly he would say something that would go to the very heart of our discussions. He had, and has today, a great gift for the telling phrase and our meetings would always be good fun. The British Aerospace flotation was imminent and Norman took a firm hold of the matter and within a few weeks we saw a majority of the shares in public hands: privatisation was on its way.

The other change at Minister of State level was the departure of Adam Butler and the arrival of Kenneth Baker. Adam had never looked comfortable with the hi-tech side of the Department but Kenneth took to it like a duck to water. This was Kenneth's first job in the Government for until now he had been identified with Ted Heath whose Parliamentary Private Secretary he had been up to the last leadership elections. He had been an industrial consultant before and knew much about the computer industry. He had made a number of powerful speeches during the last year about the need for a coherent policy on information technology, and in many ways created the need for the job he was now to hold.

He swiftly transformed himself into the Minister for IT – Information Technology. IT quickly became a household term although whether anybody really knew what it actually meant was quite another matter. He made it his task that all schools would

49

have one of the personal computers that were now becoming available. I had always been a computer freak going back to my banking days. I taught myself to use a programmable calculator, and used it all the time for financial assessments. One day in late 1977, flying back from the United States, I saw an advertisement for an Apple computer. They were made by a Californian firm which I rang the very next day. With some surprise they told me that they had just appointed agents in London and had consigned some computers. A day or two later I became the proud possessor of the second Apple II computer in the country. Subsequently I found that I was using it more and more for words not figures so I had taught myself to touch-type on the machine. I now found it invaluable.

During the last year I had been talking to Sight & Sound, a company who specialised in teaching touch-typing using equipment that they had devised many years before. I wanted them to create a mobile unit that could go round schools and teach pupils to touch-type. I did have one set of ongoing discussions with a Local Education Authority for I was convinced that familiarity with a keyboard would go a long way to help the acceptance of computers. During my recent holiday I had been proudly telling an American friend of my bright idea when he exploded with laughter. Thirty years ago, he said, half of our school work that we sent in was typed. By the time I went to college, he went on, they would not accept hand-written work. That made me realise how far we had to catch up.

Within a few months Kenneth had seized hold of the issue. Acorn Computers, a fast-growing new British company, collaborated with the BBC to produce a machine which was very suitable for schools. Clive Sinclair produced a cheaper machine which became very popular. We devised a scheme that would ensure that all schools had a computer and it was taken up with alacrity. Computers entered the schools to the puzzled concern of the teachers.

Tate & Lyle announced that it would be closing its Love Lane works in Liverpool. This caused a tremendous outcry as Liverpool had become a great concentration of unemployment. I went there to see the plant and with Tony Pender and English Estates worked on plans to redevelop the site into a series of small workshops and give other help from the Department to encourage the start of new businesses. The company was aware of the social consequences of its decision and I managed to extract a promise of help which ran well over a million pounds.

Within a few days of our being able to announce the new scheme Michael Heseltine announced out of the blue that he was going to purchase the site and take over responsibility for the project. That put the entire cost on the Government, let Tate & Lyle off the hook and brought my discussions to an untimely end.

There were other problems in the Department. Cable & Wireless was a famous old British company that had originally cabled the world when the Empire was at its height. It had been nationalised in 1947 and had gone into steep decline. As our influence in the Gulf diminished, so all the Gulf states decided that they could undertake their own communications. I went to C&W one day for lunch and all the senior executives boasted to me how much compensation they had been able to negotiate for withdrawing from state after state. It did not seem to occur to them that they could expand.

C&W had flourished in Hong Kong where they had grown and kept pace with the enormous increase in commercial activity in the colony but now even this was in disarray. As a result of a monumental row with Hong Kong Telephones, C&W were not even receiving the income due to them on their overseas calls.

Keith Joseph had decided to change the Chairman and had appointed Eric Sharp (now Lord Sharp of Grimsdyke). One day I received a phone call from Eric and we met for lunch at the Athenaeum. Eric was a former civil servant, who had worked for Manny Shinwell in the Ministry of Power, and then had left for a life in industry. He had been with ICI and then moved on to Monsanto, where he had just retired as Chairman of their UK subsidiary.

There were many problems to solve and a fair degree of urgency since C&W were high on the privatisation list. Eric asked me to work with him and I was happy to do so. Over and above the litigation problems with Hong Kong Telephones, the licence with the Hong Kong Government only had a few years to go and I was asked to go over and help with the negotiations. In February I went out to Hong Kong. I had spent much time in Hong Kong during my time with Manufacturers Hanover and I was a great admirer of the 'can do' approach that passed for normal over there. I had many friends in Hong Kong and soon settled down to the negotiations. Before too long the difficulties were solved.

Gradually Eric Sharp overcame all the formidable problems. Merchant Bank advisers were retained and work carried on for the sale of just under half of the shares scheduled for the autumn.

I had spent much time during the year on the privatisation of British Telecom. I had argued that we should split the company into a number of regional companies with a long lines and an international company as well. The Americans had just split Ma

51

Bell along similar lines and if we did that we would have sufficient competition to act as a stimulus to development and efficiency. I had lost that battle for a rather odd reason. The accounting systems of BT were such that at that time they could only produce separate accounts for the whole group or Prestel, which was a small subsidiary employing less than five hundred people. It would take years to create the separate accounting systems so it was decided that it would have to go as a whole.

If we could not split BT up, then we still had to give it some competition. It was proposed that we create a competitive telecommunication network: thus Mercury came into being. Mercury was originally a consortium of C&W, British Petroleum and Barclays Bank, although after a year or two the other partners withdrew and only C&W remained.

Within a few weeks it had earned its place under the sun. BT had planned a digital network for the UK that should be in place by the end of the nineties. A few weeks after the announcement of the formation of Mercury, BT brought forward the date for their digital network to the early nineties. We had just saved over seven years. Over the next few years Mercury was to supply a stimulus to development that would ensure that BT would remain on its toes.

The CPRS, the Central Policy Review Staff, was a central government organisation based on the Cabinet Office that was originally set up during Ted Heath's time to advise the Prime Minister of the day on policy options. To think the unthinkable was how it was described to me, and the Prime Minister had charged the staff with taking a look at the nationalised industries.

They had been looking at BT and when I first saw the draft report I was delighted. It was radical, but above all it proposed a division into competitive units. Unfortunately they decided to pass it around Whitehall and seek the views of Permanent Secretaries and Secretaries of State. That might be the right way to get consensus but it did not do for a radical document. I saw the proposal become more and more anodyne, until the final document emerged with a set of bland proposals that contained little more than the status quo.

I realised after that that the CPRS had been in existence for far too long. When it was formed under Lord Rothschild it did come out with radical proposals. Whether they were too radical or not was up to ministers to decide, but at least they would have the option. Now the Whitehall machine had been at it and no radical solutions would emerge. I was not surprised when sometime later the Prime Minister decided that she could live without it and it was disbanded.

52

John MacGregor had come in with the reshuffle and had replaced David Mitchell as Small Firms Minister. I worked very happily for John and we fought a number of battles with the Treasury to launch schemes, like the Loan Guarantee Scheme, which gave guarantees to small companies to help them provide additional finance.

This work was getting even more urgent. Unemployment was approaching the two and a half million mark. Firms were closing down all over the West Midlands and the North East and the North West began to look as if they were blitzed. We looked at schemes that would help people start up their own businesses.

By now I was spending so much time with ministers that I was given new quarters. Now I had a ministerial suite on the seventh floor, a large room with windows on three sides, and next door I now had my own private office. My first Private Secretary came from Treasury but my second was Alex Rae from the Department. Alex (pronounced Alec he told me at our first meeting) was a Scot from Livingston, just outside Glasgow. One of a large family, 'and we are all in work', he had entered the Service in Glasgow and then transferred South. He was married with a small child.

I had been spending more and more time with English Industrial Estates Corporation. It took me back to my old love, industrial development, but I wanted to encourage them to experiment with different types of projects. At a time of industrial recession large vacant factories would not do much for jobs and gradually they were converted into small workshops and even offices. The board meetings took place every month, sometimes at Team Valley in Newcastle where their Head Office was, and at other times elsewhere in other parts of the regions. On the board I struck up a friendship and a rapport with Jack Eccles, the statutory Trade Union member.

I went over to Northern Ireland for a few days. David Mitchell had gone there after leaving Industry and he asked me if I could look at a problem he had. I found a most curious situation. All factories for rent were built by Government for there was no private sector. Once a year, in the autumn, an official in the Department of Commerce would fix the rents for the next year. He would say, literally, that all factories in Belfast were worth say 88p per square foot whilst over in Londonderry they were worth 48p per square foot. The Government had a building programme but not sufficient resources to expand it and wanted to get the private sector in to add to it. It was quite impossible at those rents. But there was something odd. The Government refused to build warehouses. This was a hangover from the attitude that we inherited from the last

53

Government that held that manufacturing was good and services were bad. Of course there was a demand for warehouses and there was a flourishing market at rents in Belfast at about £1.75 per square foot. There was no shortage of private sector developers building to cope with the demand.

I told them that if they wanted to improve the supply of factories they should stop building them! It would only take a matter of months and there would be a plentiful supply at a higher rent. That was a very good example of how a businessman must be careful in politics. Undoubtedly it was a correct solution but it was simply impossible politically. With soaring unemployment, Government must be seen to act – even if it destroys the market. When I had the facts of life gently explained to me I went home a wiser man.

Whilst I was in Belfast I was shown around a number of large and derelict factories. They had all been built by past governments in an attempt to persuade industry to go to Belfast. One had been used for the manufacture of toys, another for electronics when the technology demanded hundreds of women soldering transistor radios. If only a similar effort and cash had been put into small and new businesses many would still have been there. Indeed some may well have grown into medium companies.

I continued to spend much time working on a solution for the closed Philips works at Lowestoft. My original idea was to convert the property into a workshop estate and undoubtedly Philips would have assisted us. The more that I looked at this the less I liked it. Over 1,000 jobs had gone and the small workshop route (although much safer in the long run) would be just too slow. I then went to one or two importers of high-tech products to enquire if they could persuade their suppliers to set up production here. That seemed to be a much more promising avenue to explore and at first I had some hope. However that failed but I did hear that Sanyo might be persuaded to come to the United Kingdom and I made contact with them.

The time had come to appoint a new Chairman of British Steel as Charles Villiers was due to retire. I heard rumours and then had confirmation of a surprising choice. Ian MacGregor was a Scot who had lived and worked in the States for many decades. He was older than Charles Villiers but the real surprise was his remuneration package. It was not his ability or his age that would be controversial. He – or rather the American bank Lazard Frères he was attached to – would receive a total of some £1.8 million over the next three years. Even more than that, the larger part of his remuneration was based on results, an unheard of principle at the time. It was not

54

quite as radical as it could have been. He himself would only receive some £48,000 per annum, the rest going to his firm where he remained a limited partner.

That was an inconceivable amount to pay for management at the time. Our salaries had always been ludicrously low compared with other countries, although with tax at 83 per cent there was little point in paying more. Instead many schemes of great complexity and dubious legality were devised to give employees benefits that would survive penal taxation. It was a system that had to be broken and when Keith Joseph stood in the House to announce his decision it was I think one of the bravest political acts of the decade. There were critics in plenty on both sides of the house but it marked a watershed. Before many months were out the changes that MacGregor brought in stemmed the losses. Long before his term was up he was saving his total remuneration package every single day! From that time onwards the principle of letting market forces determine pay, although not followed through in the public sector, began to penetrate the private sector. The process only gathered pace after we had reduced taxation to more sensible levels.

In May I had a short break. I flew out to Gibraltar with an old friend of mine Gerry Lavender. We jointly owned a forty-two-foot ketch, the *Rake's Progress*, which we were sailing out on the instalment plan to the Aegean. The boat had come as far as Gibraltar and we wanted to spend the next seven or eight days seeing how far we could get. We arrived in the late afternoon and made the boat ready. That night it really blew and I was quite apprehensive about our passage the following morning. For the first two or three hours we had an interesting time of it with the wind against the tide but as we rounded the Rock the wind died. Thereafter we had no wind at all, and we spent day after day chugging up the coast on our diesel across a glassy blue sea. We went up the coast as far as Barcelona and then over to Minorca and finally to Andraitx in Majorca. We left the boat there and planned to come back in September to sail across to Italy and then through the Straits of Messina to Greece and the Aegean. There was bound to be wind then, at least around the Greek Islands.

On my return we started a series of dinners with the Chairmen of the nationalised industries. I had heard a few weeks before that they felt that they could never talk to Keith Joseph without the ever-present civil servant. I persuaded Keith that we should have a series of dinners without officials. That idea went down like a lead balloon in the Department and over the next few weeks all kinds of ingenious suggestions were made for introducing officials, from a

Private Secretary, just to keep notes, to the Permanent Secretary himself. Keith stood his ground and we then had a series of dinners starting with George Jefferson from British Telecom, Michael Edwardes from British Leyland, Ron Dearing from the Post Office and the new Ian MacGregor at British Steel Corporation. The dinners went very well. It is important for ministers to be able to obtain impressions and information at first hand, and not to always have them sifted through the Department – but departments hate it!

The unemployment figures came out for April. The headline figure now exceeded 2,500,000 for the first time. In eight months it had gone from 2,000,000 to 2,500,000 and nothing seemed to be able to stop it. Seasonally adjusted it was a little lower but the really bad news was that, even then, it now exceeded 10 per cent. A very gloomy day indeed.

Meanwhile there were other disturbing incidents. There had been trouble for three successive nights in Brixton in April. All had gone quiet for some months but at the beginning of July there was trouble in Southall. The television played it up and almost immediately there were repeat incidents in Brixton, in Toxteth and in Birmingham. Unemployment and concentration of ethnic minorities were making a heady mixture in what the papers began to call the 'inner cities'. They were not, of course, for some were the decaying suburbs. Nevertheless this was a new phenomenon for Britain and we began to consider what could be done. I thought that it was more to do with idle hands and began to think how we could get employment going in these areas.

One morning towards the end of July we were having a routine meeting in Keith's room on steel. Norman Tebbit was there and after the meeting was over I walked out with him. We were both going out to lunch and we stood waiting for the lift idly chatting. I said to Norman that the rumour was about that he was going to the Department of Employment. He merely shrugged his shoulders. If you do, I said, then I will help you sort out the Manpower Services Commission. Norman merely grinned.

I did not go away that August. There was much to do in the Department and I was also engaged in showing all that ORT could offer in technology training. I invited both Peter Morrison (who was Parliamentary Secretary at Employment) and Kenneth Baker for a presentation by ORT at their offices.

My discussions with Sanyo were now hotting up. I was acting as a sort of middleman between Philips and Sanyo with Jim Prior taking an understandably keen interest in all that happened. Philips were

56

not too keen to sell to a competitor but were aware what this sale could do for jobs in the area.

September came and the Department came back to life. It was difficult to get used to the enormous change that came over the Department in August. During my banking or property days August could be a very busy month indeed but in Government, as in the outside world, hardly anything happens. Parliament would rise at the end of July and all ministers, save the luckless Junior duty Minister, would flee to their homes or get away with their families on holiday. So would all the senior officials. On 1 September all the senior Ministers and officials would reappear and we would carry on exactly where we left off a month earlier. I learned to follow suit, and each future August, I would disappear as well.

One Sunday evening in the middle of September I received a phone call which shook me. Strong rumours were around about a reshuffle due the very next day but my caller was adamant that Keith Joseph was leaving Industry and going to Education and would be replaced by Patrick Jenkin. I had never met Patrick Jenkin and this came to me as a bombshell, for Keith had given no indication that he might be on the move. My caller insisted that was not so; Keith had asked to go since he believed that his job at the Department of Industry was done and if more was not done with Education all our work would be wasted.

I was frankly incredulous for I had heard no whisper and had no indication from Keith. The next day carried on as usual. A reshuffle was certainly on and the story was around that Norman Tebbit was in the Cabinet. That was confirmed when his Private Office was asked by the Cabinet Office to clear 11 a.m. the following Thursday for a meeting. They did not say what sort of meeting but it could only be Cabinet. At the time Norman was waiting for his summons to No. 10, which duly came.

The day carried on with its usual complement of meetings. At about 4 o'clock Keith Joseph held a meeting on the future of British Telecom. We were agreeing the progress to be made if BT was to be brought to privatisation. Keith took an active interest in the discussion and mapped out steps to be taken over the next few months. He was due to go to Japan the next day and was very interested in what made Japanese industry so efficient. He handled the meeting as if nothing were to change. By then I was sure that he was not going to leave the Department.

The meeting finished at about 5 o'clock. I was about to go when Keith asked me to stay. He asked to be excused for a moment as he had a letter to finish. He carried on writing for a few moments. At exactly 5.15 p.m. he looked up and told me that at that very moment the announcement was being made that he was going to the Department of Education and Science and would I come with him as his Special Adviser?

In spite of the warning that I had had I was at a loss for words. I mumbled something to the effect that I was not too sure if I could really help at DES and said that I would be in touch. I asked who his successor would be and he said Patrick Jenkin.

I then had to go to a meeting in Kenneth Baker's room. During the meeting Kenneth's Private Secretary handed me a message saying that I should go immediately to No. 10. I excused myself and left. When I got there I was shown into David Wolfson's room who passed on the request from the Prime Minister that I should continue my work in the Department for Patrick Jenkin as his Special Adviser. He had agreed and I was then introduced to him. We arranged to meet the next morning. Later that evening Kenneth rang me, full of curiosity, to enquire if I had got a job!

Norman Lamont came to replace Michael Marshall, the junior Minister, whilst Norman Tebbit duly went to Employment. All the ministers had changed since last Christmas! By now I was getting used to the system which was so different from anything I had experienced in the outside world. I had now been in the Department for well over two years, far longer than any of our ministers and in many cases I had been dealing with issues longer than the officials themselves. At the beginning I had come in with a healthy contempt for ministers. They were not managers and in words that John Hoskyns was to use in years to come, I could not see them running even a medium sized multinational. After a while I developed a healthy respect for them and the system. Time after time they would show that they had the political feel for the possible that I lacked. They really were the interface between the possible and the people.

We were due to go back to collect our boat from Andraitx in Majorca where we had left it in May. I thought about it overnight and felt that I could not go away for ten days within a few days of acquiring a new master. I rang Gerry and reluctantly we cancelled the trip. I never went back. By the time the next spring came I had other responsibilities and there was never the time. Five years later we sold the boat. I have never sailed since.

I now started working for Patrick Jenkin. This was a very different experience from working for Keith Joseph. For one thing I had worked for Keith for years and presumably he only selected me once he was satisfied that he could work with me. Patrick, who had been at Social Security, had me thrust upon him by the Prime

Minister at the very moment he was offered the job. No one refuses in those circumstances!

Patrick was far more pragmatic than Keith. But the change that really amazed me was the change in the Department itself. Within a few days we had our usual state of the union monthly meeting. All those civil servants who used to speak in an impeccable monetarist dialect suddenly changed. No more did they speak of the importance of reducing public expenditure, of containing the money supply, of not allowing the public sector to expand in any circumstances. Instead they went back to where they were in 1979 and I could see that they were tempting Patrick to be as interventionist and as wet as they could.

Of course there are differences of attitude and approach between different politicians. I found the changeover a trying time. Policies did change but in the end not as much as I had feared. I quickly became used to the new regime. But what I learned from the incident is how a department will try to read the mind of a minister in order to provide him with what they think he wants. If a minister is not definite, if he does not lay down clear policy guidelines, then the department will give him what they think is best. That way lies disaster since policies that emerge from the depths of a department without the political steer of a minister are often a weak compromise of differing strands within the department. I learned a great lesson over this incident which I did not forget although I never dreamed that one day I could put it to good use.

I became part of a small group under the Prime Minister looking at the problems of Liverpool. All sorts of remedies were suggested. Michael Heseltine submitted a paper entitled 'It took a riot . . .' and ended up with special responsibilities for the area.

The unemployment figures for August were released. They now exceeded 2,900,000 for the first time. Unemployment had increased by over 400,000 in the last four months alone. The whole idea of unemployment offended me. The waste and the moral degradation of hundreds of thousands of people, the depression and the sense of uselessness that a futile search for employment engendered seemed to me to be against all that we stood for. All the opposition bleated for, day after day, was for the Government to spend more and more money. I knew it was not the answer. There is an old saying from the Talmud that continually went through my mind: 'Give a man fish and he will soon be hungry. Teach him to fish and he will never starve.' All that the opposition would have us do was to hand out more and more fish. I suspected that the more that people became dependent on the state, the happier the opposition would be.

59

There was also much concern about school leavers and the Youth Opportunities Scheme was being extended in an effort to help. I could not help thinking of my experiences in Israel and France and many other countries with ORT. Wherever I now travelled around the country I would hear complaints about the quality of young people leaving our schools: undisciplined, illiterate or innumerate were the mildest criticisms of them. But these very people had all benefited from the longest period of compulsory education in Europe, if not the world. But I knew that the fault lay not with our young people but the quality and type of education they had received. Yet all we were offering was the Youth Opportunities Programme which to my mind was no more than giving a young person the opportunity to watch those in work without training them. If it was ever more than that it tended towards exploitation.

The arrangements for the flotation of Cable & Wireless were now in full swing. As we got near to the flotation date the market went into decline. The price was to be settled over the weekend in early November and Kenneth Baker called a meeting. I had received a strong warning from the merchant bankers that it might be difficult to place the underwriting in the current state of the market. This warning is almost traditional on all underwriting, but I was still concerned. The price was settled and agreed on the Sunday evening. In view of the market conditions it was at the lower end of the range and the Treasury agreed. The following morning the market improved: I was torn between delight and horror. I watched prices going up day after day for the ten days before the flotation. The issue was a great success but in the Commons we were criticised for setting the price too low. That was the first time that I discovered the great facility that the Opposition had with the exercise of hindsight!

In the meantime Keith Joseph had appointed me a part time Special Adviser to him at the Department of Education. I invited him, together with Sir James Hamilton the Permanent Secretary, over to ORT for a demonstration of the latest in vocational and technical education. I did not think that they would allow the experience of ORT to help his Department, although that would be easily possible, but I wanted to bring to the attention of senior officials and ministers how our educational system differed from those of almost all industrialised nations.

The unemployment figures for September were announced. The headline total now stood just under 1,000 short of three million. The seasonally adjusted total had increased by over 100,000 in the last two months alone and the percentage was now 11.3. The prospects were getting very depressing and commentators were now talking about the end of jobs, especially for the young.

In the middle of November I was called to a meeting late one afternoon in Keith Joseph's room in the House. When I got there I found Norman Tebbit and Peter Morrison. Norman said that he was looking for a new Chairman for the Manpower Services Commission. Sir Richard O'Brien, the present Chairman, was on the point of being re-appointed when he arrived at the Department but he had decided that they needed someone new. We had a long inconclusive discussion thinking of names, but no one satisfactory to Norman was suggested. We left agreeing to meet again.

It was quite late so I said goodbye to Keith and went home. On the way I was thinking of names I could suggest when suddenly the thought came to me that I should try for it myself. Why not me? I thought. I had been in the Department of Industry for two and a half years and much of the foundations of my work had been laid there. Privatisation was becoming established, the Small Firms side of the Department had a good minister in John MacGregor and now priorities were changing. Seasonally adjusted unemployment had stuck at about 2,800,000 but all sorts of wild allegations were being made that it was really far higher. Far worse was the spectre of youth unemployment looming on the horizon. It was rapidly becoming *the* political issue.

The next day I sought out Keith who was back in his room at the House. I told him that I had thought again about our meeting and that I wanted to put my own name forward. His first reaction was to say no. It is an impossible job, he said, it is this terrible tripartite organisation. We discussed it for a few minutes and when he saw that I was serious he said that he would telephone Peter Morrison.

He did so immediately. Peter told him that it would be possible to have control of the Commission – with three union representatives, three from the CBI (Confederation of British Industry), the balance of control would lie with the local authority representatives. Two of the three should be ours, he said. Above all there was a real job to be done.

'On that basis,' said Keith, 'let David's name go forward.'

Chapter 5
WAITING

I put any prospect of the Manpower Services Commission out of my mind for the time being and got back to my work in the Department of Industry. In the meantime my negotiations with Sanyo came to a head and were finally agreed. Now very nearly half the jobs would be restored and there would be prospects that in time all of them could come back.

In early December a press conference to announce the new plant was called at the Grosvenor House Hotel. I turned up and instead of my usual seat in the back row I found that they had reserved a place for me in the front. Jim Prior, the former Secretary of State for Employment, was there and to my considerable embarrassment I was given credit by Sanyo and by Jim in very generous terms. Some mention of it appeared in the papers the next day. That was the very first time in nearly three years that I had any public mention of my activities and I resolved that it would not happen again. An adviser's job fails if people realise that he is there.

I kept an eye on the plant over the coming years. At first it continued to manufacture television sets but before too long it became the first video tape recorder plant in the country. Where labour relations had been bad in the old days they became good. Productivity soared. The Sanyo management insisted that all employees, from the Managing Director onwards, started at the same time, ate in the same place, worked the same hours and parked their cars in the same car park. They even insisted that they wore the same clothes, a company uniform, and everyone complied. Furthermore they actually communicated with their workforce. Each week everyone was told how the plant was progressing, were asked for suggestions for improvements which they actually put into practice. The same workforce that had been so troublesome in the past was welded into a productive unit working to high standards.

I thought back to my early days in Great Universal Stores. I had started working in a Rego Clothiers factory on the North Circular

Road. For the first fortnight I ate in the canteen and had a perfectly respectable lunch for one and threepence. For the next fortnight I ate in a roped off portion of the canteen with the foremen where we had the same food but with waitress service – and for ninepence. After two weeks I went upstairs to the Directors' dining room where we had all that we could eat and drink – and it was free. The factory started at 8.00 a.m., the office personnel started at 9.00 a.m. and the Directors came in at 10.00 a.m. We all ate in different places, used different toilets and practised an apartheid as effective as any in the world. No wonder labour relations were always difficult and productivity and quality poor. My experiences of British industry were typical of the times and left me with one indelible impression – privilege. Yet here was another way. That it worked, and worked better, was plain to see.

A day or two later I went with Kenneth Baker on a visit to Acorn and Clive Sinclair in Cambridge. We were frankly impressed with what we saw of the innovation coming out of this new wave of companies that had grown up out of the graduates of the Cambridge computing schools. What we were not to know at the time was that our manufacturing skills did not keep up with all this innovation. Whilst we were with Clive Sinclair he showed us his plans for an innovative small electric car. It would have a special battery (which was secret) and a new type of small electric motor, one on each wheel. When it came out it had neither and unfortunately it failed.

The unemployment figures for November were announced. The headline figure had dropped and I wondered if we had a chance to avoid exceeding three million. It was not all good, however, for the seasonally adjusted figure increased to just over two and three quarter million.

With just a week to go before Christmas the Department of Industry began to slow down. On the Tuesday afternoon I got a sudden call to go and see Patrick. He had just returned from a Cabinet sub committee where the agenda had dealt with Ian MacGregor's latest project. I knew of it since I had been with Peter Carey when Ian came in to see us on the previous Friday. Ian had proposed that BSC be allowed to buy Kaiser Steel, a company in California which looked like a tame customer for semi-manufactured products from the UK. The snag was that it would mean a considerable expansion of the public sector and British Steel Corporation was nowhere near the privatisation stage. Patrick asked me to go to the States, investigate and report back.

Ian MacGregor was in Chicago but was coming back overnight. That did not surprise me for his activity was legendary. Only a short

64

time before, on a Friday, he told me that he had a lunch appointment in Los Angeles over the weekend. We fixed to meet to carry on our discussions on the Monday morning. He turned up bright and cheerful. Over the weekend he had flown to Los Angeles, had had lunch and had flown back. He was nearly seventy.

I telephoned Ian and arranged to meet him as he landed at Heathrow. His plane was on time and he briefed me on the people I was to meet in New York and the latest details of the Kaiser Steel project. I then took Concorde to New York and went straight from Kennedy to the lawyers. That took most of the day and in the early evening I went over to the bankers who were handling the terms of the deal. The purchase price would be some two hundred million pounds but the real problem was the commitments that the company had entered into some years earlier for the provision of health care for their employees. The costs of this looked horrendous but Ian had a method of solving the problem.

Just before midnight I finished with the bankers, and was satisfied with the position. We had a deal that would run if ministers so decided. By the time I got back to my hotel it was already early morning in London. I decided that I could not trust myself to go to bed but I would wait up until Patrick Jenkin came into the office. After I had reported the situation to him he told me that he was going into Cabinet and would ring me immediately thereafter. I settled down to wait and I sat rereading the papers until he rang. Could I please come back to London and bring the lawyer and the banker with me? he said. There would be meetings that evening where we would be required.

By then it was just after six in the morning in New York and nowhere was open to book the return flights. I rang Ian in London and he reserved seats for us on Concorde, and then I telephoned the lawyer and banker with the news that they were required in London that day. As soon as they heard they would be meeting the Prime Minister they agreed and we met at Kennedy airport.

We were met off the plane and rushed to the House. The Welsh and Scottish Secretaries were waiting for us in Patrick's room and I went through the position. About midnight we adjourned to the Cabinet room at No. 10 where the Prime Minister was waiting for us. The Treasury was not very keen but I thought they could be persuaded – but not the Prime Minister. She was adamant that the public sector must not be enlarged. Gradually any support died away and finally I was the only one left to argue the position. After an hour and a half even I gave up and we all left. As I went out I said to Geoffrey Howe that I had been up forty four hours, crossed the

Atlantic twice, spent an inordinate amount of time agreeing the terms and all for nothing. 'No,' said Geoffrey, 'you have had the experience!'

At the time I thought that the Prime Minister was wrong. She was, if you were thinking as a businessman. But not as a politician. Once this Government, of all Governments, started to enlarge the public sector there would have been no containing it. As it happened Ian MacGregor found other means of solving the problem; Ravenscraig remains open to this day and, I trust, for many years to come. It was a good deal, though, and one that would have been done had British Steel been in the private sector.

After that it was all downhill for a few more days until the Christmas vacation. I felt that I had earned it; yet I spent the holidays in an agony of impatience. I had heard no word from Norman and Keith knew nothing. On my return I enquired but all I could find out was that I was still in the running. There was a short list of two or three, and I was definitely on it. The newspapers (for I now looked out for references to the Manpower Services Commission) were talking of a Youth Task Force that was looking at an upgrade of the Youth Opportunities Scheme.

I went back to New York, as we had an idea how we could achieve the Kaiser purchase using outside partners. That took two days but in the end it came to nothing. Whatever we did would still be dependent on a Government guarantee and that would bring in the public sector. Reluctantly we filed our papers. Margaret Bell telephoned me whilst I was in New York; Norman Tebbit's office had come through and she had arranged for us to meet on the following Tuesday. It was going to be a very long weekend.

As soon as I went in to Norman's office he offered me the job. The more we talked the more I realised that he had intended me to have it all along. All I could think at the time was that it would be very good to be working with Norman again and with Peter Morrison who would be the Junior Minister responsible for the Manpower Services Commission. Only afterwards did I recall my conversation with Norman Tebbit the previous July when he was still at Industry, and my offer to help sort out the MSC.

I walked back to Ashdown House floating on air. I would not take up the job for another three months so I had to plan how I would spend the time. I had promised the Department that I would go to Japan early in February. It would be my very first visit and I was looking forward to it. I agreed with Norman that we would announce it before I left. If I left the country straight away that, at least, would stop me getting into trouble until I had actually started.

On the way back I made up my mind that I would play the job in a non-political way. If I succeeded that would help the Government enough, but I had to be able to work with the unions and Labour authorities.

I went in and told Patrick Jenkin the news. He became quite upset and said that he would complain to the Prime Minister, but realised soon that there was nothing to be done. 'Find me your successor,' he said, 'otherwise you just can't leave.' Peter Carey also tried his best to persuade me to stay but I think that he realised that after nearly three years of being an adviser I really did want to go and run my own show.

The following morning Geoffrey Holland, the Chief Executive of the Manpower Services Commission, was on the telephone and we arranged to meet. I had to go off that weekend to a World ORT executive meeting in France. It was to be my last meeting as I would have to resign as soon as I took up my new post, but I could not tell them about it for a few days.

All was not plain sailing at the Manpower Services Commission. Sir Richard O'Brien, the present Chairman, produced a report that shed doubt on the unemployment figures produced by the Department of Employment. It inferred that unemployment was way over three million and the Opposition was saying that it was over four or even five million. Far too many political statements had come out of the Commission for anyone's liking – the sooner I started the better.

Geoffrey Holland came to see me. He is a most unusual civil servant and is typical of many who I was to meet in the Manpower Services Commission. His first words to me were that he had agreed a deal within the Youth Task Force, the group representing employers, trade unions and local authorities, for the creation of the new Youth Training Scheme. Much of it was Greek to me, but I found myself carried away by his evident enthusiasm. We were to work together for many years and I never once found him unenthusiastic about any new project.

The December unemployment figures were announced and my heart sank. The headline figure had shot up by 130,000 and now exceeded 3,000,000. Seasonally adjusted it had only gone up by some 43,000 but the Opposition made enough fuss as it was. I began to wonder if I really knew what I had let myself in for. Was unemployment capable of being reduced? I did not have the faintest idea if it was but at least, I thought, I will have a good try.

The press conference was fixed at Caxton House, the offices of the Department of Employment. Peter Carey calmed me down over

67

lunch and afterwards I went over to the Department of Employment. I met Adrian Moorey, Norman Tebbit's Chief Press Officer and whilst I was with him I was asked to go and have a chat with Sir Kenneth Barnes, the Permanent Secretary. It was the first time that we had met.

I went into the press conference. For the first time I was the centre of attraction. I had attended many conferences over the previous three years but never played a part, except for the Sanyo conference and even there I had nothing to say. About twenty journalists turned up, all wondering who this unknown person was who was replacing the existing Chairman so unceremoniously. The general attitude was that Richard O'Brien was a much-loved figure who was being displaced by this right-wing property developer. Some of the papers thought that this might be acceptable, but the majority did not. *The Times* in a leader two days later were to take the line, followed by the majority of commentators, that Norman had given great offence by not consulting the unions although in the end they, like most of the other papers, gave me a cautious welcome. That only came, I thought, from not being known.

At the press conference itself there were few difficult questions. Geoffrey Goodman, the Industrial Editor of the *Mirror*, asked me if I had ever been unemployed. I could only reply limply that I did not think it was a necessary qualification for the job. In the main there was genuine curiosity about this unknown who was taking a job in the very centre of public concern.

As soon as the conference was over I was taken into a studio next door. Before I knew what was happening I was giving interviews to BBC News and to ITN. It all happened too quickly for me to get nervous, although when I saw the results in the evening I reminded myself of a frightened rabbit.

There was quite a fuss in the House. An Early Day motion was signed by over 200 Labour Members protesting at the sacking of Richard O'Brien. Greville Janner (a Labour Member) and I had grown up together. When I was first a solicitor and he a barrister we worked together on my one and only criminal trial. It should have been an open and shut case of shop lifting. My client, the shopkeeper, had long suspected a particular customer and had stationed his staff around the shop. They allegedly saw the accused take some goods. Alas, she engaged a leading criminal silk of the day who merely had to look at our witnesses to reduce them to tears. Our case collapsed within the hour and I decided on the spot that my future did not lie in criminal court work. Greville's father, Barnett Janner (later Lord Janner) was the first politician that I had ever met. He convinced me for a time that the reforms of the 1945–50 Labour Government would really work.

Greville told me afterwards that he was approached in the House and signed the motion; then he asked who was replacing O'Brien. When he was told that it was me he scratched his name off the list!

When I got back to my office I thought of the line of questions at the press conference and telephoned Jack Eccles, the union member of the English Industrial Estates Board. I told him of the announcement and asked him to tell his union friends that I was going to play the job straight down the middle. My concern would be the Commission.

The following day, after I had got over the shock of seeing my picture plastered all over the front pages of the papers, I went into the office. There were a whole series of interviews arranged for the Sunday papers – I was certainly getting on the job training for my new life. At the end of the day Geoffrey Holland came in to report on how the news was received in the Commission. I began to realise that Richard O'Brien had been a very popular Chairman and that I would have my work cut out over the next few months.

On Saturday I left for Japan. Originally Patrick had asked me to go, not only to see how the electronic companies were progressing but to do what I could to encourage other companies to follow Sanyo's example. It was a fascinating trip; I quickly learned that Japan's famed lifetime guarantee of employment only applied to the great companies. Every factory I visited – and I spent day after day going from one industrial plant to another – relied upon a whole host of small suppliers, the component manufacturers. They were asked to deliver many times a day and with zero defects. Zero defects was a new expression to me. It meant exactly what it said. Their suppliers would provide the components which would be assembled and not be checked until the product was finished. And then they were all expected to work.

I laughed to myself the first time I heard this thinking back to my days when I ran small component manufacturing companies in the UK. I knew the general standards of quality and thought their targets impossible. During the sixties I had a factory supplying Rolls Royce at Derby. Despite all the extra checking that went into parts for the aircraft industry we still supplied components that were returned. We were no worse than the industry norm yet here was a television manufacturer insisting on no faults at all. With mounting admiration I realised that it was true, and that they were really achieving it.

Some of the electronic companies showed me their products

under development and I began to have some idea of their lead, at least in the consumer electronics field. Of course, not everything was perfect. One day when travelling to yet another plant I was in the company of two Sanyo executives. We got to talking about pension schemes. Their scheme started at sixty-five. 'Is that the retiring age?' I asked. 'No,' was the reply, it is fifty-seven. When I asked what happened for those intervening eight years there was an embarrassed silence. Our families keep us, was the eventual reply.

I began to realise that there were great gulfs between us even though we spoke the same language. What impressed me most was the amount of resources devoted to training. NTT, the telephone company of Japan, had a number of university campuses around the country. All graduates who qualified with a two-year degree would go for a one-year course on joining the company whereas those with a four-year degree would go for six months. In addition every year all employees would have to devote a number of weeks to more courses. Yet it all paid.

I calculated the number of lines and subscribers that NTT had compared with British Telecom. On that basis they were managing with about a third less in the workforce. It was this saving that would pay for any training. Fujitsu, a computer company that was the Japanese answer to IBM, sent all their middle ranking executives on reaching forty to a Pacific island and made them take a three-month course together on liberal arts. When I asked what that would do for their business performance, I was told that spending this time together would ensure that for the remainder of their working lives in the company they would know all their peers and internal communications would be much improved.

When I came to the real reason for my trip, I did not have much success. As much as I would draw on the things we had in common – our both being islands, our great abundance of golf courses, in fact on any selling line I could think of – I would get the same reaction: the climate.

The first time I heard this it was pouring with rain outside. I pointed out that here again we had much in common. Once more, it was made very clear to me that we did not. It was the industrial climate that concerned them, and the behaviour of our unions was driving them to the continent.

I went home through Hong Kong. Cable & Wireless had settled down very well. It was always stimulating to be in Hong Kong. Attitudes were so different. Everything was possible and could be done quickly. If only we could import more of that attitude at home my new job would be very much easier.

On my return I had to deal with the task that Patrick had given me – finding a successor for myself. I telephoned Jeffrey Sterling who was intrigued by the idea: he knew Patrick at the DHSS as a result of his involvement with Motobility. I arranged for them to meet and they hit it off: my problem was solved. Jeffrey served as Special Adviser with distinction for many years. He was never a full-time adviser, his work precluded that, but worked on particular projects.

I started to prepare for my new life. I arranged a series of meetings with the senior officials of the Commission. I also thought that I should see how our European Community neighbours were coping with similar problems.

Out of the blue I received a call from Lord Scanlon. One of the 'terrible twins' of the union world of the seventies, he was at that time Chairman of the Engineering Industry Training Board. We arranged to meet and I was amazed at our conversation. Very practical, down to earth, he knew just what was necessary for the industry. I could detect little trace of the political views for which he had once been notorious.

I then went to Bonn and looked at the very impressive Jobcentres that were run by the agency equivalent to the MSC, the Federal Institute of Labour. Ford of Cologne showed me their programme which concentrated on rescuing school drop outs. They were convinced that in the future all companies would be held back by the extreme difficulty of recruitment as the number of school leavers declined sharply. I could only wish that we had that concern: youth unemployment was turning into a major political issue at home and the decline in school leavers would not come until the end of the decade.

I went on to Paris. Whilst I was there I called on the Minister who was responsible for training. My French is inadequate so I was relying on an official from our embassy. The Minister would make a long speech in French and my companion would give me a five word precis. I would make a full statement back and he would say a word or two to the Minister. It was not a satisfactory meeting and I learned little, save one thing: as I took my leave the Minister walked me to the lift; when I got in he wished me well in faultless English!

I had never met Richard O'Brien. We arranged to meet at my old bank offices. He appeared rather concerned about his own future but he had no need. Before too long he was to follow Hugh Scanlon at the Engineering Industry Training Board.

Patrick gave me a farewell dinner. All our ministers turned up and it was a jolly occasion, marred only by a number of divisions in

71

the Commons. The next day I gave a drinks party to all the colleagues that I had worked with since the last election. Easter was coming up and my new job started immediately afterwards. I had already told the MSC that I would be taking my secretary, Margaret Bell and Alex Rae with me. There was no problem where Margaret was concerned, but the transfer of Alex, a mere Executive Officer, was unheard of; no one at that lowly grade was ever transferred. 'There is always a first time,' I said, and the matter was settled.

The time had come to make my farewell call on Peter Carey. After reminiscing a little about the many changes that had taken place during the last three years I said to Peter that I thought that I had earned a place in the *Guinness Book of Records*. I had come to the Department as a Principal and was leaving as a Permanent Secretary. All in under three years, I boasted. 'Oh David,' said Peter, 'you won't be a real Permanent Secretary.'

Nor was I.

Chapter 6
CHAIRMAN

The Manpower Services Commission made the Easter weekend longer by taking an additional day. I went down with my family to Graffham taking with me a great pile of reading that Geoffrey Holland had prepared for me. The more I read it the less I seemed to understand. The papers used terms and initials that were not only strange but seemed devoid of meaning. That feeling was not to leave me for many months.

I had arranged that Margaret Bell and Alex Rae would go ahead of me on the Wednesday to get everything ready at the Commission's offices. Richard O'Brien was still the Chairman as my term was not due to start until Thursday 15 April. During the day I received a number of anguished telephone calls from Margaret.

When she and Alex had arrived Ken Moody, the Secretary of the Commission, showed her her desk in the Private Office next door to the Chairman. 'Where is Alex?' she asked. 'Oh, he will be most comfortable. I have a room specially for him on the floor above.' When Margaret protested that it would hardly be convenient he looked most surprised. After all it was a room directly above the Chairman, she was told. When Margaret told me I asked if he meant that Alex would bang on the floor to communicate with me. The exchange was worthy of the very best of *Yes Minister* but after one phone call they were both established in my Private Office.

Other little difficulties were overcome and gradually everything fell into place. On the following morning I arrived at the Commission's offices. At that time they were in Selkirk House, a very undistinguished eight-storey building in Holborn notorious only for the extreme unreliability of the lifts. I arrived at precisely 9.15 a.m. by arrangement and there waiting for me at the door was Ken Moody. 'Good morning Chairman,' he greeted me.

I did not realise it at the time but at that precise moment I lost my name and was not to regain it for many years. I was known, at least to my face, as the Chairman. At all meetings, both public and private, I would be called Chairman. Quite often in the Commission I would be addressed in the third person: the Chairman wants this, or the Chairman thinks that. It was quite disconcerting but after a while I got used to it.

There was much to get used to in the Commission. Conceived during the Heath Government it was born out of wedlock during the Wilson Government in 1974. By one of life's better ironies it represented all that I came into government to change, and yet here I was charged with the task of running it. It was the corporate state personified and yet, at the end of the day, few other bodies could have dealt with the emergencies of the early eighties.

The original concept was flawed. It assumed that government could better discharge its duties by abrogating them to a series of agencies at whose head would be tripartite Boards (representing the employers, the unions and the government) who would bind in whole sections of the working population. It further assumed that the CBI spoke for the average employer whilst the TUC spoke for the average worker. Over the years it became apparent that all they did represent were their own sectional interests. Neddy, the National Economic Development Council was the supreme tripartite body of them all. In fact it was no more than a talking shop and I was destined to serve on it for seven long years. The MSC, the Health and Safety Executive and ACAS, the conciliation service, were also tripartite bodies formed at the same period.

The Employment and Training Act of 1973 had brought together, in the Manpower Services Commission, the government training agencies, rather trendily renamed Skillcentres, together with over a thousand Jobcentres, as the unemployment exchanges were now called. As well as the Commission itself there were Manpower Services Committees for Scotland and Wales each with their own Chairman.

The Manpower Services Commission had evolved over the years into a Kafkaesque bureaucratic nightmare. It was made up of an Employment Services Division, a Manpower Intelligence and Planning Division, a Special Programmes Division, which ran all the YOPs and other schemes, a Training Services Division and finally a Corporate Services Division. Under all of these was a whole labyrinth of committees dealing with the disabled, with employment rehabilitation, with executive recruitment and with almost any activity known to man. We employed over 24,000 people. The more that I looked into it the more I became convinced that nothing less than a wholesale pruning and simplification of the organisation would suffice.

74

But having said all that it still worked as an organisation. The Manpower Services Commission came into its own with the rise in unemployment, particularly the rise in youth unemployment which came upon us with alarming suddenness towards the end of the seventies. In the summer of 1978 the school leavers poured out of school – and went straight into unemployment. Nearly a quarter of a million young people were unemployed at a time when the general level of unemployment was still well below 6 per cent. There was something wrong and the MSC set to work to find an answer. At the beginning it proved to be far harder than anyone realised.

The YOP, the Youth Opportunity Programme, concentrated on giving young school leavers work experience but no training. Too many employers were abusing the scheme and using it as a source of cheap labour. 162,000 school leavers were provided for in the first hectic year of this programme in 1978/79 and had continued to grow until no less than 553,000 were due to enter in 1982/3. Yet it was only a palliative and only six months in duration. With no training and no real work it was only just better than nothing but it had fallen into disrepute. Even this would not have come about without real cooperation between all parties on the Commission. At a time when unemployment was rocketing unions and employers alike were not too keen to see jobs taken and costs rise through taking on young trainees. Yet something had to be done.

I spent the day going over the problems facing the Commission. They were formidable. First there was the Youth Task Group Report. The group, representing the employers, unions and local authorities had been sitting for some months when, in a massive negotiating session just before Easter, Geoffrey Holland was able to persuade them to come out with an agreed report. Now all I had to do was to get the Government's agreement and make it work. That would be no light task for it was a massive scheme with the simple objective of offering all sixteen-year-old school leavers one year's training and work experience. That would cover about 350,000 school leavers.

Then there were the proposals by the Chancellor in the last Budget to enable long-term unemployed to get work. The long-term unemployed were those who had been out of work for over a year and were becoming a real problem. There were signs that their number would exceed a million. Once out of work for a long time it became progressively more difficult to get a job. What all employers wanted to see was an up-to-date reference from an employee. Whether this was true or not was in many ways irrelevant, since the evidence was that the long-term unemployed believed it was and gave up looking for work after a while.

The Community Enterprise Programme gave full-time jobs for a year to the long-term unemployed doing work for general community benefit. It was good, but far too expensive. It only covered 30,000 people and the problem now facing us required a far more ambitious programme. The Chancellor had proposed giving a supplement of £15 over the benefit rate unrelated to the kind of work, but the TUC were firmly wedded to the rate for the job.

These were the main political problems. Over and above these was the reorganisation of the Commission itself. As the days wore on, and I met more and more of my senior officials, I realised that this was going to be a full-time job.

I began to meet my Commissioners. First I encountered Elizabeth Carnegy who chaired the MSC Committee for Scotland. She proved to be a tower of strength and common sense within the Commission, even if she did not guard her words too carefully at all times. Don Stradling was the Personnel Director with John Laings; and Sonia Elkin who accompanied him was an official with the CBI. The third CBI representative was Terence Lyons who was another personnel director but this time with a bank. I met with Sir Melvyn Rosser who chaired the Committee for Wales, Roy Helmore who represented Education and Roy Thwaites who represented the Association of Metropolitan Authorities and was the leader of South Yorkshire County Council. So far I had not met any of the union Commissioners for it was proving quite difficult to arrange a convenient meeting. Eventually I did agree to call on Len Murray at Congress House just before the next Commission meeting.

But before then I had to go to Sheffield. In the early seventies, Ted Heath had decided that government offices should be dispersed to the regions. This initiative quickly ran into the sands as few senior officials wanted to leave the home counties. The MSC was an exception, or else being new had little clout. It was decided that they go to Sheffield and they had commissioned a great building there. In 1979 the incoming Government had reviewed the position and as building work had commenced the transfer continued. There had been great dismay within the Commission as many officials had to uproot themselves; but all that was in the past. The new offices were just opening and would be fully operational by the year's end.

My first sight of Moorfoot, the office building in Sheffield, was daunting. Its architecture was typically PSA, the Property Services Agency, which was the government property agency. It certainly would not have received a commendation from the Prince of Wales. It was an enormous red slab of a building. It was rapidly known as the Kremlin by local inhabitants but the inside, once you had mastered the labyrinthine layout, did provide excellent working conditions. I had a far more impressive office than I would ever have in London.

Richard O'Brien had decided that he would move up to Sheffield and not use his London office. That gave me great difficulty. Moorfoot certainly would be the administrative headquarters of the Commission. But the political decisions would be made in London. Both the CBI and the TUC had their offices within a few hundred yards of Selkirk House. I decided that I would stay in London but visit Moorfoot frequently. This did not enhance my popularity with those who had already moved to Sheffield and in practice I was never to be in Sheffield often enough.

Each evening I was there on my early visits I gave a small dinner for different Commission officials. We would have a wide ranging discussion when they would let their hair down. I became more and more impressed with the quality of those working there. They rose to a challenge and there was a 'can do' spirit that was not always evident in Whitehall. It seemed to me as time went on that all those in the service who wanted to do things had asked for a transfer to the MSC.

In becoming Chairman I had been given one of the more difficult management tasks. Here I was, in charge of 24,000 people, without the power to hire, fire or promote any one of them. All jobs in the service were graded. The job went with the grade and if you did not have the grade you could not have the job. All permanent civil servants had tenure and provided that they did not commit any one of a short list of rather heinous crimes they had a guarantee of life-time employment.

Just how did you ensure that someone, say, in his late forties, who knew that he could get neither promoted nor sacked, continue to be interested and motivated in his job? The answer lay in the intellectual content of the work. You were rarely bored, since every three years jobs were rotated. Providing variety solved one problem but created another: few people had been in any job for any length of time and experience was always at a premium.

This was a management challenge quite unknown outside. I suspect that if I had not served an apprenticeship as Special Adviser I would have been lost. Change – especially of an unpopular nature – would only be carried out through persuasion. A large part of my time was to be spent with our own people gently leading

77

them through the changes to come and ensuring that they would adopt the ideas as their own. For the one lesson of life I had learned over the years is that ownership of an idea is essential to its adoption. If people think that the idea is theirs then they adopt it with enthusiasm – but if you try to persuade them to accept *your* idea the difficulties multiply.

My other problem was the realisation that the role that Richard O'Brien had adopted would not suit me. He had acted purely as a Chairman, spending a great deal of his time going around the country, visiting Commission establishments, chairing the CMC, the Chairman Management Committee, and building up a great reservoir of good will. He was a very kind man and took great pains with all our people. But I felt he was not an initiator and I wanted to initiate change. That would mean that I would have to be an executive Chairman. Although in practice I would sometimes encroach on the job of Geoffrey Holland, he never minded. Our only problem was to be that as two hyperactive enthusiasts we would sometimes encourage ourselves to set unrealistic targets and at the end of the day work very hard just to scrape home!

I held my first meeting of the CMC and was the more able to judge my new colleagues. Instead of accepting a broad consensus of their views I would on occasion sum up in an entirely different direction. After the first shock they accepted it with good grace.

My real test would be the first meeting of the Commission. The Commission always met on the last Tuesday in the month, and my first meeting (which was by chance to be the hundredth since its inception) was to take place at the end of April. There was going to be a very long agenda with many contentious issues.

First thing that morning I called on Len Murray at Congress House. It was my first meeting with the unions and with him was Ken Graham, Assistant General Secretary (subsequently Deputy General Secretary) of the TUC and a member of the Commission since it was founded in 1974. They received me cautiously but without any hostility. I assured Len Murray that I was determined to play the job straight down the middle. The fact that I had been a political adviser, a Director of the Centre for Policy Studies, would not affect my work now. I wanted to see the programmes we were on the point of introducing succeed. I would put politics aside in this job. As he walked me to the lift he told me that I had the most important job in the country.

Ken Graham was a bureaucrat, a long-time official with the TUC. He was the opposite number of Sonia Elkin of the CBI and was a very enthusiastic member of the Commission. He was short, approaching his sixtieth birthday, with a passion for racing, military history and Elgar. In political terms he was right of centre and we became good friends. Bill Keys was the General Secretary of SOGAT, one of the printing unions. You could not describe Bill's politics in any terms other than left wing. He was mild, calm and very contained until the wrong word was said. Then he would gather himself together, the rest of the Commission would sit back and he would explode in a torrent of self-righteous indignation; ten minutes later he would be calm again. Elizabeth Carnegy had the unconscious knack of setting Bill off and I would always listen to her contributions with bated breath. The odd thing was that they were the best of friends.

There was one occasion when a question of racial discrimination came up. We all sat back and waited for the explosion. We were not disappointed and when Bill subsided I looked firmly at him and said, 'Bill, that is nonsense. I am the only racial minority sitting around this table.' Bill gave me a hard look, followed by a broad grin. From that moment he became my best friend in the Commission and over the years always spoke up for me outside. The third representative of the TUC, Ken Graham, was not able to make that meeting and I would not see him for a few weeks.

The Commission meetings would start at 11 o'clock and break for lunch. The TUC members would meet first over at Congress House and agree a line on every item. The CBI would do the same but it was very evident that they were not as well prepared. Indeed the TUC outgunned the CBI, and at times this was embarrassingly evident. Then we had the Third World, as the other members were known throughout the Commission. They could be rather unguided but at that time we had the support of Elizabeth Carnegy and Roy Helmore. Roy Thwaites would always be against us so that, for most issues, I could count on the support of the Commission by five votes to four. I was never to find out if I had a vote. Some said 'yes', some doubted it, but at that time it was not important.

Meetings were not to be taken lightly and the first meeting brought that home to me. We started off with a rather long and sterile debate about the *Annual Manpower Review*. This was an annual publication which was a minefield for the unwary. The newspapers and the politicians would quote selectively from it and in the past it had caused the Government much embarrassment. I was determined that this should cease. It was not a matter of hiding facts but it was more that opinions about the future of work and work practices should be expressed positively. The TUC were in the business of being Jeremiahs. They were all doom and gloom and

79

wanted us to say so. Whatever I wanted the TUC wanted the opposite. In the end we achieved an uneasy compromise and this pattern was to be continued in the future.

I asked Geoffrey Holland to introduce the Youth Task Group Report. This was not a difficult issue since the report was agreed between all parties but it dealt with by far the biggest programme that the Commission had ever tackled. The compromise agreed was very different to the scheme advanced by the Government. There were some ritual exchanges about compulsion and the report was approved; I was authorised to send it immediately to the Secretary of State and publish it on 4 May 1982.

Compulsion was a code word for an issue that was to dog us for years. Sixteen-year-old summer term school leavers were entitled to register for benefit early in September. It was bad enough that they came on the count of the unemployed, but I believed that we were undermining them morally by paying them benefit for doing nothing. Sixteen pounds a week was not much, until you compared it with the likely pocket money from their parents when they were at school. Not only was it more than they had ever had in their pockets before but we were indoctrinating them in the great lesson of the welfare state – do not worry about yourself, the state will look after you.

The new Youth Training Scheme would pay an allowance that would be considerably greater than benefit. Norman Tebbit had said that young people refusing to go on the scheme would have their benefit stopped. All my sympathies were with him but I knew that if we did that we would lose union support. The state of industry was so parlous at the time that we would lose our employer support as well if there was any danger of the unions blacking the programme.

After lunch – always a buffet where senior officials from the Commission would join us – we reached the more contentious items. A paper about the future of area boards, or what sort of consultative machinery we would have throughout the country, came before us. This sounded innocent enough but it would determine the future shape and success of the Commission. In future all individual schemes would have to come for approval before these area boards. How were they to be made up and who would dominate them? In the end the best we could hope for was one third employers, one third unions and then the remainder made up of local authorities, education interests and voluntary agencies. These boards would have the power to black schemes and it was important that we keep politics out of it if at all possible. In the end we agreed the shape of the review and that the new boards would come into being by the following April.

Finally we came to the most contentious item on the agenda. What should we do about the Chancellor's offer for help for the long-term unemployed? The TUC thought that £150 million was not enough and we should provide far more money and extend the existing Community Enterprise Programme. The CBI thought that it was enough, and in any event were not most of the long-term unemployed single? If they were married they would be eligible for housing allowance and other benefits. Then what sort of projects would be carried out? Would they destroy jobs?

I could see that there was no prospect of any agreement. I had already agreed with Geoffrey that we should aim to keep the discussions in play. We agreed to carry the item over to the next meeting. There were a few miscellaneous items but at about 6 o'clock the meeting ended. In times to come I was to realise that that was about average for Commission meetings.

One day I went into No. 10 for the first time since I had arrived at the Commission. The last occasion had been before Easter when I had gone to say goodbye to the Prime Minister. At the time she had appeared very tired, had a bad cold and gave every appearance of longing for Easter week so that she could have a day or two off. Then the Falklands had intervened and she had recovered overnight. Despite all the gruelling work and worry of the last few weeks she appeared fresh and untired.

I had been invited to a reception in my new capacity. As soon as the Prime Minister saw me she asked me to come into her study for a chat and tell her how I was getting on with our new programmes. After she had left the reception I made my way to her study. She was sitting, avidly reading the *Evening Standard* which had banner headlines rumouring the loss of our aircraft carrier at the Falklands. After a minute or two I said, 'Prime Minister, surely they would have told you.' She looked up, gave me a look which said, if only you knew.

On Tuesday 4 May we had the press conference to launch the Youth Task Group report. Geoffrey Holland and I did the first of our double acts. I was nervous and rather unsure of myself and he took over and did it in style. The press coverage was rather good which was just as well as I had been summonsed before the Commons Select Committee that day. Their ostensible reason was to examine evidence about the Youth Training Scheme but I suspected that the real reason was to investigate this man who had replaced Richard O'Brien. Their Chairman was a Labour member, John

Golding, who had been the Parliamentary Under Secretary of State in the Department of Employment during the last Government. As such he had many dealings with my predecessor and considered himself an expert on the workings of the Department.

I had upgraded my Private Secretary to Principal. Alex Rae still remained with me but the volume of work and paper escalated enormously, so I had acquired Alan Wright. He had been warning me for weeks about this forthcoming ordeal. The Chairman of the Select Committee would eat unwary amateurs for breakfast, I was told. He regaled me with tales of poor officials who walked away broken men after appearing before them to give evidence. The press would be there in force and the proceedings would be broadcast. I was given enormous piles of reading to commit to memory. Teams of officials would surround me hurling quite inappropriate questions. In short I was prepared for the grand inquisitor himself.

The reality was quite tame. I knew the report backwards having spent so much time on it over the last few weeks. I found that I had a taste for verbal gymnastics and could deflect the really awkward questions without too much difficulty. It was not the most memorable hearing of that select committee. I suspect that listeners would have considered it boring, but I enjoyed it and what is more, I survived. What did come out of the hearings was the acceptance that I stood behind the report. Jonathan Aitken, one of the Tory members of the Committee, attacked the report and I strongly defended it. It stands or falls as a complete package I said. The press began to report me as having an argument with the Government. Was I really Mr Tebbit's hatchet man?

On my first or second day in the Commission it had been suggested to me that I should go on a television training course. I had agreed and in due course I found myself at the Hendon Hall hotel for a one-day course run by Barry Westwood. Six rather nervous strangers, executives from nationalised industries or large corporations, gathered together to receive what I consider to be by far the most valuable single day's education of my life. Indeed I acquired more knowledge about life in that one day than I think that I gained in most years. I learned about body language, useful in all situations not just on television. 'Remember that you know more about the subject than the interviewer,' was dunned into me. 'You are the expert not him. All he or she wants is a fluent interview, not to turn you into a stumbling wreck.' By the end of the day I had acquired a confidence on television that was to stand me in good stead in future years. Of course, that one day's course did not do it by itself. I would appear on television two or three times a week (mainly in the regions) for all the time I was at the MSC, and eventually all this practice paid off. What it did to the teatime of millions of good viewers was quite another matter!

I then continued my visits around the country, concentrating at first on how our own area offices and regional offices worked. That gave me a few surprises. Whilst I was in the Department of Industry I was used to regarding a Principal as a sort of 'gofer' – an official who did a great deal of the drafting but not someone of consequence. Out in the field it was quite different. I met one Principal in the Jobcentre service that had over 1,500 people reporting to him. I was under no illusion that his people regarded him as far more important than me. As time went on I began to appreciate the artificial distinction that the Civil Service makes between policy people and those who carry out the policies. In the private sector the doers were highly regarded, in Government it is just the opposite.

I also came across pilots for a new programme, the Enterprise Allowance Scheme. One of the hallmarks of the welfare state was that it looked after you from the cradle to the grave. If you were unfortunate enough to lose your job then you received unemployment benefit for one year. As soon as that expired you were on social security. There were housing allowances, single payment benefits and a plethora of other benefits that ensured that a goodly proportion of people were in receipt of 85 per cent or more of their net take home pay. There was only one snag. If you were so reckless as to start up your own business, or work for yourself in any way, then all of these benefits would be cut off immediately. Not only would you have to take all the risks involved with starting up a new business, or becoming self-employed for the first time, you would lose the prop of all state aids. It was a very efficient device to keep people on the register.

These pilots had been set up towards the end of the previous year. Originally the TUC and the CBI had been against the scheme – the TUC because they were little interested in small businesses and self-employment and the CBI were more interested in reducing National Insurance Surcharge. However, thanks to the spirited advocacy of Mel Rosser, the Chairman of the Committee for Wales, we had embarked on five pilots.

The scheme was simplicity itself. As long as you had been out of work for at least thirteen weeks, were in receipt of benefit, could get hold of £1,000 even by loan and were prepared to work full-time in the business we would give you £40 a week in lieu of benefit for a year. The scheme was immensely popular. On one of my first visits to Scotland I went to one of the pilots in North Ayrshire. I visited a small factory where five or six supervisors, made redundant in the steel industry, had set up their own factory. All they needed was the ability to borrow £1,000 each and we would give them the allowance. When they told me of the difference this had made to them and to their families it reminded me of my early days. 'It is not the money,' one of them said to me, 'it is the self respect.' Unfortunately agreement had been reached with the Treasury that we would pilot the scheme for two years before extending it. I resolved to do something about it if I could.

In another major departure from accepted practice we would take no interest in the type of business that people wanted to start. As long as it was legal, did not involve gambling, politics or religion, it was up to the applicant. John MacGregor, back in the Department of Industry and Peter Morrison had taken a great interest in the scheme and it was due to them that it had got so far.

One day I was driving to Ashdown House for a meeting on the pilots with Roger Lasko, one of our officials. We had a real problem. The system of government control would not allow a switch of expenditure from programme to running costs. We only had sufficient in our budget for staff to either run the programme or pay out the allowance. Of course we needed both. I suggested that we get the banks to take over this work from us. After all, they always wanted new accounts and here people would be starting their own businesses. The banks, I thought, would be happy to pay out the allowance.

The next day I rang John Quinton, Chairman of Barclays Bank. He was encouraging and within a fortnight we had agreed to make the payments through the Banking Automated System. It proved to be very cheap and efficient. This was the first time that banks had been used in this way and it set a pattern for the future for many different government programmes.

I was making good progress with Norman Tebbit on the Youth Training Scheme. Norman's original scheme would only give £15 a week to trainees but our scheme would involve a substantial contribution from the employer. However the result would be that the trainee would receive about £28 a week and it would also ensure thirteen weeks' training in the year. That was an enormous increase in the provision of training, about 100,000 trainee years for the country as a whole, and would make great demands on the further education colleges. Norman accepted that we needed the agreement of the unions, if only to keep uncommitted employers on side. On the other hand I was making very little progress on the programme for the long-term unemployed. Not only did I have agnostic unions I also had very hostile Labour local authorities.

Life had become very hectic with meeting after meeting. As I had made it clear that I was interested in all that was going on, all the problems facing the Commission came on my desk. The sheer volume was immense. No sooner had I mastered one brief when another would hit my desk. After a few weeks I suddenly felt that I could not cope; I started to panic. Had I finally taken on too much? I cancelled the next meeting and had a hard look at my diary. What could I change? I decided just to work through it and see what would happen. As the weeks, months and years went by I found ways of stretching myself and taking on more and more. One day I was to look back and realise that my workload at that time was quite light, at least by later standards. It certainly did not feel it at the time.

I was introduced into a new phenomenon, the Centres for the Unemployed. They had started as places for those out of work to meet but some had been taken over by left-wing activists who used them as a focus of political activity. Jim Prior had come to some arrangement with the TUC whereby we were funding about a hundred of such centres which were run by the unions. These were not supposed to be political for such activities were forbidden. In the main our troubles were often with the centres funded by local authorities who paid for them themselves, not the unions who received funds from us. Over the years many of these centres specialised in advising the unemployed how to work the benefit system. How that was to help the unemployed other than to ensure that they kept living off the state I never found out.

Youth unemployment was top of the agenda and the only way we could help was with the existing Youth Opportunities Programme. We arranged a series of presentations at large industrial employers such as ICI and Hanson Trust to recruit them to provide places. What we were really selling was the forthcoming Youth Training Scheme. Whenever we had an opportunity to explain what it was, what it would do for young people, how it was really in the self-interest of all employers, we had no difficulties. But I realised very soon that we were taking on a great gamble. The Government was going to offer a guarantee of a place on the new programme for each and every unemployed sixteen-year-old school leaver by the Christmas of the first year of the scheme. The way unemployment was going we might have to find hundreds of thousands of places to ensure that guarantee.

The Skillcentres were another difficulty. Formed to help the war effort the Government Training Centres continued after the war to train the returning soldiers. Decades later they had become a good example of an institution that had outlived its purpose. I visited six Skillcentres around the country and was appalled by what I found. They concentrated on the sort of skills that were rapidly being overtaken by technology. Computer numerically controlled lathes were being introduced throughout industry and each would do the work of six or eight of the old machines; yet we were training unemployed people in the old skills. The construction industry was depressed; but we were training brick layers and carpenters to a standard not accepted by the industry. I suspected that most of them would end up in the informal economy. Not only were the skills wrong but the costs were far too high.

But it was not a simple decision. There were considerable political costs as the Skillcentres were regarded as a symbol of training. If we were to try to close one down then there would be a storm of protest from the local council, questions would be asked in the House and it would be raised at an endless succession of Commission meetings. We spent over four years closing down just one Skillcentre in South Wales. There were nearly one hundred around the country.

The May meeting of the Commission still saw deadlock on the programme to help the long-term unemployed. The difficulties were considerable. On the one hand the CBI were concerned that the work done would destroy jobs in many small jobbing builders around the country. On the other the TUC were concerned to put the programme on an employer/employee basis with the rate for the job being paid. The money simply would not run to this, not if we were to try to help the numbers involved. The Association of Metropolitan Authorities, in the presence of Roy Thwaites, was cool on all the alternatives but in the end we did take away for further study a part-time scheme which could help as many as 100,000 people.

I spent the next few weeks working hard on devising an alternative that would be acceptable. Finally I found one that would be acceptable to Norman; I even persuaded Leon Brittan, the Chief Secretary. I went into the next Commission meeting in a confident mood and, after congratulating Elizabeth Carnegy on her peerage, we went straight into our discussions. The CBI and the TUC were in favour but I ran up against a brick wall with the Association of Metropolitan Authorities which was Labour controlled. Roy Thwaites was adamant: the AMA would not endorse a scheme that did not give at least four days' work a week. We were proposing two and a half days. I might argue that the long-term unemployed required an up-to-date reference even more than the money but Roy was unmoved. In the end we agreed to stand the discussion over until the next meeting.

By now we were beginning to run out of time. This had started as a suggestion in the Budget by the Chancellor who was wedded to the idea. He wanted the long-term unemployed to work for a supplement over the amount of their benefit monies. We were beginning to move a long way away from that scheme and I still did not have anything agreed.

Jeremy Surr was the Commission official who had spent most of his time working out the details. After the Commission meeting we sat down and considered the alternatives. In the end I asked Jeremy to arrange a meeting with the Association of Metropolitan Authorities.

The good news was that the Government had accepted our proposals for the Youth Training Scheme in full. We could now go full steam ahead with preparing for its introduction next year. After the initial publicity we would have to go slow on any further publicity as we still had this year's YOP to deliver. We had to find places for the school leavers for this summer but I did authorise a number of pilot schemes for the Youth Training Scheme. We also made arrangements for an Advisory Group on Content and Standards, under Peter Reay of Cadbury Schweppes, to supervise and approve of the training arrangements for the new scheme.

On the 1 July Jeremy Surr and I drove to Sheffield to meet with the AMA in Sheffield Town Hall. On the way up I said to Jeremy that if we pulled it off we would call the new programme the Community Programme if only to maintain continuity with the existing Community Enterprise Programme. Jeremy filled me in at length with the difficulties he was having with the voluntary sector who were opposed to the programme. We did not need their agreement to launch it, they were not represented on the Commission, but they would have to organise about half the projects if we were to deliver.

The meeting was over surprisingly quickly. After we had all rehearsed our positions we sat and just looked at each other. David Blunkett, now a prominent Labour MP, suddenly suggested that we should offer the rate for the job for the number of hours worked. I jumped at this and we quickly sketched out a scheme which would continue to have as many full-time places as the existing Community Enterprise Programme and allow a large number of places to be made up of part-time jobs paying the appropriate hourly rate.

This suggestion was approved by Norman Tebbit. It was not very different from the scheme that I had had approved by the Chancellor. I had said then that it would ensure that long-term unemployment would not exceed one million. I was wrong, for despite the introduction and success of the Community Programme, long-term unemployment continued to rise, albeit at a slower pace. I was still some years away from finding the real way to deal with this problem.

At the July meeting of the Commission the new programme went through, with the grudging consent of the TUC and the enthusiastic endorsement of all other parties. I suspected that the TUC had only supported the programme in the past because they knew that the local authorities were opposed. Once we overcame that hurdle they were forced to accept.

That was not the end of our problems. Over the next year Jeremy Surr, David Price and many other Commission officials would work unceasingly to overcome the hostility and suspicions of the voluntary sector. They spoke at meetings up and down the land, often seven days a week. They were so successful that in the end the voluntary bodies adopted the programme as their own and would not be parted from it. All over the country hundreds of schemes opened up. It was said that there was not a scout hut in the land that was not rebuilt during this period, no village hall unpainted and a host of environmental schemes started. At its peak the Community Programme was to have over 200,000 people working in it. It made a real contribution to helping those out of work for over a year to maintain, or rediscover, their self respect. Many went into outside jobs during the second half of their year on the programme.

By now August had come and I went on my break well satisfied with my first few months. The Youth Training Scheme and the Community Programme were now accepted. We still had to deliver but the immediate political problems were over. Internally though there was still a great deal to be done. I had announced at my third Chairman's Management Committee meeting that I thought that I was the only person who worked for the MSC. Everyone else still talked in terms of their being part of the Special Programmes Division, the Training Services Division and Employment Services Division. With the new programmes coming up that had to change and I set about reorganising the Commission.

Chapter 7
DAWN RAID ON EDUCATION

I spent the early days of August giving interviews on my first months in the Commission. As soon as those were over Lita and I went down to our house at Graffham for a fortnight. On the whole the press was supportive and I appeared to have established myself as an independent Chairman. My relationship with the TUC was surprisingly good and on occasion the left wing press was kinder to me than our own.

Keith Joseph had suggested that we get together at some time during the summer to discuss future policy. I invited him down to the country to stay for a day or two and he came down in the middle of August. We hit a short patch of good weather and we spent the time sitting in the garden talking. Although he was largely concerned with educational policies, our discussion did range over a whole number of other issues.

At the end he asked me if I had anything to raise. There was and I was bursting to get it out. I told him of the progress we had been making towards the development of the Youth Training Scheme, how we had been developing fairly rudimentary training programmes for young people who left school with not much to show for eleven years of compulsory education.

I had been down to one of the early pilot schemes in the West Country. In one factory a young trainee had proudly showed me all the measurements he had taken in the quality control department and how he had calculated the variances. He then showed me about thirty charts and graphs neatly produced in coloured inks. I had asked him if he had passed any exams in maths. 'No,' he replied, 'I failed the lot.' In an odd way he was almost proud of it. Had he been any good at maths at school? I had asked. 'No,' was the reply. At that point his supervisor told me that he had taught him everything in ten days. 'When they see the point they always learn,' he had said, 'it doesn't take long.'

That incident had left a very deep impression on me. I remembered the first visit I made to the ORT schools in Israel. Since then I had seen many similar schools around the world. Young people, not academic by nature, had come alive as soon as their education had changed to technical or vocational subjects.

I then came to the idea that had kept me awake at night for the last few weeks. I suggested to Keith that we open a series of technical schools around the country. 'Let them be outside the existing state system if we have to,' I suggested. We could run the programme through the MSC. I was sure that we could open a number of demonstrator projects for the 1983/4 school year. 'Let them succeed,' I said, 'and we will infect the system. Then they will all want to change.'

I told Keith that to be successful these schools would have to combine a normal education with technical and vocational subjects. 'It is not the schools themselves which are so important,' I concluded, 'we must find a way to motivate the majority of young people who simply don't benefit out of the existing comprehensives with their watered down academic system.'

Keith Joseph sat and thought about it for a moment and then just said, 'Yes.' I do not think that any other colleague as Education Secretary would have agreed. We had discussed vocational education over the years and he knew my long-term commitment to it. But I doubt if Keith would have agreed for any other colleague than me. Although his main interest was in increasing academic standards, he was also aware that there was a dissatisfied minority whose needs were being ignored by the present system. The politicians in education would hate the whole idea although many teachers would be enthusiastic from the start. Unfortunately both would detest the thought that any responsibility for education would go outside the DES. Although he said nothing to me he knew full well that he would be subjected to a shower of abuse by the whole of the educational establishment for selling his birthright to the dreaded MSC. Once again he was right.

I then sketched out some plans I had for opening these schools. For a start I knew of two or three apprenticeship schools that were now closed. We could buy them and convert them in good time. I was sure that we could find more. But this would only be there as a threat. If we could persuade the Local Education Authorities to create the new projects it would be better. But I was doubtful. In the end we agreed that we would keep this to ourselves, as if it leaked the resulting publicity would prevent it ever happening. I told Keith Joseph that the only person I would discuss our conversation with would be Geoffrey Holland. I had to get his assurance that we could deliver. After I had been to Norman I would come back to Keith.

When I returned to the office I found that Norman Tebbit had taken a late holiday so I awaited his return with some impatience. In the meantime we had a great deal to do. I went to York to address a section of the Civil Service Union about our plans to reorganise the Skillcentres. I felt like Daniel walking into the lions' den but they turned out to be very kind to me. After we spent some time, and consumed much beer, in the bar after the meeting I began to feel that we might be able to make some progress.

The September unemployment figures only added to the general gloom. The headline figure was now well over 3.3 million. It had increased by 370,000 in the last four months alone. Seasonally adjusted the figure for the UK now exceeded three million and that was without 289,100 school leavers. The underlying rate of increase for the second quarter of the year was between 30,000 and 40,000 per month but this had accelerated to 45,000 a month for the last two months. Worse of all, long-term unemployed had finally exceeded one million. By now a third of all unemployed had been out of work for over a year. Even I, a professional optimist, began to wonder what we could ever do to reverse the rise.

In October we were due to launch the new Community Programme. By combining it with the old Community Enterprise Programme we were able to create 130,000 jobs, some full and the remainder part time. This would be a massive effort, far greater than anything attempted before, which could only work with the voluntary sector right behind us.

The announcement went well in the party although there was a wave of criticism from the voluntary bodies that I had feared. Of course Labour politicians attacked it as well, but that was neither surprising nor serious. I had to do something about the voluntary bodies so I took Peter Jay to lunch. He had started to build up TV-am which was yet to open.

My brother had been the Chairman of the losing consortium for breakfast television and was quite upset at the time. Within a few months he had been invited to become a Governor of the BBC and found that fascinating. But television, interesting as it was, was not the reason for lunch.

Peter Jay was also the President of the National Council of Voluntary Organisations who were leading the opposition to our new Community Programme. I think that he was sympathetic to our plans but I doubted whether he could really deliver his organisation.

At the same time our real challenge was the preparation for the new Youth Training Scheme. It was frustrating; as we were in the build up for the final year of the Youth Opportunities Programme we could not distract our people in the field. There were just too many school leavers with nothing but their YOP places waiting for them to take attention away from our job of placing them with employers. As for the Youth Training Scheme, the major effort had to be behind the scenes. The Youth Training Board (which had the task of supervising the entire programme) came into being and I chaired the first of a long series of meetings. We made arrangements to ensure that we offered quality training.

Many large companies wanted to deal centrally with their commitments to the Youth Training Scheme. We set up a large firms unit who were given the task of obtaining over 100,000 places. I asked for weekly meetings to report progress.

One day I took Terry Beckett, the Director-General of the CBI, to lunch at a rather good restaurant in Covent Garden. We spent almost the whole lunch discussing how the Youth Training Scheme would work and what they could do to help. As we parted in the street Terry said to me that he could offer no guarantees, no promises, that the CBI would deliver. All that I could think was that it was a waste of a good lunch.

Other organisations were more optimistic and I had tremendous support, not only from large employers but also from unions. As I went around the country I gradually became more cheerful about the outcome. But until we had delivered our places for this year's school leavers for YOP we could not be too public about the new scheme.

Adam Thomson, the Chairman of British Caledonian, invited me down to tour his offices in Gatwick. My brother Stuart had been a non-executive director for years. At one point we went into a large room where about thirty girls were taking telephone bookings from the public for tickets. They were sitting in front of VDUs connected by satellite to their main booking computer in San Francisco. They were using the Continental Airlines installation during the night hours on the West Coast. I suddenly realised that, in the future, service sector jobs could be the subject of import penetration if we were not careful. With the latest forms of communications, back offices could be in any part of the world. If we did not have the necessary skills there were jobs that could be exported in the future.

But by then Norman Tebbit had returned and I went to see him. Michael Alison, his Minister of State, was there with Peter Morrison. When we had finished our agenda I asked the officials to leave and launched into my idea. Norman took to it immediately.

He knew, by instinct, that it was what his constituents wanted. He asked me if I really could deliver ten new schools, each with a thousand pupils, within a year. I replied that the first year's intake would only be 250 a project. It would take four years to build up to 1,000. In any event I hoped that we would only have to use the new schools as a threat. It would be better if we could persuade the existing system to run our new programme provided that we retained control in its entirety. On the other hand if we were boycotted by the education system I now knew of at least six places where we could buy suitable premises to house the new schools. I was sure that we had a good chance of completing the ten projects in time.

A few days later we all met with Keith Joseph. We agreed to ask the Prime Minister to announce the programme. That would settle any demarcation dispute between departments that the journalists would otherwise create. The educational press were already complaining about the Youth Training Scheme and were arguing that the responsibility for it should be transferred to the Department of Education and Science.

The Prime Minister had a very busy schedule and it was proving difficult to get in to see her. I complained to Norman Tebbit once or twice that we were rapidly running out of time if we were going to open these schools in time for the next school year. An appointment was finally made for the second week in November.

We met in the Prime Minister's study with Norman Tebbit, Keith Joseph and Leon Brittan. Happily the Prime Minister took to the idea straight away. But she was a former Education Secretary and still remembered many of the pitfalls of the Department. 'What about legislation?' she asked. Then I revealed our secret weapon. By a happy accident of drafting – and it was no more than an accident – the 1973 legislation that set up the MSC allowed us to run our own schools. I was told that it was never planned but the unintended by-product of sloppy drafting. Whichever way it arose it was still good enough, at least so the lawyers advised us. After that it was plain sailing. The Prime Minister accepted the need to reintroduce technical education and accepted that she should announce the scheme to prevent any talk about machinery of government.

Leon Brittan was there as Chief Secretary and he did his duty. He insisted that I find the cost out of my existing budget. I agreed for the first year cost would be well under £10 million and I was already sure that we would have an underspend on the Youth Training Scheme. We had the draft of a written question and we agreed that it would be announced the following day.

93

We went back to our offices to tell our departments. Geoffrey Holland had been in on the secret all the time but we had not told anyone else. It would be a considerable understatement to say that it came as a surprise. One of the more senior of my officials merely said 'How curious.' He seemed more upset that this could happen without him knowing than excited by the new scheme.

Keith Joseph rang me and asked if I would see some of his people. Early the next morning three senior officials from the DES came round. I could see that they were utterly shocked and rather fed up. After a while they came to the point of their visit. Could we run the programme within the existing system and let it be administered by the Local Education Authorities? 'Yes,' I replied, 'as long as we make sure that it does happen and it will not be taken over and treated merely as extra money for the present system.' A name was dreamt up by one of our people and the New Technical and Vocational Educational Initiative came into being. It was a terrible name but it quickly became know just as TVEI.

In the country at large the announcement attracted little comment but it burst like a bombshell in the world of education. Many educationalists at that time were insisting that the world of school and that of work should be kept separate; our programme sought to bring them together. Again, the funds for this programme would be administered by the MSC and not by the DES. For some reason I was never able to divine why that was considered a heinous crime. I was to be told time after time in the months to come that it would be alright if only DES paid out the monies. Finally, we wanted to enter into a contract with the Local Education Authorities. Not only would they be obligated to provide the appropriate courses, but we actually proposed to check up on them.

The Local Education Authorities themselves had no such inhibitions. We had our first expression of interest the very next day and by the end of January no less than two thirds of the LEAs had indicated preliminary interest and over half had submitted outline ideas. At that rate there would be no difficulty in getting our ten pilots. Politics now entered the scene. A number of left-wing authorities refused to have anything to do with the MSC and the Labour education spokesman went around the country making speeches about the evils of producing 'factory fodder'. I met him once at a conference in the Midlands but nothing could shake him from his views. I did not think that he had the faintest idea what vocational education was about but he had a good speech and he was not going to be confused by the facts. He never was; his name was Neil Kinnock.

At the beginning the local authority associations thought that here was a pot of money merely for the taking. They were quickly disillusioned. We set a tremendous pace; by the end of November we convened the first meeting of the National Steering Group, assembled a national management team and issued public invitations to LEAs to come and take part. Then before Christmas we asked for and received outline proposals, judged them and selected the projects' localities. By mid-February we appointed local chairmen and put project teams in place. By the end of the month they were all up and working. By mid-March we had Exchequer funding agreed for each local project. Then all we had to do was to make local preparations, staff development and in-service training and open our doors in September: This in the world of education, where progress was usually measured over decades!

We also asked the Local Education Authorities to cost their programmes and then come to us to justify their proposals. That was a new departure for, from all accounts, we were the first people to ever ask them about costs at the school level. It seemed very odd to me but the system of education in this country ensured that individual schools had no idea of their own costs. The Local Education Authority dealt with all these matters – until we came alone. Even where LEAs dealt with costings they never worked out the cost per pupil, let alone where some schools were more efficient than others. When the proposals came in we had a panel of experts to judge them.

I had originally planned the programme for a four-year course, starting at fourteen. I had hoped that one result would be to encourage more and more young people to stay on at school after sixteen. I knew that if we could only motivate them sufficiently in school they would learn, and do so because they would see that it would be helpful in later life. Many of the projects included high-tech subjects and I had little doubt that the courses would be popular – they were. The following year I was to go to see the first project in Hertfordshire.

It was the end of a long day and I arrived at the school over an hour late. It was now a quarter to five and the school should have closed at 4 o'clock. The class (all girls) were present and totally absorbed. They were operating small computer controlled lathes and, although they were under sixteen, had all learned to programme and use them in a few weeks. When I apologised for being late one of the pupils thanked me. 'This way we have more time,' she said to me. Many of the others nodded vigorously. As a child I never volunteered to stay on after school, but one of the teachers told me that, for their TVEI courses, they look for any excuse to stay on.

The first set of proposals was for the fourteen to sixteen age group. Each project provided for 250 entrants at fourteen, and then an annual intake of 250 pupils until the full complement of 1,000 per project was achieved. The individual applications showed a great deal of variety and there was no doubt that we had captured the imagination of many teachers. Many of the projects found new and imaginative ways to bring schools and colleges of further education together for the very first time. But they would not be technical schools.

With the help of the DES officials we formed a National Steering Group to oversee the applications and another group to look at the curriculum. This brought into the commission a whole group of people from the Local Education Authority world. Time after time they seemed obsessed with politics when I thought that they should have been interested in education. Slowly, carefully and painfully we agreed the way ahead. We had to make some compromises but the package we ended up with was far more realistic and vocational than anything that had existed up to now in the school system.

We ended up with applications from sixty-six Local Education Authorities and some even submitted multiple applications. The selection group worked heroic hours to whittle them down to ten, but failed. In the end they could not reduce the selection to less than twelve. The Commission looked at the geographical situation of those selected and increased it to fourteen. I realised that I could find enough money to pay for them all and sent it on to Norman Tebbit. The more the merrier, was my view.

In order to drive this programme through in the time allowed I went outside the service for someone to run it. I secured from W. S. Atkins, the international consultants, one of their senior partners, John Woolhouse. John was a great enthusiast who was quite seized by the importance of this programme. He came in like a breath of fresh air and revolutionised the way it was introduced. Originally, I persuaded him to come for a two year period. He did so well that in time we managed to persuade the Civil Service Commissioners to allow him a three-year extension. Just when we were about to go national, at the end of his five years, the Civil Service Commissioners insisted that we advertise the post before giving him another extension. Quite rightly he refused to go through the indignity of applying to an advertisement for the job he himself had created over the previous five years. John went off and became the Director of the Centre of Education and Industry at Warwick University. His sacrifice was not in vain, for the rules were subsequently changed. But we were denied the best qualified man for the job by a bureaucratic nonsense.

During the early months *Panorama* decided to make a programme about TVEI. They followed me around the country for a day or two and interviewed all those opposing the scheme. I was innocent enough in the ways of television to allow them to interview me for a half hour or so at our area offices in Coventry. I was rather worried for a while until I saw the programme. They had cut my interview up, salami fashion, all through the programme, but to good effect. It turned out to be a powerful recruiting agent for the scheme. I was told that the Prime Minister recommended everyone to see the programme at the party's Central Council meeting. There could be many worse recommendations than that.

All the projects opened on schedule at the start of the next school year. They became so popular with pupils and teachers that year after year we were able to extend the programme just to cope with demand. Eventually we were able to go national and at a cost of £1 billion over a ten-year period all schools would have their TVEI programmes. Over two million young people would be in TVEI in the early nineties and teachers all over the country would boast about their own projects and regard the programme with pride. We did infect the system although we still do not yet have modern up-to-date technical schools in the system. We have the new CTCs, the City Technology Colleges, but they are outside the main system. I hope that by the end of the nineties we will have a school system fit to enter this century, if not the next! If so, it will have an extensive vocational training base as part and parcel of the educational system.

All the time that this was going on we still had to fill all the places in the old Youth Opportunities Programme. In the end we did rather well; we found places for 325,000 entrants and by Christmas we were down to only 7,880 of the summer school leavers waiting for a place. That was under half the previous year's figure. I thought that we were making good progress. Before I could get too complacent I realised that YOP was only a six-month programme and we used many places twice a year. The new Youth Training Programme would have to provide for a full-year place for all school leavers. In practice that meant more than double the places.

At times I felt rather like a trainee music hall juggler with rather too many balls in the air at any one time, for we could not afford to ignore the new Youth Training Scheme. We ran nine pilots to develop the new system, covering some 600 school leavers. I went around the country asking to see exactly what we provided in the thirteen weeks' training. The answer was 'not enough'. Time after time I would see that what we were really giving was remedial education – not training.

I sat on a committee, chaired by Michael Alison, the Minister of State at the Department that was concerned with the employment prospects of ethnic minorities. There were representatives of the various groups in the Asian and Afro-Caribbean communities as well as the Chairman of the Commission for Racial Equality. I would sometimes ponder how representative members of a committee like this actually were of their own communities. One day one of the Asian members said to me that the world was much easier at the turn of the century when the Jews were arriving. 'They would all help each other,' he claimed, 'in Leeds and in London they all worked together.' I thought back to the Jewish bakers' strike for a sixteen-hour working day, and wondered. In fact they did not work together as a community but – and this was a very big difference – they did not expect the state to do anything for them either. They did have charitable organisations, but that was for the less fortunate members of their own society. It did bring home to me how destructive the welfare state could be. A perfectly respectable desire to help the less fortunate ended up in the discouragement of incentive among the majority.

The three-year terms of the Commissioners were due to expire at the end of the year. The TUC, being very conscious of protocol, duly renominated the same Commissioners, for they held the post of the Chairmen of the Labour and Education Committees. Ken Graham and Sonia Elkin were also renominated since they were part of their respective head offices but we did not give the CBI the same luxury. Norman Tebbit and I plotted together and then proposed the names of new Commissioners which the CBI accepted with good grace: Norman Payne, who ran the British Airports Authority and Hamish Orr-Ewing, who ran Rank Xerox, could easily give the TUC a run for their money. At long last I felt that the odds had evened up. It was not all good news for on balance we were far worse off. We had certainly lost political control of the commission. Elizabeth Carnegy had had to step down following our electoral losses in Scotland although she still chaired the committee for Scotland. Her place was taken by Dr Malcolm Green, a very sensible Labour councillor from Strathclyde. Although we now had Alistair Lawton from the Association of County Councils who was a Conservative and a tower of strength, control of the Commission actually lay in the hands of Wilson Longdon, the education representative. It was thought that he was a Tory, for his wife had been a Tory councillor. Alas the information was not quite accurate. They had divorced and I never found out what he really was for his voting record was quite erratic. We never knew from issue to issue which way he would jump and thus, whether or not I had command of the Commission on any issue.

Christmas came and went. All through the Christmas period I was worrying about the launch of the Youth Training Scheme. We had set ourselves a really ambitious target. To give our guarantee to each unemployed sixteen-year-old school leaver we had to find 400,000 places. We arranged a great press conference on 17 January.

It would not be easy. In the old scheme the small companies would take their 'YOP' as someone they could use at no expense to themselves for six months; there were no other commitments. This time, in order to make up the cost of the training, the companies would have to pay part of the overall cost, although they could now use the trainee to work in the business.

Not all school leavers were employable. Where they were not we would run our own schemes with the help of the voluntary agencies. As there was no employer we would have to make up the additional costs. We had calculated that the national companies would provide over 100,000 places. The remainder would have to come from smaller companies in the regions.

We started work before Christmas and by the time of the launch the large firms had promised 50,000 places: 100,000 could be converted out of the existing YOP programme but that still left us a quarter of a million short, often in difficult areas. There was a too evident mismatch between the demands of industry and commerce and the areas of highest youth unemployment.

Saatchi & Saatchi had been acting for the MSC since 1977. We spoke to them about an advertising campaign and when they came in I met Tim Bell. I took to Tim right away. Puffing away on an inexhaustible supply of cigarettes, he is imaginative, enthusiastic and the archetypical 'can do' man. They produced a very dramatic newspaper campaign and a marvellous sixty second television commercial which, with just the right touch of humour, brought home the need for the Youth Training Scheme, both for school leavers and their employers. The campaign quickly became a talking point and I spent a great deal of my time appearing on radio and television. After our press conference I spent the early months of 1983 anxiously travelling the country checking up on progress.

The Enterprise Allowance Scheme had proved to be a runaway success in the five pilot areas. It captured the imagination of ministers, Members of Parliament and the general public. There was something about helping unemployed people to work for themselves that went to the very heart of the policies of the Government. In his Budget the Chancellor extended the scheme nationally from 1 August. It was initially limited to 25,000 places but I was sure that if we could show that the demand was there, I could get it extended.

As time went by I became increasingly fed up with the selective briefing coming from the TUC after each Commission meeting. I would always read their version of events in the following day's papers. I decided that, in future, I would hold a press briefing after each Commission meeting. From that moment onwards our press improved. The TUC still gave their version but it was now balanced by ours. I learned from that incident how important it was to ensure that you communicate with the media first. Give your story, for if you don't the other side will surely give theirs: journalists abhor a vacuum more than nature.

By the end of March we had just under 40,000 places filled in the Community Programme and a further 40,000 approved. We were processing a further 85,000 places and were well on course for our 130,000 filled places in the autumn. Our initial problems with the voluntary bodies were now behind us and a wave of enthusiasm was building up around the country for the programme.

Outside the Commission other great events were taking place. Arthur Scargill was trying to recreate his heady days of 1974 and had brought the bulk of the miners out on strike. Ian MacGregor had gone to the Coal Board and was locked into a propaganda war which he was losing. I would meet him from time to time for breakfast and talk over the latest situation. One day I suggested to him that he should have an adviser to help him with his public relations. He agreed and asked me to suggest the right person. I went back to the office and rang Norman Tebbit. He suggested Tim Bell and I rang Tim who met with Ian MacGregor the same day. From that time on Tim Bell was to spend a great deal of his time with Ian MacGregor who I fear never mastered the art of dealing with the media.

The campaign to sell the Youth Training Scheme was now in full swing. I would be embarrassed from time to time speaking to employers to be asked what we, the Government, were doing. I could only shrug my shoulders because the Government had decided that they would not take part themselves. Eventually we managed to persuade ministers to allow the Civil Service to enter the programme and one day I created a major coup. I went to see the Prime Minister. She had always been lukewarm about the

100

Youth Training Scheme in Government. I persuaded her to take her own trainee in No. 10. I came away delighted but suddenly sobered by the realisation that now I would be responsible for the behaviour of the trainee. We had better pick a good trainee, I worried, when once again we were saved by the unions. As long as the Government said 'no' the Civil Service unions were pressing us to take trainees. As soon as we said yes they blacked the whole programme. The Prime Minister never had her trainee.

Easter came and went and election fever was on the rise. There are strict conventions regarding government activities during an election and there was a blanket restriction on all forms of advertising. We were now in the most hectic phase of our Youth Training Scheme advertising and I asked Norman Tebbit to see whether we could negotiate an agreement with the opposition to allow us to continue. Peter Morrison spoke to Harold Walker for the Labour party and Shirley Williams and Cyril Smith for the Alliance. To their credit they all agreed – Harold Walker on the specific understanding that the Commissioners were happy. Ken Graham studied the scripts of the television advertising, found no political content and was happy for it to proceed. Just when I started to relax something went wrong in 'the usual channels' and it was all stopped. In practice I had arranged a natural break in the television advertising between 22 May and 9 June on the offchance of an election so it did not matter too much.

I went in to the Department of Employment and had a farewell drink with Norman Tebbit and Peter Morrison. Norman certainly did not expect to return afterwards but I was not sure about Peter. I had greatly enjoyed working with both and I wondered who I would get after the election. Of course, if the unthinkable happened, I would be working with a Labour Government. However with Michael Foot as the Leader of the Opposition I quickly put the prospect out of mind.

One Sunday there was a highly publicised council of war at Chequers. The television news was full of pictures of Cecil Parkinson and Norman Tebbit leaving and we expected an imminent announcement. I went to Sheffield for a meeting of my Chairman's Management Committee. It was hard to concentrate on the work in hand and the morning dragged on. I had a slightly discreditable reason for wanting an immediate announcement. The following day I was due to go to the North East for the first flight of an aircraft built by YOP trainees. I thought that it was just a publicity stunt until I was told that it was going to be flown by a Concorde pilot. Then I realised it was not. The aircraft was a two-seater. I would volunteer whatever anyone said and I did not fancy the idea. Just before lunch the announcement came. I was saved. All public events were cancelled for civil servants and I could not go. I found out afterwards that the pilot made one circuit of the airfield and came down ashen.

It never flew again.

Chapter 8
PROBLEMS AND SOLUTIONS

As soon as the election was called we burst into frenetic activity. All public meetings had to be cancelled. This had all the makings of a disaster as we were in the middle of marketing both the Youth Training Scheme and the Community Programme. We had arranged numerous meetings with industry and the voluntary sector – all those had to go. So did all advertising. We were very worried about the break in the marketing effort of the Youth Training Scheme at this most critical period but we could do absolutely nothing about it. As soon as all the publicity and all the meetings were cancelled we just stopped.

I had to be very careful that no one in the Commission said or did anything that could become a political issue during the heady days of an election campaign. That included me, so for a few days I went down to the West Country for some fishing.

When I did go into the office there was little to do. It was not the same in the Department of Employment. There officials were manfully studying the manifestos of all parties and preparing position papers in the event there would be a change of government. Even if there were not there would almost certainly be a change of ministers and they would have to be brought up to speed. But that would not apply to the Commission.

About twelve days before polling day the TUC Commissioners asked to see me. After a general discussion, Ken Graham said that he had a message for the Prime Minister and Norman Tebbit. He wanted to assure them that whatever the result of the election the TUC would work with the Government of the day. After they left I telephoned Norman. The TUC have just thrown in the towel, I said. I never had any doubts about the outcome. Of course it appeared quite different to those actually involved, as I was to discover the next time around.

The result of the election was a tremendous victory for the Government. That was no real surprise, but the return of Norman

Tebbit to Employment was. The reason became public months later but I was happy to see Norman and Peter Morrison back. Peter had been promoted to Minister of State when Michael Alison left to become the Prime Minister's Parliamentary Private Secretary. There were no charges at the Commission, save it was now all systems go. There was no doubt that the considerable majority gained by the Government worked wonders in terms of getting policies through. Within weeks, policy decisions which had seemed very difficult, if not impossible before, slipped through, almost unnoticed.

Almost as a bonus unemployment stopped rising. The Budget excluded those over sixty on long-term benefit from signing on, since the evidence was that few if any of them were really in the labour market, but there was a real fall for two or three months. But my worry continued: long-term unemployment now exceeded 1,100,000.

Marketing for the Youth Training Scheme continued in earnest. I met with the senior managements of Imperial Group, Chloride, British Steel, Rowntree Mackintosh, Ford and Tesco. The Lord Mayor of London offered his help. Public interest continued unabated and we began to catch up on our targets. By the end of June we had identified over 90 per cent of our Youth Training Scheme places although we had only contracted for a third of them. In many areas we were over our target, often in the most difficult employment areas. Our greatest area of difficulty was in London. In the areas of highest unemployment people worked together. In more prosperous London, that did not happen. Unfortunately there were many pockets of high unemployment in London.

By the end of May 1983 we could report that 200 ITECs (Information Technology Centres) had been identified. These training centres, which made so many young people computer literate, had started as a result of a visit some years before by Kenneth Baker to a Notting Hill project when he was the Minister for Information Technology at the Department of Industry. He had persuaded the MSC at the time to accept 90 per cent of the cost, with the Department making up the rest. When I arrived at the MSC I expanded the programme fourfold although I was unsuccessful in persuading the Department of Industry to increase their share of the costs.

We had now identified all our places for the Community Programme and were on target for the autumn.

Before the summer I reported to the Commission that we now had over 400,000 places on the Youth Training Scheme. Not all were in the right place, or even signed up but we had broken the back of the work. It had been a tremendous effort by thousands of MSC officials up and down the land. There had been extraordinary public interest. Even BBC Radio One had devoted a week in June to selling YTS to school leavers. Just as well, for the testing period was right ahead of us.

At home there were other changes. The time had come for George Howard, Chairman of the BBC to step down. He had been in indifferent health and was keen that my brother Stuart take over from him. Stuart could think of nothing better and resolved that if it were to happen he would retire from his accountancy practice. To his (and our) great joy and pride it did happen and it was announced that on 1 August he would become Chairman of the Corporation. I have on my desk the photograph that was taken on the day he entered Broadcasting House for the first time as Chairman. Alas, our joy was soon dimmed. Only a few weeks later he complained of a persistent cough. The diagnosis confirmed the worst, and he was operated on and commenced chemotherapy. The prognosis, which they confided to me alone, was very gloomy indeed, but he seemed to make a good recovery. The unthinkable is simply put out of mind; before long I just forgot it ever happened. But in the still of the night it would return.

As soon as August came we went down to the country. I had by now learned the great lesson of political life – to take a break whenever an opportunity presents itself. But there was still too much to do in the Youth Training Scheme to really relax.

By the September Commission meeting we were over the worst. We could report over 380,000 approved places with a further 71,000 places anticipated. We had achieved our target! We also had 86,000 trainees in training at the end of August. The real rush came in September and October but now we were ready for it. I began to relax. We now had all the 130,000 approved places for the Community Programme although only 83,000 were filled. As soon as the summer was over the places would be occupied.

I spent much of September travelling around the country seeing what was happening on the ground. One day I was at our Skillcentre just outside Liverpool. The manager told me how he would see trainees, especially those in plumbing, carpentry or bricklaying, the cowboy trades he called it, come back for technical help a few months after leaving. 'They would be driving their own vans,' he said, 'and still drawing benefit.'

I was down on one occasion in South Wales visiting one of our Jobcentres in a small valley town. The manager told me that he would sometimes ring one of the unemployed on his books with an

105

offer of a job. 'Funny,' he said, 'how often they would be out until after six.' He then told me a story, apocryphal or not I never found out. He was told by a wife that her husband was out working. 'Could he see him tomorrow?' he asked. 'No,' was the reply, 'he works during the day.' 'Never mind,' he said, 'when he comes in just give him a message. Ask him to report to the benefit office first thing in the morning as he has just come off benefit.' 'The next morning,' he said to me, 'there was one housewife in the town sporting a brand new black eye!'

The conference season came round. From the moment I came to the Commission all party conferences were out of bounds for me. Instead I would go to the TUC conference in September and the CBI one in November. Bill Keys always gave me a good reception at the TUC, and by now I had quite a number of friends in the union world. However I suspect that the vast majority were rather wary of me. The MSC was an object of suspicion to most of the left-wingers, who seemed more and more in control.

The Conservative Conference caught all the headlines. Cecil Parkinson resigned and that caused a small reshuffle. This time Norman Tebbit did go to the new Department of Trade and Industry and Tom King came to Employment; Peter Morrison remained so not much changed. Peter was a remarkable minister. When he first came to the Department he rapidly became extremely unpopular with most of the officials who dealt with him in the Commission. I got the impression that he was not exactly popular with his own officials either. He was very enthusiastic, and a workaholic. He looked into detail in ways that few ministers ever did. He called civil servants Martians, beings from another planet. Whenever a particularly impenetrable minute or letter would appear before him he would call for a translation from Martian to English. He was an old Etonian and came from a very comfortable, political family. His father and both grandfathers had been in the House and an elder brother was there with him now. He was one of the first supporters of Margaret Thatcher and helped to organise her leadership campaign.

Gradually as time went by attitudes towards him changed. People began to recognise him for what he was – a dedicated and hard working minister who had the interests of Government, and therefore the Department at heart. He had a great sense of humour and delighted in appearing other-worldly. Stories about him abounded. It was said that on one occasion his official car broke down and, in company with his Private Secretary, he dived down the Underground. When the train came in he said, 'Right, to the bar. I am dying for a drink.'

A year or two later he was on a guided tour of Moorfoot, the

Commission headquarters in Sheffield. It was a Friday afternoon and my people had carefully worked out a tour which ended, as arranged, at 3 o'clock so he could leave to drive to his constituency. Peter was cleverer than that. Just before three, just as they were preparing to bid him goodbye, he announced that his car was coming at four. My people were lost, as they had come to the end of their prepared tour. 'Never mind,' said Peter, 'let us go anywhere at random.' The official told me that with a sinking heart he followed Peter to another floor. Peter opened door after door to find empty rooms. 'It was after three on a Friday afternoon,' my official lamely explained, 'and we work Flexitime.' At last there was one room occupied with one official concentrating over a computer. Peter walked into the room; the official did not look up but carried on. Peter walked behind him and looked at the screen. He was playing space invaders! At that point my official gave up. 'I didn't mind,' Peter was to complain to me later, 'that he didn't acknowledge me, nor even the fact that he was playing space invaders. But why, oh why, did he play so badly?'

By the end of October 1983 we could report that 240,000 young people had entered the Youth Training Scheme. We now had well over 400,000 places and wound down our search for more. Early in October we conducted a survey and found that there were still 66,000 school leavers waiting for a place. However we were now confident that we would meet our target by Christmas.

But the system was not really working well. When we first started on the Youth Training Scheme we were aware that we would be creating an enormous demand for a type of training that had never existed before. This demand, for about 100,000 man-years of training for young people, some of whom would have left school with CSEs whilst others would leave with nothing. At first we looked to the colleges of further education but the more I visited them the less I liked what I saw. Many of the faults that we had in the Skillcentres were there in the colleges. Courses were being run because they were there, not because they were wanted. By and large the colleges were insulated from the real world of supply and demand. Young people on leaving school would go down to their local college and sign on for a course in engineering because it was there. Only when they finished did they find out that the skills they had acquired were not those demanded by the market.

We allowed private sector trainers to provide the Youth Training Scheme training. There were few private sector trainers in existence but we thought that it might help a little. As the scheme got underway we were very glad. The colleges proved very inflexible; they

107

provided their courses and the employers could take them or leave them. Many left them. When we added up the results at the end of the first year the private sector trainers provided just over half of all the training. Now we had a flourishing private sector training establishment. Training managers, made redundant, had started up new companies. Existing companies opened their run-down apprenticeship schools to the new trainees. A whole variety of new arrangements came into being. Collectively they provided just the training that the market wanted. As the years were to go by they would play an ever more important role in the training scene. That was a lesson I remembered and was to put to good use in an entirely different context a few years later.

By November all seemed well. *The Times* could report in an editorial that the Youth Training Scheme was an enormous success. They went on to draw a distinction between the German system and our own. The Youth Training Scheme would cost the taxpayer some two billion a year (they exaggerated somewhat) but in Germany the employers would invest seven and a half billion themselves. I thought that I would go to see for myself. By the end of the year the workload had slowed down enough for me to visit my opposite number.

Dr Stingl was the President of the Federal Institute of Labour in Nuremberg, a tripartite body but with independent status. It did not appear to be immediately answerable to a minister. We spent two days in talks and compared notes. The system of dual education in Germany is one of the reasons for the German economic miracle. Like many things in Germany it is very stratified. Young people who were not academic could leave school at fifteen and spend the next three years enjoying two days full-time education and training at college and three days with their employer. I thought that it provided a far better system of education than our system, but I doubted that we could introduce it at home. Our training effort was rudimentary compared with theirs, so much so that it became quite depressing. We finished our talks with a few hours to spare before my flight.

Dr Stingl was a Bavarian, larger than life and still full of his experiences during the war. He had been a fighter pilot, 'on the Eastern front, naturally' and seemed to think that that would make everything all right. He asked me if I would like to do any sightseeing. When I agreed, they took me to the Nuremberg parade ground a few kilometres outside the town. I doubt to this very day if they understood why I did not appreciate being taken up to the podium and stood on the very spot where Hitler would review his troops.

By the end of the year unemployment (which had seemed to be on the decline) resumed its steady, inexorable advance. There was now an ageing pattern in unemployment and evidence was coming through that people were beginning to adjust to being out of work. Certainly there was little social unrest and the Community Programme was doing heroic work in alleviating distress. I was not satisfied that we had the answer: there was something fundamental that I was missing.

I was becoming increasingly aware of the many defects in the way that the colleges of further education worked. Keith Joseph and I had discussed this many times to see what we could do to improve the situation. The colleges were just too insulated from the market. It is one thing to guarantee the independence of the education system from interference from politicians but quite another if that results in an unchanging, inflexible system. I would visit colleges around the country and time after time I could see that courses were run simply because they were there. Lecturers had tenure and there was little incentive for change. Even worse, young people in their last few months of school would visit their local colleges and sign on. They assumed that, because they were there, there was a need for them. Only too late, once they had finished, would they find out that the skills they had acquired were in little demand.

I looked at the *taxe d'apprentisage* in France. This is a payroll tax and employers can either spend it on their own training or give it to the college of their choice, or in the last resort the Government takes it. That would be hypotheticated taxation (earmarked for a specific purpose) and would be too great an innovation for the United Kingdom. Even then, after the poor experiences of the Industrial Training Boards, I doubted that it would work. Eventually I thought that it would be better if we were to let our area boards act as some form of substitute for the market. This would not be a perfect solution but would be better than nothing.

The existing system gave funds for education to local authorities who would then hand them on to their own Local Education Authorities. The LEAs would then divide the funds, first between schools and colleges, then the colleges' funds would be further divided between advanced and non advanced, that is work-related, further education. I suggested that we should take part of the funds for non-advanced further education away from Local Education Authorities and give it out from our area offices on a contractual basis. By entering into individual contracts we could be sure that the courses would change to those we thought would be in demand. We would use our local employers, through the area boards, to look at the local labour market and examine local skill shortages. Keith Joseph was happy with that and so was Tom King.

109

All this was eventually enshrined in a White Paper 'Training for Jobs' which was published at the end of January. The Government provided that the Manpower Services Commission be given some £200 million per annum, about a quarter of the annual spend on non-advanced further education. The MSC would look at their local labour market information, take the advice of local employers, and determine what courses should be run. Then they would negotiate with the colleges and enter into a contract. No contract, no money, no courses.

This was another great shock to the world of education but perhaps they were getting used to it, for the reaction (at least initially) was not too violent. Our sternest critic, the *Guardian*, admitted on 1 February that vocational education had an abysmal track record and that it made sense for central government to take a hand in trying to remedy the situation.

We were all then thrown into a great round of negotiations with the authorities. The Labour ones, at least, tried to fight the decision politically. Even our own Conservative controlled authorities seemed to balk at the new system. As time went on tempers shortened and a very difficult situation seemed inevitable.

Keith Joseph once again became the target of attacks from the educationalists for selling his birthright. He shrugged his shoulders, paid tribute to the good work that the colleges were doing and then dipped into his seemingly inexhaustible supply of patience and pointed out where they were not in touch with the market. 'This is where the MSC comes in,' he added.

We held all the cards. The White Paper was published and we had the funds. In conversation I would drop hints that we could always make monies available to private sector training establishments if the local authorities did not take it up. In time the problem was resolved, although not until after I had left the Commission. Today the system works very efficiently. For some months I would wonder why we had so much difficulty with this particular White Paper. After it was settled I concluded that I had simply tried to change too much in too short a time. I had been the author of too much innovation in a very conservative system and it took Bryan Nicholson (my successor at the Commission) to win them over. But that was a long way ahead.

In the meantime TVEI was spreading like wildfire. At the January meeting we were able to report that sixty-eight LEAs had submitted applications. To my surprise no less than forty-six were good enough to support. We had stormed the citadel of education and from now on our only problems would be coping with the demand.

The results of the Christmas undertaking on the Youth Training

Scheme came in. Out of nearly 500,000 summer school leavers only about 3,000 were waiting for a place at Christmas. Most of the remainder would be entering the programme in January. It was a triumph, and confounded all the critics of the scheme who had been forecasting disaster all year. It was a considerable tribute to the way both the business community and the unions had worked together in what was perceived to be a time of national crisis. Commission officials had worked heroic hours and had achieved miracles in some parts of the country where employment was very difficult and unemployment chronic.

I had been travelling the country examining the way the Enterprise Allowance Scheme had been introduced. The Chancellor had given us sufficient funds for 25,000 places for a national scheme from 1 August. With no experience of the scheme to fall back on we had allocated places in proportion to those claiming benefit around the country. Within a few months we had 23,000 people, previously unemployed, working for themselves. Long waiting lists were now building up in some parts of the country. But the results had been variable.

In the South West it had been an immediate success. There were few large employers but they did have a long tradition of small businesses. From the very first there were never enough places. Before many weeks were out the area directors were clamouring for more. In the North East it was very different. There there was no tradition of self-employment and the going was very slow. In the North East you either worked for the large steel mill, coal mine or shipbuilder, often following father and grandfather into the same company, or else a very few owned the corner shop. It took a number of years before we saw the North East catch up with the rest of the country. Gradually, their native entrepreneurism came through and as the months and years would go by the numbers accelerated until today there is little difference from the rest of the UK.

On 1 April I went down to Chequers to see the Prime Minister. It was a lovely spring day, I was on top of the world and, alas, in such an ebullient mood that I started off our meeting with words I was to regret for years afterwards.

We met in her study. 'Prime Minister,' I started, 'Youth Training Scheme – delivered, Community Programme – delivered, TVEI – delivered. Both the Enterprise Allowance Scheme and our Further Education programmes are now established and running well.' I went on to describe the reorganisation of the Commission that was now completed and to say that, apart from some work on the Skillcentres, my work was done.

111

The Prime Minister just smiled broadly at this and went on to discuss other ways in which I could help. We discussed the prospect of my coming into No. 10 as her Chief of Staff. I said that I was quite content to do the job in any way that she would like. There was a whole spectrum ranging from a Special Adviser, a Civil Service Chief of Staff, to a minister who would carry out the same job. I said that I would be content with whatever she decided.

Within a day or two of our meeting there were stories on the front pages of the *Financial Times* and some of the other heavies. 'Thatcher considers MSC Chairman for Downing Street role' was the leading story in the FT. I was to become a minister in the Lords and head up a Prime Minister's department. Luckily I was away at the time, so the stories died out after a day or two. But the really damning comment was contained in an article by Alan Pike in the *Financial Times*. 'Other people come to me with their problems, David Young comes to me with his achievements.' Over the months to come the media was to change 'achievements' to 'solutions' and I was to be stuck with the label for the rest of my political life. I have no idea whether or not the Prime Minister ever made the statement; certainly she did not do so in front of me. I am equally certain that few statements could have helped me less with my colleagues.

By the time I came back all this had died down. I went back to work and spent a great deal of my time travelling around the country visiting schemes and looking at changing work patterns. I went out on a rig on the North Sea, a visit which was only memorable as the helicopter lost one engine within a dozen feet of landing and had to veer off and return to Aberdeen. I went back on the next flight thinking little more of the experience. That evening I was entertaining the local large employers when my neighbour at dinner said to me that they had had quite an exciting morning at the airport. One of the helicopters had engine trouble and all the emergency services were put on full alert until it had landed. 'It was a close run thing,' he said to me. I quite lost my appetite when it dawned on me that it had been my flight!

Unemployment continued to be a problem and the April figures showed nearly 3,100,000 out of work. Despite all our efforts with the Community Programme long term unemployment continued to rise. It had now reached 1,200,000. What would it have been like without our programmes? I would wonder.

I would lunch from time to time with Michael Quinlan, the Permanent Secretary at the Department of Employment and with David Hancock, the Permanent Secretary at Education. We would take turns as host and meet every six weeks or so for a general discussion. Initially I suspected that they were both rather fearful what this rather blundering amateur would be up to next, but after a time we became good friends.

I had been asked to give the annual Haldane lecture by Birkbeck College. 'Knowing How And Knowing That, A Philosophy of the Vocational' was the title I chose, and I devoted a great deal of time and effort to attacking the academic bias of the present educational system. Considering, as I suspected, that very few of my audience agreed with me, I was received with great courtesy.

Hamish Orr-Ewing, who was Chairman of Rank Xerox as well as being one of my Commissioners, had offered help with my speech writing. He had arranged for David West, who came to help me. We started to use the latest communication methods. David would put the draft of a lecture on Telecom Gold and late at night I would turn on my computer, dial the service, and down-load the draft into the machine. When it was finished I would send it back. It did not work perfectly, but it was a start. From then onwards I would use computers for all of my writing and I was grateful for my enthusiasm for these devices that had made me teach myself to touch-type.

As the weeks went by we made all the arrangements for the second year of the Youth Training Scheme. It was now becoming routine and I could see a need for a two-year scheme. Quite a few young people were leaving the programme before the end of the year to go into a job. Whilst I welcomed this since it certainly helped the unemployment figures, I was really interested in them receiving a good foundation training, as far too many employers still did not provide any form of training.

The end of the summer term came round again and school leavers started to take up their places. In July I went around North Wales and spent a day or two in Snowdonia and Central Wales. We hit a spell of idyllic weather, the scenery was spectacular, the schemes we visited looked worthwhile and I knew that this would be one of my last tours in my present job. It was, I thought, a good time to go on to another challenge.

Chapter 9
CABINET

August came around again, the House rose and ministers disappeared. I went down to the country. As the month wore on speculation started again about the coming reshuffle. I had been asked to call on the Prime Minister at the end of the month. The days dragged by.

At last the end of August came. On the day, since Norman Dodds was still away, I took a taxi to Downing Street. Downing Street always had a very deserted air during the holidays. Gone was the hum of activity, the continual flow of visitors and the occasional grouping of photographers waiting patiently for the colleagues to arrive or the famous to leave. Even the police at the entrance to the street and the attendants at the front door went about their duties with an uncharacteristic lethargy. In an almost deserted Private Office I was told that the Prime Minister was in her study and waiting for me. I climbed up the stairs, this time having no time for the serried ranks of past Prime Ministers that lined the walls, all in black and white save for a solitary James Callaghan in glorious colour.

I knocked on the door and entered her study. She was in a very relaxed mood and well rested from her holiday. She had the secret of getting more benefit from a few days away than most of us did in a month. 'David,' she started, after we had compared notes on the way we had spent August, 'I have made up my mind that I would like you in my Cabinet. You will come into the Lords, well you have nearly earned it anyway, but you will not have a department. I would like you to take a special interest in job creation. Unemployment must be dealt with.'

I had often read the expression the 'floor opened up' and discounted it as pure hyperbole, but this time it actually happened. I am not too sure that I heard the rest of the conversation, although afterwards I thought I remembered that we discussed ways that I could encourage employment creation. All that was running

115

through my mind was 'Cabinet – Cabinet', and wondering what that would entail.

It had been a rather poor summer but the day had turned warm and humid. I left Downing Street in a daze. Left into Whitehall, I walked past the Cabinet Office (my future home!, I thought to myself with slowly diminishing disbelief), between the Welsh and the Scottish Office, up Whitehall towards Trafalgar Square. I had meant to get a cab but I was still in such a turmoil that before I knew quite where I was I had walked right across the West End up Regent's Street into Regents Park and then to our home. I arrived quite hot and sticky from the long walk, told my wife Lita, swore her to secrecy, and then went back to waiting.

The following Monday I was back in the Manpower Services Commission preparing for the second year of the Youth Training Scheme. On the Thursday I went down to Brighton for the TUC conference. The left-wing was steadily getting more strident. There was a strong element that wanted to pull the unions out of all government training and unemployment schemes. I was not too worried because we all knew that the delegates at Congress were not too representative of their members. Those unions that did black the Youth Training Scheme, at least those in the private sector, found that schemes simply started at individual plants around the country. Their members were dealing with their own, and their workmates', sons and daughters. That counted more than any annual conference resolution.

That weekend, reshuffle speculation ran riot. Although there was some mention of the earlier story about my going to No. 10, security seemed to have held. At first I was relieved but before long, having had no word from No. 10, started to worry in case there had been a change of mind.

The next morning I went into Selkirk House. It was still soon after the summer break and there was little to do. My paperwork was quickly finished and I paced around the office. Every few minutes I would go to my private office and ask, quite innocently, 'Any calls?' Margaret and the others knew full well why I asked, and would merely shake their heads. In desperation I called a meeting to review progress on the Youth Training Scheme. It had hardly started when David Vere, my Private Secretary, interrupted the meeting with a note. 'It's come,' it said, 'Appointment to see the P.M. at 2.45 p.m.' I finished off the meeting as quickly as possible and continued to pace up and down.

After a quick sandwich I left early to go to Downing Street. Today was not a day to be late. The deserted air had evaporated.

There was a buzz of activity and the policemen at the barricade at the top of the Downing Street were expecting me. Scores of photographers and television cameramen were herded in their compound opposite the front door to No. 10. They paid no attention to me, presumably thinking that I was some sort of official. Well, I still was. I went in and walked through to the Private Office at the back. Robin Butler, the P.M.'s Principal Private Secretary, was waiting for me and we climbed the stairs once again to her study.

This time our meeting was rather more formal. I was to come into the Cabinet as Minister without Portfolio and I would be in the Lords. I was to have special responsibility for enterprise and wealth creation. I would have an office in the Cabinet Office, evidently the one previously occupied by Arthur Cockfield, who was leaving the Cabinet to go to Brussels as a Commissioner.

Just as we were finishing the Prime Minister said to me, rather tentatively, 'David, there is one more thing. I am afraid that you will have no salary.' There was a statutory limit to the number of salaries that could be paid out to members of Cabinet and my joining exceeded the limit. As I had worked for Keith Joseph and Patrick Jenkin for nearly three years for nothing I thought that one more year would not be the end of the world. Before I knew what had happened, I was out of the office. On the way out Robin Butler told me that he hoped that the announcement would be out by 6 o'clock but I should keep it to myself until then. 'Accidents can happen,' he added rather ominously.

I went back to the office for a few minutes. They could see by my face that I had something to tell them but I said little. I told Margaret that we were moving and went home and told Lita. Stuart telephoned me and knew merely by the sound of my voice. I asked my parents to come over for a drink and to see the *Six O'clock News*. I refused to tell them and teased them to wait for the news. When it came on there was no announcement. We waited for the *Seven O'clock News* and still no announcement. Then about 7.30 p.m. it came. The big news was the fate of Jim Prior. He had left the Government and Douglas Hurd was going to Belfast. Grey Gowrie was to become Minister for the Arts and the Civil Service in the Cabinet. Arthur Cockfield was leaving to go to Brussels and I came in. 'Lord Who?' Eleanor Goodman described me at the tail end of the programme. Then the phone started to ring.

The following day *The Times* did me proud but most of the other papers had hardly heard of me. I thought it a little strange until I later realised that all the articles were written by the political correspondents, the lobby, and I was only known to the labour correspondents. I went into the office to clear my desk.

I had not been in long when David Hancock rang. 'Congratulations Minister,' he began. 'Come off it, David,' I replied. 'No, from now onwards you are Minister,' and nothing could shake him. Indeed from that moment onwards I was 'Minister' to all. Now I had lost my name even to those few remaining civil servants who still thought that they could call me David.

I went down to 70 Whitehall, the Cabinet Office and my new home. There I came up against my first obstacle. Lord Cockfield had refused to leave his offices. He was not going to budge. He was going to Brussels at the end of the year and until then he was going to stay put. I had assumed that it was only to be for a day or two but in the end he refused to leave before Christmas. He held on to his official car as well. He got his way. Where would I go? I was shown some rather unsatisfactory accommodation on the ground floor at the front. It was about the same as my original accommodation when I first arrived at the Department of Industry but I resolved to put up with it and not complain. After all, I thought then it would only be for a few weeks. In the end I had to camp out in this temporary accommodation until the end of the year.

At this stage I had absolutely nothing. I had no office, no private secretary, no staff, no job description and nothing to do. As there was no car, I held on to my MSC car. Happily Norman Dodds and Margaret Bell came with me, but that was all. There were not even any ministerial boxes as it had been many years since there had been a previous Minister without Portfolio. At first I was quite upset and then I sat down to think through the situation. The more that I thought about it the more that it seemed to me to be a great opportunity. If there were no rules there would be few limits to what I could do and so it proved.

Robert Armstrong, the Cabinet Secretary, told me that he was arranging for me to have a Private Secretary and I was given two or three names. I was also told that a trawl was going on around departments for people to help me set up my office.

I went over to see Willie Whitelaw who, as Lord President of the Council, worked in another part of the Cabinet Office. I always liked Willie and found him straight with me. He wanted to welcome me and said that he would do all that he could to help me settle down. He was Leader of the Lords and had arranged that I would speak for Employment and probably for the Treasury as well. He asked me to make contact with the Privy Council office as there was going to be a Privy Council the very next day to swear me in.

My grandfather, c.1935

My parents, 1927

With my mother and
brother Stuart, Torquay
1941

First meeting with
Margaret Thatcher, at the
ORT Businessman's lunch,
1978

My introduction into the House of Lords, with Baroness Carnegy of Lour and Lord Thomas of Swynnerton, 1984 (*Copyright Universal Pictorial Press*)

On the Great Wall of China, with Margaret Bell and interpreter, March 1985

First meeting with Premier Zhao Ziyang, March 1985

Launch of 'Pleasure, Leisure and Jobs', 1985 (*Copyright Press Association Photos*)

Introducing Keith Joseph into the Lords, 1987

The Family Rally, Wembley, the Sunday afternoon before election day, 1987
(*Copyright Financial Times Photography*)

'Action for Jobs' breakfast, with (*from left*) John Lee, Kenneth Clarke and David Trippier (*Copyright Press Association Photos*)

Election triumph, with Norman Tebbit, 1987 (*Copyright Srdja Djukanovic*)

(a) Lord Young as depicted by G. Ian Williams

(b) The race for the chairmanship of the Conservative party

First day at the Department of Trade and Industry, with Kenneth Clarke
(*Copyright Press Association Photos*)

With ministers from the Department of Trade and Industry (*Copyright The Times*)

At the Privy Council office I was initiated into the rather formidable ritual of being sworn in before your sovereign. First we would have to line up in order outside and then come in, bow and form a line. When my turn came I would have to kneel on one knee on a small stool and take the oath holding the Old Testament in my right hand and then advance, kneel on a second stool and kiss hands. Then I was to retire backwards until I was back in line. Just to make me even more nervous the Privy Council, which is always called for the purpose of handing over seals of office and swearing in new Councillors, was to be at Balmoral for the first time in decades. Normally the Queen would come down to London but this time we would go there.

We were due to meet at Northolt Airport at 9 o'clock in the morning. When we drove up to the gate and the guard saluted me I realised for the first time that my life had really altered. I was shown to the waiting room where Willie Whitelaw and Arthur Cockfield were waiting. Grey Gowrie then arrived, and we were told that Douglas Hurd would be going direct from Belfast. We soon boarded a plane from the Queen's Flight and we were on our way.

We landed at Aberdeen and were put on a coach. We had to endure a very bumpy drive of about an hour and a quarter until we arrived at Balmoral. Helicopters were not allowed, I was told, and this gave me all the more time to worry and fret about getting the ritual of swearing in and kissing hands right. As it happens all went faultlessly. Any meeting of the Privy Council is over in a few minutes. It is, I suppose, the oldest form of council in the land and the meetings are always taken with all the participants standing throughout. I could think of many other meetings which could only be improved in that way.

As soon as it was over we adjourned for a drink and what turned out to be a very jolly lunch. Afterwards we were shown over the house by the Queen. It had been carefully restored over the years to the decor it had when it was occupied by Victoria and Albert. It was obviously a greatly loved home. After we had made our farewells we were taken on a tour of the estate ending up at a remote lake with a semi-derelict house which was sometimes used by the family for picnics. The dining room still had pictures on the wall and I noticed that all were rather gloomy Victorian paintings which, without exception, featured death! By the time our tour was over it was time for our return and we drove back to Aberdeen airport; we were back in London too late to go back to the office. So far membership of the Cabinet had not proved too onerous!

The following morning I interviewed Leigh Lewis. Leigh was a

119

Principal at the Department of Employment and I took to him immediately. He seemed to know, almost by instinct, not only the machinations of Whitehall but the way to present any statement likely to be acceptable to my colleagues and irritate the Opposition. Like most civil servants, his political opinions were shrouded in mystery and remain so to this day.

I agreed to his appointment as my Private Secretary on the spot and over the next few days I acquired a small group of civil servants from all over Whitehall. I tried to make it as representative of the economic departments as possible. Robin Linguard came over from the Department of Industry to head up my unit. Those who volunteered to come to the Unit tended to be those who relished a challenge. They had to be, for to volunteer for what I was about to do was likely to provide more than a little irritation to the Departments they left behind and would one day have to return to.

That afternoon I received a telephone call from Nigel Broakes of Trafalgar House. He told me that he wanted to come and see me with Ian MacGregor about the Channel Tunnel. As I had very little else to do I agreed to see them. They told me that they were part of a group that wanted to build a part-bridge, part-tunnel using only private sector resources. Even Ian at his most persuasive had some trouble in convincing me with this rather bizarre notion but after some time I gradually came to accept that they not only meant what they said but there was a good chance that it might happen. I said that I would speak to the Prime Minister and some of my colleagues.

My embryo department was not grand enough to have its own press department, or even a press officer. Robert Armstrong kindly arranged that I would be helped by John Stubbs, who ran the press department of the Cabinet Office. He had arranged a series of interviews with the lobby correspondents who were rather curious to see what I was made of. During my time at the Manpower Services Commission I had dealt with the industrial correspondents and knew them all well. The lobby, which included the Sunday lobby, consisted of the journalists who dealt with all parliamentary matters. They had the run of the lobby in the House of Commons (hence the name lobby) and thought of themselves as a journalistic elite.

The interviews went well considering that they were all trying to make much of my new role. What were my responsibilities for job creation and enterprise?, they all wanted to know. How did I fit in with the existing Departments of Industry and Employment? Was I some sort of overlord, set up by the Prime Minister over the economic departments? Then I had a happy inspiration that served me well over the months to come. 'Oh, no,' I replied, 'I am much more an underlord, working for Tom King and all my colleagues.' That captured their imagination and in all the subsequent interviews I became known as the 'underlord'. I made much play with the fact that I was number twenty-two (out of twenty-two) in the Cabinet. 'Only just a little worse than I used to do at school,' I would tell them.

The following week continued with a whole series of firsts. I attended my first Cabinet Committee, met with Bertie Denham (Lord Denham), the Chief Whip of the Lords, who told me how I was likely to spend my evenings until the next summer, met the Garter King of Arms and had my title provisionally approved. Then came my first Cabinet.

Cabinet was always on Thursday mornings and on 20 September it started at 10 o'clock. Both Grey Gowrie and I were the new boys and I noticed that we were both among the first to arrive. All the Cabinet colleagues congregate in the waiting area outside the Cabinet room a few minutes before the hour. I knew nearly all the Cabinet and received congratulations from most of them, some, I thought, warmer than others. I could not help noticing that Grey was carrying a sheet of paper with just the two words 'Shut up' written in large capitals. I thought it a good tip and resolved to follow suit, although without the visual aid. Just before the hour we were shown a seating plan, each place marked with the name of our office. I found that I was sitting at the far end of the Cabinet table on the side that faced the Prime Minister.

Cabinet turned out to be a far more formal affair than I had imagined. Everyone was addressed by the office they held. There was always a set agenda, opening with Parliamentary business, followed by foreign and then home affairs. After some years home was promoted before foreign. Anything else would be dealt with in Cabinet sub-committees and only come to a full Cabinet if it proved impossible to resolve there. As a result Cabinets rarely took more than an hour or an hour and a half. The Prime Minister acted as a good chairman, sometimes taking the lead on a subject she felt strongly about but other times listening carefully to the views expressed. At that time the Cabinet was less homogeneous than it was to be in later years, although this would vary according to the subject under discussion.

Both Grey Gowrie and I managed to keep to our new resolutions and the Cabinet passed without any significant happening. I had one thought running through my mind and it took me back a long way. When I was just eleven and living with my parents in Finchley,

I surprised my parents and shocked my teachers by passing the eleven plus sufficiently well to be accepted for Christ's College, the local state Grammar School. When I arrived in the first form I was quite convinced that the fifth formers were gods. When, in the fullness of time, I arrived in the fifth form (I left school before the sixth) I found to my horror and great disillusionment everybody behaved just like the first formers. As time went by all life seemed to be made up of the same sort of people that I first met in the first form at Christ's College. There were the hyperactive and the lazy, the popular and the solitary, those who belonged and those who wished that they did and tried too hard. Wherever I went there seemed to be only first formers. So it seemed to me that first day I sat in Cabinet.

That weekend Stuart had invited Lita and I to share his box at the Albert Hall for the last night of the Proms. When we arrived we found Leonard and Ruth Wolfson in the party. As soon as Leonard saw me he could not contain himself. 'David,' he said, 'if only I knew that you would work for your present salary I would never have let you leave the group.' Like all really funny remarks it had more than a grain of truth in it.

I have often looked back on that evening as being the one when everything in life seemed to fall into place. My brother had achieved his ambition and loved the BBC with a passion that fulfilled his days. All thoughts of his illness had been banished as had my memory of the doctor's gloomy prognosis. We still enjoyed both our parents and they enjoyed what was happening to us. We were all close to our children. As the marvellous traditional jingoistic ritual of the last night washed over us my thoughts soared away and I could not help thinking that life could scarce improve on that evening. I was right.

By the following morning all the unreality had gone and the euphoria evaporated. It was back to my temporary office and down to work. Robin Linguard had suggested that I call my new unit the Enterprise Unit and I had put in a minute to the Prime Minister the previous weekend. It came back approved, so at least we now had a name. There were few ministers in Whitehall who could meet with their entire department each Monday morning but that is what I could do, and did for the entire year we were together. As I sat back that Monday morning I felt that I was back in the days when I first started my own company. Here I was, with a desk and a small office and the whole wide world outside. The only asset I had, never to be underrated, was a weekly meeting with the Prime Minister. Otherwise I was only limited by what I dared try to do.

I had first met Robin Linguard when I was in the Department of Industry where he had been dealing with small firms. It was hardly surprising that we would both look towards small firms as a very job productive area and one that we should concentrate on, at least at the beginning. Then I thought that I should try to take my crusade for young people a stage further and try to eliminate unemployment for all the under eighteen year olds. If we could extend the Youth Training Scheme to a two-year programme then no school leaver at sixteen need ever fear unemployment. With a look at competition and additional work on deregulation I thought that this would make a start and I drafted a minute to the Prime Minister.

I ran into a slight embarrassment. That Thursday and Friday was the Jewish New Year. I asked Leigh Lewis to arrange for a leave of absence from Cabinet on the Thursday morning. No, came back the answer, there are few occasions when you would be excused from Cabinet and certainly not for a New Year, which I suspect from the tone of the reply, they confused with an obscure form of Hogmanay. Nor indeed, I was told, had anyone asked to be excused for that reason before. I was not particularly observant but I had never worked in my life on our New Year nor did I think that at this time, when the eyes of my community would be on me, that it would be a good time to start. I asked the Prime Minister's office to refer the matter to her and she agreed at once. By chance, the same circumstances were not to arise again during my time in Cabinet.

We were now only a week away from the Party Conference at Brighton and I was anxious to settle my precise job description and responsibilities before we entered the hot house atmosphere of a Party conference. After much comings and goings between Robert Armstrong, Bernard Ingham and the Prime Minister's office a press release was agreed and issued. This referred to my policy interest in small firms, measures to increase competition and the reduction of controls and regulations, and the coordination of policies to promote the education, training and employment of fourteen to eighteen year olds. It went on to say that the list was not exclusive. I would be free to pursue other matters within my general remit at the request of the Prime Minister or at my own initiative.

In my innocence I thought that our discussions did not involve any other parties. That week's *Economist* thought otherwise. I learned with some interest that a fierce Whitehall struggle had been taking place over what, if any, specific functions I should be allowed to exercise. Victory for the *status quo* was the conclusion of the journalist since I was to have neither executive functions nor a budget. Swords were being happily sheathed at Treasury and at the Departments of Employment and Industry. Time would tell, I thought to myself, as I read the article.

Then we were off to Brighton where I rediscovered the joys of our Party Conference. It had been some years since I had last attended and then I had merely been a Special Adviser, not a Cabinet colleague. Despite my new found eminence I found that I was back in the team drafting the Prime Minister's speech for the final session. I was to help with the section on unemployment. On the Wednesday evening we started a drafting session with the Prime Minister which carried on until half past three in the morning when we all staggered to bed. Not so the Prime Minister who still appeared remarkably fresh and was even heard to call for a dispatch box.

The next day I sought out Nicholas Ridley who at that time was the Transport Secretary. I told him about Nigel Broakes's suggestion about the possibility of a privately financed Channel Tunnel. I said that I would still take other soundings. I got rather similar reactions from Nigel Lawson and Norman Tebbit.

On the Thursday evening I was back in the Prime Minister's suite for another speech-writing session. At about 12.30 a.m. we finished the section on unemployment and I asked to be excused. I wanted to go back to our home at Graffham that evening to take Lita to the Conference on the final day. The Prime Minister readily agreed and I drove my weary way home getting to bed at about 2 a.m. I had hardly closed my eyes when the phone rang. Peter Morrison told me of the bomb. 'We may have lost Norman,' was his chilling conclusion. I switched on the television and saw the wreck of the centre section of the Grand Hotel.

We sat glued to the set waiting for news. After a while we tore ourselves away and drove in silence across the Downs. Early on we learnt from the radio that Norman and Margaret Tebbit were safe but badly injured. At the outskirts of Brighton we found all roads leading to the front were blocked off by the police. We had to walk a very long way before we finally made the conference hall, arriving just before the first debate was due to begin. By an odd irony it was about Belfast and it was carried out in a subdued atmosphere. Lunch came and the Prime Minister appeared and then we were ready to go in for the final session.

I was sitting in the row behind my Cabinet colleagues. I had been impressed earlier in the day how smart they all looked. When we all sat down the reason became quite clear. I could now see that, without exception, all my colleagues wore brand new shoes. Two or three still had the price ticket stuck to the sole. I had another look. They were all wearing what were obviously new suits. There was a simple explanation.

In the early hours of the morning the word came that they would not be allowed back into the Grand Hotel to get their clothing. At about 5 o'clock Alistair McAlpine had telephoned Marks & Spencer in Baker Street in London. At that time in the morning he had only been able to speak to a security guard, who asked him to leave it with him. Within a half hour the message came back. The manager of the Brighton store was on his way to open the store for them. As a result I doubt if the Cabinet will ever look as smart as they did that day.

Despite the triumph of that afternoon and the heat and emotion of the hour, the effects of the bomb were to last. The rather free and easy days of the conferences of the early years of the decade are now no more than a memory and with it these occasions have lost a great deal of their value.

The next day I drove back to Brighton to pay a quick visit to Norman Tebbit and John Wakeham who were both in intensive care. Margaret Tebbit was also in intensive care but was far too ill to be seen.

Monday saw us back in London. The Parliamentary scene was about to begin. I was to be introduced as soon as the House resumed and my introduction was scheduled for the Wednesday. On that day my new title would be gazetted and I would formally become Lord Young of Graffham, and bid farewell to David Young. The introduction of a Peer into the Lords has its origins shrouded in the mists of antiquity. It is a complex ceremony that requires two sponsors. I thought carefully and decided to ask Elizabeth Carnegy (Lady Carnegy of Lour), since she would represent the Manpower Services Commission period of my life and Hugh Thomas (Lord Thomas of Swynnerton). Hugh Thomas had become the Chairman of the Centre for Policy Studies in 1979 after Keith Joseph had entered the Government and, as well as being a friend, I thought that his presence would demonstrate the debt that I owed to the Centre for my subsequent career.

The great day dawned and we gave a lunch for the family at the House of Lords. My brother, our wives and all our children were able to be with us as were our parents. My father had become partially sighted a few years before and had just developed lung cancer. Although he was in fairly continual pain we would never hear him complain. It was a great family occasion and as I stood at the Opposition dispatch box preparing to take the oath I caught sight of my father. What, I suddenly wondered, was he thinking? What would his father have said if he had been told that this would one day happen to his grandson when they both arrived at the Port of London nearly eighty years before?

Chapter 10
BEVERIDGE AND BEIJING

The day before my introduction in the Lords, Leigh Lewis came to me with a broad grin and told me the Opposition had put down a motion on training and I was to take it. Even more, as it was a two and a half hour timed debate, I was to both open and wind up. Not for me the agony of indecision about the timing of my maiden speech, worry about its contents or even the sheer luxury of nerves on the day. The debate was the following Monday and that was that. It was on me before I realised.

Officials from the Department of Employment gave me a fully written out text for my opening speech. I had the impression that they thought that I knew more about the subject than they did and I felt quite at home. In the Lords, as distinct from the Commons, there is a convention that whoever is winding up a debate will listen to all the speakers. I was told that as long as I sat there during the debate, and mentioned all speakers by name in my winding up, all would be well. So it was, for it went all right on the day. I did not think that I did very well but everyone was too polite to tell me otherwise. At least it was over.

The principal item on the agenda in Cabinet at that time was Norman Fowler's review of Social Security. Ralph Howell, one of our backbenchers, asked me if I had ever read the Beveridge report. Sir William Beveridge (later Lord Beveridge) had been a predecessor of mine as Minister without Portfolio during the war years. It was during this period that he published his famous report, 'Social Insurance and Allied Services', which laid the foundation of the welfare state. I asked for a copy. This caused much consternation in the Cabinet Office but eventually a rather ragged one turned up. It was, I was told, the only one left and I had to treat it with great care. I took it home for the weekend and what I read gave me much to think about.

It expressed, in rather forthright language, what I had come to feel instinctively during my time at the Manpower Services Commission.

In his introduction Beveridge laid down three guiding principles.
First, his proposals should be revolutionary. Second, a full system
of social insurance

> '. . . may provide income security: it is an attack on Want. But
> Want is one only of five giants on the road of reconstruction
> and in some ways the easiest to attack. The others are Disease,
> Ignorance, Squalor and Idleness.'

His third principle was that social security must be achieved by
cooperation between the State and the individual:

> 'The State should offer security for service and contribution.
> The State in organising security should not stifle incentive,
> opportunity, responsibility; in establishing a national mini-
> mum, it should leave room and encouragement for voluntary
> action by each individual to provide more than that minimum
> for himself and his family.'

I re-read Norman Fowler's draft White Paper and the supporting
papers. The more I thought about the position the more I realised
that, over the years, we had fallen into the trap that Beveridge had
cautioned us against. Successive generations of ministers and civil
servants, doubtless with the best of intentions, had tinkered with
the system to increase benefits and help those in need. All this
additional expenditure had to be found so up went taxes. In 1950
income taxes did not start until one and a half times the average
industrial wage. Now income taxes started, for a single person, at
one quarter of the average industrial wage! In combination the
mixture was lethal to incentive. Today many, if not the majority, of
unemployed people would get at least 85 per cent of their net take-
home pay in work as benefit. Some could take home more in social
security than they could earn. No wonder, I thought, so many
found it sensible to supplement their benefit with a cash income,
and then found that they were actually better off than in formal
work.

What post-war Governments had started out to provide was a
safety net for the least fortunate in society with ladders of opportunity for all. Alas for good intentions, for what had evolved was a
system that placed the net firmly on top of the ladder. The unemployed and low income groups were trapped in the web of state
support, unable to climb free. If they worked harder and their
income increased they would lose benefit and would end up worse

off. If they gave up work they might find that their income hardly changed. All the stories I had picked up during my travels around the country during my time with the MSC now fell into place.

Beveridge was also forthright on the question of Unemployment Benefit. He was adamant that it should not be paid indefinitely, that there should be compulsory training for all the unemployed after six months. Otherwise there was danger of what he called 'habituation', people becoming discouraged and ceasing to look for work. This fitted in exactly with all my experience and was one of the most powerful reasons for introducing the Community Programme: I had seen time and time again the way people rediscovered their pride and initiative once they came back to work.

'Young people,' he wrote, 'should not get unconditional unemployment benefit at all. Their unemployment should be made an occasion for further training.' That was exactly what I was trying to do in my committee.

I studied the papers about the new review of social security. I found to my dismay that it did little to change this. In fact the new system, by concentrating on the after tax position, was at best neutral to incentive. Far from increasing the incentive to work, in many cases it actually reduced the difference between in work and out of work pay. There was one graph with the draft White Paper that showed the gap between in work and out of work pay for a particular combination of parents and young children had increased under the new system. I asked my people to work out other permutations. Every other combination showed the gap diminishing rather than increasing. The more I thought about the problem the more I thought that the way out of our difficulties would be to take a very large proportion of lower paid people out of taxes; let us get back to the position of 1950. We did some calculations and then I realised that the cost would be enormous and take many years.

I wondered what we could really do to improve incentives. I thought to myself that as more and more people would begin to realise the advantages of not taking a formal job and drawing benefit, unemployment would simply climb and climb. The White Paper was published, the legislation passed and in time the new system was introduced.

Despite this setback I continued with my work in the new Committees. We set up a group of ministers to look at all the measures taken by all departments to help small firms. Before long it became apparent that there was no need for any more measures. The number of small firms was increasing at an ever accelerating rate,

129

helped, I suspected, by a number of causes including the great success of the Enterprise Allowance Scheme which encouraged the start of self-employment for unemployed people. Progress was also being made in the group looking at the fourteen to eighteen age group and I hoped for an agreed report before too long.

One morning I was woken very early by a telephone call from a good friend of mine from Hong Kong, David Li. We had been friends for many years and now he ran the largest Chinese bank there. A great break through had just been made in the negotiations over the future of Hong Kong and the Prime Minister was due to go there to sign the agreements in early December. He told me that he had just returned from Beijing and had a message for me. They wanted to show the Prime Minister the high regard they had for her, I was told. I should go with her and take a trade delegation. There was a great deal of business to be done and much of it was going to the Japanese.

The more I thought about this the more sense it seemed to make. At my next meeting with the Prime Minister I raised the matter and received her enthusiastic agreement. A few days later there was a message from the Foreign Office. They were concerned at the prospect and feared that it might offend the people of Hong Kong who would think that we were selling our birthright for the prospect of some business. I thought that the people I knew in Hong Kong would think less of us if we did not take advantage of the circumstances; but there was no shaking the Foreign Office. I then suggested that I take a delegation to China before the Prime Minister's visit and that we finish the mission in Beijing at the time of the signing of the accord. That was just as bad in their eyes. We had reached an impasse when the situation was resolved in an unusual way.

Lita and I had been invited to the Lord Mayor's Banquet for the first time. By chance I happened to be sitting opposite Anthony Ackland, the Permanent Secretary of the Foreign Office. A few minutes conversation quickly settled the matter. We agreed that I would not go with the Prime Minister but some weeks later, and that she would announce the trade mission during her visit. That satisfied all the proprieties and when the Prime Minister was in Beijing she announced that I would be taking a trade mission in February.

I also underwent one of the ritual trials of all ministers and appeared on Robin Day's *Question Time*. This is, quite rightly, taken seriously by all ministers who appear on the programme. When in Opposition, or if you happen to be a non-political on the programme, then you could take the programme quite lightly. If you are in Government then you are speaking on behalf of the Government and must be briefed on all aspects of Government policy. When I first saw the briefing my heart sank. It was at least two feet high and covered all departments from Agriculture to Social Security. All this just for a television programme! In the event it passed off well and afterwards Robin Day was quite complimentary.

Life had become very hectic. I was now a member of a large number of Cabinet sub-committees and received the papers. The work of my own unit was in a formative stage and required quite a lot of thought. I thought that the demands of the MSC were great but I now found that this was far greater. From time to time I would go and see Norman and Margaret Tebbit who were now at Stoke Mandeville hospital. Norman was mending slowly but Margaret was gravely paralysed.

One Saturday morning I was driving up the M40 to see them when I started to have bad chest pains. By the time I arrived at the hospital I had quite convinced myself that I was having a heart attack and could hardly leave the car. I attracted the attention of a passer by and before long I was in the emergency ward. The attack soon passed and they could find nothing wrong with me. Some form of indigestion, they decided, and so it proved to be. Norman heard where I was and threatened to come and see me so I carried on with my visit. I soon forgot all about it but I did decide to pace myself better. During the following week the Prime Minister told me off. 'You should take it easier,' she said, 'You have now arrived.' I did not want to disagree with her but it did not feel that way.

In the middle of December we had a visit from Mr Gorbachev. The General Secretaryship was still some weeks away but he was known to be the coming man. The Prime Minister had said publicly that 'she could do business with him' and I was curious to see what he was really like. Geoffrey Howe had invited me to a lunch he was giving at Hampton Court.

The day turned out to be one of those wet gloomy December days when you rather wished that you hadn't bothered. If it was cold outside it was even colder and damper inside. Mr Gorbachev was busy with talks with Geoffrey Howe and was running late. By the time they arrived we were all frozen. We sat down to lunch at a long table for about twenty. Mr Gorbachev had Elspeth Howe on one side and Leon Brittan on the other. I was sitting opposite Leon with both the Russian Ambassador and Geoffrey Howe on my right. As

131

the conversation and the lunch wore on I became more and more impressed with Mr Gorbachev. He did not appear to be the usual stereotype of a Soviet leader. At one point I apologised to him for the weather and for Hampton Court, which I said was rather like many English buildings, colder inside than out. He smiled and remarked that there were many buildings like that in the Soviet Union. 'We have good Soviet central heating,' he said and picked up his glass. 'Vodka.'

There was only one difficult moment. At one point Elspeth Howe asked me if I was a lawyer. When I admitted I was she said to Mr Gorbachev that we were all lawyers here. Geoffrey, Leon and I were, as was she, and evidently so were both the Russian Ambassador and Mr Gorbachev himself. Then Mr Gorbachev turned to me and asked why there were so many lawyers in the United Kingdom. 'Ah, Mr Gorbachev,' I replied, 'you see we are a society founded on individual rights.'

Elspeth looked up at the ceiling as if to save herself from this gauche newcomer. But I did know exactly what I had said and in fact was looking for an opportunity to say it. At that time emigration from the Soviet Union had reached new lows. I did not use the phrase 'human rights' quite deliberately as, over the years, it had become a term of art in politics.

Mr Gorbachev gave me a look that made me realise, quite suddenly, that there was a lot more there than the surface charm would suggest. Then he laughed and raised his glass to me.

At my last meeting with the Prime Minister before Christmas I raised the question of a Channel crossing. I told her that by now I had raised the matter with most of our Cabinet colleagues. We agreed that it would now be left to Nicholas Ridley, and many months later when the prospect of a Channel crossing came before Cabinet there was not one dissent. I wondered at the time what would have happened if I had not just entered Cabinet with nothing to do when I was approached by Nigel Broakes of Trafalgar House. The great irony of all this was that his consortium was unsuccessful in the competition and the benefit of their work went elsewhere.

Christmas, which included Boxing Day at Chequers, came and went and we took our break away. On my return, my proper accommodation was waiting for me and I moved into a very pleasant room overlooking Horseguards Parade. The whole of my unit now occupied the offices once used by the old Think Tank, the Central Policy Review Unit. I hoped that this would not be a bad omen, but it was far more convenient to have the unit all together.

132

Now I had to arrange my trade visit to China. I wanted to take a first-class team of businessmen and I started to ring round my friends. Eric Sharp of Cable & Wireless, John King of Babcock and BA, Dick Giordano of BOC, Arnold Weinstock of GEC were quick to say yes. I was able to include the Chairmen of NEI, Plessey and Simon Engineering as well as chief executives and senior directors of British Aerospace, Davy McKee, Rolls Royce and Sedgwick. It was thought to be the strongest team that had yet been put together for an overseas trade mission. The Prime Minister agreed to receive us at No. 10 for a drink, where she put them all through the mill and left them in no doubt of the seriousness of her desire to improve our export performance.

Whilst I had been away on my Christmas break I had been brooding over my defeat with the Social Security White Paper. At one of my Monday morning meetings, when I would sit down with almost the entire Enterprise Unit and plan the week ahead, I launched into a vigorous attack on the black economy and its interaction with the tax and benefit system. I ended up with a request that we do some work on possible solutions to the problem and in particular the effect it might have on the future unemployment figures. As I waxed enthusiastic I became aware that instead of the fairly continual, always irreverent, interruptions that was the hallmark of my weekly meetings, they all kept quiet. When I came to the end there was an embarrassed silence. They simply did not believe me, nor did they see that the problem even existed.

I brought the meeting to an abrupt end and another piece fell into place. The Civil Service, rather like ministers, came from that strata of society that had retained the old values. Collecting Benefit was shameful. At that time the level of taxes was such that tax avoidance schemes were entered into by the rich. That they knew and tried to stop. Why not, I thought, the less well off? Surely anybody would not pay taxes if they could get away with it? I was talking about nothing more than a general tax avoidance scheme for some people. If my own unit, who were by far the most sceptical of civil servants, did not see the problem, then I could not see how others, more conventional, would. But it did not get me any nearer to a solution.

My contacts with the Commons were rudimentary to say the least. I spoke to the Chief Whip and asked him to recommend a Parliamentary Private Secretary. He came up with Robert Atkins, the Member for South Ribble. I arranged to meet Robert and we hit it off from the start. Robert had two abiding passions in life, cricket and aviation. Neither were to be found in the Cabinet Office, but he had the great gift of getting on with everybody in the House. He

133

really was a House of Commons man and ensured that from the day he started I was available for all who wanted to meet me in the Commons. He was the PPS for Norman Lamont at the time, but Norman agreed to the transfer with good grace.

The date of our departure for China was fixed for 27 February which also happened to be my birthday. There was considerable press interest in the forthcoming mission and I held a press conference in the Cabinet Office. Expectations began to build up over the kind of successes we were likely to achieve. We certainly had an extraordinarily strong team, for when Arnold Weinstock pulled out a few days before our departure Jim Prior, his new Chairman, came in his place. What a case of role reversal, I thought. Now I am the politician and Jim the businessman. The press interest was such that Bernard Ingham transferred one of his Press Officers to come to China with us. Even after China I would have the White Papers to announce.

However before I could get away we had to agree the first fruits of my Committee on the fourteen to eighteen age group. I was determined to see a two-year Youth Training Scheme introduced and there would never be a better time than now. Concern for unemployment was rising steadily. Tom King was working on a White Paper on employment and unemployment, but it would announce no specific measures. As a result, it had no real impact.

My committee was making good progress. I was trying to bring together all the elements of the small revolution we were creating in education and training. We took the changes introduced at the start of the year in Non-Advanced Further Education and put them in context with TVEI. We agreed a new scheme to improve teacher training and, most important of all, we were preparing to announce a review of vocational qualifications.

I had long worried away about the great number of vocational qualifications, over 750 of them. They simply did not relate to each other. How would any employer be able to value the qualifications earned by any potential employee? I wondered. I had long dreamt of a system that would compare and evaluate all the vocational qualifications in the country. The review I was to announce was to establish the National Council of Vocational Qualifications. That led, a year or two later, to the Certificate of Vocational Qualification and the five levels on which all qualifications were graded.

All was going swimmingly until we hit a road block in the week before my departure for China. I had one overriding ambition. The elimination of all unemployment for those under eighteen. I knew that this could be achieved by introducing a two-year Youth Training Scheme and at the same time taking away benefit from those under eighteen. Young people would no longer be faced with the tempting offer of money from the state for staying at home. Instead they would have the opportunity of earning more for taking a two-year training scheme. That is exactly where we ran into trouble.

The Treasury agreed with me; they also thought that my idea would work. Young people, they believed, would not stay idle if there was no money. They would all flock to join the scheme. 'Good,' I agreed, 'that is what we are about.' 'No,' said the Treasury, 'that is not what we are about. The two-year scheme costs the Exchequer far more than unemployment benefit. We want another £200 million if we are to go with it.' I was appalled but I had no budget of my own and thus nothing to offer up. Other departments were, I found, not as keen on this as other parts of their existing spend so I had no help from them. After a sleepless night or two I agreed. The best must not become the enemy of the good, I reasoned to myself. Then the roof fell in. The message came to me that the Prime Minister did not like the compromise. If it still meant paying benefit to young people, she would rather forget the whole idea.

I arranged a meeting with a number of colleagues to be chaired by the Prime Minister on the morning of the day before my departure. The draft White Paper would be going to print during my absence in China so this was the very last opportunity to agree its contents. I knew that without a two-year scheme the White Paper would be an empty shell. The Prime Minister was adamant, the Treasury and the remainder of my colleagues were not moved and after about an hour we broke up without any change. I went to see the Prime Minister privately before lunch but all I succeeded in doing was making her really angry. Everything she stood for was offended by our proposals. She knew that paying benefit to young people was wrong and she was not going to endorse it in this manner. On the other hand I knew that we must introduce a two-year scheme for the benefit of young people and I hoped that we could abandon benefit at a later date. I went to lunch very depressed and resolved to try again.

I went back three more times, in the middle of the afternoon, before dinner and for the last time at about midnight after voting in the House. On the first two occasions I made no progress whatsoever; but on the last occasion, in the early hours of the morning, either she became persuaded by the force of my arguments or else, very uncharacteristically, she was worn down by my persistence. Either way, she suddenly agreed. What a birthday present, I thought! I returned home knowing that my first White Paper was safe, and that we now would have a two-year scheme for this summer's school leavers. Five meetings – and I had incurred the undivided wrath of the Prime Minister for as many hours. Still I knew that she never held a grudge – that, having agreed, she would take the decision as her own. Then my elation evaporated; I had yet to pack for China and we were leaving in a few hours time.

The journey was uneventful except for one incident. The Department of Trade & Industry had been nagging me to meet a certain foreign businessman who allegedly had great influence in China. All my other preoccupations had prevented me from doing so. I said that I would try to find time to see him in China. On the flight out to Hong Kong I idly noticed an empty seat next to me. I had left my briefing papers to read on the lap from Hong Kong to Beijing. At Hong Kong this businessman suddenly appeared and occupied the seat next to me, and quite prevented me from doing my reading. He now had me at his mercy for the remainder of the flight. It was easy to see why he had become a great success.

Although I knew the Far East quite well, this was my first visit to China. I was met with great courtesy and plunged into a great round of meetings, one an hour, on the hour, between 8.00 a.m. and 5.00 p.m. The businessmen would invariably be with me, either separately or together. In a state trading nation, like China, ministers performed a vital role. Business decisions were inseparable from political decisions and my presence ensured that the businessmen, and their local representatives, met ministers and senior civil servants at least three rungs higher up the ladder than they would otherwise meet. When they returned to China in the future they would be able to put this to good use.

We met Zhao Ziang, the Prime Minister and Li Peng, one of his deputies. Our meeting with Zhao went very well; he reminded me irresistibly of a rather prosperous Californian, Chinese yes, but a prosperous businessman rather than the heir of Mao. Wherever I went I found two ritual responses: great admiration for Margaret Thatcher and then following very swiftly a request that our prices be more competitive! Over the years I was to find that the latter came as naturally to the average Chinese official as bidding good day. We met with Citic, their joint venture company run by a group of businessmen from Shanghai. They had kept their fortunes, and in this way the Chinese showed that they were more pragmatic than the other socialist centrally controlled economies. The Citic people were certainly as shrewd and as entrepreneurial as any group in the west.

They worked me so hard that I had little time for sightseeing. I visited the Imperial Palace as the Forbidden City was known. That was very impressive, even if the chill factor made the temperature at least twenty below and hardly ideal for sightseeing. It did remind me very much of the chateaux in the Loire valley: very impressive on the outside but almost nothing inside. All the treasures had been looted in China's turbulent past. I was taken out to the Wall on a cold bright Sunday morning. The road on top of the Wall was covered with ice and very slippery to walk on. I manoeuvred myself for a photograph, whipped out my camera and took one. There was an enormous crash and clatter. I looked up; I was surrounded by at least thirty press photographers who had just snapped me taking a photograph. Sadly I put my camera away.

After Beijing we went on to Shanghai. In the winter Shanghai is south of the line where coal is supplied for heating. During the day it was about 2°C outside and hardly any warmer inside. Happily our hotel was kept splendidly warm. When I went out for my first meeting on the first morning I could not believe how cold you could get sitting in a meeting. We sat, huddled in our coats, clutching a mug of tea in both hands, peering at our hosts over the steam of our breath and trying hard to raise some enthusiasm for the project under discussion. I could not help noticing that our hosts would invariably wear a Mao jacket; and when I looked closely I could often see no less than seven layers of clothing underneath. After an hour, as soon as the meeting ended, we rushed back to our hotel and put on as much clothing as would fit for the rest of the day.

All the meetings seemed a repetition of Beijing, save that we were now dealing with the provincial officials. They even had their local Citic. There was far less rebuilding compared with Beijing. I was told that this was due to the Gang of Four having come from, and been supported by, Shanghai. If that was so, it was in the past for there were many projects for my team.

There was one incident that I doubt I shall ever forget. One morning I was due to pay a visit to the container port, over an hour's drive outside Shanghai. We left our hotel before daybreak on a gloomy, bitterly cold morning. The Deputy Mayor accompanied me and we travelled in their version of a Russian limousine, upholstered in velvet with antimacassars. Next to the driver, seemingly a long way away and behind an open partition, sat my very pretty interpreter. As if to compensate for what lay ahead the car was overheated, and far too warm for the amount of clothing I was wearing. To help me keep awake (and besides she was very pretty) I started to chat to the interpreter. I asked her where she had learned her excellent English. In Shanghai University, she told me, where she only finished last year.

She then went on to tell me that in her first years she had had a teacher from England and he had given the class an excellent English accent. I agreed. 'But then,' she went on, 'for my last year he left and his replacement was an American from New York. We did not like his accent, but he did teach us a number of American slang expressions.' 'Which ones?' I inquired idly. 'Oy vey,' she replied, and let rip with a number of expressions in Yiddish with an American accent! I gritted my teeth and looked intently out of the window, nearly exploding with laughter. It kept me warm all day.

We went on to Canton, which was already looking more and more like Hong Kong. The people wore brighter clothing and Mao jackets were noticeable by their absence. The Governor of the province even asked me over dinner if I played golf. By now I had spent nearly two weeks with a continual round of meetings and banquets for lunch and dinner every day. England seemed so remote that I hardly remembered what golf was. Evidently they were building two golf courses to encourage tourism. What would Mao have thought, I wondered.

On our last morning we discovered that the hotel in Canton, quite up to the best of world standards, served English breakfasts. We had been living on Chinese food for the last fortnight so we all took advantage of the opportunity and had a late breakfast. Leigh Lewis, my private secretary, told me that he had over-indulged and asked to be excused from the first meeting in order that he could write up his notes. At 10 o'clock I went with Eric Sharp of Cable and Wireless to witness the signing of a joint venture agreement with the province. To celebrate the occasion they had laid on a celebratory banquet luncheon – at 10.45 in the morning! Leigh was on the invitation list and had to eat his way through fourteen courses, and innumerable toasts, with the rest of us.

We left Canton by car to the new town of Shenzen. This was one of the new special economic zones created in the coastal areas. It had made spectacular progress in just a few years and the Hong Kong entrepreneurs were setting up factories, taking advantage of the lower wages and absence of regulations that prevailed there. When we entered the zone we passed through a gate in a long barbed wire fence that separated the zone from the rest of the province. That was to keep people out, I was told, not to keep them in. I thought of the other Wall in Berlin.

We took the hovercraft over to Hong Kong. On the way over Margaret Bell, my secretary, who had come with us to prepare all the speeches, took me aside. The press were very restive. My new Press Officer had been protecting me from the journalists who had come with us and they were furious. It had cost their papers quite a lot to send them with us, and they had not had many stories. Even worse, Margaret told me, this had helped to encourage them to file unhelpful stories, and the publicity back home was not all good. I had been so occupied during the trip that I had quite forgotten the press. I then spent the rest of the journey giving them all separate interviews and resolved to do something about the situation when I returned home.

Our arrival in Hong Kong was spectacular. The light at the end of the tunnel was the way I thought of Hong Kong all the way through China. At first the light was far too faint to see but during the last few days I could not wait to get to a world where I could carry on a conversation without an interpreter. By arrangement, we arrived at the ferry port on Hong Kong Island and when I climbed the stairs there was the Governor surrounded by a great crowd of people, journalists, lights and television cameras. After a short statement I was hurried away in the Governor's Rolls Royce to the Mandarin Hotel for tea. We went up to the Penthouse apartment and sat on facing sofas in an elegant drawing room. An immaculately clad butler loomed above me carrying a long thin tray balancing four teapots.

'Tea, M'Lord,' he said. Yes, I indicated. 'Jasmine, China, Indian or Ceylon?' he inquired. I was back in Hong Kong.

Chapter 11
BACK TO EMPLOYMENT

When we returned from China I found that the press comment, whilst not bad, had been not nearly as good as the visit had deserved. We had opened up quite a number of opportunities in a very encouraging way. I thought that there would be a good chance that we could place an order for at least ten BAe 146 jets, although other capital projects were subject to very intense competition from the Japanese as well as the other Europeans. There was little doubt that our partners in Europe had taken full advantage of the years we had spent negotiating the agreement on Hong Kong.

I had become convinced, mainly by the strong persuasion of all the businessmen on the mission, that we must have a system of soft loans to encourage the start of capital intensive projects. A soft loan, a loan at below market rates, would get orders that should lead to repeat contracts. That business would be at normal commercial rates. When I reported back to the Prime Minister I raised this and started a series of discussions that was to lead to our first soft loan package. Zhao Ziang was due to come to London on a visit in June and that seemed a good target to aim for.

Unemployment had continued to climb during the last few months. The pace had slowed down but nothing seemed to halt its relentless advance. The Manpower Services Commission continued to perform and all but 3,000 school leavers had been offered a place on the Youth Training Scheme by Christmas.

The Prime Minister, during one of our weekly meetings, suddenly went back to the whole question of deregulation. She had just returned from Washington where she had had a long discussion with Ronald Reagan who had emphasised the necessity of deregulating if we wanted to get the economy going again. I received the go ahead to form my group. Grey Gowrie was to be in it and I thought that with two Cabinet colleagues my task would be much easier. So it proved, for I enlisted Grey's help for the vital first meeting of the committee and he came through splendidly. I was under no illusions, however, for my committee consisted of Junior Ministers and as a general rule they could only speak to their departmental brief. I did warn the Prime Minister that, although all involved were taking a positive attitude, it might be necessary to arrange a meeting under her chairmanship.

One of the early results of my committee on Urban Policy was the formation of City Action Teams. I knew from my time in the Manpower Services Commission that out in the field there was a tendency for the various Government departments to act as if they were members of competing Governments. In Whitehall the contact between different departments was minimal – out in the field it was a little better but only if, by chance, they were housed in the same building. We dreamt up the idea of creating City Action Teams (CATs). They were small committees of the regional directors of the major departments in five areas: Newcastle, Manchester, Birmingham, Leeds and London. Their job was to coordinate their actions within their areas and improve the way that departments worked together. To give competition, they put each CAT under a different Chairman, two from Environment, two from DTI. In Newcastle the first Chairman was Peter Carr from the Department of Employment.

I went with other ministers to launch the new CATs. We left after Cabinet one Thursday in the middle of April and opened Birmingham in the afternoon, Newcastle the following morning and Manchester during the afternoon. It was the real beginning of the public face of our Inner Cities policy and taught me a great deal. For one thing, if you could only get rid of all the turf battles then government becomes more efficient.

All announcements about new programmes encourage the cry about new money. There was little new money in this particular programme and as soon as the press heard this they tended to discount the programme. I found this most odd for I was never sure what magical properties new money had that made it so much more desirable than old money but there was no denying the concern about mounting unemployment.

In Newcastle, for the CAT launch, I was asked about the future course of unemployment. John Biffen, as Leader of the House, had forecast that unemployment would shrink before the next election. I was getting so fed up with the continual tales of woe that were being spread by the Labour local authorities that, on the spur of the moment, I decided to go out on a limb.

'Unemployment will fall,' I said, 'in a year or eighteen months. As a result of the firm foundations laid by the Government we will

see unemployment go down.' Leigh Lewis looked at me in horror.
It made a certain amount of coverage the following day, and luckily
for me Patrick Jenkin at Environment followed suit, although Tom
King was more cautious. He stressed that nobody could predict
what would happen.

I now had a difficult decision to take. My Press Officer had not
worked out, at least for my purposes. But she had been recommended by Bernard Ingham who had always been very helpful to
me. I had no wish to upset him nor, on the other hand, could I let
matters rest. I had a number of White Papers to launch, for I had
now obtained the Prime Minister's agreement to set up two further
groups, one on tourism and one on deregulation. In the end I
decided that I would have to make a change.

Press Officers were a distinct group, a separate grade in the
service. I resigned myself to once more relying on the Cabinet
Office services. Then I had a minor brainwave. I could appoint a
Special Adviser. After all, I had once been a Special Adviser and as
a Cabinet colleague I was entitled to one myself. I did not need one
to help me with political advice but with dealings with the press. I
rang Tim Bell to ask him for some help. Straight away he said that
he had just the right person for me and within a few days, Howell
James came to see me in the House.

Howell came from Wales but had lived in London for many
years. He had worked for Capital Radio and had moved on to
TV-am just as they ran into their troubles. He used to claim that he
had been Press Officer for Roland Rat! He had survived that baptism of fire, having to deal with the press every day at a time when
the very survival of the television station was a matter of great
doubt. He had left them when the troubles were over, had gone to
the Dorchester, but did not think that there was enough there to
keep him occupied. I thought that his previous experience would be
just right for the job and I said 'yes' on the spot. It was one of the
very best decisions of my time in Government. Howell had an
ability to become part of any scene. With the civil servants he was
one of them, with ministers he was one of us, and with journalists
and the world of television there was hardly anyone he did not
know. From the moment he joined my team I could relax about the
media, although there were mutterings from the ranks of the Press
Officers, and one or two unfortunate diary stories appeared as a
result.

In the meantime I was becoming fully immersed in my committees. Paul Twyman was the Assistant Secretary who joined me in
order to deal with deregulation. Paul was just the sort of official (he

143

would object to the description) whom I saw as ideal for the job. When he first came for an interview I was warned off him. Difficult, I was told. He was a member of a building society, I was told, and he objected to their policies on opening branches. As a result of the campaign he ran, he ended up on the board. Just the chap, I thought, and so he proved to be, for the committee dealing with deregulation was particularly difficult. As a general rule if the abolition of any regulations would incur a hostile press then my colleagues would allow me to include it in the forthcoming White Paper. If, on the other hand, there were votes in it, then the particular department would suddenly find a very good reason why it had to be the subject of a separate announcement. This was simple politics and all part of my continuing education.

I would spend quite a time in the House. Although I had no department of my own I was given the task of speaking for Employment, Treasury and Industry. The system in the Lords is quite different from that of the Commons. In the Commons all the departments come first for questions about once every three weeks and then all the ministers turn up for about forty-five minutes in order to answer questions. In the Lords there are four questions every working day at the commencement of business. They are put down a few days before and can be on any subject. If they were to fall within one of my responsibilities then I would appear, read out a short answer and then deal with any supplementary questions in what was, in effect, a short debate for five or six minutes. I greatly enjoyed answering questions and found that the more party political I made the answers the more my own side enjoyed it.

One day in the House, Christopher Soames took me aside. He was very kind and gave me good advice. 'David,' he said, 'get a department. No one ever makes it without a department.' I was quite aware of that but I also thought that someone coming into the Cabinet at my age and with my political experience would never command a department. I told him so and he just looked at me pityingly. 'Without a power base you are lost,' he said, and wandered off, gently shaking his head.

The Opposition Chief Whip, Lord Ponsonby, had put down a motion on tourism and I was asked to take it. That gave me a chance to announce that my group on tourism would publish a report before the summer recess. In my speech I said that too many people thought that 'service' was somehow the equivalent of 'servile'. The profession of waiter was honourable, and giving good service in a hotel or restaurant was an honourable way of earning a living. I argued that a hotel was the equivalent of a factory, earning

144

foreign exchange from overseas visitors the same as exports and creating wealth by employing people just as a factory would. The hotel might even last longer than a factory. I could see that I did not convince all those sitting opposite; they still thought of tourism as a candy floss occupation and assumed the only way to create wealth was to make things.

As part of the preparations for the return visit of Zhao Ziang, the Chinese Premier, Geoffrey Howe had asked me to accompany Zhao on a visit to Cambridge on the Friday of his trip. We were to go to Trinity and then to the Science Park after lunch. I remembered how we travelled throughout China. Preceded by a police car, with officers leaning out of their windows waving little red flags and blowing whistles, all traffic would stop immediately and we would drive on unimpeded. Once, arriving in Canton in the afternoon rush hour, we must have snarled up all the traffic for hours.

I was now due to pick up the Premier at 11 o'clock on a Friday morning and drive to Cambridge. My heart sank when I thought how long it could take and I suggested a helicopter. That was vetoed by the Chinese on security grounds, so in the end I reconciled myself to driving.

The visit went well. The meeting with the Prime Minister (to which I was invited) was the occasion for announcing the soft loan facility of £100 million. We were also able to announce the landing of the BAe 146 contract. The Lord Mayor gave a lunch and to my slight surprise I was sitting next to the Japanese Ambassador. The Japanese were our rivals for business in China. We talked about education and I found he was envious of our system. 'We do not get enough innovation,' he complained. 'We do not get high enough standards,' I replied. On the spot we agreed to exchange systems for the next twenty years. If only we had been able to!

My visit to Cambridge also went well, and all my fears about the traffic proved groundless. We were given a police escort of a dozen police outriders who managed to get us from Claridges to Trinity College without stopping! I hated to think what that must have done to the traffic throughout the whole of East London, and sat well back in my seat hoping not to be spotted.

On the way we talked in the car. Premier Zhao told me that the growth rate of the People's Republic was averaging over 10 per cent per quarter and they had to find ways to slow it down. I said to him that we were having lunch at Trinity College; they had no more than 800 people in the college at any one point in time but they had won no less than twenty-six Nobel prizes for science. Incidentally, I added, Japan has only won two. He laughed at this and repeated the remark once or twice during the day, but we both knew that Japan had won all the prizes for product development. We still did not have the secret of taking our excellent research and turning it into new products.

Over lunch the Foreign Minister inquired about Marks & Spencer. I gave him full instructions on how to get there from Claridges and he promised to go later that day. He subsequently told me that he found his way there but found the prices too high for him.

That evening Grey Gowrie and I took the party to a performance of *La Fille Mal Gardée* at Covent Garden. Throughout one entire interval I had a talk with Vice Premier Tien, who had accompanied Zhao. He told me how he had spent five years of his life studying Marxism. Karl Marx may have been right for his time, he said, but times have changed. 'The systems that the Russians put into place in the early fifties set China back for decades,' he went on. 'The only way to run an economy is through the market,' he finished, poking me painfully in the chest with his forefinger. I had never before been lectured on the advantages of the market, but luckily I was saved by the end of the interval before I could think of a reply.

Once or twice a week Robert Atkins would bring a number of back bench MPs to my room in the Lords for a drink. There was mounting concern over unemployment and the attitude of the Government which was seen as uncaring. Tom King was in a very unenviable position with increasing unemployment figures to announce month after month. There was a great shortage of good news and when we did stress the increasing employment figures they were ignored. All the opinion polls showed that unemployment was the most serious issue in the minds of the electorate. I rather doubted it, for that never came through in all the conversations I had when I would go out on my visits to the regions. But there was no doubting the importance placed on this issue both in Parliament and in the media. All I could do was to talk about tourism and deregulation and the effect that they would have on the creation of new jobs. The new two-year Youth Training Scheme would have a very good effect on the levels of youth unemployment.

In the meantime, my committee on deregulation was making good progress thanks to the help that Grey Gowrie would deliver at critical moments. Nicholas Ridley at Environment arranged that we would synchronise my White Paper with his circular to local authorities which would stress again the existing presumption in favour of development. This was a very important circular and would have considerable effect on planning decisions in the future.

146

One other recommendation that we were able to get through was the setting up of a central task force in the Cabinet Office, which would include outsiders, to overview deregulation generally with the establishment of deregulation units in all departments charged with the task of preparing the compliance costs of all new regulations before they were introduced.

This was to be my first (and for all I knew, my only) White Paper. I wanted to make sure that it went well; I took the draft home and rewrote the first chapter. By now I was very happy that I was able to get everything put on a floppy disk and work on my computer at home. It certainly saved time. I reasoned that the average journalist would not be likely to read more than the first few paragraphs, and that would set the tone for all the comment. We also put the summary of all the many proposals in the second chapter so there was no excuse that they, or colleagues for that matter, would not read them.

We had a competition in the unit for the name for the paper. I won with my suggestion 'Lifting the Burden' which was hardly surprising since I was the sole judge. In the first paragraph of the paper I wrote

'It is the growth of enterprise, the efforts of millions of our people engaged in the creation and development of businesses large and small that is the real driving force of the economy.'

I went on to say that deregulation must be done with care. 'The line between licence and liberty is fine and can easily be crossed'. The whole paper was a careful exercise in driving through deregulation without alarming those who were concerned that this was no more than an excuse to let development rip.

Finally it was all agreed and a date was set for publication, Tuesday 16 July. Howell swung into action and lined up a whole series of interviews with all the heavies. Even more surprising Bernard Ingham allowed me to take over his morning lobby briefing. I went over to No. 10 for the 11 o'clock briefing and then had about twenty minutes to explain to a rather bemused set of political correspondents why deregulation was so important for jobs. I pointed out the independent survey quoted in the White Paper which showed that excessive regulations caused job losses of over 200 in the sample of 200 firms and that there were over 1.6 million firms in the country today – then they appreciated its importance.

I went down to the House to make a statement straight after questions. There is nothing that our House likes more than to have a minister who can make statements, rather than repeat statements made by other ministers in the Commons. This White Paper was mine, with my name heading my other, far more senior, colleagues. For this reason it went well in our House, although the Opposition did question what it would really do to help solve the problem of unemployment. There was no doubt that unemployment really was a thorn in our side.

I followed Howell's advice and fully briefed the *Evening Standard*. The paper came out with banner headlines which helped to give me good coverage on all the television bulletins. When the next day's papers came out we scooped the pool. All the heavies gave it the front page treatment, with the *Daily Telegraph* doing me very proud with a banner headline and a rather good cartoon. Without exception all the editorials were enthusiastically supportive. I invited the whole unit to my office for drinks before lunch and we did little work that day. In time stories appeared in the papers of how other departments briefed against us before the launch. I did not think that this was anything to do with my colleagues but merely the natural desire for civil servants to play turf battles. Whatever I did must by definition cross another department. In any event it ended up as the most positive statement of the action we were taking about unemployment that we had made for a long time.

The following day I was due to see the Prime Minister at one of my weekly meetings. She was delighted but becoming more and more concerned with the unemployment issue. She asked me to start thinking about a new approach. I said that I would but I could think of little more than we were doing already. I told her that my last paper, due to be launched on the following Monday, 'Pleasure, Leisure and Jobs', would be very positive about the employment potential of tourism.

The following Monday we launched the paper. This time there was no need for a statement in the House and we went to the Dickens Inn down by the river. We had a very good turnout and plenty of picture opportunities. The following day we had a good press again. My paper was very positive, emphasising the job and wealth creation potential of the tourist industry. It was printed in full colour with many photographs and charts illustrating the growth of jobs and earnings from the industry. There were not too many new announcements although some rather important steps forward were taken. We let it be known that at last we would recognise the importance of tourism in the need for new roads, and we also introduced a new system of 'Brown Tourism' signs for major roads and motorways.

There was no doubt that the dozen or so of us in the Enterprise Unit had come through with two very positive announcements at a time when the Government as a whole needed them. Robert Atkins came in to see me before the summer break and he was delighted. The only downside was a certain amount of political comment in the press about the pending reshuffle which often had me heading up some form of 'Super Ministry'. The commentators always had Tom King being transferred to other departments, and this did not help my relationship with him, although in all the circumstances we did get on well. That was a tribute to his personal qualities.

Parliament rose for the vacation and I had my last meeting with the Prime Minister. I found her tired and worried about unemployment. She thought that we were losing the battle for people's hearts and minds on the issue. We were halfway through the term and she knew that the changes she would have to make this time would take us through to the election. Before we parted, I arranged to come to Chequers on the last Sunday in August for a further chat.

August came and with it the migration of boxes for at least three weeks. We went on a walking holiday with my elder daughter Karen and her new husband Bernard. Westminster was a long, long way away as we enjoyed the fairy-tale charm of the Swiss lakes and the upper slopes of the Alps. Alas, the longest of holidays come to an end and this was all too short. I was soon back in London preparing for my meeting with the Prime Minister.

We had had a good first year in the Enterprise Unit. The dozen or so officials who made up the unit had been responsible for the White Paper introducing the two-year Youth Training Scheme and the working party recommending a structure of vocational qualifications. We had introduced deregulation as a concept to a deeply sceptical Whitehall, pushed it through and had a good chance of making it work. We had put tourism on the map. On the other hand, we had accomplished very little towards the reduction of unemployment. I had failed completely in my efforts to increase incentives and I had come up with little that we could do about the black economy.

But I had learned how Cabinet worked. I had also learned that you cannot make positive announcements out of monthly unemployment figures that continue to creep up. Tom King had been on a hiding to nothing for all the time he had been at the Department of Employment. My papers had made a far more positive impression, and there was a moral there. I drove to Chequers for tea in rather a pensive mood.

I found the Prime Minister fully restored. I would always marvel how the shortest of breaks would bring her back to full form. The day was sunny and warm and we walked briefly in the gardens. Norman Tebbit would become Chairman of the Party she stated, and that cheered me up right away. I thought he would be splendid and restore our fortunes very quickly.

We then went on to discuss what changes should be made this time. She was very concerned about unemployment and told me of some suggestions that had been made to her about departmental amalgamations. I said that I agreed with her that we must do something. 'Let me go to Employment,' I offered, 'but let me take tourism and small firms from DTI.' Because of my work both during the time I was at the Department of Industry and more recently for my committees, I knew that there were only about one hundred people involved in a transfer. 'If you give me that,' I went on, 'I will have some positive stories to announce with the more difficult news about the figures.'

I went on to say how all the employment creation was coming out of these two areas – that Tom had no tools at his disposal and that was why his White Paper had sunk out of sight overnight. It had offered no hope whilst my minor tourism and deregulation papers were still being talked about and could be referred to when asked what Government was doing about unemployment.' 'Could I create a strategy to deal with unemployment?' I was asked. Without having any clear ideas I said that I could. 'Good,' the Prime Minister replied, 'now leave it with me.' We chatted for a while about other dispositions that she was contemplating. It also became quite clear to me that we had at the most two years to the next election. If she followed her preferred course we would have one in less than twenty-one months. Unemployment was becoming an urgent issue.

The next week was Bank Holiday week and there was little to do. Monday 2 September marked the real return to work and it was obvious that it would also be reshuffle day since all the papers had little else in them. I passed the time as best as I could, pacing up and down my office again and unable to concentrate on what little work I had. Leigh Lewis came in at last and just said to me '2.15.' At least it was the afternoon. The morning was reserved for those who were going. As I was in the Cabinet Office, I could walk in through the dividing door and that way I was able to fool all the television cameras outside No. 10.

I followed the Private Secretary up the stairs to the Prime Minister's study. I wondered where the last year had gone. As soon as I had sat down she said, 'David, I want you to go to the Department of Employment and you will take small firms and tourism from

150

DTI.' 'Thank you,' I replied. Then came a small bombshell as I was then told that I would have Kenneth Clarke as Paymaster General in the Cabinet to act as my spokesman in the Commons. I had never met Kenneth; he was then on his way down from his constituency. Once again, the Prime Minister asked me in a slightly embarrassed way if I could continue without pay. I just nodded, but I did begin to think that it was getting a little beyond a joke. It had been many years since I was last at work in the outside world.

A moment or two later Kenneth Clarke came in. He appeared slightly shocked when he found out his new job, but cheered up immediately as soon as he realised that he was in Cabinet. The Prime Minister asked us to develop a strategy for dealing with unemployment and I said that we would be back to see her within eight weeks.

At that we left and we arranged to meet the following day at the new Department. I went back to my offices and was told that Michael Quinlan had asked to come to see me at 4.30. He arrived and brought a short note that started 'Welcome back'. I found out from him that my dawn raid on DTI had caused a certain amount of annoyance and that we had better work carefully to make sure that we got enough resources to cover their programmes. At that stage I could not take any problems very seriously; all I could do was sit back and wait for the formal announcement. Against all the odds, and to my own surprise, I had ended up with a department. True it was the department at the heart of the storm, but I was home again.

Chapter 12
RESTART

The Department of Employment is not one of the historic Departments of State. Its origins are humble and go back only to 1893 when the then President of the Board of Trade, A J Mundella, created a small labour Department responsible for industrial relations and statistics. Winston Churchill expanded the Board's role whilst he was President by setting up sixty-two Labour Exchanges in 1909 to make it easier for employers to meet with prospective employees. But it was not until the First World War that the Ministry of Labour came into being as a separate department with John Hodge, a trade union leader, as its first Minister. The Labour Exchanges were promptly renamed Employment Exchanges.

There were no further changes until the Second World War when the Ministry of Labour and National Service was formed with the added responsibility of mobilising manpower for the war effort. The wartime Minister was Ernie Bevin. There was a rather well-worn tale of his first day as Minister. As soon as he arrived in his new office he took off his jacket and said, 'Let's get down to work.' My favourite cartoon of my time in Government appeared on the day after my appointment and showed me, as another Ernie Bevin, taking off my jacket and getting down to work. I bought it and hung it in my office. It was not that I compared myself with Bevin, far from it, but it was the way that unemployment had escalated into the national consciousness that made me feel the same sense of national emergency.

The name of the Department remained unchanged until 1959 when the name reverted to the Ministry of Labour with the end of National Service. Both the Wilson and Heath administrations demonstrated a continuing passion for institutional change. Unkind souls would allege, with some confidence, that it was a substitute for action. For whatever reason, the Department became first the Department of Employment and Productivity in 1968 and then in 1970 simply the Department of Employment. The irony was that throughout the seventies UK productivity sank like a stone. In 1974 the structural changes conceived during the Heath administration, but carried out during the second Wilson administration, split off the MSC, the Health and Safety Executive and ACAS (the Advisory, Conciliation and Arbitration Service) into separate tripartite agencies leaving a small core Department behind. Small it might be in terms of policy civil servants, but it still contained the network of over a thousand benefit offices around the country administered by the Department.

Under Labour administrations it had always been an important post for, in reality, it was the Department of Trade Union Affairs. It continued to hold the centre stage during the first few years of the decade as we restored a better balance between employers and employees. That had been accomplished by the three main trade union bills, carried through by Jim Prior, Norman Tebbit and finally Tom King.

Now the priorities were different. Unemployment was at the top of the agenda and we had to operate in a very pessimistic climate. It was very odd. The pessimists, who were in the majority, said that nothing could be done about unemployment. We should find ways to encourage early retirement. Detailed plans for job splitting, marvellous ways in which we could educate for leisure, ingenious reasons why employment would never return, were always being aired. Even the optimists, a small group indeed, felt that nothing could be done about employment save different forms of Keynesian expansion. I felt to the very core of my being that both were wrong. I knew that the United States had created over twenty million jobs during the last few years whilst the whole of Europe had created less than one million. I had to find a way to make the Department concentrate on employment and enterprise. When that had been achieved I then had to find a solution to our present problems. But in the still of the night there were times when I began to feel that my friends were right and that it really was a hopeless and thankless task.

The transition was considerable, for I went from a mini-department of not more than a dozen to one of nearly 60,000 people (including the MSC). In financial terms the change was even bigger. I had moved from having no budget at all to being given charge of a department with a budget of over £3,000 million. But it was good to be back with a large command again and particularly one where I knew so many of the senior civil servants. I decided that before I started to look at them I should change ministerial jobs around and I gave Peter Bottomley race and sex, and thus liberated Alan Clark

154

from a job he was not comfortable with. Alan instead had the Jobcentres and employment programmes.

On our very first morning Leigh Lewis, who had now returned in triumph to his old department, came to me with a press release about Job Clubs. This was an idea that had been picked up from the United States. It was a simple concept: we would provide office accommodation and advice and help to unemployed people who would have to turn up at regular office hours every day to the Job Club. They would then spend their time applying for jobs, with expert help and supervision and, it was said, by encouraging each other they would prevent despondency and depression and maintain their enthusiasm. It was said that the success rate was very high. I thought about this and I decided that this proposal was dangerous. I could see how this scheme could be misinterpreted, even by critics on our side. I decided not to put the release out.

The very next day Kenneth Clarke came to me and asked me if I minded if he issued it. I agreed, and in the course of time it turns out to be one of the very best self-help ideas of the decade. In the future we were to create hundreds of Job Clubs around the country and they proved to be a very cost effective method of getting people back to work. So much for my political instincts!

I started a series of briefing meetings with our officials. Kenneth took responsibility for Industrial Relations and Health and Safety. I also gave him the MSC, as I felt that it would be unfair to the present Chairman if he had his predecessor breathing down his neck, although I kept my interest in the programmes. However even if Kenneth did take on certain responsibilities I could not shed them. At the end of the day I was the Secretary of State and had to answer for all aspects of my Department. Kenneth, also, had to speak in the Commons for the whole Department and so he had to keep up to speed on everything I was up to. It says a great deal for him that in all the years we worked together he never complained or made a mistake. Sometimes the nature of our work was such that he would only find out about a development at the last possible moment, but he always coped splendidly.

Kenneth asked me if he could also deal with the EDU, the Enterprise and Deregulation Unit, which was the new name of my old Enterprise Unit which was now moving over from the Cabinet office. Steel House, the office building immediately opposite my office in Caxton House, was to be their new home. I knew Caxton House from old, for it was here that I had my first press conference when I was first appointed to the MSC, and where I would come to report from time to time, first to Norman Tebbit and then to Tom King.

155

We had much to do on my side of the house. As well as the MSC programmes, which had changed little in the year I had been away, I had the whole of the benefit service and a number of employment programmes directly administered by the Department. But before I could get down to looking at our strategy I was given an unpleasant surprise.

At almost my first meeting I was told that, as a result of a Rayner Scrutiny, a proposal had been made to change the frequency of the unemployed signing on at benefit offices from fortnightly to once every three months. 'Rayner Scrutinies' were the outcome of the work that Derek Rayner, now Lord Rayner and the Chairman of Marks & Spencer, did for the Prime Minister. He had instituted a large number of investigations that were concerned with the Government getting value for money. The Efficiency Unit investigated all aspects of departmental work across Whitehall and had been responsible for savings, over the years, of hundreds of millions of pounds. They had now focused on one aspect of my Department.

Almost all the unemployed receiving benefit would have to attend at a benefit office on the same day each fortnight just to sign the register. This was all that had remained of the original, pre-war system. In those days the unemployed had to sign on twice a day, once in the morning and again in the afternoon, just to make sure that those receiving benefit did not work as well. That had been eroded over the years, first to daily signing, then to twice weekly and then, after many years, to weekly signing. It had finally been changed to fortnightly signing.

It was quite a formidable operation. Over three million unemployed now had to sign on at one or other of the one thousand benefit offices around the country every other week. That meant that each office had on average about 1,500 signings a week, carried out on the Mondays through to the Thursdays. The Fridays were kept for catching up on the massive paperwork involved. Unemployment was not the static situation that most people imagined. The number of people becoming unemployed each year was about four and a half million with almost as many getting back to work. That was about 350,000 each way every month. It was an enormous clerical job merely to keep up with the changes. Individual records on each claimant had to be kept so that there would be a record for the next time they came in to claim unemployment benefit.

The Rayner Scrutiny changes would, so it was claimed, result in considerable savings in manpower and some £6 million a year. At first sight the case appeared irresistible. But all my instincts were against the change. Everything in me told me that if we were to relax the conditions for signing even more, let alone relax it as far as making it quarterly, then the fairly tenuous moral hold we had to prevent even more working and signing would go for ever.

I rejected the proposal. In fact, I wanted to tighten up the procedures and asked if we could reintroduce weekly signing on. It quickly became clear that would be too expensive to go back to. I continued to brood over what we could do and how I could develop a strategy to deal with unemployment. I did not have very much time before I was to go back to the Prime Minister. However the whole incident set me thinking. Finally I had the glimmerings of an idea. Like all ideas that appear to be the result of a flash of inspiration, the thought had been at the back of my mind for some time. Gradually all the parts began to fit into place. I began to realise that there was a way ahead, but the ideas were still vague and ill-formed. If extending the signing on periods would encourage working and signing then we should do something to reduce that temptation. Besides, I knew full well from my time with the MSC that too many of the long-term unemployed give up looking for work and learn to live within their benefit income.

The first Cabinet since the reshuffle was now due. I was no longer twenty-second out of twenty-two but had moved three places up the pecking order. This order was of no consequence except to your pride and your civil servants. There was simply no way any Private Office would allow you to visit any Cabinet colleague lower in the pecking order than you – they had to come to you. It was all part of the turf games that all offices played. As the only three Cabinet colleagues below me were Kenneth Clarke, John MacGregor as Chief Secretary (and no Treasury Minister had ever been known to leave his office!) and Kenneth Baker at Environment, I would still spend my time visiting my colleagues. Still I now had one of the economic departments to run and the one that was consistently top of any opinion poll of public concerns.

When we arrived in good time at No. 10 the seating position was there waiting for us, just like any good dinner party. I was sitting next to Kenneth Clarke, this time at the other end of the table, still facing the Prime Minister. As we went in I said to Kenneth that he should listen very carefully to Geoffrey Howe. Geoffrey was so soft spoken that we all had great difficulty in hearing him. Even Lord Hailsham, who actually sat next to him, would sometimes ask Geoffrey to repeat himself. 'Who knows,' I said to Kenneth, 'one day you might leave Cabinet and only find out afterwards that we had declared war!'

Once a month, when the unemployment figures were due, I

would have to leave Cabinet early, at about 12.15 p.m., to give interviews on radio and television. The first time that this happened I was told that, back in the seventies when we were in Opposition, the then ministers in the Department would refuse to appear on programmes with our shadow ministers. As the unemployment figures were consistently disappointing and I had nothing convincing to say, I refused to appear on any programme with John Prescott. After the first month or two, he realised what I was doing and for the following months would spend most of his valuable air time complaining bitterly that I would not appear with him. The public was simply confused by all this complaining and, in contrast, I was able to appear calm and reasonable in our explanation of the problems. In due course I did appear with him, but that had to wait for many months.

We called a series of brainstorming sessions. Bryan Nicholson, my successor at the MSC, came in with Geoffrey Holland. We included our ministers and of course Michael Quinlan, my Permanent Secretary, together with a number of officials I had worked with during my MSC days. I had these half-formed ideas which I kept to myself. I suppose that in the old days of the Manpower Services Commission I would have bounced them off Geoffrey Holland, but now he had a new Chairman and I had to keep my distance. All sorts of training programmes were discussed and extensions of the Community Programme were proposed. The Community Programme was designed for those out of work for more than a year but I found to my horror that whilst I had been away a survey had shown that only one-third of the long-term unemployed even knew that it existed.

I raised the problem that nearly all unemployed people experience. At first a period of elation, as they took their redundancy payments and realised that they had some capital for perhaps the first time in their lives. That elation tempted them into an unexpected holiday or even the new car that they had always wanted but later on would be unable to afford. After a time they would start to look for a job and, after repeated failures, depression and a profound sense of uselessness would set in. That depression would deepen and many would then stop looking for work, lowering their expectations and reconciling themselves to living within their new income.

Not all, of course. I was well aware of the existence of the black economy and part of it was certainly being carried on by the unemployed. We could not talk about it openly, for whilst unemployment was going up our opponents would only attack us for being uncaring and using the black economy as an excuse. But I was sure that not a few of the unemployed would find other ways to top up their income. For many, working in a pub for twice a week at lunchtime and one evening each week would provide them, not just with more than they used to get when they were working, but more than they could get from any job open to them. I could not blame them, for tax avoidance schemes are not the sole prerogative of the wealthy; but until we could change the system of tax and benefits I had to devise a method of discouraging them.

During the meeting we began to sketch out a short course designed to remotivate those out of work for over a year. I was now a fan of Job Clubs and we planned a nationwide extension with a training programme for the supervisors. I made a joke about discovering a unified field theory (the vain pursuit of which had occupied most of Einstein's life) when the pieces suddenly fell into place in my mind. It was simple but all my experience in business had convinced me that only simple things ever worked. I could visualise it as a whole. It could work as a strategy that would bring down the count. I left the meeting for a few moments, pleading a telephone call. I paced up and down my office. I went through it again; I knew exactly what had to be done. Would it work? I worried. Yes, I said to myself again and again. I returned to the meeting. Now was not the time or the place to explain the purpose, but I could lay it all out and I began.

'Why don't we invite all the long-term unemployed in for an interview,' I suggested. 'Let us put every scheme we have together. We would have something to offer to all. Besides,' I could not help adding, 'it will stop them working on the black economy.' At that some of my officials began to look uncomfortable and shortly afterwards the meeting broke up so officials could work out the details.

After the meeting I sent for Adrian Moorey, my Chief Press Officer, and Howell. Something else had occurred to me during the meeting, particularly when we had remarked how few of the long-term unemployed knew of all our programmes. I reminded Adrian of all the advertising we had done in the MSC and how it really had put the Youth Training Scheme on the map. I asked him how much the Department presently spent on advertising. I was quite surprised at the answer. We were spending many millions a year, generally in totally forgettable advertising. The system was quite familiar to me. Different parts of the Department would advertise their own programmes. Advertisements crafted by officials were invariably forgettable and of course they would not follow a common house style. I asked Adrian Moorey to speak to the Central

159

Office of Information (COI) people and go out to tender for an umbrella campaign that would put all the Department's programmes together. I was sure that for the amount that we were presently spending we could have more impact. 'After all,' I finished, 'if only one-third of the long-term unemployed have even heard of the Community Programme we are hardly doing our job.'

The Party Conference came around, only this time I would not be a spectator but would have to speak. I could not claim that I was an inexperienced speaker, but I doubt that I had ever spoken to an audience of more than a few hundred. Now I was to be facing 3–4,000 and taking the debate that was clearly seen to be the weak spot of the Government. Conference speaking is an art form really quite unrelated to any other form of speechmaking. You have to be prepared to ham it up, and that was not my nature. I wrote and rewrote my speech. At last I had it in a more or less final form and gave it to Harvey Thomas (who was responsible for conference presentations) for inscribing on the prompter. At least I would not have to learn the speech off by heart.

The night before I went up to my room and started to practise. Jeffrey Archer took me under his wing and heard me read it again and again with mounting desperation. He tried to teach me about timing, about stressing words correctly, about waiting and pacing an audience. Howell looked on trying to encourage but not really succeeding. Bruce Anderson, now Deputy Editor of the *Daily Telegraph*, had helped me with the final form of the speech and subsided on the bed listening with his eyes shut. The longer this went on the more tired and depressed I felt. In the end I brought it all to a halt.

When they had all left with assurances of how well I was doing, assurance which sounded very hollow to me, I tried to sleep. I knew that I could do the job, at least I thought that I could and now I had a good idea how to tackle unemployment. But I was not sure that I could succeed as a party politician. I did not want to let down the Prime Minister who had gone out on such a limb to give me this chance. Then I thought – if I mean that I should say it. I got out of bed and wrote some words down on a sheet of paper.

The next morning I met Howell for breakfast. I showed him what I had written and he agreed with it. The day dragged on. Every now and then I would get out my speech and look at the words until they lost all meaning. I went for one more practice with the prompter. Eventually the time of my debate approached. Howell and I went over to the Conference and waited behind the platform. As the applause for the debate before mine died down Harvey Thomas led

me on. The hall looked even more immense than I had feared and I
could see that I had a very full turnout. All my team wished me luck.
I doubt to this day if they ever realised how nervous I was or what a
step in the dark that speech represented.

The Prime Minister turned up and sat, on my right, in her usual
place next to the minister replying on the platform. I was pleased,
of course, for she only turned up to more important debates, but in
some ways I would rather have gone through my ordeal without
her. She wished me good luck (afterwards I realised that probably
she was as nervous of my debut as I was) and the debate started. Sir
Basil Feldman, an old friend, was Chairman of the Conference that
year and took the chair for my debate. Geoffrey Howe, Nigel
Lawson and Norman Tebbit turned up and sat on the platform.
Jeffrey Archer was there looking a little nervous, but he knew my
speech.

I forced myself to listen to the debate. Sitting there in the centre
of the stage looking at that enormous audience strangely calmed
me. The house was full, with people now crowding all sides and
standing at the back. Tory Party Conference debates are not real
debates, for there is rarely any dissension: they are more a chance
for ministers to address and encourage the faithful.

The debate was not particularly distinguished and all too soon
my time arrived. For the last few years we have had a podium that
rises automatically at the end of the debate when it is the minister's
time to reply. On the podium is a glass of water, a rather elaborate
stop-watch, which I never mastered, and ahead of you, half right
and half left, are the two screens of the prompter. Hopefully they
contain your speech and even more hopefully the operator down in
the bowels of the stage will run the machine in time with your
words. Over the years I learned to master the machine. After one
moment of absolute terror at a Scottish Party Conference at Perth,
when the operator lost my place and I just dried up for fifteen
seconds that lasted all eternity, I always marked the script with page
breaks and solemnly turn the pages of the speech in front of me.
You can never tell, and I would not be caught twice.

I started off by giving credit to Tom King and introducing my
team. I drew attention to the number of those claiming benefit. I
went into the labour force survey. I showed that, according to the
survey, nearly one million of those unemployed were not even looking for work. I announced the 100,000th firm to start under the
Enterprise Allowance Scheme. I had the ritual go at the Opposition.

I came to the end of my speech on the prompter. I picked up my
glasses and read the words that I had written the evening before.

'Chairman, I conclude my first debate at our Conference conscious of many different emotions. There has rarely been any issue that has so gripped our hearts and our minds, not only of our great Party but of the Nation itself. I have been concerned with young people and unemployment for many years now. I consider it a privilege that Margaret Thatcher should have entrusted me with this responsibility at this time. I will not let her down, nor you. Thank you.'

I finished and there was a moment's silence. It seemed never ending and then the applause started and I sat down. In two or three parts of the hall people jumped to their feet and applauded vigorously. I willed more to join them and gradually, all too reluctantly it seemed to me, others got to their feet. When about a third of the audience were standing the Prime Minister stood and so did everyone. I had my standing ovation, albeit not the most spontaneous in the world. I stood again grinning broadly and waving to one or two friends I could see in the crowd. My only thought was that I had survived – until next year.

All too soon we were down behind the stage again. The Prime Minister congratulated me. 'You have your own style, David,' she said to me, 'you speak in such a quiet, conversational manner. It is very different.' That shook me, for I had deluded myself that I had ranted and raved with the best of them. Oh well, I still have a lot to learn, I thought to myself. When I saw the tape of it I realised that I really did.

After my debate was over and I had recovered, it was full swing into the round of parties that start at the end of the afternoon session and finish in the small hours. I could not enjoy myself too much for I still had one further task to perform. I had been asked by the Conservative Political Centre to give the CPC lecture at the conference. I had worked for much of the summer preparing for it and I called the lecture 'Enterprise Regained'.

It developed a familiar theme of mine. I recounted how we had evolved an entrepreneurial spirit at the start of the Industrial Revolution and then lost it as we developed Empire. I compared 1776, the loss of the Empire in the West, in the same decade as the start of the Industrial Revolution, with 1876 when Disraeli made Victoria Empress of India in the same decade as the evolution of the public schools system designed to produce administrators for the Empire, with 1976 when the IMF came to London and we had to rediscover enterprise.

The lecture was delivered at the Royal Opera House. I cracked a rather weak joke about always wanting to appear in opera, but despite that it seemed to go down well. The lecture was subsequently printed and I was told later that it sold in considerable numbers, at least for a CPC lecture. At least I was getting the message across to a wider audience.

I returned to London with renewed determination. I had made a few telephone calls from Blackpool back to the Department and gradually put the package into some sort of shape. I called one more meeting of the group. I decided to call the new programme Jobstart. It was very simple, and would be exactly as I had visualised a unified programme during the last meeting of the group.

We would write to all the long-term unemployed and invite them into the Jobcentre. When they came in they would have an interview and be offered one out of a long menu of choices. By putting everything together we thought that we could guarantee something for everyone. A place on the Community Programme, entry into a Job Club, a place on the new weekly course that we were going to set up, help under the Enterprise Allowance Scheme, or a new programme we wanted to pioneer which would offer £20 cash in hand for anyone who had been out of work for over a year and who would take a job at under £80 a week. I hoped that after working for six months they would stay on, or at least get another job with an up-to-date reference.

The great unknown was the effect of counselling on those who should not be on the register in the first place. My own expectation was that a number of long-term unemployed who were working and signing would think that the game was up and would come off the register. Our economists, with a little prodding from me, produced graphs that showed that if we started straight away we could have unemployment below the magic three million early in 1987. It all depended on whether the counselling would have the effect I had hoped for. Unemployment would never come down sufficiently far without the counselling. We could question suspicious cases closely, and ask them back for another interview if necessary, but I knew that little would really be achieved in this way. I tidied up my paper and arranged to see the Prime Minister.

The meeting was fixed for Thursday 7 November. Cabinet that morning had been a particularly bruising occasion. It was the autumn White Paper Cabinet and all the colleagues had to agree their spending for the following year. I had been the first to agree my bid for the next year but that had not been too difficult as, in view of the situation, I was being given almost all that I had asked for. There would be a good increase in the Community Programme and I was quite content. Unhappily, that did not apply to all of my colleagues and there had been a Star Chamber.

We met that afternoon in the Prime Minister's study. Kenneth Clarke came with me and the Prime Minister had invited Norman Tebbit as well as Nigel Lawson and John MacGregor as the Chief Secretary. I had prepared a full presentation accompanied by coloured charts that showed the cumulative reduction of unemployment as a result of each programme. I even forecast unemployment dropping beneath the magic three million level just over a year after the start of the campaign. If we were to achieve our target before the next election, we had to start immediately.

I ended with the surprising statement that this was the one programme that would save money, if only for the DHSS. I estimated that the savings from the reduction of benefit payments would outweigh the cost of the programme many times over. I finished my presentation and looked at my colleagues. I am not sure if at the time I convinced them or not. Perhaps it was merely the absence of any alternative!

I got the go-ahead but only grudgingly. They were against any immediate start. No matter how many times I emphasised that this programme would actually save, not spend, it was felt that we must have a trial, a series of pilots which should be evaluated by the Treasury in the usual way. I could see the force of this argument and went quietly although I knew that I would have to find a way to speed up any evaluation if we were to see any results in time for the election. That would only give us eighteen months from that day, let alone from the end of any proper evaluation period. However the progress we had made was sufficient for one day and we returned in triumph to the Department.

The very next day I met with John MacGregor in the Treasury. From the outset John made it quite clear that there was no further money. In the end we agreed that I could announce the new six-month pilots for the long-term unemployed on 13 November. There would be seven of them in different areas around the country, unless the Scots and the Welsh wanted their own. I did far better with the evaluations of the pilots, for I persuaded John that they should be continuous. I could get no commitment to any expansion of the pilots, nor if they ever were expanded, any commitment to Treasury funding. I would have to find all the costs myself. We also agreed the extension of the Loan Guarantee Scheme to the end of 1985/6. I think that gave us both a great deal of pleasure. Back in the early eighties when John had his first job as Small Firms Minister at the Department of Industry and I was Special Adviser, I

164

worked for him in a long, drawn-out battle with the Treasury to get the original scheme established. Now we could both extend it in good conscience.

The next few days were filled with furious activity. I met with the Financial Secretary but could not agree any way we could make the Jobstart allowance tax-free, although I did win the concession that it would not count for National Insurance. Our officials burnt the midnight oil and agreed the form the evaluations would take. I wrote to Bryan Nicholson and officially informed him of the scheme and the work started on training our people in the pilot areas. The only changes that the Commission made was to insist on one pilot in each of the seven regions. With Scotland and Wales bound to come in, that would increase our pilots to nine. However by dint of careful selection of areas we were able to cover the same number of long-term unemployed as before.

In early December the results of our beauty parade of advertising agencies were in. I spent one whole day listening to presentations made by each of the four agencies. All the agencies had been selected by the COI and had been asked to work to a standard brief. The results were very different. They were simply not positive enough – save one that stood out from the crowd. Davidson Pearce came forward with a campaign based upon self help with a logo of an opening door and a slogan of 'Action for Jobs'. They also relied on a secondary slogan, 'Action opens doors', and produced a number of mock-up advertisements showing unemployed people getting through impenetrable barriers to employment through a door opened by training. Their campaign proposed more than just newspaper advertising and included radio advertising.

I could see right away the potential of the slogan 'Action for Jobs' and the logo of an opening door. It had the positive approach that I was looking for. It would also serve to give a corporate identity to the Department as a whole and a sense of unity to the Government's programmes. I selected Davidson Pearce as soon as we had seen all four presentations and over the next few days I spent some time with them. The campaign, costing some £3 million, would run from early April until the end of the year with three bursts on radio. I saw no need to change their plans at this stage but I knew that if all my plans came to fruition we might expand on this base. This would complement our new programme should the pilots work as I hoped.

I had arranged to take another trade mission to China and Leon Brittan, who was now at DTI, was quite happy for me to go. We put together another high-powered group and this time we agreed to go to Tiengen as well as Canton. Going back for the second time in the same year had a powerful effect on the Chinese and the visit went well. I thought that Howell deserved one trip and I arranged for him to go to Hong Kong and wait for us there. His task was to arrange for my press conference when we came out of China.

All went well and this time we went by car from Canton to Hong Kong and our arrival caused little stir. Howell had arranged for the press conference to be held at the British Trade Commission offices.

We had a new Trade Commissioner. He had only arrived the day before me and, poor chap, had to deal with me before he had even unpacked. The continual complaint of British businessmen was that the Hong Kong Government never preferred British contractors. Of that I had no doubt for the Hong Kong Government had recently thrown out all their Jaguars and replaced them with Mercedes! Our European Community partners would never have done that, was the complaint I heard. I could only agree, but on the other hand I doubt if any other attitude would have created a Hong Kong. The press conference promised to be a sticky one, for there were some in Hong Kong who saw in my trade missions to China a tendency for the UK to prefer the emerging market in China to our obligations in Hong Kong.

I took the press conference with the British Trade Commissioner by my side. I also asked some of my businessmen that had come as far as Hong Kong to join us. It started quietly enough although there was one sticky moment when a journalist in a rather emotional state stormed out of the conference because I would only confine my remarks to trade issues and refused to deal with passports. The conference wound down and I called the last few questioners.

A journalist from Taiwan asked me about Jenkin's Bill. I had no idea what it could be and looked at the Commissioner. I said that I was sorry but I had not heard of it. At that point the whole room exploded in anger. I quickly gathered that the Jenkin's Bill was some legislation that had passed Congress and was before the President. I tried to explain that I was an Employment Minister, not a Trade Minister and anyway it was American not British legislation. The more I said the worse it became. I learned during the next half hour the real value of the advice 'when in a hole, stop digging'. When I finally stopped the damage was done.

The television that night was appalling but the next day's papers were even worse. I was ignorant, a disgrace to the Cabinet, was about the kindest comment. The irony was that by lunchtime

166

President Reagan had vetoed the Bill and the issue was no more. Poor Howell was disconsolate, for Adrian Moorey had looked after all the press arrangements throughout China without any undue incidents. I returned thankfully to London, happy in the thought that there were only a few days before the Christmas break.

When I returned I asked for the latest news on the pilots. As I thought, the seven pilots expanded to nine as the territorial ministers got into the act. The pilots would be held at Crawley and Horsham, Ealing, Plymouth, Stoke-on-Trent, Preston, Billingham, Huddersfield, Dundee and Neath. They would all start early in the new year and there was nothing for me to do until the first results were out early in February.

Outside the Department a difficult situation had been building up between Leon Brittan at the DTI and Michael Heseltine at Defence. Bizzarely it was about Westland, a small helicopter company in the West Country. It appeared to have calmed down when, after Christmas, Lita and I flew off with Karen and Bernard, my elder daughter and her husband, to the Caribbean for our break. The one promise which I had made to Lita when I started at the MSC (and kept) was that we would take one holiday away from it all each year.

It was not a simple journey. The timing was such that we had to spend one night on a neighbouring island and then wait for a small boat on the following morning. We arrived at our destination at lunchtime and before I could even start to unpack I was given a note to ring the office. When I did, they asked me to ring No. 10. There I was told that the situation had deteriorated and a special Cabinet had been called for Thursday. I was told that the Prime Minister would quite understand if I did not return as I had just gone on holiday. I said immediately that I would come back as I gained the clear impression that the Prime Minister would need all the friends she could get.

By now it was late on Monday and the only flight that I could get that would get me back in time was the Wednesday morning Concorde from Miami. The only way to get to Miami in time would be to charter a small plane to take off from the landing strip on the island, and a twin-engined light aircraft flew in late on Tuesday afternoon. We would have to leave at first light and the following morning we sat in the aircraft waiting for sun up. We took off for Miami, and I noticed nothing amiss. A year later I was at Antigua airport when I met the pilot again. He said that he would never forget that takeoff. Evidently we missed some rocks by a few feet and he told me that he vowed there and then never to take off in the half-light again. Luckily, I was ignorant of all this and only knew

167

that we were experiencing strong head winds and were getting later and later.

It took well over five hours to reach Miami and we landed with just half an hour to spare. A van arrived and I hurried to a hut at the side of the runway to clear customs and immigration. The official was as all officials are when you are in a hurry. He took his time and he took pains to ensure that all the paper work was in order. I contained myself as much as I could but I was in a frenzy of impatience. All I could think was that I must not miss the flight. Eventually he agreed that all was in order and I could enter the United States for a few minutes. We (for the pilot had entered into the spirit of things and insisted on showing me the way) dashed around the airport perimeter, into the British Airways building, through Customs and Immigration again and up to gate.

The flight had just closed but with some fast talking they opened the gates for me. I was just about to board when they stopped me. As I had no ticket I had given them my Visa card and the machine had rejected it. My limit was not high enough and they were not letting me on the plane. At that point, I lost my cool and invoked all the deities even up to the Lord King himself. By then they must have realised it was serious and they let me on the flight. We were in Washington before I had calmed down but happily there were no more incidents and that evening I was back in London.

Chapter 13
TRIUMPH AND TRAGEDY

By the time Concorde landed, all thoughts of the holiday were behind me. Norman Dodds was waiting for me and filled me in with the news on the drive back from Heathrow. All London was agog with talk of the monumental row that had broken out between Michael Heseltine and Leon Brittan. When I got home I telephoned some of my friends. The general view was that the crisis was now over and that Michael was looking for a way out. But Thursday's papers were still full of it and by the time I turned up to Cabinet there were crowds outside No. 10.

We went impatiently through the routine business and it was not long before we were on to Westland. At first I was quite sure that Michael had come to Cabinet determined to settle the matter. A full discussion commenced. There is a convention which I shall not break, that Cabinet discussions remain confidential. However, the papers later reported that the cause of disagreement was slight, descending to mere trivialities. Michael, it was said, whilst willing not to continue the argument in public, wished merely to repeat the statements he had made over the past few weeks. It was reported that this argument found little favour with his colleagues. Suddenly I noticed that Michael had closed his papers. I turned to Kenneth Clarke and remarked with alarm that he might be serious. A moment or two later Michael gathered his papers, got to his feet and said, 'Prime Minister, if this is how it is to be I can no longer serve in your Cabinet.'

He left the Cabinet room. After an embarrassed silence we carried on with the next item on the agenda as best we could. A few minutes later a Private Secretary passed a note to the Prime Minister that she promptly read out. Michael had gone to the media waiting impatiently opposite No. 10 and announced his resignation. At that point the Prime Minister said that she thought that this would be a good time to break for coffee. It was.

We had coffee outside the Cabinet room discussing the events with, on my part at least, considerable disbelief. Rumours abounded – Michael was to call a press conference, make a statement in the House and many more. After about twenty minutes we were called back into the Cabinet room. The Prime Minister said, quite simply, that George Younger was now our Defence Secretary and Malcolm Rifkind would take Scotland. Cabinet continued, although we finished early.

Kenneth Clarke and I evaded the press outside No. 10 and we walked back to our Department. Although that was not the end of the story (for both the resignation of Leon Brittan and the rather pointless campaign run by Michael was yet to come) it was for me. If I was back early and had lost my holiday I could at least put the time to good use. That afternoon I called the first in a series of meetings to make sure that the pilots would succeed.

I had been left with a rather difficult problem. The Treasury had taken ministers' words literally. If ministers had decreed that there would be a six month evaluation period for the new programmes then that is what we will have, was their attitude. They did not want to even look at the results until the summer. I knew that with next year an election year we had to be ready to start the national programme as soon as possible. There were less than eighteen months to go. We had agreed joint monitoring of the pilots and we had computerised the programme to ensure that the results would be out quickly. Our statisticians selected the control areas and started work on the basis of comparison before Christmas.

On top of that there was a hidden agenda. The Manpower Services Commission was willing to run the pilots and would do so conscientiously. It was convinced of the good that this new scheme would do in providing an interview for each long-term unemployed in the pilot areas. The guarantee of a wide choice on offer to every one of them would ensure that, first and foremost, each interviewee would feel that they had a chance, that we were interested in their welfare. I was sure that even the combination of the week's training course coupled with a place in a Job Club would work wonders. Time after time, over the years, I had been told of those long-term unemployed who had just given up and reconciled themselves to living on benefit, especially when there was, so often, little difference in net take home income. The Jobstart allowance might allow some people to price themselves back into employment. All this was worth doing for its own sake.

The hidden agenda was the effect that the receipt of the letter and the invitation to attend the counselling session would have on some of the unemployed. My hunch was that there were quite a number of claimants out there who were either working and signing or had just given up and were 'resting' on the register. My simple idea had been that merely the receipt of the letter would persuade some of those cheating that they had been found out. It would take a very brazen claimant to wish to face an interview. Time would tell, but this element of the programme was not emphasised to the MSC. As a tripartite organisation I did not wish to put my people there in too difficult a position. For many years the left had adopted a curious attitude to unemployment. You would have thought that they would have done all in their power to help the unemployed. They often did, but mainly to keep them on the register. I could only assume that they thought that, if high unemployment embarrassed the Government, it would advance their cause. Time after time, they attacked anything that would resemble an assault on benefit fraud. Indeed, there were a number of centres for the unemployed that had fallen into the hands of the far left that specialised in giving out prepared answers to our questions merely to keep a few more people on the register.

Meanwhile, the newspapers and the television worked themselves up into a frenzy, day after day, night after night, about the Westland affair, with revelation after revelation. I just ignored it and busied myself with the pilots. I went on the radio and television whenever I could just to talk about them. I reasoned that if people knew that we would be coming into their area to call on them then they would act all the quicker when the letter came. I asked all my ministers to make day trips to the pilot areas and arranged with our information people to ensure that they got good local coverage.

The pilots started on 7 January. We had made good use of the period between Christmas and the New Year. Most of the country may have been on holiday but my people were busy preparing the letters, sending them out as soon as the Christmas rush had subsided. Within two days the first results came through. We had assumed for all our estimates that the overall response rate would be only 50 per cent, that is only half of those we wrote to would come in to the Jobcentres. The first results showed that over two-thirds were coming in, and that increased the effect we were having considerably.

By 15 January I had the report of the first week. Everyone who had come in to a Jobcentre had received an offer of some sort. There were sharp North/South differences. Where unemployment was highest the response was greatest. Not only that, in the South East, in that first week, there were no less than twenty-two references to DHSS for benefit sanctions. These were quite separate from any referrals to Social Security for not turning up for any interview. They would be given a second or even a third chance. These were referrals for the attitude adopted by those who did turn up! More than that we found a substantial number who lived a long way away from the area where they were registered. They would have to travel a long way to their benefit office each fortnight but, if they were working, there was less likelihood of their being spotted out of the district where they were registered. Quite significant numbers claimed to be working part-time or in education which prevented them looking for work. Were they, then, unemployed? They were certainly included in the figures.

At this stage it was far too early to see any effect on the count, but my people thought that we had a chance. By the end of the second week, across all the pilots, some 847 left the count of whom nearly one fifth did so after receiving their letter. This percentage varied widely, from 6 per cent in Plymouth to 75 per cent in Crawley! At this stage we had sent out over 5,000 letters out of the stock of 28,000 long-term unemployed in the pilot areas. Out of 2,341 interviews we had failed to make an offer only sixty-six times. Some of the anecdotal evidence was very surprising to some of my officials, if not to me. In Plymouth the lead singer in a pop group admitted working six nights a week and still signing on as unemployed. In Ealing, a 25-year-old refused a job offer of £98 a week despite being on only £20 benefit. In Crawley and Horsham one third of those on the list turned out to be living in places like Tunbridge Wells and would travel long distances just to sign. Our people thought that their hope was that they would not be spotted working by our staff. From then on, that was one of the first signs that our fraud teams would look out for.

There was even evidence that other Government departments were encouraging people to sign on. In Plymouth, one man admitted working and signing just to get his children free school meals. All over the country, evidence came in that claimants were encouraged to register by DHSS in order to claim housing and other benefits.

Finally, reliable figures began to come through. The new programme had an effect, and if anything it was bigger than I had dared hope. We took the first few weeks' results and left them to the tender mercies of our statisticians. They submitted them to rigorous analysis. At this stage much of the benefit of the MSC's work to help the long-term unemployed in the pilot areas was still to come through. We had no direct way of measuring those placed in jobs, for it would take weeks before the evidence filtered through from the Social Security offices. My Department paid unemployment

172

benefit for the first year only. After that the liability was transferred to DHSS as the claimant went on Social Security. The records were then kept at the local DHSS office and the details took a long time to filter through to our Department.

Even with the final results still to come, the effect was clear. The increase in those leaving the register in the pilot areas was 10.6 per cent greater than in the control areas. We analysed those who left anyway, or left before they received the letter, or who left and went back a fortnight later. We looked at the results every possible way. Finally, towards the end of February, my statisticians came to me. Despite the smallness of the sample there could be no doubt about the result. If a national scheme were operating we could expect roughly 23,000 extra to leave the register each month! That would be more than enough to completely reverse the whole direction of unemployment.

I could scarcely contain myself; we had a strategy and it worked. I went through the figures. A scheme to provide a national guarantee would be an immense task. There were about 1,300,000 long-term unemployed. Between now and March of next year another half a million would join them with a slightly smaller number leaving the register. That would give us the herculean task of over 1.6 million interviews between July and the following April. We would have to build up to well over 40,000 interviews a week at peak. With 1,000 Jobcentres that would mean 400 interviews that week, or 80 a day for each Jobcentre! After that there would be a running programme of about 650,000 interviews a year. The interviews were only one part of the problem. We also had to make sure that we had a full menu of offerings. Then again it would take over 2,000 additional staff. That would have an effect on the figures by itself!

We made our plans and our officials met with the Treasury. The results of the pilots were so clear and unambiguous, and improving week after week, that we had no real difficulty in persuading the Treasury officials to cut short the appraisal period. About ten days before the Budget I met with Nigel Lawson. I offered up a number of smaller schemes and agreed to end the redundancy rebate for all but the smallest firms immediately after the Royal Assent of the Wages Bill. In return, Nigel gave me all I asked for.

First, we would have a national scheme, starting on 1 July with the declared aim of interviewing all long-term unemployed by the end of the following March. The demands of this crash programme would mean that we would be given even more places under the Enterprise Allowance Scheme. Only the previous November I had managed to get an increase to 65,000 places for 1986/7 – now this would be increased to 80,000. The Loan Guarantee Scheme would have its premium halved to 2.5 per cent and we also introduced a new scheme, the New Workers Scheme, to help those leaving the Youth Training Scheme by giving a subsidy of £15 a week to those taking their first jobs under specific wages limits. The Jobstart allowance would not be taken out of the pilots but put on a national basis and, of the greatest importance to the MSC, the Community Programme would be increased again to 255,000 places by November. That programme, which I agreed in Sheffield Town Hall, had grown to an immense programme costing well over a billion a year. Almost as an aside, the number of Job Clubs would be increased to 450. No one would ever be able to say that I was afraid to change my mind, I thought to myself, when the time came for me to announce that.

There was a small price to be paid. For some reason the Treasury objected strongly to the name Jobstart. There was a day of high level discussions involving both ministers and officials which finally resulted in the name being changed to Restart. The name Jobstart was kept for the Jobstart Allowance Programme.

A week before the Budget I went to Toynbee Hall in the East End of London to deliver the annual Barnett Lecture. I had been invited by John Profumo, who had spent many years rebuilding Toynbee Hall to meet the demands of a new wave of immigration. I reminded my audience that my grandfather and father had come to settle only a few hundred yards from where I was speaking that evening. It did not occur to them to demand that the Government gave them a job. They knew that, if they did not look after their own, no one else would. I spoke of the need for enterprise, for new employment and the opportunity that the explosion in new activity that the Big Bang in the City of London would provide. This time there were more than a few in the audience who appreciated my remarks. I began to feel that slowly and surely the message was getting through, although there were still some who thought that Government should provide just what they wanted. It is remarkable how Toynbee Hall has continued, decade after decade, to carry out very necessary work for a population that has totally changed as one wave of immigrants gives way to the next.

All my programmes were announced in the Budget, although they were overshadowed in the fuss and excitement of Budget day. The next day I went to town. 'A three pronged attack on unemployment' was how I described it and it did represent a formidable package with a first year cost of £200 million and £300 million in 1987/8. It would help over one and three quarter million people, including all school leavers, for we were now starting my two-year YTS, as well as the Restart programme for the long-term unemployed. It contained considerable help for those leaving YTS, as well as those starting to work for themselves.

The following Monday I gathered all the officials in my Department, from Principal grade upwards, and spoke to them. I told them that at long last we actually could do something about the evils of unemployment. No longer would we have to take it lying down, waiting like Mr Micawber for something to turn up. They now had the ability to reverse the rise of unemployment. I also spoke of the need for the enterprise elements of our new programmes and that it would only be the continued increase in the number of new companies and the growth of self-employment that would permanently reduce the figures.

It would be difficult to exaggerate the effect that all of this had on my Department. For years the staff had been deeply demoralised. Month after month, year after year, they had seen unemployment continue its apparently inexorable rise. There had been deep pessimism about our ability to do anything to halt it, especially with a Government that set its face against a Keynesian spending spree. Suddenly everything had changed. There was something that they could do. I had seen the change on the small inner group that had worked with me in creating the programme. Most, but not all, had been doubters, going along with this new Secretary of State with his fixation with the black economy. As the first results of the pilots had come in the change could be felt. Enthusiasm for the new programmes began to spread like wildfire. Soon it was hard to restrain the new ideas and spirit of 'can do' that now permeated Caxton House. Gradually knowledge of what we were doing, and what was in store for the future, spread throughout the regions and the area offices around the country. No one minded the long hours and the considerable sacrifices that the rushed start of the new programme entailed. I still had one more card to play. The advertising campaign in the national press was to start in April.

I launched the booklet 'Action for Jobs – opening more doors' at the press conference which announced the start of the campaign. I pointed out that we were spending over £3,000 million a year to promote enterprise and jobs. Even as we spent that amount of money surveys recent surveys that we had made disclosed that five out of ten employees could not name a single scheme, and seven out of ten employers said that we did not do enough to publicise schemes. We had also found in running the recent pilots that far too many of the long-term unemployed were in ignorance of the very

175

schemes that could help them. I announced that we would be spending over £3 million on a campaign on radio and in the press by way of coupon adverts to publicise the booklet.

When it came out it had an electric effect on our officials around the country. They could see that they were part of a national effort to deal with the evils of unemployment and that they too, at long last, could do something about it. I would spend long hours travelling around the country ensuring that the arrangements would be in place for the start of the national campaign. In the meantime the pilots continued to show good results. I would also take every opportunity to get out and visit benefit offices and Jobcentres. Every time I did so I would find another loophole in the system.

I had a few nervous days as the campaign started. I remembered all too well back in my Eldonwall days in the sixties when I was developing industrial estates entering into an advertising campaign in the national press that also featured coupon advertisements. The agency had told me to get temporary staff installed to handle the rush. In the event we only received a dozen or so replies most of which came from friends or business rivals! This time I was not to be disappointed. The requests came flooding in and hundreds of thousands of the booklets went into circulation in the first few weeks of the campaign. By the middle of April we were ordering a reprint of 1,250,000. I wrote to the Chairman of the Joint Stock banks who agreed to display the booklet in their branches for a week or two. Surprisingly the Post Office were more commercial and charged us £20,000 a month to put it in all their main offices. Before long I was boasting that I was selling more than Jeffrey Archer!

In the meantime, Westland had sunk back into well deserved obscurity and we had had two brief, but painful, rows over the interest that Ford and General Motors showed in Rover and Land Rover. I was at Chequers on a Sunday for an early meeting on election strategy when the Prime Minister excused herself for a few minutes. She came back looking thoughtful. Afterwards the press reported that she had taken a call from President Reagan. That evening the Americans bombed Libya and we had another painful, but mercifully brief, row. It died down as the days and weeks passed and people realised that it had worked. Gaddafi stopped his more public support of terrorism. Until that became apparent there was quite a field day for all the harbingers of doom and gloom amongst us, particularly at the BBC.

Two by-elections were called. We were defending both and I was asked, at the commencement of both campaigns, to go and speak in support of the candidates. One Monday in mid-April I went in the early morning to Sheffield to spend time with my people in the Manpower Services Commission. Late in the afternoon I travelled over to Derbyshire West where the Tory candidate was one Patrick McLoughlin. Patrick, whom I briefly met, had started life as a miner. Later he had moved into the sales side of the Coal Board and away from the pit face. He was still under thirty and was representative of a new breed of Tory candidate. My task was simple. He had three meetings in remote villages in his constituency. I was to go ahead and warm up the audiences. As soon as I saw Patrick arrive I was to break off my speech and introduce their new member. Then I was to go on to the next meeting.

It was a foul night, pouring with rain and the villages were difficult to find. The first meeting boasted an audience of no less than fifteen. I did my bit and when Patrick arrived I moved on. The next meeting was down to a dozen and the last was little more than half that number. I spent my time wondering what it was all about. After I had finished I was driven for about an hour and a half through pouring rain to a lay-by on the motorway where I was to meet someone, I never found out who, driving down from Ryedale. I was due there in the morning for a press conference.

Driving through the pouring rain with minimal visibility, my driver told me about the '79 election. He was accompanying one of my Cabinet colleagues. He had my job, acting as the warm-up speaker. Arriving thankfully at the last meeting of the night, in a barn in a distant farm, he found a high, rather rickety, makeshift platform at one end and a total audience of one! He went up to his audience and presumed that he did not wish him to go ahead and give his speech. On the contrary, his audience did. So my driver climbed up the high platform and delivered his standard speech to his audience of one. A few minutes later the candidate arrived and asked the same question. He did what he was told and duly climbed up the platform and delivered his speech in full, feeling, he confessed afterwards, more than a little ridiculous. On the way out he stopped by his audience and hoped that he could count on him for the election. 'When I came here I was going to vote for you,' was the reply. Then, after a pause, 'but now I have heard you, I will not.' From that moment on I have never asked anyone in my audience how they will vote afterwards.

Ryedale was quite a different experience. I made much of all our work dealing with unemployment in the morning press conference. I could not understand the total lack of interest in anything I said until I realised that, in Ryedale, unemployment was still under 4 per cent. That was another view of the so called North/South divide.

177

That became all the more unreal when the candidate offered me a lift back to London in his private plane.

When the results came through, we lost Ryedale in a landslide defeat but we won West Derbyshire. Patrick was destined to become my PPS in due course and, after I left Government, the second youngest Minister in the Government. He was beaten to the title by Thomas Strathclyde (Lord Strathclyde), who was even younger and who had been my Lord's Whip.

The unemployment figures for April continued to be disappointing. It really was frustrating, for I was now sure that we could reverse the seemingly irresistible rise in the figures. Besides, I knew that there were a great number of people out there who had simply given up hope. Our new programme would change their lives and I could not wait for it to start.

We were now well into our advertising campaign. I was very happy with it as well as the Action for Jobs booklets that were now being heavily featured. But how many people read the papers? I wondered. I thought that we should do something more, so I sent again for Adrian Moorey. We worked out an idea for having a series of breakfasts around the country featuring ministers. I thought that we would get good coverage on regional television and local radio as well as the local press. We would also get to meet a few hundred local businessmen and local authority representatives but that was not the main issue. What I really wanted was the coverage on the local media. Adrian had some ideas and I asked him to get a presentation ready for me.

By then it was Whitsun, and the House was rising for the week. I was to go fishing in Scotland but before we left I arranged to go and record an interview with Jonathan Dimbleby at TV-am. Howell came with me and sat outside during the interview. It all seemed to go swimmingly and I fenced around the subject for fifteen minutes without, as I thought, giving any hostages to fortune. I knew that the whole scene would change in the autumn but I could say little. When we finished I walked out of the studio with Jonathan Dimbleby and we said goodbye. He told me later that he had noticed nothing out of the way. Howell, I thought, looked and sounded rather restrained.

When we were safely away in the car Howell said to me that he thought that this time I had really done it. Evidently, I had said, in an aside, that even the unemployed had never had it so good as benefit had gone up faster than inflation. I shrugged it off and thought that he was worrying too much. I went away in good humour.

Lita and I stopped for the Saturday night at Kirkby Fleetham

Hall in Northallerton in Yorkshire and the proprietor told me over breakfast that he had just seen me on the television. He said nothing else so I assumed that Howell had been worrying overmuch. That afternoon we arrived at our hotel on the Spey and I started to think about fishing. Later that evening the onslaught began. I was considered uncaring, with no feeling for the unemployed. As I was unelected I had no political touch. The next day's papers were even worse. I made headlines on the front pages of most papers, and cartoons in all. The press were out in force to find me. All they knew was that I was in Scotland. They did come to the place I was at but the proprietor protected me. As the week wore on the furore subsided. By the end of the week there were even some editorials saying that I was right. I wonder what they would have said if they knew that I had spent the week up to my waist in the River Spey!

It was the first time that the press had been really unkind about me, and I did not like it. I suspect that one effect of years of political exposure that all my colleagues had enjoyed, was to get used to knocks from time to time. My life had been far too sheltered. Even when I was in the Manpower Services Commission I only asked for publicity to sell my programmes and it had never turned back on me. I now had to get used to it backfiring. It was something that I would get used to in time, I thought. I did not.

I continued my practice of going out at least once a week to visit both the Jobcentres and the benefit offices. I would meet with our people, but I was more interested in examining actual case studies. Almost every time I would come across something wrong, not with the administration but with the system. One day I went out with Howell and Adrian Moorey. On the way back we started to discuss the success of the advertising campaign. It was going well, with our press advertising combined with extensive use of radio commercials generating a demand for the Action for Jobs booklets now running into the millions. Nevertheless I was concerned that we were not making real impact. Adrian and I started to reminisce about the success of the television campaigns we ran back in our MSC days. We had used it then to launch the Youth Training Scheme, and as much as anything else it had contributed to the success of the launch. 'Right,' I said, just as we arrived back at Caxton House, 'come on up to my office for a few minutes. We will use television for our programmes.'

I sat down with Adrian and told him that I would find the resource for an advertising campaign to back up our new programmes. If we wanted to get on air by then we should have to go out to tender quickly. Adrian said that he would contact the COI and they would recommend the agencies and he would discuss the brief with them. I found out that, rather like newspaper advertising, the COI controlled the choice of agencies. They would make sure that the most suitable agencies competed, although I would be permitted the choice of which agency best fulfilled the brief.

Hu Yaobang, the General Secretary of China came for a visit and Geoffrey Howe asked me to greet him at Heathrow. He was a small man with tremendous vitality. It was a fine Sunday afternoon and he came bounding off the aircraft and into the VIP suite. As soon as we had settled down for the obligatory cup of tea he told me off for deserting my wife on a Sunday afternoon just to meet him. I wondered how many other ministers of his rank would have even thought of that. I took to him immediately, and saw him for two trade meetings during his visit. He brought Li Peng, a Deputy Premier (now the General Secretary) with him who was responsible for power installations. One morning I took them both on a boat trip down the Thames. I thought that docklands looked very dramatic seen from the river.

My pilots made good progress. Unemployment continued to climb, for the pilots were far too small to have any effect. My worry, now, was that we had concentrated too many resources on the small pilots. Now that we were going national would they have the same effect? Would the quality of staff throughout the country be able to achieve the same effect? Our training programmes were accelerated and I rushed around the country worrying and fussing. We could not actually open everywhere on 1 July. It would take some weeks, as gradually we spread the programme around the country. We would not see the effect probably until the late autumn.

I had not seen my brother Stuart for a few weeks, for he had been on a trip for the BBC to the Far East. He had a slight cough when he left and it was still with him on his return. At first I paid little attention until he went in for a check up and they hurriedly repeated the chemotherapy. Suddenly all the doctors' doom and gloom of two and a half years ago came back to me. I had put it firmly out of mind, partly because Stuart had had frequent treatments and check ups without incident, and partly because the time limit they had given me had long since expired. Now all my fears returned. I simply could not contemplate anything serious happening and the doctors still appeared confident. He went into the Royal Marsden for a few days but when he came out he still had the nagging cough.

Adrian came to me and told me that he had arranged for a demonstration from a company he had found who would like to present our Action for Jobs breakfasts. One Thursday in July, after

Cabinet, I came back to Caxton House and found that the press conference room had been taken over by a massive audiovisual display. The technology was largely based on slides, with some television added in, and it was overwhelming. Just as it got to a climax the equipment fused. There was much coming and going but they could not get it going again. I found later that our power supply was not sufficient but I had seen enough. I told Adrian to proceed. The presentation we evolved formed the basis of our campaign to take Action for Jobs to the people.

We booked over twenty breakfasts, all around the country, at almost weekly intervals. They would start at 8 o'clock sharp and be finished by 9. A very simple breakfast would be served but the presentation, which lasted about thirty-five minutes, was spectacular. No less than 1,700 slides were used, and we would bring it up to date as the programmes evolved. The real climax to the campaign was a breakfast for nearly a thousand at the QE2 Conference Centre. This time the Prime Minister came, as well as my other ministers, and we received tremendous coverage.

Geoffrey Holland came to me one day with an idea of forming a College of the Air. His suggestion was that we would use the down time of the television stations, that is the time they were closed at night, to broadcast training programmes which could be recorded and played back during the day. They could even use some of the unused daytime hours. I thought that it was a tremendous idea, which could be self-supporting by the private sector. Geoffrey asked me who I thought should be Chairman. Instead of the same old names of the great and the good that get trotted out all the time I thought of Michael Green, the Chairman of Carlton Communications, and I invited him to breakfast. I had known Michael for many years. He had come to see me when he had a small printing company and he wanted to dispose of a spare site. Stuart had helped to float his company some years before.

It had grown tremendously fast, from a capital value of just a few millions to nearly a billion pounds. Over breakfast I told Michael that he had made enough money and the time had come to put something back. He was very keen about the uses of television and I was sure that I had sold him the job.

The results of the beauty parade of the advertising agencies came in and I spent two days looking at the results. Davidson Pearce were the winning agency and we agreed a series of commercials that featured the opening door and Action for Jobs but also concentrated on the Community Programme, on Job Clubs and our other programmes. At the end of June I agreed three bursts of television, in

181

July, October and the following January featuring a forty-second commercial and backed up with press, radio and an outdoor poster campaign. From that moment onward no one would be able to say that we did not bring our programmes to the people.

Restart commenced on schedule on 1 July. There would be a rolling programme as it gradually spread around the country. I would spend all the time I could away from London tracking its introduction. There was a very real constraint on the amount of time I could afford to spend away from Westminster – I sat on many Cabinet sub-committees and I had my duties in the House. Normally it was only on Fridays, or on Monday mornings that I could slip away. I took the chance whenever I could.

I then felt that we should get the maximum use out of our advertising. The Manpower Services Commission was just about to start a substantial advertising campaign on television for YTS and it was also a substantial advertiser for its other programmes. There then followed some awkward negotiations to persuade the Commission to adopt the open door and Action for Jobs. I was told of the independence of the MSC and how it could be compromised by advertising in common with the Department. 'Rubbish,' I could say, secure in the knowledge that I had once run the Commission and could make a few suggestions as to how they could achieve it. They did and from then on we had achieved a corporate identity for both the Department and the Commission. That would be worth an untold amount in reinforcing the message of the advertising . . .

For some weeks the papers had been running stories saying that Norman Tebbit and the Prime Minister did not get on. Whenever I spoke to Norman or to the Prime Minister I could find no reason for any suspicion. The stories began to have a life of their own and got worse and worse. Eventually the Prime Minister made a well-publicised telephone call to Norman. All the papers ran the story that they were now reconciled and, just as suddenly as it had arisen, the story died. It did not bode well for the election, now less than a year away.

In the meantime Stuart's cough did not improve. The doctors decided that he should go back into the Royal Marsden for further tests. The cancer had definitely come back and the doctors were now really worried. Stuart wasn't and had all the confidence in the world. While he was waiting to go into the Marsden he spoke to me about the Deputy Chairmanship of the BBC. He was very concerned to remove the BBC from the political arena. He asked me about Joel Barnett (Lord Barnett), who had been in the last Labour Cabinet. I thought that he would be splendid and I approached him for Stuart. He accepted, after clearing the position with his whips. I told him that we only did it to stop him criticising me in the House! He was only able to speak to Stuart on the telephone, for he was now too ill to go to work.

The House was now in its final week. I had one last political dinner, for Giles Shephard on the 22 July. Robert Atkins came in to see me in my room in the Lords for a chat but I could not really concentrate. Stuart was having treatment and had just had more tests and the results were imminent. The phone went and it was our doctor, Joe Joseph. Robert saw my face, excused himself, and went on to check how the dinner was going.

Joe just said, 'Bad news, very bad. In fact the worst.' Stuart now had secondaries. 'How long?' I asked. 'Six weeks at the most,' was the reply. 'There may just be a chance with one more treatment,' but I could tell that even Joe did not believe it. I put the phone down and sat, looking blankly at the blotter on my desk. I just could not understand how this could happen. I simply refused to believe it. Just then Robert put his head round the door and I had to go downstairs and greet fifty perfect strangers and make an upbeat political speech. I did so, but all the time I tried to understand what I had just been told.

The next day, and every day for the next few weeks, I would spend a few hours with Stuart, and then make an excuse to go away for a few hours to a non-existent office. We would sit in his garden and make plans for Christmas and for all the years ahead. He wanted a second term at the BBC. He had a great strategy for their future development, for the new people he wanted to bring on. He had bought the site for the new White City building and talked of how it would bring all parts of the Corporation together. We talked of the future of our children, of what he would do after his second term.

Eventually he had to return to the Royal Marsden. The treatment did not work and when it became obvious that there was nothing further to be done I went with him in an ambulance to the Wellington clinic. None of the family knew how bad his condition was, except Denis, his son-in-law, who had always known. In the middle of August my father, who had been sinking steadily, died in his sleep. Despite all his pain, we never heard him complain. I told Stuart, who was distressed that he could not even go to the funeral. He lasted a further thirteen days, although to the very end he thought that he had it beaten, that he was getting better. The day before I told the family. In the middle of the night the telephone rang. I went to say farewell to Stuart and then to tell our mother. She gave us all strength. Ever since that day the telephone falls strangely silent, each morning at 8 o'clock.

As soon as that dreadful month of August was finally over I returned to the Department. I threw myself back into work with a mindless passion. There was much to do. The Restart programme was slowly becoming national, and we had finished the first burst of national advertising on television. Our surveys showed that now a quarter of the people recognised the open door symbol. We were on our way to becoming a national brand. Meanwhile unemployment continued to climb, although the pace had begun to slow.

Michael Green had accepted the chairmanship of the new Open College and we announced it at a press conference. Some of the papers made much of the fact that we were related – Michael was still married to my second cousin although they were separated and destined to divorce – although how nepotism worked when you gave away an unpaid job I was never to discover. Michael was a fully paid-up member of the band of enthusiasts. If enthusiasm and drive could make this work I knew that we were in good hands.

The party conference season was with us again. This was clearly a pre election Conference and Norman Tebbit was treating it as such. He spoke to us after Cabinet one day in September and unveiled his plans for all our speeches at the Conference. We were to use the phrase 'The Next Steps Forward' in all our speeches and that common theme would be a unifying thread running through our Conference.

Labour were holding their Conference at Blackpool whilst we had decided to go to Bournemouth for the Grand at Brighton was still being rebuilt. On the Thursday morning of the Labour Conference week the unemployment figures were due to come out. When I had been given the advance figures I had exploded with frustration. I called an immediate meeting with our statisticians, Paul Dworkin and Anne Wheatcroft. On a headline count of over 3.3 million they calculated that unemployment had increased by merely 200. In vain I told them that the margin of error was far greater than that. That an increase of just 200 in over three million was meaningless. That normally we took our figures to the nearest thousand and why not now? Quite rightly they were not to be moved and there was nothing I could do about it.

For some months now unemployment had been steadily increasing, albeit by a gradually diminishing amount. Unfortunately each time the figures came out they established another record level. Labour usually made the most of it. This time they excelled themselves. When the figures came out at 11.30 on the Thursday morning they interrupted their Conference and, in a dramatic gesture, John Prescott rushed to the podium and announced the new record figure. Flashing lights completed the scene and it made all the news bulletins that evening. I was privately furious, for in truth unemployment had really stood still. The newspapers ran stories of Neil Kinnock drinking champagne on the train down from Blackpool, celebrating his forthcoming victory in the election. They had had a good Conference and the press came to Bournemouth quite prepared to write us off.

I had been working hard on my speech. This time I was able to announce some new programmes. I had worked hard, both on the content but this time on my delivery. At one point, in a rather flamboyant spontaneous gesture that I had practised for hours, I said, 'I have a message for the unemployed, we have not forgotten you – you have my word on it.'

That extract made all the television bulletins, but when I saw it I felt more than a little ashamed of myself. What ever it was, it was not really me. Still, I did mean it, I could comfort myself, even if I did think my delivery more than a little forced. This time my speech obtained a far better reception, with great praise being showered on me during the debate for the success of Action for Jobs. I was given a far more spontaneous standing ovation but at the end of the day I had to explain that unemployment continued to go up.

The Conference started slowly and with each day it improved. I believe that the foundation for our great victory the following year was laid during that week in Bournemouth. The credit belongs firmly to Norman Tebbit, who was at his best, not only in his speeches but in the way he persuaded all the colleagues to follow the same theme. By the time the Prime Minister came to address the last day it was clear that our Conference had been a triumph.

I stayed behind to do some television and it was about 5 o'clock as I was being driven out of Bournemouth on our way to Graffham for a quiet, and long anticipated, weekend that the phone in the car went. It was my Private Secretary. The statisticians had been working hard. There was a revision of their figures and it affected the last month's count. Unemployment, instead of going up by 200, had really gone down by 1,200! I do not know what they did, or why they had to revise the figures, but what would I have given for them to have done it in good time for the conference. It would have made all the difference if I could have stood there and said that unemployment was finally on the way down. Of course we could not announce anything, that would have to wait for the next month's figures to come out. Still, I began to wait impatiently for them, for this would be the first month that would show the effect of Restart on a national basis.

The days dragged by. I got a whisper that the results of the last count were showing dramatically different results. Then I was told that the results varied from area to area. Eventually they came through and they were better than I could ever have hoped. Unemployment was 35,000 down. We had never had such good results in the entire history of the Department. The flash figures came through on a Friday and I sent a message to the Prime Minister that the tide had turned. I had to be very careful that I did not let the cat out of the bag and this time it was very difficult indeed.

It was an anxious weekend for me. The Sunday papers had nothing so I breathed a sigh of relief. The figures were so good I wanted them to be a complete surprise. There was little chance of a leak. As the unemployment figures were always regarded as important economic indicators very few people knew in advance. Even my junior ministers were not in the know. The Prime Minister, the Chancellor and Kenneth Clarke were among the few colleagues to see the figures.

Monday morning brought a surprise. The *Daily Mail* was in the habit of forecasting the unemployment figures on the Monday of the week they were due. It was just an informed guess, but at times it had got so close to the mark that we would suspect a leak. Not this time. They forecast that I would be announcing an increase of over 100,000 to bring the total to over 3.5 million for the first time. I could not help smiling over my breakfast and my enjoyment even increased when Roy Hattersley, later that day, accused me of deliberately leaking the figures in order to prepare everyone for the bad news.

I said nothing. There was nothing I could say, for I would be damned if I did and damned if I didn't. I got the office to issue the usual denial and concentrated on ignoring John Prescott when he repeated the charge.

The next day some of the other papers ran the story and the general impression was that Thursday would bring with it very bad news. I was asked to go on the *Today* programme on the Thursday morning about another subject and I neatly sidestepped any reference to the figures by saying that we would have to be patient until 11.30 a.m. I tried hard to sound neither excessively gloomy or glad. When I came into the office I found that Neil Kinnock's adviser had been on asking for an early sight of the figures. I asked what reply he had been given and was told that he had the standard reply – he would have to wait until 11.30 and not a moment before.

Cabinet that day was fairly routine. When it came to Home affairs the Prime Minister turned to me with a smile and asked for the figures. There was a perceptible gasp when I revealed all. I pointed out that this was now the second month of a fall, as my officials had revised the last month. I got slightly carried away, for I went on to say that I was now sure that unemployment was going to fall for the next five months at least. I was told later that when my statisticians in the Department saw the relevant extract of Cabinet minutes they became gravely concerned. When they came to me, I told them not to worry. I had made the forecast as my opinion, not theirs.

I left Cabinet early as usual. This time the interviews were a delight. After television I went on to do *The World at One*. When I was there I was told that John Prescott had cancelled his appearance. He was rewriting his statement.

From that day onwards I would accept any invitation to appear with John Prescott. The figures were set on a firm downward path. To gild the lily, my statisticians continued to revise the figures until today, if you look up the record, it appears that unemployment turned down from June 1986. I only wish it had. It would have made my life very much easier.

At my next meeting with the Prime Minister I gave her a graph that showed the probable decline in unemployment over the next nine months. It showed that unemployment would probably drop below the three million level in May – and be announced just after the likely date of a June election. If only we had had an immediate go ahead on Restart!

I expanded Restart and unemployment continued to drop. For the remainder of my time at Employment I would continue to press home Restart and plan to extend it, first to those who had been out of work for just six months and later to all unemployed. Today it is a valuable tool in the hands of the Department, not only in the battle against those abusing the system, but as a worthwhile method of helping the unemployed back to work before despondency sets in.

How successful was the whole Action for Jobs campaign? I was always concerned that, with such a high profile campaign, I could justify the expenditure involved. We instructed MORI to conduct a continuous tracking survey and the results were published in July 1987. The survey was a large one, a sample of about 2,000 and taken on ten separate occasions between July 1986 and April 1987. The survey focused on four questions: did people recognise the 'Door' symbol? How aware were they of the existence of the 'Action for Jobs' booklet and how many of them had read it?

Over the period public awareness of 'Action for Jobs' advertising increased from 10% to 56%. Recognition of the 'Door' symbol rose from 7% to 44% and awareness of the booklet from 7% to 46%. Those who claimed to have looked through the booklet rose from one in fifty to one in eight.

The report went on to say:

'Throughout the campaign, young people aged 15–17 were significantly more aware of all aspects of the campaign than were the public as a whole. By April 1987 a staggering 87% of this age group spontaneously recalled government advertising to do with jobs and almost as many (84%) recognised the "Door" symbol. Seven in ten said they were aware of the "Action for Jobs" booklet and about one in four (23%) claimed to have looked through a copy.

The shift in awareness levels among 18–24 year olds has been almost as dramatic as for the younger age group: advertising awareness rose from 12% in July 1986 to 75% in April 1987 while recognition of the "Door" symbol rose ten-fold over the same period from 7% to 70%. Awareness and penetration of the booklet by the end of the campaign stood at about the same level as for 15–17 year olds (68% aware of booklet, 24% penetration).'

How successful had the campaign been with the unemployed? The report said:

'Awareness of "Action for Jobs" advertising among the unemployed rose from 15% at the start of the campaign to 74% in April 1987 when 73% also said they were aware of the booklet and one in three (34%) had looked through it (compared with 9% in July 1986). Shifts in awareness levels among the unemployed and young people have been consistently higher than for the general public as a whole, indicating the effectiveness of the advertising campaign in reaching these target audiences who are among the main potential beneficiaries of the "Action for Jobs" schemes.'

What about our success with employers and small businessmen? The report said that we had increased awareness here but not to the extent achieved for young people and the unemployed. In fact they fared little differently from the general population. This report put paid to all the criticism that the campaign was overtly political. It was focused entirely on our client group, the young and the unemployed, neither of whom were likely to vote for us, and was

188

completely successful. Of course, the rest of the population were now fully aware that the Government was tackling the problem of unemployment with some vigour!

One day Adrian Moorey came to see me. He had put in for a job at the Department of Trade and Industry. Colette Bowe, who had been one of the figures in the Westland affair, had decided to leave the service. DTI was a considerable promotion for Adrian and I recommended him warmly to Paul Channon. He got the job and I was sorry to see him go as we had worked together since my early MSC days.

Both Kenneth Clarke and I had long been concerned at the way the figures were calculated. I did not believe that they gave a fair view of unemployment, and every time the yearly Labour Force Survey came out it would throw up considerable discrepancies. By then the figures were historic, but they did give a far better idea of the nature of the workforce and the real extent of unemployment. They were calculated, not as a head count, but by way of a survey. I knew that the Americans, the Canadians and the Australians also calculated their unemployment by means of a survey.

I would have taken this up far earlier, but one of the attacks that the Labour Party always used was that we had 'fiddled the figures'. We had not, but the way in which they were both collected and refined from time to time to give a better idea of the extent of unemployment could certainly give that impression. I wanted to change the system but I had to wait until unemployment was on the way down. Now this had started I could look seriously at the problem.

As soon as I could get away I went to Washington via New York where my younger daughter was working. I flew down to Washington on the Sunday afternoon. My only appointment was to have tea with Vice President Bush and his wife. When I arrived at the airport I found that the Ambassador was out of town, which I knew, and that the Embassy car was out of action, which I did not. The Embassy had hired a chauffeur driven black limousine of a length found only in fiction. When I got in I could hardly see the driver. I found myself with a television set, a bar and enough room to throw a party – all for a ten-minute journey.

Vice President Bush lived in a house, with a small circular drive, on an Air Force base close to the centre of Washington. The driver tried to enter, had to back, tried again, succeeded and then got stuck. I looked up and saw George and Barbara Bush splitting their sides with laughter standing on their front porch. I baled out of the car and endured much good natured ragging.

The next morning it was down to business. I found out that a sample unemployment survey would have to be at least 60,000 to have sufficient accuracy and as time went on we decided that we should leave well alone. Whilst I was there I spent some time looking at the way they carried out training. I came across Private Industry Councils, voluntary bodies that carried out many of the tasks the Area Manpower Boards did imperfectly for the MSC. They were run by employers and I could see that they would be more relevant to a post election world. I commissioned a report from one of our civil servants who had temporarily left the Department to follow her journalist husband to Washington. That report formed the foundation for the TECs, the Training and Enterprise Councils.

Gradually the political temperature began to rise. One week I had to take part in both Oxford and Cambridge 'No Confidence' debates. To the great surprise of both Presidents we managed to win both! The last time we had won such motions was before the last election. I took this as a very happy omen. From then on I concentrated for the changes that would come after the next election. I now had a clear idea where we should be going, not only in programme terms but also in the way we would organise the Commission.

All now depended on the manifesto.

Chapter 14
MANIFESTO TIME

As 1987 came in I found that I had less and less to do. Restart was now a clear success and month after month unemployment continued to come down. All eyes now turned towards the forthcoming election. The changes that I planned for my Department now had to be part of a manifesto and brought in on the crest of a good election victory.

Two events happened in the middle of March, one public and the other private. The public event, although it remained confidential for some time, occurred when the Prime Minister asked me to help at Central Office for the duration of the election. Her relationship with Norman Tebbit had greatly improved since the last summer, but there was still a residue of unease. She wanted me to deal with some details of the campaign planning and my friendship with Tim Bell would ensure that she would still be able to rely on his advice from time to time.

The second, private, event was that for the first (and probably the only) time in my life I kept a diary. Every night, no matter how late it was, or how tired I felt, I would go to my study. There I would switch on my tape recorder and for ten or fifteen minutes dictate the events of the day. I started this diary not with any idea of publication, indeed the major part will long remain private, but to give my grandchildren some taste of what I thought would be a momentous period of my life. I am still slightly surprised that I managed to keep it up throughout the election until the first day of the new Parliament.

It is difficult now to recreate the atmosphere of the frenetic activity at the centre of an election where paranoia is the order of the day and the world is seemingly always about to end. My diary is not the story of the last election; that will have to wait for another time, perhaps another age. In any event the true story, if that is not a contradiction in terms, would need to be told by a far more dispassionate observer than I could ever be. But a dispassionate observer would not have tasted that cocktail of utter fatigue laced with the adrenalin of sheer terror, let alone lived on it for day after day, week after week, until election day.

Here are some extracts from that journal.

Tuesday 7 April

After I finished last night's work I prepared three copies of a critical path network, a detailed agenda for what we would have to do for the manifesto. My first appointment this morning, after a haircut, was the regular one with the Prime Minister. That was now fixed at 9.30 on Tuesday mornings after she finishes the press review of the papers. She was in a good mood. She said she had a good meeting with Norman Tebbit and asked how was I getting on. I said it was difficult, but I was making good progress. I had clearance to deal with the three items – the tour, the manifesto and now party political broadcasts. I told her that I had been working on the tour and would get the details to her. On the manifesto I said I was going to settle down with Howell and start to get the detailed charts and graphs done and look for the artwork. I would have it all for her – at least the first sight of everything – by Easter. We chatted a bit and then I showed her my critical path network. I went through it in some detail very quickly.

I said, 'What's more, I want to have a special candidate's conference,' and she burst out laughing. 'Oh,' she said, 'it was your idea, was it?' I then produced my note headed 'Autumn Special Conference', and we went through it. She told me she wanted to have a special meeting to discuss campaign issues on the Thursday before Easter and on the Tuesday after Easter, when I was to be there all day. We first discussed holding it at No. 10. I suggested we make it at Chequers because she would be less bothered by the Private Office, and she agreed.

The rest of the day carried on being pretty horrendous. I gave the keynote address at the Human Resources Development Week at the Barbican and then dashed upstairs and launched the prospectus for the Open College with Michael Green. Back to the office for a variety of different appointments, including a slightly fraught meeting with the TUC.

That evening there was a marvellous dinner to celebrate the 30th Anniversary of the Institute of Economic Affairs. There were many speakers, including Keith Joseph, who received warm tributes. The Prime Minister was the eleventh speaker, which wasn't quite as bad as it sounds because most of the contributions were reasonably short and all entertaining. She ended up saying, 'I may be the eleventh speaker, but I want to remind you all – the cock may crow, but only the hen can lay an egg.' It brought the house down – there's no doubt that in this particular company she was a great hit.

Incidentally, one of the speakers was Joe Grimond (Lord Grimond), and I found it very odd that he should be a speaker at the IEA since he had given me so much trouble earlier that week in the Banking Bill, when he had come out with the most protectionist speech. He thought that everything was all right as long as it ensured that Scottish companies could not be taken over by anybody else, particularly by the English!

Thursday 9 April

This morning started off with a minor crisis. For the last few days industrial action had been building up in the North West and in Wales with both the Society and the CPSA (the two main Civil Service unions). I had started the week by going to an Action for Jobs breakfast with Nicholas Edwards (the Secretary of State for Wales) in Newport. The breakfast was being held in the exhibition centre and I walked straight past pickets who hadn't even recognised me – indeed Nicholas came in a few minutes later laughing all over the place because the pickets hadn't even recognised him. I stopped laughing when I realised that if we weren't careful the unemployment count figures – the count day was today – would be delayed in coming out on 14 May. I couldn't think of anything worse than the figures being delayed during an election, with allegations flying that we delayed them for political ends.

I called a meeting first thing this morning to solve the problem. Roger Dawe was there – in fact all my crowd were there. Leigh Lewis had drafted a splendid press release – it was so way out, so political, that even I couldn't use it. I think he had his leg pulled quite a lot by most people in the Department.

Friday 10 April

After a splendid night at Ashby Castle and a marvellous breakfast cooked in a little private kitchen near our room, we went off to a very good meeting in Northampton Jobcentre. I must say the quality of our people on the ground in the Jobcentres who are administering Restart really has to be seen to be believed. Then on to Tony Baldry's meeting in the Cherwell Valley, then back to Caxton House in London in time to agree the precise form of the statement that I'll

193

be making about the industrial dispute on Sunday night (embargoed for Monday). The more I think about it, the more worried I get about the prospect of postponing the unemployment figures during an election period.

Not all bad – we now have the very good news indeed that the unemployment headline figure will be 82,000 down. Seasonally adjusted, 30,000 down. This means unemployment's now at 3 million and 43 thousand – it looks quite clear that if we have a June election unemployment will come under the three million just about a week too late. Still . . . you can't win 'em all.

Tuesday 14 April

This morning at 9.15 I had a meeting with John MacGregor, ostensibly to go through the manifesto. John was very concerned that it was too long and had to be cut down. I produced my timetable and I showed him what we had to do, and he agreed that although the dates were tight it would be possible. I really needed the words, so we could fit in the graphs and the pictures. He also thought the Prime Minister was still very set on having pictures in the manifesto.

I did briefly raise the letter I'd written to him about the three guarantees for the unemployment part of the manifesto. He told me about Robin Harris's points of achievements of the last seven years. I had the idea on the spot that we should produce another book which should be full of achievements.

Wednesday 15 April

I then came back to the office to meet Jimmy Savile. He was the President of Hands Across Britain, a movement run by Molly Meacher, which was going to demonstrate on 3 May. They were planning to get 350,000 people to hold hands to demonstrate their concern about unemployment. Well, I'm not sure what good it will do, but I was very worried that it was in the week of the local elections. Molly Meacher had been to see me and had tried to get me to sign a ridiculous note saying I would press Government for more resources for unemployment, as if that was the answer.

When Jimmy Savile came in he insisted on kissing everybody in the office – I think he kissed every girl he ever saw. There's a very shrewd brain behind that jazzy exterior. I arranged with him – after a very long chat, I wouldn't persuade him to stand down as

President – that at Stoke Mandeville he would give away 500 Action for Jobs leaflets. Perhaps I will arrange to telephone him during his programme.

Tuesday 28 April

Strategy Group meeting. Willie Whitelaw was there, but he didn't stay for the whole meeting, as were John MacGregor, Norman Tebbit, Kenneth Baker and Norman Fowler. I said right at the outset, 'Prime Minister, my objective in the next parliament is to get unemployment down under two million.' I don't think anybody had ever spoken to them in that way. I produced a chart which showed that if we did that, we would be saving some £2.75 billion a year in reduction of benefits. We then had a rather difficult conversation. John MacGregor is totally supportive but he does feel, I think, that he's got to take the Treasury line. He objected to the Public Expenditure Survey transfer – the transfer of resources from DHSS that I would need to give my three guarantees.

We went through the three guarantees. The first was to make YTS universal by taking benefit away from under eighteens and that was agreed, as was the PES transfer. The second which didn't require a PES transfer was to guarantee all those who had been unemployed for between six and twelve months a place on the Job Training Scheme, and that was agreed. The third one, which was to guarantee a place on all programmes for those between the ages of eighteen and fifty, was not agreed. After some dickering I agreed on a formula that we would move towards the provision of such a guarantee. Well that was fine with me because that was the most I suspect that we would be able to do for some considerable time.

We then moved on to structural changes and right away I could see the Prime Minister was very nervous over the proposal to abolish the MSC. In one of those rare moments of brilliance – even if I say so myself – I suddenly suggested that instead of abolishing the MSC we could substantially increase employer representation. This got general agreement, and the more I thought about it the better it actually appeared. At which point I dashed out of the meeting and went back to the office to see Geoffrey Holland and Roger Dawe, and Clive Tucker [one of my civil servants] and John Turner. I explained to them that what I really envisaged was an MSC with an amended constitution that would have 75 per cent employer representation, and 25 per cent would be the unions and educational training interests. The employer interests wouldn't necessarily be the CBI but other bodies as well. I think this was received with some relief.

195

Wednesday 29 April

I was tired last night and went into a deep sleep, to be suddenly woken by the telephone – it was Greville Janner, the Labour MP, who rang on his way to Leicester. He told me that after my big write-ups at the weekend, one of his colleagues on the Labour front benches said to him, 'I didn't realise that David Young once voted Labour – it's a pity we let him go.' I dashed into the office – I was due at 9 o'clock at the Queen Elizabeth Centre Conference Centre for a big NEDO conference in which I made the opening keynote speech. Norman Willis was there from the TUC and when I saw Norman I thought how glad I was that in the end we'd kept the MSC on the basis of changing the constitution rather than abolishing it entirely. They will certainly be easier to deal with later.

Friday 1 May

When I came into the Department there was Anne Wheatcroft with Paul Dworkin (my statisticians) in the waiting area outside my office. My heart sank. 'Oh God,' I thought, as I invited them in, 'the unemployment figures are going to be bad.' Then Paul Dworkin said, with a smile, 'Secretary of State I think you'd better sit down.' I guessed immediately from his manner that the figures were going to be marvellous – under the 3 million I thought. I sat.

'I shouldn't have done that to you,' Paul said, when he saw how white I had gone from suppressed excitement. They told me the headline total was 40,000 down, the seasonally adjusted 20,000 down. The statisticians had rejigged all the seasonal adjustments, so in fact this would be the tenth consecutive month they would be down. The figure looks like it could be 3 million and 19 thousand – slightly higher than it would be otherwise because of the effect of the strike of our officials. At least that problem is out of the way. It certainly made me happy but I swore everyone to secrecy. I cancelled the ensuing meeting dealing with the figures because there were still two weeks before the results and I didn't want anyone to know.

I went to see the Prime Minister. It was a small meeting, Christine Wall, Peter Morrison, Stephen Sherbourne, Roger Boaden and myself. The Prime Minister was fairly relaxed. Peter gave us news about some amazingly good by-election results that had just come in. I just took out a scrap of paper and wrote on a note that said – 'Prime Minister, the very early flash result – next month's figures are going to be all right.' I passed it to her, she unfolded the note, looked at it and just passed it straight back to me without even twitching. I know it must have been a great relief to her.

I started off with the manifesto and the tour. It was an amazing meeting – best part of an hour – and with one or two small exceptions she was very happy with the whole tour. We may have to make contingency plans if she goes to Venice, to the Council of Ministers' meetings.

I went off with Peter Morrison to White's and we had a jolly good lunch. We both felt very relaxed and in high spirits. The manifesto–achievements book was now with the printers, the tour was virtually agreed and over lunch with Peter I went through what our roles would be during the campaign.

Sunday 3 May

Hands across Britain flops!

Tuesday 5 May

A final manifesto meeting, and the Prime Minister was in pugnacious form – criticising the work that had been done so far, having a go at a great deal of Nigel's part – part 1 – while I was sitting back. Once I did intervene – there was one part in the draft which said that when threatened we had gone in to protect the Falklands, and I said, 'No, no, what we want to protect is the *people* of the Falklands, not the Falklands – people not property.' 'Oh no,' she said and gave me a terribly fierce look, 'Georgia, South Georgia *was* about property, the islands *were* about property – we're about protecting property AND people' – and that was an end to that.

So it went on until we came to the chapter about employment and jobs. Trade and Industry and the Employment and Jobs sections had now been put together.

This is where my whole world suddenly started to become unstitched. Out of the blue, they suddenly produced a brand new paper – one that I'd just not seen before. What made it worse was that it quickly transpired that the Prime Minister had redrafted the whole section on employment and jobs – she had done it at a session they'd had the evening before and of course she was very much wedded to it.

Well, there wasn't too much wrong with it. She had put it, I must confess, in much better shape and rather more tersely than I'd written it. I did try to point out, gingerly, but no one paid much attention, that at the Chequers meeting I'd been asked to pad it out.

Then it came to the third guarantee. This was the great bone of contention between the Treasury and me as to whether we could give a guarantee of work – or even use the words 'work towards a guarantee' – for all those between eighteen and fifty unemployed for more than two years. My proposal was that they could have a place on either the new Community Programme or in a Job Club or on the Enterprise Allowance Scheme – she'd rephrased it so that the third guarantee appeared merely to give a place on the Restart programme, which is the interview. I fairly exploded at this point, and said, 'I'm sorry, if you really want to have my great prize – which is unemployment to come down to two million – then I really do need to have this guarantee.' To no avail. In the end the Prime Minister did agree on a fairly soggy form of words, which said that after the third guarantee (applying particularly to the Restart interview) we could say it is our aim within the lifetime of the Government to move towards a position in which we could offer to all those under fifty and over eighteen, etc, etc. At which point, realising that sometimes you can never win, I decided to keep quiet.

Friday 8 May

I woke up slowly and painfully. John Turner was waiting for me downstairs and we went off to fly to Middlesborough for the day. When we reached the raised portion of the M4 we could see it was at a standstill, so we cut off down the A4 and that was almost as bad. By ten to nine it was quite clear we weren't going to make the 9 o'clock flight, which was more than embarrassing because I was going to see the two bishops – the Bishops of Whitby and Middlesborough – that I'd had to cancel in January because of snow. We went to the Hounslow Suite and to my surprise we were just a couple of minutes after nine. They rushed us out to the DC9 which had already left the gate. It stopped, opened the door, put down a ladder and we joined the flight. All that caused some delay and when we landed I thanked the Captain for enabling us to catch the plane. 'Thank you very much,' said someone behind, 'for making us all so late as well.' So I suppose that it could cost us a hundred votes, which is an expensive way to fly.

We had a very good visit and I was able to satisfy the bishops. On the way back I went to see John Hall, the developer of the Metro Centre and I took him aside and told him that we were probably going to go to the Metro Centre in Gateshead during her tour which really bucked him up enormously.

We were back in London by 2 o'clock and drove in to the office.

198

Norman Blackwell came round with Howell, and they had rewritten our part of the manifesto. We went through to make sure it was all OK.

Saturday 9 May

We had a quiet and fairly peaceful time, and late in the afternoon packed up and dropped Tiffany (our dog) over at Karen and Bernard's and drove down to Dorney Wood. It was a gorgeous summer's day, and still very warm when we got there at about 6.30 in the evening. Willie and Celia Whitelaw were there sitting in the garden; he had been speaking up in Droitwich and had his jacket and tie off, enjoying the summer's evening. After a drink and some political chit chat, we went up to wash and get ready for dinner. The Hurds were there for dinner together with Kenneth and Mary Baker.

It was a very enjoyable dinner in which everything came round time after time to political matters. After dinner, we adjourned to the study. Willie was full of reminiscences about earlier elections – after all, this was his eleventh election. He fought his first election – the first two or three I think were unsuccessful – in 1950, so he goes back a very long way.

As we all broke up to go, I took Kenneth Baker aside and told him to ring me Sunday evening when I would let him know how things were going. We went off slightly unsteadily to bed. I slept through to about 9 o'clock the following morning.

We came down for breakfast; all the papers were there, full of this meeting which was to take place, they thought, at No. 10. I wondered just how many photographers would have a wasted day standing outside Downing Street waiting for us to arrive. Some papers went very heavily for election day on 4 June. The rest went for the 11th. Two or three said we would be having steak for lunch, which slightly surprised Willie and I because as far as I recall the Prime Minister never has steak for lunch. We went through the papers; one thing which amused me particularly was an article by Robert Taylor in the *Observer* which described the Strategy Group – which was Willie Whitelaw, Douglas Hurd, myself, Nigel Lawson, Norman Tebbit, John Wakeham and Geoffrey Howe – as the Seven Dwarfs.

We spent a pleasant morning sitting reading all the papers comparing the stories and admiring Peregrine Worsthorne's leader in the *Sunday Telegraph*. At about 11.30 a.m. we set off for Chequers. I went with Willie in his government Daimler with his driver and security man. My wife Lita went off with Celia Whitelaw to spend the day sight-seeing. We got quite close to Chequers about noon; we were obviously half an hour early, so we took off up a side turning and went on a long detour right up into the hills, and got thoroughly lost. We ended up only a hundred yards from where we had started off.

We arrived at Chequers; John Wakeham was ahead of us, Norman Tebbit arrived shortly afterwards, then Nigel, Geoffrey and Douglas, and we were all set.

We had drinks in the downstairs room and she started to talk through dates. The first date we really went through was 4 June – and then had a far longer discussion about 11 June. The Prime Minister knew the unemployment figures were due out the next Thursday, the Retail Price Index figures the following Friday; we had a clear idea about unemployment and a vague, sensible sort of guess for the RPI. The only other figure to come out would be the balance of payments figure, which was impossible to even guess at. Then we considered 18 June; but then there were some arguments about letting the campaign go on too long.

We went round, and she concluded quite firmly that it would have to be 11 June. We went on to discuss administrative arrangements, and particular roles that people would be playing. The political issue now seemed to be absolutely clear and at about a quarter past one we went in for lunch.

I sat between Nigel Lawson and Douglas Hurd, and contrary to all the stories in the papers we didn't have steak – we actually had turkey. Denis Thatcher joined us for lunch; it was his birthday and I clean forgot to wish him happy birthday. Denis does not like steak, he prefers a stew, so I now know I can never expect to ever have steak there. It was a cheery lunch, everybody was very relaxed and, at about ten past two, we went into the hall to have coffee. Over coffee I saw my chance and went up to the P.M. No one else was with her, so I asked if she had had a good meeting with Tim Bell. She looked startled, and said 'Shh' – evidently it had been a very good meeting with Tim – but she didn't want Norman to hear. I told her it was going to be my task to deal with the media and the newspapers and everyone else over the period of the campaign and she was very happy about that.

Norman and I walked together upstairs – on the way up he said, 'David, I see from the papers that you're now the favourite to follow her and you're prepared to renounce your peerage and fight a by-election.' 'What a lot of rubbish,' I replied. Now I think this was a story that was in the *Evening News* the week before – obviously Norman was half-joking with me, but I shall have to be very careful about that sort of thing.

200

We found the meeting was downstairs and went down where the atmosphere was still quite relaxed. The Prime Minister wanted to go into all the details of the campaign. It was quite clear that she'd agreed the list of those who were going to be at the press conferences each day, that she and Norman were going to be out and about during the day, and it was agreed that I'd stay behind in Central Office. I would also work in with John Wakeham on television, but John would be in charge of those going on the box; Willie was in charge of matters of policy. Norman [of course] would be there, but he would be out. That part went very well. The Prime Minister was also concerned about the party election broadcasts, and about Norman. I think the impression she was getting was that things weren't far enough advanced. There was obviously still a great deal of tension between her and Norman.

After about an hour we'd cleared up all the administrative details. Norman then gave a first-rate resumé of all the polls, including our private polls, and of the significance of the local government elections. He said that they'd looked at the local government election results for 1983, and calculated the shift between them and the General Election. They had taken this year's local government election results – unfortunately there had been no elections in London or Scotland – and then he had looked at all the polls. He produced a variety of calculations that produced a range that went from one at only an eight seats clear majority (which was just taking the straight local government results), up to some which went as high as a majority of 126. Norman summed up that in his own view we were looking at a majority of about nineteen.

We discussed that over and over again – this took about three quarters of an hour. In the end, the P.M. said, 'Right, I've got as much as I need now. I shall sleep on it.'

Willie and I returned to Dorney Wood and there went for a walk in the garden. He proceeded to show me the way in which the National Trust had been building up the property. After about half an hour Lita and Celia came back and then we went in, had a chat and a drink, and watched the news which was very amusing. The BBC news mentioned us but didn't have pictures and the ITV news had a fairly spectacular shot. He said now comes the Lordly car, the car with the two lords, and they managed to freeze frame a picture and highlight it. There was Willie and I sitting looking very relaxed in the back of the car. All the programmes were speculating on 11 June and taking it as a pretty foregone certainty but saying that she'd decide tomorrow.

Monday 11 May

Cabinet had been called for 11 o'clock, and I was invited for lunch with the Strategy Group. There was an enormous crowd of photographers in Downing Street calling to us as we came in. We went into Cabinet. The Prime Minister was in a very calm mood, and said she had met with a few colleagues over the weekend. Since then, she had considered all the implications and concluded that the time was now right for us to go for an election. She had also concluded that 11 June was the right date. The reason she was going to the country was partly because of all the pressure in the media, but more, much more, because we had now almost completed this year's work and we had a very exciting and imaginative and radical manifesto. 'We have a great deal to do and we should now call an election and get on with it. There are things on the international scene which really need the stability of knowing who the next government is going to be.'

We went through all the business, and then she asked me to report on what figures would come up during an election campaign. I told the colleagues the unemployment figures would be out on Thursday. I couldn't give the exact figures, but I think I smiled. Then I said that on the Friday there would be the cost of living figures and that looked all right; then Paul Channon reported on the Trade figures. Then the Prime Minister turned to the Chief Whip, John Wakeham, and we went through all the business in Parliament – with a certain amount of dickering about what should or should not be done. She then asked us to leave and look confident, but not to give a clue about the date or timing of the election because that was not going to be announced until 2 o'clock; she was going off to see the Queen.

Again there was an enormous crowd shouting out, 'Can you give us the date of the election?' We just waved cheerily and went back to the Department. I gave John Turner the manifesto – it was quite improper I suppose – and asked him if he could see Roger Dawe and just make sure that the wording hadn't changed and we could live with it. John Lee and then David Trippier (two of my Junior Ministers) came in for a chat. A few minutes later it was time to return to No. 10, and again the photographers were outside. Another cheery wave and in I went – I think they are probably getting a bit fed up seeing me!

Willie and Norman and John Wakeham were waiting – the Prime Minister was still at the Palace – and Willie said he thought, as Deputy Prime Minister, he would take executive authority and we could go up and help ourselves to a drink. She came in a few minutes

202

later and said, 'Yes, Her Majesty has consented that an election be called.' The announcement was going to go out at 2 o'clock. We had a drink and chatted away – it was a big crowd, it wasn't just the Strategy Group. John Sullivan, Brian Griffiths, Stephen Sherbourne from No. 10 – in fact, the whole team responsible for writing the manifesto. We went in and it was a relaxed sort of lunch, with not too much serious business discussed.

The P.M. nagged away a couple of times – probably quite rightly – about the party election broadcasts, but otherwise was fairly calm. At 2.30 p.m. we broke up.

I went back to the Department and John Turner suggested it might be tactful if I were to then meet Michael Quinlan to discuss the arrangements during the election. Michael came in and told me that Howell would have to leave almost immediately, and that I was much more limited in the use of the government car than Norman Dodds had led me to believe. I discussed briefly where Margaret Bell would go.

I settled down to do some box work. Howell came bustling in to say Central Office had been on and would I do the 7 o'clock news – Norman Tebbit was caught up in a meeting. I would be on with John Smith and John Pardoe, the Chairman of the Alliance campaign. I did a bit more box work, and then went over to the studio and both Johns were there. We were all quite friendly and civilised. I did the interview, and I think it was all right – the other two tended to argue with each other, while I tried to stay a bit above it. Walking back to the hospitality suite, John Pardoe suddenly said to me that the reason why he was chairing the Alliance campaign was that he was the only chap with whom the two Davids got on well. I thought that was quite revealing for the campaign!

The phone went again and Central Office asked me if I could do what I thought was *Newsnight*, as Norman Tebbit might be tied up. I arranged that they would ring me at 8.30 p.m. to let me know. I went home and Howell rang and then said, 'It's on, you're doing it.' I couldn't quite recall if it was ten to nine or ten past nine that I was being picked up. I went dashing down and Dodds just rang up – he'd been there since ten to nine, but hadn't bothered to ring, so I got in a frightful tiz as we charged off – got there just in time to find out that it was in fact a 9.35 p.m. special programme as an extension of the News – it was on BBC 1, not 2, and I was on with Roy Hattersley and Roy Jenkins.

It went quite well, and afterwards I went back to the hospitality suite. Michael Grade was there as well as David Attenborough, and all the people in the programme. Hattersley is a bit strange with

203

me – Roy Jenkins is charming, but he looked very old, and in fact during the programme he lost his microphone and got carried away on all sorts of points – I don't think he made too much sense. I went home feeling rather shagged and thinking, my God, this is the very first day! I'd been invited to do TV-am for the following morning, so I would have done the *Seven O'clock News*, the *Nine O'clock News*, *Breakfast Time* the following day; and the campaign hadn't even started!

Chapter 15
ELECTION CAMPAIGN

Thursday 14 May

Went over to Cabinet, which was at 10 o'clock. It was fairly light-hearted – apart from Geoffrey reporting on a revolution in Fiji. We finished home affairs, and I reported on the unemployment figures, which were being announced that morning. I said we should concentrate on the figure that shows 177,000 down since last year, because that equates to the three million and twenty thousand. Towards the end of Cabinet the statement from Central Office arrived. Howell had drafted it and I handed it out; then one or two of my colleagues – I think with a certain amount of ill-concealed glee because I suspect they reckoned I'd got too many things right recently – pointed out that the statement said that unemployment was 200,000 down. We had confused the headline figure with the seasonally adjusted figure.

I said that as it was only about twelve minutes past eleven it wasn't too late, I would get it stopped. The Prime Minister said that she wanted to talk about some political matters, but she'd excuse me. I was in such a tiz about getting this wrong and feeling so sick about it as I went out; I rang through to the office and in no uncertain terms got them to get it right. Then I came back in as the P.M. was coming to the end; she wanted to thank everybody for the work they did, to wish everybody luck, and looked forward to meeting us all in six weeks' time. This last comment caused general amusement, and off we went.

I did ITN and John Prescott was there. Howell told me that Prescott had criticised my use of the phrase 'stagnant pools'. In a debate in the Lords, and on one or two other occasions, I'd used the expression that as unemployment went down it would leave some 'stagnant pools' – inner cities, sometimes the suburbs in the North or the South that would be a much more difficult problem to solve. In the next interview, I turned the conversation around, repeated the 'stagnant pools' line, and explained it in full.

The interview seemed to go all right. I then went back to the Department, still hopping mad about the way in which the arrangements for the unemployment figures had gone. I was in a thoroughly bad mood, and asked to see Michael Quinlan. I complained that the civil servants had decided that the moment the election was called they couldn't even issue the press releases. We were going through the ridiculous situation that in order to get them printed and distributed by Central Office, we had had to send the blank press statements over to the Department, who had duplicated them on our paper and reissued them to us at 11.30 a.m. All this because they contained financially sensitive information. No wonder there were mistakes in them.

I said to Michael that it was all nonsense, because in Cabinet half a dozen other colleagues had also complained about the same ruling and said they'd not known it before. All of this made not the slightest difference . . . but I did feel better!

I went over to Central Office because I was getting more and more worried about accommodation – I couldn't see where Margaret Bell was going to sit, and I wasn't sure where I was going to sit myself. My arrangement with Peter Morrison was that I was going to use the Prime Minister's room. It was set up for about thirty or forty seats as it was the morning conference room, but in addition there was someone there with a computer and a printer. I gathered they were going to stay there. That would clearly not work, and in the end Howell and I shared the office of Emma Nicholson, the Woman's Vice President. Emma was off fighting a seat, so the room would be empty. Margaret Bell would use a cubicle not far away.

I arrived home and as I walked in Lita said, 'Oh, you're going to be in trouble, this is going to run against you.' I asked her what she meant. 'Stagnant pools' she said; it was a phrase of mine David Blunkett had used a couple of times on *Question Time*. I went to bed rather depressed, thinking I had made a mistake which would run during the election.

Tuesday 19 May

An early start. Howell picked me up with Norman Dodds at 7.15 a.m. and we arrived at Central Office at about 7.30 – I was due to do an interview for *Breakfast Time* Television. I did the interview, which was fairly innocuous stuff; they kept on asking me what was going to be in the manifesto and I kept on dodging the answers but occasionally teasing just a little bit. I went back, and saw Alistair

McAlpine [Lord Mcalpine, Party Treasurer] who always seems to be in very early, and an avid watcher of breakfast television. I saw John Prescott being put down very effectively by a business-man from the Midlands, who kept on asking for his plans for employment. Every time Prescott went on, the businessman said, 'That's absolute nonsense – that's not going to help me at all.' I realised for the first time that non-politicians have a considerable advantage, and I began to think of ways in which we could use suitable ones.

There was quite a crush in the Prime Minister's room, as we had seven or eight Cabinet colleagues sitting around the table. We started the meeting – everybody was in a very genial mood. There was a lovely incident. Labour were proposing to set up a Ministry for Women, and the Prime Minister said she'd had this question in the House. She had then said that having looked at the Honourable Gentleman sitting opposite, 'I think it's about time we had a Minis-try for Men,' which broke us all up. About five minutes later we were reporting from the papers that both Neil Kinnock and David Owen were photographed on the front pages kissing babies – the Prime Minister said, 'That's another reason there should be a Ministry for Men.'

The polls look as if we are keeping constant, with Labour rising slowly at the expense of the Alliance – that's probably as good an outcome as we could get. We were due for an 11 o'clock launch of the manifesto. Harvey Thomas came in and said he'd agreed that the photographers had a run for the first three or four minutes, and would then withdraw.

We all filed down waiting for Norman Tebbit, who would bring the Prime Minister. I have never seen such a crush – the photo-graphers were piled four or five deep. You couldn't see anything of the rest of the room – suddenly saw I Sally Soames of the *Sunday Times* at the centre of the crush – many years ago I had shown her how to load her first camera. She got into a good position, and was taking pictures of all of us – but there was such a crush that I doubted whether they would be any good. Then the Prime Minister and Norman came in, and there was a continuous battery of flashes. After three or four minutes Norman asked everybody to have some mercy on the Prime Minister, who was being blinded by all this, and eventually the press conference started.

The Prime Minister made her statement – then she asked three or four of us (but not me) to say a few words, and then she went into questions. There was one question about the inner cities which she asked me to answer, and then at the very end I managed to get

207

something out on unemployment. It was quite obvious that no one was very interested in employment or unemployment. It looked as if I had been totally successful over the last eighteen months. We'll see.

Wednesday 20 May

Over to No. 10. When I came in, she was in Stephen Sherbourne's room with Michael Alison, talking about how well the candidates' conference had gone. Stephen and I went upstairs to her study. I found out that after I left, David Wolfson told her that the tour was far better than last time's, so at least she's quite happy.

We discussed the conduct of the campaign. It had been reported to her that Kinnock was coming up in the polls, and was actually getting the best of the media coverage. I said, 'Look, Prime Minister, we decided the strategy was that we would run a short campaign; you are not really going out until tomorrow, Thursday, and Friday's the first of the tours – we start then, it's much better this way.' She agreed, and I then managed to raise with her the question of the last day of the campaign. If we weren't careful (because of Venice), she would not be able to do Robin Day's Final Election Call, and it would go by default to Kinnock. We discussed a complicated procedure in which she could manage both.

Then I rang Michael Grade, and suggested to him that perhaps he could bring the Robin Day Programme forward to 8.30 p.m., which would give the Prime Minister time to do everything.

Friday 22 May

Robert Atkins rang. He was rather nervous about the way the campaign was going; I was inclined to dismiss his fears because I was feeling better about it. David Hart rang and expressed considerable worry about what was happening and about coordination; then John Wheeler MP rang to complain that he couldn't get any manifestos in his constituency; – evidently they just didn't have enough of them.

At about a quarter to midnight the Prime Minister called. She said that she'd had two disturbing phone calls – one from Tim Bell and one from her daughter Carol. Carol had told her that we were about to lose the election, and the P.M. was very concerned about coordination, about the way things were actually going. It was one of those occasions when the line was bad and I could hardly hear her, but I had got too far into the conversation to tell her this, and it was all rather unsatisfactory.

208

I did agree that I would come in to see her with Tim Bell when she returned the next day. I went to bed in a very unhappy mood about the election campaign.

Saturday 23 May

Keith Britto popped in; the *Daily Telegraph* poll is rather good, we are still about forty-two to their thirty-four, and I'm getting some more briefing which will help me for *Weekend World*, which I've got to do tomorrow.

I was wandering through to Norman Tebbit's office when I saw Steve Robin. I said I would like to have a chat with him; I went upstairs and spent a few minutes looking at his great big board. I was appalled at what I saw – there seemed to be an enormous amount of Nigel Lawson, and quite a lot of some worthy and valued colleagues who were not necessarily the best people on the box. Steve then took me into the television monitoring room where there were four televisions going, recording everything that took place all day long. I had a sudden idea and asked, 'Look, can we dub? Can we make tapes up at the end of the day?' and he said, 'Yes.' I said, 'Right, what we've got to do at midnight each night is get someone along here and during the night they have got to put on one tape (we can have two or three copies – I can have one and Norman can have one) – but the Prime Minister's got to have one which will show all the political bits of the news programmes of the day before. Can we get this done?' 'Yes,' said Steve, so I said, 'All right let's go and do it.'

By now it was already twenty-five past six, and I drove round to Tim Bell who was waiting for me at the corner of the road, picked him up, and went in to what otherwise was a very quiet No. 10. The porter downstairs showed us into the lift, and took us up to the flat. On the way in I said to Tim, 'Do you know, Tim, in all the years this is the very first time I have ever been to the flat upstairs.' Tim looked amazed – though probably not as amazed as I was – at the thought that someone who was reputedly a close colleague had never been there before.

We went in – the Prime Minister was there, her daughter Carol, Denis, Stephen Sherbourne and myself. We sat down and had drinks. The Prime Minister said, 'Well, it's not been a good week for us. Kinnock had a marvellous programme – it's hardly worth bothering, let's give up, it's the end.' She was playing the devil's advocate role in which everything was exaggerated. 'Nonsense Prime Minister,' I said, 'there's everything to go for, we've just got

209

to get our act in order.' We started talking about what we could do. I said, 'What we've got to do is organise television.' 'John Wakeham's a total disaster,' she said, and really went on about it. Denis kept on encouraging her to listen to us.

Eventually I said, 'Prime Minister, this is what we will do – this must be the strategy.' She told Stephen to take notes. I said, 'Prime Minister, what we've got to do is simply this. Unleash Norman, he's got to go for Kinnock – we've really got to destroy this nonsensical image that Kinnock has created. *You* must go – not against Kinnock, but against the Labour Party, and show what their hidden manifesto really is. The party election broadcasts have to show Kinnock making the speech about how he's got rid of all the militants, and then *we* have to show Bernie Grant, Ken Livingstone – all the others, one after the other. Then go on to the hidden manifesto and show all the things that he's done one after the other. It's really got to attack him.

'We have to select the right people for television. I can't do it by myself, I must do it with Norman because he's the Chairman.'

Tim Bell said, 'Use responsible people – like David, like the Home Secretary, like Douglas. Then you've got to have the combative people – Kenneth Baker and Kenneth Clarke. Geoffrey Howe would be one of the quiet people.' – He went down a list of five or six people. 'We've got to concentrate on those for television, and use *only* those.' She accepted this, and we talked a bit more; by now it was about 8.15, and I had David and Susan Wolfson at home for dinner. Carol was very kind about it, and said, 'I'll ring Susan,' and helped me to get away. The Prime Minister said she would speak to Norman – not that evening, but the following day, and she agreed that next week we had to go out and we really had to go and attack Labour. 'Prime Minister,' I said, 'if we do this, if you unleash Norman, if you go and make the speech you are going to make, if we get the party political broadcasts right – if we really go and attack them, I promise you by the end of the week the whole position will be very different.'

I think gradually she was becoming more relaxed, but I slipped away with Stephen leaving Tim there, and went home feeling that things now would change more than a little.

Sunday 24 May

Norman Tebbit came in. He had been with the Prime Minister. At the beginning of the meeting he said, 'Yes, we've got to do some things differently. I've just got instructions from the Prime Minister

210

about the next phase in the campaign. David and I have got to deal with that.' He was very cheery.

I was called out twice from the meeting – once because Kenneth Baker had telephoned, and I told him about the change of strategy. He was quite happy about it. A few minutes later I got called out again, and it was the Prime Minister. She told me of her meeting with Norman. Then she said, 'People have told me how appalling our ministers look. Nigel's got to get a haircut – will you tell him.' 'No, Prime Minister,' I said, 'you've got to tell him.' 'All right, I will, but what about Kenneth Clarke; he's got to smarten himself up.' I said, 'Don't worry, I'll tell Kenneth.' And then she went on about how we've all got to look good, and she concluded by saying, 'Well, I hope I look all right,' and I said, 'Prime Minister, oh yes, you look all right, there's no problem with you or Norman.' Obviously some people have been talking to her.

I returned to the meeting. Norman outlined the way he would be attacking Kinnock in a speech on Tuesday night, and she would be attacking the Labour Party, also on that night. Everyone was quite cheered by this. The polls looked as if we had levelled out – Labour had been catching us up, but we hadn't actually moved very much. We thought a bit of attack might move them down again. Afterwards – I said to Norman, 'I must talk to you about the appearances on television.' We went on to agree who would go on, and what sort of posters we would be having.

Monday 25 May

The press conference went reasonably well. Nigel Lawson put up a very good performance, and there weren't many questions. After the conference, I asked, 'Prime Minister, can we have a word?'

I went in with Norman and sat down. I said, 'Prime Minister, you will have to tell John Wakeham,' and she said, 'Yes.' Norman and I went back to her office bringing John Wakeham and kept everybody else out. We sat down, and in the end she fudged it. All she really said was, it has got to be run from the centre, television appearances must be run by the three of us; then she left it at that and went off for the day.

After that I went upstairs with John Wakeham, saying, 'Come on John, let's have a look at what we're doing.' We sat down with Steve Robin, who was responsible for the schedules, and I sort of took charge of things, and we agreed everything together for the next few days. I said to John, 'Look if there are any changes during the day, I'll give you a call and see what we can do.'

Tuesday 26 May

Woke up feeling very weary indeed. I had to be in Central Office early, in fact I got a phone call about 6.50 a.m. from Steve Robin to remind me I was on breakfast television at 7.30 a.m. I did the interview in our own studio, and the interviewer asked aggressively, 'How can you as a Government expect to be re-elected when crime is up, unemployment is up, rape is up?' I snapped back, 'What a very facile question.' I don't think I came out of it very well.

I dashed over to have a quick meal at the canteen – which made me feel rather ill. I then ran up for the morning meeting – I was there a minute or two late, but the meeting seemed to be going all right. We weren't doing too well in the polls, but not that badly, and I think there was a feeling around that we were beginning to get our act together.

Howell came in to see me and said that Norman Blackwell had suggested we should thin out the morning meeting. It was far too crowded and it was not the right atmosphere to prepare the PM for the morning press conferences. I agreed, so I took a copy of the minutes in which we fixed who should be in the morning meetings, and crossed through a number of names. I left the list with Norman Tebbit, and when he rang me back at 11.30 p.m. that night, he told me he had dictated a minute reducing the number of people who would be at the Prime Minister's briefing meeting. I said I would put it into effect.

Thursday 28 May

The Prime Minister came in for the pre-press conference briefing meeting, which went very well. I must say the new format of having fewer people seems to be much better. We were able to get a short break between the end of the briefing and the start of the press conference. When we went down to it, our music was blaring away – the marvellous theme music that Andrew Lloyd Webber had written for us.

When Norman Fowler turned on his illuminated panel during the press conference there was a spontaneous round of applause – I suspect it may have been started by our own people. The conference wasn't well attended at the start because Kinnock was having one of his few press conferences in London; he was being hounded by those journalists who were asking him awkward questions on defence. We were determined not to let our conference start late, even though there was a fairly small number of people at the beginning;

however, it filled up later. When we came near the end of questions on the Health Service, the Prime Minister asked Norman Fowler to do his presentation all over again; which he did, and fingers crossed, the lights worked. There was a slightly less spontaneous round of applause this time.

I spent much of the day with Howell and Norman Blackwell working out what I would be saying at my Employment press conference. I went in to watch the *Six O'clock News*; I felt it was totally biased. Our monitoring people came back to say it was about six minutes twenty seconds for Labour, three minutes and a bit for the Alliance, and only one minute twenty for us. I got straight on to the BBC to speak to Michael Checkland, but he was away in Finland until the following Monday. Then I asked for John Birt, with whom I had a rather amusing conversation. I said, 'I want you to understand this is not an official complaint – but have you seen the *Six O'clock News*?' He said, 'No,' and I said, 'Well, please do look at it.' He replied, 'I'll go and watch the *Nine O'clock News*.' I said 'No, no, please look at a tape of the *Six O'clock News*'; this he refused to do. I gave him the reading, saying that the balance seemed to be out, and he said, 'I didn't think we had to balance it.' It was my understanding that they did, but he promised that the next day he would be looking at all the news throughout the day with an eye to balance.

When I watched the *Nine O'clock News*, I felt sick because the first seven minutes were totally us; I don't for one moment believe it had anything to do with my phone call, but it certainly gave some comfort to our people to think perhaps it did!

Howell and I went down with Norman Dodds to Teddington – we got there about 10 o'clock. I went into the green room and watched the end of the news. I was going to be on the programme with John Prescott, who I was told was having his hair washed, and Bill Rodgers who seemed quite a pleasant chap. They were both wearing rosettes and I wasn't, but I suppose that was appropriate as I wasn't standing for election.

We eventually entered the packed studio – the presenter said last week's edition had been very dull, and he hoped this one would be more lively. When I first went in my heart sank because it seemed that everyone in the audience was wearing either a red rose or an SDP/Alliance yellow lozenge; but in the end it worked out to be a marvellous programme – just a pity it wasn't national. I think I did quite well, and it was interesting that a number of people wearing roses turned out to be our people, who had put roses in their lapels and got called for questions thinking they were Labour supporters!

213

When the programme finished and I was waiting for a car, I was buttonholed by someone who had a go at me because I'd sounded off about books like *Young, Gay and Proud* and *Black Lesbian and White America*, which had got into the schools in Brent. He asked me if I had seen the books. I said, 'Yes.' Have you read them? I said, 'I've glanced at them.' 'Well, what's wrong with them?' he asked. 'They're not for children, my friend,' I said. That didn't leave him very satisfied, and the security guards came along – just in case, I think, they thought he was going to beat me up.

I finally got home at 12.15 a.m. When I got home there was a little note on the front door, saying, 'Nine and three quarters out of ten.' I gathered that my mum had been watching and had jumped up and down clapping her hands when I said my mother lived in Brent. That had obviously gone down well!

Friday 27 May

It was a good press conference; we had restricted it to just over half an hour, when at the very end the men from *The Independent* and John Cole from the BBC raised some questions about VAT. The P.M. managed to fudge her way through, and I had arranged that after this press conference we were going to let Sally Oppenheim have a few words with the P.M. about pacing herself, slowing herself down.

I then received a message asking me to go upstairs. The P.M. was in a right state about what to do about VAT. Norman Tebbit was there, and we got Nigel Lawson on the phone, and eventually it was fixed that she would see Nigel over the weekend. I know Nigel did not want to limit his options in the future, but she was very keen that we shouldn't allow this VAT issue to run and build up into a scare.

After she left, I arranged to have a few minutes with Tim and Gordon and Alistair at Alistair's house later on that afternoon.

Tim produced the storyboards that he was going to use for the meeting. I thought the strategy absolutely right that we should start attacking Labour for the first three or four days (I was much keener on attacking Labour for its trade union policies than anything else), and then become positive towards the end of the week. This did mean changing press conferences from departmental conferences into ones which were much more thematic.

Tim and I went up to the P.M.'s flat. She was there with Denis and Carol, and the five of us sat down to talk. Quite obviously, she

214

With my wife Lita, having just received an Honorary Doctorate of Science at the Cranfield Institute of Technology

With Mr Takashi Ishihare, chairman of Nissan, after the company announced it was to invest further in its Sunderland plant, bringing 1,400 jobs to the area by 1992 (*Copyright Press Association Photos*)

Launch of the two-year Youth Training Scheme (*Copyright Press Association Photos*)

Demonstrating 'Spearhead' to the Prime Minister at the Lancaster House launch, 1988 (*Copyright Press Association Photos*)

Opening the first Mercury call box

My last box, taken in the garden at Graffham (*Copyright The Times*)

was very tired – she had had a drink and was in a fractious, irritable mood. She was kind enough to say that when we met a week ago we had got the strategy right, but it looked very different now. Then Tim got out his storyboards, and started going through his presentation.

I think that we got through to her, although it was quite difficult to tell. However, we did establish what the next party political broadcast should be, and how we should go over to the attack. Then we went in to have dinner; the P.M. was fussing a bit over Carol, who was due to go off at 9.30 p.m., as I think she had a date; the Prime Minister was being very much a mother towards her. After dinner we went back into the other room to have coffee. The P.M.'s eyes kept closing, because she was very tired indeed. Denis and Carol had been very kind about my performance on the Thames television show the night before. When Tim and I got into the lift, we just looked at each other and shook hands, and I said, 'Thank God we've got that strategy set right.'

Saturday 30 May

I spent a few minutes with Norman Tebbit and managed to talk him into the strategy line which we'd agreed with the Prime Minister the night before. I said I had to go down to the country to deal with the marginal constituencies of West Sussex. I told Shirley [Norman's secretary] where I was going, and exactly what time I would be back.

Lita said she'd made a sandwich, and we drove down to Graffham to go to Glyndebourne. On the way I realised I'd left my bow tie behind, so when we arrived I called our neighbours, who said they would bring one round. Before they could do so, the phone went and it was Michael Dobbs, who said, 'David, we've just got the script of the new party election broadcast.' I said, 'Yes,' rather suspiciously. He said, 'It's going to be attacking the trade unions and we'd like you to be in it.' 'Oh good,' I said. 'We've got to shoot it tonight,' he added. 'Oh – !!! [four letter expletives] can't you do it tomorrow? I'll come back whenever you like.'

But as soon as he put the phone down I knew I'd had it. John Sharkey (of Saatchi's) rang a few minutes later and said they couldn't do it tomorrow. They were shooting it on film and they had to do it today. I agreed. I asked him to get a car to take Lita to Glyndebourne and back. Then in the midst of all this, our neighbours came round; I got the bow tie and thanked them every much. Off I went back again to London. On the way, Ken Baker rang me in the car. He'd been ringing me most days to see how it was going

215

on – and he couldn't stop laughing when I told him my story.

We went to some studios in Blandford Street where we shot the last part of the party election broadcast over and over again. I didn't actually think it was particularly good. It was all about somebody doing conjuring tricks (the Labour Party), which always failed; I was part of the audience. We will see how it turns out. I must confess, though, that for the last few days I've been feeling more and more despondent about the outcome of the election. Afterwards, I took Howell off to a local Chinese restaurant and we had a very good meal. Got back about 11.30 p.m. and went to bed still feeling rather worried.

Monday 1 June

This is my day for the press conference. I arrived at 7.30 a.m. and went first to inspect the conference room. Howell was there putting up the titles behind the podium. I was very pleased with the way the press conference room now looked, and I thought the graphics which I had seen the night before had come out very well. At 7.45 a.m. I went upstairs to the morning meeting. The polls had not changed very much – it was slightly worrying, attacking on defence all week and not getting much change in the polls. We carried through the usual routine business. I told Norman Tebbit exactly what the slogan was and what the graphics were, and then at about twenty past eight the Prime Minister arrived. In the Prime Minister's meeting we agreed the press notice, but I thought she was in rather a tense mood. We went through all the questions arising overnight – there seemed to be far too many points of detail – but she does want to master every single detail, to show she's on top of everything.

We went into the press conference at 9.30 a.m. – I must confess for the first time in a long time I was feeling more than a little nervous. I had organised a tie mike so I could move around rather than hold anything, and it all went extremely well. When we had the visual with the dead rose, there was a titter around the audience of fairly hard-bitten journalists. The questions were quite slow in coming, but in the end I thought I managed to get nearly all the points through. We finished about ten past ten and I went upstairs.

I went into Norman's room. Willie Whitelaw was sitting there with John Wakeham and Norman. Willie congratulated me very warmly on my performance – almost made me blush!

I went back to my room. Howell spoke to me about taking up an invitation in Southampton that had originally gone to Nigel Lawson. I thought it was for a television programme, and quickly agreed to do it. It turned out to be a public meeting; they had now made arrangements to increase the size of the meeting from 300 to 350. I asked Howell to see if we could get some television there.

Tuesday 2 June

Went into the 7.45 a.m. strategy meeting – much more relaxed as this was not going to be my day, it was really Nigel Lawson's day.

The Prime Minister came in – a minute or two late. The polls didn't look very good. After the press conference I saw the Prime Minister for a few minutes who looked worried – had a quiet chat with her and with Norman, and eventually she went off on her tour.

After lunch Michael Dobbs [Chief of Staff at Central Office] had the party election broadcast ready. I was very disappointed indeed with it. It started off with the theatre scene, and went on to show a magician (the Labour Party) failing in all his tricks. It ended up with about fifteen or twenty seconds of me sitting in the audience watching the tricks being performed, and then it immediately switched to a three-minute film all about the Prime Minister, and how she's an international statesman and everything else. I couldn't quite believe it; I think for two reasons. First of all, it was clearly two entirely separate films. Secondly, I'd given up the whole of Saturday night for something of which only fifteen or twenty seconds were used.

The *Nine O'clock News* announced a *Newsnight* marginal poll which showed that we could be heading towards a hung parliament. There were difficulties with this poll – firstly, it was *Newsnight*, and secondly it was a poll by a company which quite frankly wasn't a recognised one, and we did not know enough about it to trust it. Nevertheless, the prospect that Labour was somehow catching up with us in the marginals was rather disconcerting, to put it mildly. It was certainly rather depressing, particularly as I now had to go over to BBC for *Newsnight*, and I had to think hard how to react to it.

I went over to *Newsnight* with Howell a little early. John Prescott had made some excuse about phoning his wife (it's about the second or third time I've heard him do that), and then he came in with his rather jolly woman assistant and two or three earnest young people. On *Newsnight*, we first had the poll, together with all the health warnings which I felt had made it very suspect. They said, 'It looks as if we are heading towards a hung parliament.' I said, 'Well, of course, we take all polls seriously, it's going to make us work harder.' John Prescott went very upbeat and started to talk about outright victory.

217

After that we went on to *Newsnight* proper, and I found to my absolute horror that the film they had prepared included Professor Story of Newcastle (allegedly an expert on small businesses but who I felt was avidly against them), and Richard Leyard, professor of Labour Economics, who was really an Alliance politician – the film was stacked all against us. When the film finished, they asked me a question about it. I said that the film was absolutely bizarre, and went on to give all the reasons why. I thought that John Prescott was rather better than usual, but I still think that it went quite well for us. We eventually finished at about half past eleven, and I went home. Lita thought it had been very good, but I always find after evening television that it takes some time for me to settle down; we finally went to bed about a quarter to one.

Wednesday 3 June

I got my machine out and started to write a speech. I spent from ten to one until 2 o'clock writing what I thought was quite a good speech, and printed it out on my machine. Norman Blackwell was going to put some finishing touches to it – the speech was about the choices that are facing us. I promised to visit Colin Moynihan's constituency to help with canvassing. When I got down to Colin's place, what he really wanted to show me is how they were running their campaign – in fact I found it a very interesting three quarters of an hour. I could see he had built his campaign very much on local issues and I thought it was going rather well.

When I went back, I found that Norman Blackwell had made a lot of modifications. At first I hit the roof; but then I looked at them and realised it made a pretty marvellous speech. Imagine my panic when I suddenly found the press office had issued the old speech! I managed to get it back, and send the new one out instead.

There were rumours going round the City about a rather bad poll. I went to Keith Britto, and he said the story was that the early results of the poll showed us four points ahead, but the final result could vary quite a bit.

Tim Bell and I were due to see the Prime Minister at about 10 o'clock when I returned from Southampton. To save travelling through the rush hour, I got the train. I suddenly realised to my horror that there was a train next to us at the platform and all the people were looking through the windows and pointing at me: then, people came in to my carriage, they sort of nodded and later on when leaving they wished me good luck; obviously I'd been on so much television recently that I was now quite well known.

At Southampton, the agent was waiting for me. In the car, he told me how Michael Heseltine had got a standing ovation a few weeks ago. When we got to Bittern School, it was all a bit shambolic. I had a press conference with a couple of fairly aggressive local reporters. By 7.30 p.m. we had a good crowd – it must have been well over 300 – and started the meeting. Chris Chope introduced me and I did my bit. I got rather carried away. There were hecklers there in good measure, but I think I gave as good as I got – in fact I think I probably got on top. At the end of my speech, to my complete amazement, I got three standing ovations. The Chairwoman got up and said they wanted to show their appreciation to me, and everybody stood up. Then I realised that the other MP still had to go and give the vote of thanks, and so they all sat down again. He then gave a vote of thanks, and when I got up to go everybody got up again for the third time!

I left at about 8.30 p.m. – it was still light and all the BBC technicians with their big vans outside the school waved at me and called over to me and wished me luck. I thought we were going to need it . . .

We started back to London, and lost our way going out of the town. The whole evening I had been dreading getting on the telephone to Keith Britto, but eventually I had to. 'Very bad news,' he said and my heart sank. The poll showed Labour just four points behind, and catching up fast.

We were back to London in good time and after a snack I got to No. 10 at about quarter past ten. Stephen met us and said the P.M. was very tired, with a very bad toothache. She had heard the poll result, and started talking about the prospect of actually losing. I said, 'Look, what we've got to do is to change what we are doing, get a coherent coordinated programme.' Tim Bell gave his plan for the way the campaign should be run. I said, 'Prime Minister, we will organise something for you, we'll do it tomorrow morning and it will all be done, just leave it to me.'

At this point, she looked very tired indeed and opened a dispatch box – it was now about twenty to twelve. Tim and I walked out with Denis Thatcher, who said she had had this problem with her toothache, and she was very tense. The chap at the front door showed us the next morning's *Times*, which had headlines about the bad poll results. The *Telegraph* seemed to refer to the meeting we had just been having upstairs! This was either miraculous, or else they had just been guessing very shrewdly. I got home and went to bed once more feeling depressed and very, very nervous.

Thursday 4 June

I woke up still feeling very apprehensive – I hadn't slept too well – and went in to Central Office for the 7.45 a.m. meeting. The atmosphere was tense. We went through everything; the poll was undoubtedly a shock, and there were further polls due. The irony was – this Thursday was Wobbly Thursday – that this was the day that Alistair McAlpine had been forecasting for the last three weeks. The first time I was aware of this was early in the campaign when I saw a big chart on the wall of his room plotting the polls. Towards the end of the chart was a pencil line all the way down under a date. 'That,' he said, 'is Wobble Day.' I asked, 'What's "Wobble Day"?' He said, 'We had it in '79 and we had it again in '83. You see, they'll be above us on that day – they were in '79, they moved to half a point above us, and in '83 that was the day when the campaign was going wrong and we met and thrashed it out and changed this and changed that – it will all work out all right, just you wait and see.'

The Press conference was not good at all. It went on and on – the P.M. got caught out on a question dealing with private health medicine. The meeting lasted till about five or ten past ten, and it didn't look good. There was a feeling around somehow that we were on the run. Kinnock had had his press conference before ours, and the journalists all came in after it, and were pushing the P.M. on questions arising from cases that had come up in his press conference. It really did appear as if we were on the run.

When the conference ended, we went upstairs to have the meeting which I had fixed the night before. Willie Whitelaw was there with John Wakeham; the P.M. went on about the advertising which she didn't like at all. She wanted it to be more aggressive, more anti-militant, more along the lines we had discussed the night before.

At half past three, I went over to No. 10. We went to the waiting room on the ground floor, and had a long meeting going through everything. I outlined an idea for the party political broadcast – her last one – which was to be about paths and choices – I suppose a little bit coloured by my speech the night before. To my surprise, I found when I finished doing this that it was almost exactly the script they had already written; so we agreed to take it further.

Before lunch, I had seen John Sharkey and the Saatchi people, told them the sort of advertising she wanted, and asked for it to be ready for her return at 5.15 p.m. Tim Bell told me that he had been working on an advertising campaign, and when he outlined it to me I told him that it was just the job, and asked him to go and get his campaign mock-ups.

220

'What will you do with it?' he asked. I jumped up and said, 'I'll tell you what I'll do with it. If she doesn't like it, if she doesn't take it, I'll resign.' Tim looked at me, startled, and went off with Howell to get the mock-ups. I told Stephen that what I wanted to do was to show the Prime Minister Tim's campaign, and the Saatchi campaign, and then she would have to decide which of the two she wanted. We really had to go into this advertising campaign if we were to save the election. I felt we were on the point of losing it, and I said so. And Stephen to his great credit agreed.

I waited a very nervous three quarters of an hour pacing backwards and forwards. Howell came back in a torrential downpour, and brought the boards for the campaign. He put them all out on display – they were only roughs, but they looked very good indeed. I showed them to Stephen and he loved them. I kept on ringing the office every twenty minutes but there was still no news about this rumour of a 2 per cent poll gap – rather ominously the stock market had gone down like a stone. Eventually, we heard that the Prime Minister's helicopter had landed and when she came in, I met her down the corridor.

I said, 'Prime Minister, come in here and look at this.' She looked at it, and loved it. She looked questioningly at me. 'Tim,' I replied. 'Well,' she said, 'what do I do now?' I said, 'Prime Minister, it's very simple. I have Saatchis waiting for me with their campaign – I'll bring them over, you have a look at it. If you like it, we do it. If you don't like it, all you've got to say is, "No I don't like it, David's got something better, I've got to go off and do my Dimbleby interview, David you sort it out," and walk out and I will deal with it all.' She looked very relieved at this thought and said, 'All right, I must go and get briefed up,' and off she went. I've learnt the lesson that she cannot do anything unpleasant. I've got to do it for her, and I had said I would.

Then I rang to ask Michael Dobbs over. Norman Tebbit answered the phone and I said, 'Norman, could you bring all the stuff over, and get Saatchis over.' 'Yes,' he said, and worked out we would do it for 6.30 p.m.; so I said, 'Norman, could you come over 5 minutes early?' He sounded a bit puzzled, but said he would. I paced up and down and waited for what I knew would be a very, very, difficult meeting.

The downpour continued, and the first to arrive were John Sharkey, together with Maurice Saatchi. We waited for a few minutes outside the Cabinet room for Norman, who was on his way over – while the P.M. was being briefed up in the study. Eventually, I said, 'Why don't you take the stuff upstairs and when Norman comes we can pop in?' They went upstairs and Norman came in. 'Norman,' I said, 'I must see you – there have been one or two developments.' He looked at me and I said, 'Come on, I want to show you.' I said, 'She's asked for some other things to be done,' and I took Norman into the waiting room and I showed him the programme. 'Who did this?' he asked. I said, 'Look at the programme.' 'No, no,' he said, 'tell me who did it.' I said, 'Tim Bell.' He replied, 'Well that's it then, that's it.'

I got him by the shoulders and said, 'Norman, listen to me, we're about to lose this f------election! You're going to go, I'm going to go, the whole thing is going to go. The entire election depends upon her doing fine performances for the next five days – she has to be happy, we have got to do this. Now look at this campaign, look at it!' And he looked at it and he said, 'It looks very good!' 'Yes,' I said, 'it's very simple – we'll look and see what they've got from Saatchis. If that is better, we'll use that and if this is better, we'll use this. One way or the other, we will get it done.' 'All right,' he said without enthusiasm. 'But you've got to!' I said to Norman, 'it's your future and my future and all our futures, and the future of this flaming country!'

We then walked upstairs and joined Maurice Saatchi and John Sharkey. The Prime Minister was still in her room. We started to look at their campaign and Norman's face got longer and longer. He said, 'This won't do, this won't do at all, it really won't. I don't know . . . she'll go mad when she sees it.' So I said, 'Norman come downstairs,' and I showed him the other programme again and said, 'We've got to use this one, haven't we?' 'Yes,' he said, 'we have; I can't possibly show her the Saatchi programme.' Then he said, 'Send Maurice down to me.'

I went back upstairs where David Wolfson was with Stephen. I suggested we pack the boards away because I was worried she might come up. I asked David Wolfson to take Maurice down to see Norman in the waiting room. I then took Stephen into the next room and told him what we were going to do – that we were going to get the Saatchis to adopt the other programme. He said, 'David, you would do a marvellous thing if you could get the whole thing done without even going to her, and just tell her it's off her hands.'

I wandered downstairs and there was David Wolfson waving a piece of paper and looking cheerful – I said, 'Have you got it?' 'Yes,' he said, 'We've got the poll results.' 'What are they?' They were 44 Conservative, 34 Labour, 20 Alliance! Obviously yesterday's poll had been a rogue. Immediately, I knew we had the election won and everything was going to be all right.

Norman, I assumed, was still in the waiting room with Maurice. I put my head round the door and said the polls had come through, and told him the figures – he looked pleased, and then said, 'Come in', and I looked and suddenly realised John Sharkey was there as well as Maurice Saatchi. Maurice said, 'I can't possibly do this, I can't possibly take it, it won't go.' I went up to him and said, 'Now look Maurice' – and again I got him by the lapels – 'you've got to do it!' 'No, no we can't possibly . . .' I said, 'Maurice, how much are you worth, how much are your companies worth? Do you know how much you'll be worth this time next week if we lose this election? You'll be broke, I'll be broke, the whole country will be broke! Now forget your bloody pride, this is the programme she wants, and this is the programme you're going to do!'

I literally shouted at him. He looked very sulky. He glanced at Tim's programme and said, 'Well, it's all very amateurish.' I said, 'Forget about that, just do something similar. It's what she wants, it's the positive upbeat message that she wants.' He looked again at it, and asked, 'Can we prepare something?' I said, 'Work all night, bring it round 10 o'clock tomorrow morning after the press conference. We will get it done.'

He hummed and ha'ed and, looked at Sharkey and then said, 'All right, yes.' They got their work together and I walked out with Norman. Norman said, 'I want to go and tell her.' Stephen tried to stop him, but I held Stephen back. When a few minutes later, Norman and the P.M. came down, he had told her and she looked very relieved. To be fair to Norman, he now genuinely believed Tim's idea was by far the best.

I went up to the Prime Minister as she stood in the front hall. I said, 'Prime Minister, don't worry, I will get everything done; you just forget about it – you can see it tomorrow if you want to, just relax and go and sock it to them!' Norman went off to speak in Chingford and I went back and went to her Private Office. David Norgrove was sitting reading a magazine and I teased him a bit about not having much to do. I asked the duty clerk for a piece of headed notepaper, and wrote a note to the Prime Minister, telling her exactly what I'd arranged, and left it with the front desk.

I then went and telephoned Alistair and told him that everything had worked out fine – I fixed to have dinner with him later, and also to borrow his house. I rang up Tim and arranged to meet him there in College Street.

I went there feeling absolutely worn out. I'd had two highly, emotional meetings, which had really drained me. I don't think I had ever put more into any two meetings than those. I went out to

Norman Dodds, who had been sitting patiently waiting outside since about 3.30 p.m., rang Howell from the car, picked him up and went round to College Street. We got there just as Tim Bell arrived, and Alistair's man opened a bottle of champagne – I think I drank half a bottle before I could even speak.

I told Tim the whole story. I think he was a bit shaken that I disclosed to Saatchis that he had prepared the work. In the end, he just accepted it and after about an hour's chat, celebrating the results of the polls, I told him what we were going to do. I then left and went back to Claridges, where I met Alistair for dinner and told him the entire story all over again from the beginning. I must say I was living every second of it – it really was for me a tremendous feeling of achievement. Stephen later told me it was the greatest thing in the world I'd done to take the burden away from the P.M., and get all the decisions made.

Friday 5 June

I went into Central Office for the 7.45 a.m. meeting – more than a little apprehensive. At the beginning, Norman was rather withdrawn and a bit surly but after five minutes he warmed up and it went quite well. We looked at the polls with a great sense of relief all round, since the latest one showed a much better result, and the meeting finished in good heart. I took the opportunity to say to the Prime Minister, 'Saatchis are coming around at 10 o'clock to look at the advertising,' and she said, 'No, no, I have got a tremendous amount to do, I've got to do television and all sorts of things, I can't possibly do it.' 'All right, Prime Minister, leave it with us and we will do it.' She then said to Norman that she wanted Gordon Reece, and Norman said he would be delighted, and it was left that Norman would ring Gordon Reece in order to ask him to come in.

When the press conference was over we agreed that we would wait until she left. We asked John Sharkey and Maurice Saatchi to come into Norman's room, and looked at the advertising. At the beginning of the meeting Maurice Saatchi was also a little withdrawn, but he soon changed. The advertising was very good – perhaps not quite so good as Tim would have made it, but still pretty good. Maurice Saatchi said they had three pages booked for the Sunday. I said, 'Come on Norman, let's have three pages every single day, Sunday through to Thursday – don't worry about the cost because I've spoken to Alistair and there's plenty of money.'

They then raised the question of the *Daily Mirror* and I said,

'Yes, even the *Mirror*, because it's their voters we're after!' I left that meeting quite relaxed about the way it would go; the advertising looked good, and at least we had got the whole idea in without causing the P.M. any trouble.

I then went to find Alistair to tell him how much of his funds I had committed, as I had not agreed anything with him. He agreed right away. Better to be the party in power with an overdraft than a rich opposition, was always his motto . . .

Saturday 6 June

Gordon Reece and I went over to No. 10 where we sat down with the Prime Minister, Stephen and David Wolfson. We had to agree the final election broadcast. I had previously arranged with John Sharkey that we would get the cleaned-up version by going back to the master tapes instead of using a fourth or fifth generation tape; thus all the grain disappeared and the Prime Minister looked very much better. But when they played the video tape the sound wasn't as good. That was because of a chance remark I'd made to Jeremy Sinclair at the earlier showing who had followed my instructions exactly and reduced the level of the sound; but I'm afraid it had slightly spoilt the effect – still, we can always change it.

We went through the script and the first thing the Prime Minister said when she looked at it was, 'No, this won't do at all.' She said that times change, and the campaign goes on – but of course what has happened is that she's just changed her mind. She then started to dictate to us the thoughts in her mind and Gordon Reece and Stephen Sherbourne took it down. We then all trooped upstairs. Denis Thatcher was there and we played the tape. We had the first speech cut out of it – the Prime Minister had been very conscious how her appearance had improved over the years. It had a tremendous effect. It is difficult to describe how powerful an effect it had, but it really did knock everybody out. She confirmed that we would select those films for starters and so, after a while, I left and went back to the office.

Rang up Jeremy Sinclair, and we got John Sharkey and Gordon, and told them the good news and the bad news. The goods news was keeping the first part of the film, but the bad news was a rewrite: So we then settled down for a complete rewrite of the ending. It was about 10 o'clock when we got as far as we could go with a new script, then decided to call it a day. I got home about 10.30 p.m., I suppose. Lita had left some food for me, and I eventually went to bed feeling very tired indeed.

Sunday 7 June

I took the chance to have a reasonable lie-in and didn't wake up until half past eight. Lita put on the television and we watched the Prime Minister with David Frost. She was very good indeed. At one point, he was pushing her about private health and she turned round and said rather sweetly – this is when she is at her most dangerous, 'But tell me Mr Frost, don't you use private health yourself?' 'Yes,' he said, 'but when I do I feel guilty.' That absolutely skewered him, and I thought she came away looking very good indeed. About 12 o'clock we left to go to Wembley for the big family election rally.

We arrived at about quarter past one – had a quick bite, and then went into the family rally where the atmosphere was absolutely electric. I sat with Peter Morrison near the front, and the photographers took all sorts of silly pictures of us. When the rally started, it was very good indeed – Bob Monkhouse and Jimmy Tarbuck told some excellent political jokes; it was a very warm cheerful family atmosphere. When the P.M. came on she was absolutely tremendous; as she spoke, I could see the makings of the party election broadcast, and I knew that whatever happened we would have to go back and rewrite it.

After the show was over, I went on to No. 10 and there was Gordon Reece, Tim Bell, Tony Jay, Stephen and David Wolfson. We showed the P.M. the script but even this script wasn't good enough. She had some idea how she would like it to be rewritten, and Tim and Tony Jay set to work. Eventually they drafted it out, part in longhand and part in shorthand; by now it was about 6.15 p.m., and we got a phone call asking us to go down to the studio. We went to what was obviously the two Saatchis' office – white painted, bleak, modern pictures on the wall, skylights. Then started a rather long saga.

The Prime Minister looked at the new script and said, 'Yes, that's very good indeed. But just before the final make-up, she said, 'Mind you . . .', and started looking at a word here and a word there, and the next thing I knew we were into a session which ultimately lasted about three hours. It was gone ten before the final, final version of the script was ready. Then we went down to the first floor to shoot it. The first shot failed after about a paragraph. Gordon was saying, 'No good, no good, that's good, that's good . . .' By 11.30 p.m. we got the last shot in the bag. We did one more shot on video tape just in case, which they professed to be pleased with, and we packed up for the night.

Home at midnight for a change! Quite worn out with just the nervous strain of seeing everything done. Hardly got in when the phone went at ten past twelve; it was David Wolfson. He said, 'Have you seen tomorrow's *Times*?' 'No,' I said, 'I never get it until the morning.' The P.M. had, and he started to read out the headline, evidently accompanied by a big picture of Kinnock. The headline was about a poll in the marginals which was going to make it a very close–run thing; there were also a number of very unhelpful stories. I went to bed feeling that tomorrow would produce some more problems – it was, I suppose, the last Sunday of the campaign but even by then it seemed a very, very long campaign.

Monday 8 June

I met with Kenneth Clarke and Jonathan Hill, his Special Adviser, and Howell and Norman Blackwell. We did the briefing and went downstairs to our press conference at 11.30 a.m. It was reasonably well attended – surprisingly so in fact. I used our new graphics, and thought it went very well indeed. Kenneth had a few good lines, and I was told later that the conference ran even to the news bulletins.

Eventually I got a message that we should go to a little place somewhere in Soho, so we went to a very battered, tatty sort of place. There was Terry Donovan, John Sharkey and Tony Jay (author of *Yes Minister*). The film was shown, and I thought it looked very good. On the way back, I asked Gordon Reece in the street what he thought about it; he said it would be OK.

Tuesday 9 June

We had an 8.30 a.m. start, as the Prime Minister was in Venice. Norman was to chair the meeting with John MacGregor and John Moore. It went quite well – there was beginning to be an end-of-term feeling about the whole campaign. Norman finished it after only about twenty-two minutes – and there weren't too many questions.

I found out that the Jimmy Young show which I was due to be on wasn't just an ordinary one – in fact I was appearing with John Prescott and Malcolm Bruce, down the line from Scotland. We were on for an hour between 11 and 12 o'clock, and I think it was probably my least satisfactory performance ever.

It was very odd. First of all, Prescott was his usual bullying self; but half way through I suddenly got absolutely and utterly bored with all the stale old arguments I had been using for the last five years. Although there was nothing wrong with the arguments themselves, I was just bored with them and couldn't wait for the programme to end. Afterwards, I said to Howell, 'I don't think I was very good,'; he was too polite to actually agree with me, but I think he thought the same thing. I went back to Central Office and then we waited around for the party election broadcasts to be delivered, because tonight was the Prime Minister's night.

The Prime Minister came back from Venice and went direct to Harrogate. I heard afterwards that Stephen (who faxed the speech out to her) had received the shock of his life when Charles Powell came over with the speech, and he found she had accepted the whole speech – just altering a word or two.

The Saatchis came over and showed us the final version of the tape. I thought the music in the introduction was still far too loud. But we approved it, and then waited until we got over half a dozen video tapes; then Howell and I got in the car and we went and we dropped them off at the newspapers. After that decided to call it a day, and I got home just as the party election broadcast was on. Lita saw it – but I don't think she was awfully impressed with it!

A little later, I watched *Newsnight*, where Vincent Hanna came out with a poll that went into considerable detail – though he quoted all the 'health warnings', he inferred pretty strongly that we were heading towards a hung parliament. That got me very depressed indeed, and I began to wonder whether or not our last-minute charge was actually working. Even though all the issues were going our way – tax was running strongly – I still wasn't really that confident.

Wednesday 10 June

The last day before the election. This was the wrap-up press conference day, and it was quite difficult to wake up for the 7.45 a.m. meeting that Norman Tebbit wanted first. This was the morning when the P.M. was going to do *Election Call* – the Robin Day programme which I had originally fixed to be televised from Central Office from five past nine until 10 o'clock. I went into Alastair's room where Willie Whitelaw was and we sat and watched with John Wakeham; she really did perform magnificently.

That morning's *Independent* ran a big scare story about the Jobcentres, saying we were going to privatise them. I was furious with this story, which was quite uncalled for and unprovoked. The Prime Minister came upstairs at 10 a.m. and I congratulated her – as we all did. Then we sat down and went through the press conference; she said she was going to make a very short opening statement and then leave it open to questions. Norman Tebbit said he had invited all the press corps for drinks; there was very much of an end-of-term feeling about the whole thing – it was all a bit unreal.

We went into the press conference and the Prime Minister made a short statement, then threw it open to questions. The very second question was one on Jobcentres, and I answered it very firmly, saying there was no question of them being privatised. When it finished at 11 o'clock, the Prime Minister went off to a studio to give some interviews.

I had asked Howell to book a table for lunch because I wanted to take Norman Blackwell and Jonathan Hill out for a celebration farewell lunch. Indeed, we had a very jolly time, and I thanked the boys very much. We'd run the best press conference of the campaign, were looking reasonably secure according to the way the polls were going. In fact, I was getting increasingly confident that we had done it. The press, too, was running our way.

I went back to the office and cleared up my papers – it was a rather extended lunch. I whiled away some time in Alastair's room and we waited until 8 o'clock before I finally got away. There was a variety of polls that evening – the worst showed a seven and a half points lead, the maximum showed twelve points; it did look as if we were heading for victory. But some of the polls in the marginals gave us a very slight lead, and there was increasing talk about a hung parliament. I went back that evening rather more worried than I cared to admit.

Election day

I had looked forward to having a lie-in on election day – it was the first day I didn't have to be anywhere, but at 6.30 a.m. the phone went, and it was David Li ringing from Paris to wish me luck. By ten past seven I'd had the fifth telephone call, and it was absolutely impossible to sleep. I stayed in bed until quite a bit later speaking to people; and as the day went on, I started talking myself into thinking there wasn't going to be much of a margin at all. I had a severe case of election day nerves!

Went out for a meal with my family, and came back at about 3 o'clock. I decided to go to bed, as I was due to be on radio or television for most of the night. I slept very intermittently – I kept on getting phone calls which woke me up, and I was feeling worse and worse. All I could think was that by this time tomorrow, I would know where we were.

At about 6 o'clock I got up not really having slept properly at all, and feeling extraordinarily tired. Alistair was giving a dinner at San Lorenzo Restaurant. It was a great party which we all thoroughly enjoyed – except that I had lost my appetite. I had a first course and salad, and then in the middle of it Alistair got called to the phone and came back looking very relieved. He said, 'I've got the ITN poll. The figures are looking something like 44, 32, 20.' This really was an enormous lead. I said, 'We've got it, we've got it!' Champagne appeared from nowhere.

At 9.15 p.m. I was due to leave, so they quickly gave me some spaghetti. I had very little of it and then Dodds arrived to pick me up. I then went to the BBC studio in Wood Lane where I was the first one on *Election Call*. Barbara Maxwell of the BBC was there as I came in and I said, 'What's it look like, Barbara?' 'It's grim,' she said . . . 'could be 17 seats short of a majority, or more likely a majority of just 26.' My heart sank a bit – but not too much because I knew what the other exit poll had said. I went on to the set and there was Jon Snow, jumping and cheerful, Dimbleby and all of them, happy and confident as could be. They really did think they had a great story on their hands. I also suspected that they were not too unhappy that we were not doing that well.

Jeffrey Archer was interviewed extraordinarily rudely by Julia Somerville, who asked him whether the Prime Minister would hang on if she hadn't got a proper majority. They were getting so worked up that about five minutes before the first result was due I turned round to Robin Day and said, 'Robin, do you know what they are saying on the other channel?' 'No,' he said, and I told him. 'Oh My God,' he said and picked up a phone, and they started to moderate their attitude a little.

When the first result was about to come through, for Torbay, they said on the programme, 'If our forecast is right, the Conservative candidate will have 26,000 votes.' When it was announced – and I had my fingers crossed – at 29,000 votes – that undermined their forecasts totally, and as soon as that happened the whole atmosphere changed – they went into deep depression! Within minutes, the forecast was changed from a majority of 26 to 44; and so it carried on climbing up all evening.

At about a quarter past eleven, they released me. I went upstairs to the party which Bill Cotton was giving. Shirley, the widow of my late brother Stuart, the previous Chairman of the BBC, was there with my niece and nephew, Leslie and Denis. Many of the BBC people were very glum, but our supporters were extremely cheerful. By then, our estimated majority had gone up to about fifty-five or sixty.

I spent a few minutes there, and then on to Wells Street for ITN. By then our estimated majority had gone up to 70. I said my bit and went off again to Gough Square for LBC and IRN radio. Back to Central Office, where everybody was getting more and more happy – the estimates were up to 88. At 2 a.m., I went back to Wells Street; now the estimate had gone to over 100. I was sitting there with the cameras on me when our total finally went over the 326 seats required, and we had won. That was a marvellous moment.

I went back after that to Central Office – I gave a little interview outside, got a little cheer and by then Lita had come along, the Prime Minister arrived, there was great fuss and joy, and everybody was very happy indeed.

At about 4.15 a.m. we went home. I had *Breakfast Television* and a whole host of other things still to do. I went to bed about 5 a.m. very tired – but very, very happy.

Chapter 16
THE SPECIAL ADVISER RETURNS

First day of the third term. It seemed that as soon as I put my head on the pillow the phone went. It was 5.50 a.m. and Steve Robin – who had not left Central Office all night – offered me some morning television. 'No way,' I said, and far less politely, 'this is the Chairman's day.' Later Howell came round and I found that, whatever I thought, I had to go off to do TV-am and then yet more television. It all seemed a tremendous anticlimax, particularly when John Prescott and Ken Livingstone turned up on the same programme. After all, the election was over. It felt like a great waste of time and energy to go over the same stale old arguments and I found difficulty in summoning up any enthusiasm. When that was finished there was still no respite. I was due on the Jimmy Young show.

Jimmy Young gave me a one-to-one interview which I thought went rather well and I gradually got back into the swing again. Whilst I was on, a message came through saying that the Prime Minister wanted to see me at 11.50 a.m. before she went to Central Office. I went straight back to No. 10 and walked through the back into the Private Office. I sat talking to all the Private Secretaries, teasing them a little that their holiday had come to an end. Then David Norgrove (Private Secretary for Home Affairs) said I could go upstairs.

The Prime Minister was in her study. I felt exhausted, but she already looked fully restored. She smiled and thanked me warmly for all that had happened and we spent a few moments discussing the events of the last few days. I said that the most remarkable fact of this election was that 44 per cent of first-time voters had voted for us – 'We have changed the whole face of the nation.' But, I went on, in all the euphoria of the moment and our majority of over a hundred, let us not forget that eight days ago we thought we were losing. That happened because of two things: one was the Health Service – and the other was organisation. We spent a few moments discussing both matters. I gently pointed out that Tim Bell could not be at Central Office last night. She picked up the phone and asked to speak to him but he was out. Later she tracked him down at a tennis tournament and thanked him warmly for everything.

She left No. 10 and spoke to the crowd who were waiting patiently outside and then went on to Central Office. I followed her back and walked into Central Office a few minutes later. Norman Tebbit to his credit called out, 'David, David's here' and paid me a nice tribute. Norman, myself and the Prime Minister had our pictures taken together and then we presented her with a cake. It was a tremendous, triumphant feeling. Then I cleared out my desk. I no longer belonged to Central Office, and Howell and I took our leave.

We went to lunch at a local restaurant. They made a great fuss, and almost everyone in the restaurant came over to congratulate us. It was a real carnival atmosphere. At the next table a couple from the North kept on interrupting us in a very good-natured way. Everyone was very happy whilst I was full of doom and gloom, preparing Howell for our transfer to DHSS. I wanted to stay at the Department of Employment and complete my plans. Other than that, I wanted to be somewhere where I could advance the cause of enterprise. Health and Pensions held no attractions for me. Final confirmation that unemployment would drop below three million on Thursday only made it worse. I saw Roger Dawe, John Turner, my Private Secretary, and Peter Makeham. All three also thought that I might go to DHSS. Peter said he would come with me. I went home about 5 o'clock so very tired that Lita made me a snack and I was in bed before 9 o'clock – I couldn't even be bothered to look at television.

I woke once or twice during the night and worried where I was going. In the morning I rang the Prime Minister. I asked if she could spare me some time to talk about my new job. She said, 'David, I have made up my mind, it's all settled now. I've had the best night's sleep I think I've ever had. I'll see you later on – I don't want to do it on the phone but don't worry, you're not going to DHSS.' We agreed to meet at 2.30 p.m.

In the middle of the last week of the election, an invitation had arrived from the Prime Minister for Lita and myself to attend the Trooping of the Colour. At the time it had seemed too remote an event to take seriously. I had seen the ceremony before in my Cabinet Office days when my own office actually overlooked Horseguards Parade. We had turned it into an informal family occasion, including my Private Office, but this time it would be quite different. I would be in morning dress and Lita in all her finery. We entered Downing Street and I gave a wave to the photographers waiting patiently outside. Speculation was already rife about the new Cabinet and we made the early newsreels looking rather formal and very overdressed! I wandered in to the Private Office and Nigel Wicks, her Principal Private Secretary, asked me to see the Prime Minister just before lunch.

The Trooping of the Colour is always a spectacular show but this time my attention wandered. Would I be allowed to stay on at Employment or would I go elsewhere? If so, where? I arrived at no satisfactory conclusion. After the ceremony, we went back for drinks. David Norgrove, her Private Secretary on Home Affairs, came up to me and congratulated me on my new department – then retired in confusion when I told him that I had not been told! A few minutes later Nigel Wicks asked me to go upstairs to the Prime Minister's study.

I entered the study and sat facing her. The Prime Minister looked at me rather solemnly and said, 'David, I would like you and Kenneth Clarke to go to DTI and to take Inner Cities.' I had a momentary flash of elation and then depression. I would not be able to complete all our plans at Employment. That was something I would regret for many weeks to come. Then again I would still need a Cabinet colleague in the Commons. I was delighted to be working with Kenneth again, although I had hoped that he would have his own department. What I had really wanted was a Commons spokesman who would not be in Cabinet. Later, much later, I was to realise that this need to have a Cabinet colleague in the Commons would mark the limit of my ambitions in politics.

We spent a few moments talking about the Inner City responsibility. I received the by now customary caution not to mention it until the announcement at 6 o'clock. On the way down, I had two thoughts. If only Stuart could have known – I wondered how he would have teased me. The second thought was that for the first time in three years I would be receiving a salary! For the last eight years of public life I had been paid for less than two and a half.

I rejoined the reception and muttered 'DTI with Kenneth' into Lita's ear; she looked pleased. We left early after lunch just as my colleagues arrived to learn their fate. I telephoned Howell and Margaret Bell and told my mother to watch the 6 o'clock news. The announcement was late and there on the news bulletins I appeared leaving No. 10, looking overdressed, followed by Kenneth Clarke who looked his usual cheerful, casual self.

As soon as the news ended the phone rang. Sir Brian Hayes, my new Permanent Secretary, volunteered to bring round my briefing

235

papers. I accepted and he was soon round sipping a sherry and handing over my new responsibilities. I found the whole atmosphere unreal. I was overtired, sad at the thought of leaving Employment and for the first time in years unsure what to do next. From the day I went to the MSC, I knew that my job was to fight unemployment. I had fought that battle and, against all the odds, won. Small firms, my other interest, was back at Employment and I told Brian quite firmly that I would not try to get it back to DTI. I thanked Brian warmly and said that I would see him on Monday morning.

I continued to study the papers over the weekend between answering calls of congratulations. I cheered up when Adrian Moorey telephoned. Adrian had been my Head of Information back at Employment, and I had let him go on promotion to DTI. He told me that I had been invited on to the *Today* programme for Monday morning, which I accepted. I asked him, 'What happens at the Department?' He said that he met with the Minister every morning to work out a line to take on the day's news. 'Forget that,' I said, 'it is not my responsibility what happens to every company in the land.' We will only respond to those situations we actually create. I decided on the spot that we must have a more positive public image. 'Not as easy as the old Department,' said Adrian, 'this is the Department of Bad News.' I reminded him what the old Department had been like at the beginning. We will see, was his cryptic reply.

Later on that evening I telephoned Jeffrey Sterling. Over five years before, when I had been Special Adviser to Patrick Jenkin, I had persuaded Jeffrey to take my job. He had done so, but because of his business commitments, only on a part time basis. He had continued to serve all the Secretaries of State since then, and Brian Hayes had sung his praises during our meeting. We had worked together from the late sixties and he was one of my oldest friends. He had had a most distinguished business career and was now Chairman of P&O.

'Jeffrey,' I said, 'I have never listened to you in over thirty years. I cannot think of a better person to be my Special Adviser.' Despite that comment, he accepted on the spot. This cheered me up. With Howell, Adrian and now Jeffrey, I had the makings of a team.

The following morning saw me at Broadcasting House at 7.45. I was interviewed by Brian Redhead. I had been crossing swords with Brian in a friendly way for many years and had always found him fair with me. I was still thinking in terms of my old job (I had yet to enter the 1 Victoria Street building), when he asked me what I was

236

going to do with my Department. Almost by instinct I answered that we were the 'Department of Wealth Creation'. If Industry and Commerce did not create the wealth, then the nation could not afford health care, the social services, education and all the demands of a caring society. When I left I thought about my remarks; and the more I thought about them, the more I felt that I had stumbled upon a good theme for my time there.

As I drove up to Victoria Street, I knew that I was entering a Department of Disasters. It had had four Secretaries of State during the last Parliament alone. It was clearly seen outside as a Department that had lost its way. Would I be able to find it? Even more, did those in the Department realise the reputation it had?

I walked in and my heart sank. The Private Office was immense; it looked as if there were at least a dozen working there with papers piled all over the place. I went into my own room and it was even worse. Furniture that had not only seen better days but better decades. Four tatty leather armchairs, with upholstery about to burst out, a conference table scratched and worn, other bits and pieces of well-worn furniture: this was not the office to receive any-one, let alone represent British industry and commerce. Before many weeks were out I had replaced the furniture with good British furni-ture, partitioned off the Private Office, and arranged for them to have some modern furniture. I had always known that if you cannot take pride in your surroundings then you do not take pride in your work.

Kenneth Clarke came in for a chat. I was sure that he was dis-appointed not to have his own department but at least he now had a much bigger job. I told him that he should take inner cities for himself. Despite my long interest in unemployment and inner cities, I told him that I would keep out, for here was a chance for him to make his own mark. Our photocall in the middle of the morning had Kenneth and me standing outside the Department arm in arm. It reminded me of the time we both went to Nottingham and were photographed in a similar way. The local paper had a banner head-line on the front page over a large picture of us grinning inanely which read 'Togetherness'!

Then the first meeting started. The industry part of the Depart-ment I knew well, from my days as a Special Adviser with Keith Joseph and Patrick Jenkin. I found that although the country, and the economy, had changed vastly over the last five years, my Department had not. I thought back to the changes I had wanted to introduce all those years ago. Would they still be relevant? We would have to see.

The other half of the Department, the old Board of Trade, covered the City as well as its traditional trade matters. That would be new territory for me. By now, I had been given the names of the remainder of my Department. Alan Clark, to my great delight, would continue as Minister for Trade. Robert Atkins, my Commons Whip for the last three years, now entered the Government and I gave him the Industry portfolio, reporting to Kenneth Clarke. John Butcher, who along with Alan Clark had been the sole survivor of the old Department, had first come to the Department whilst I was still Special Adviser. He must have been the longest serving Parliamentary Under Secretary of State in the Government, and I kept him on the films, design and education side. I knew that the City was going to be my real problem and I insisted on having a high flyer as my Junior Minister. Francis Maude, our old Whip at Employment, also came into Government for the first time and I was delighted to give him this very heavy portfolio. As time would pass I would load more and more on him, including our responsibilities for Europe. He always took the strain and never let me down.

Kenneth and I had decided on a total review of all policies. We would go back to basics, and attempt zero based budgeting for the Department. The first few meetings did not go as smoothly as I would have liked. Brian Hayes came into them all and either he, or my Private Secretary Tim Walker, would try to guide me through policy, often contrary to my instincts. I wanted to reduce Government intervention, to reduce spending and to release enterprise. We had to move away from civil servants and ministers telling industry and commerce what to do. Once Brian realised that I had my own ideas, he stopped coming to every meeting. He was as good as gold, and although there were times when I suspect I took steps that he did not in his heart approve of, I never heard of any occasion when he was not vigorous in support of all we were doing. He was a constant source of encouragement, and a model of what a Minister/Permanent Secretary relationship should be.

I went back for my leaving party at Employment, which only made me all the more homesick. That evening I had a quiet dinner arranged with an old friend, Eric Sharp. The Department had been negotiating for some time to get Cable & Wireless to place an order with Swan Hunter for a cable ship. Eric and I agreed the terms and shook hands before the first drink. At least I had started.

The next day the round of meetings continued. We were in the middle of the Public Expenditure Survey discussions, and by about 1 o'clock we only had the Department's pay and rations to agree. One of the officials suggested that they carry on the meeting with

Kenneth Clarke. I had lunch fixed with Norman Fowler, who had inherited my old Department, in order to go through all the plans we had made for this term. I jumped at the suggestion, and the officials adjourned to Kenneth's office, thinking that they would now have an easy ride. I went off to lunch smiling. The Department quickly found out that Kenneth was drier in money matters than was I. I was told later that he gave them a really hard time, and forced through a far lower figure than I would probably have settled for.

I had been brooding on ways to lift the morale of the Department. Eventually I decided that I would address all my civil servants of Principal grade and over. That afternoon they all assembled in the canteen and I think it went well. All my ministers turned up together with Brian Hayes. They were the Department of Wealth Creation, I told them. It was the wealth created by industry and commerce that was invested back into health, welfare and education. For the first time we had a responsibility for the inner cities. Kenneth Clarke and I were engaged on a total review of all programmes, and I looked forward to meeting many of them over the weeks and months to come. I suspect the fact that we were reviewing all the programmes raised fears more than it lifted morale!

On my way out one of my Deputy Secretaries came up to me. 'Do you know, Secretary of State,' he said, 'that has only happened once before.' 'Really,' I enquired, 'who spoke to the Department then?' 'Tony Benn' was the reply that finished me!

The next morning I had my usual meeting with the Prime Minister. She remembered the chart I had prepared on my home computer the previous February that had exactly foretold the course of unemployment over the last few months. She knew that unemployment was going under three million on Thursday, and she congratulated me.

'Now I know how Moses felt,' I said, 'brought within sight of the promised land and then translated to another place!'

Cabinet came round on Thursday as usual. I found that I was still sitting next to Kenneth, although we had both moved up one place along the table. My position in Cabinet was considerably improved. I had moved up from twenty-second to twelfth in less than three years.

At the appropriate moment Norman Fowler announced that unemployment had dropped below three million. No sooner had he got the words out than the Prime Minister and most of my colleagues turned and looked towards me. I tried to look suitably

239

modest and the Prime Minister paid a considerable compliment to Action for Jobs. I remembered how often I had dreamed of making that announcement, and when Norman left Cabinet early to make the usual television and radio announcements, I went with him in spirit.

I decided to celebrate. During the seventies we used to go racing once or twice a year. I had given it up when I first went to the MSC, but I thought that the time had come for me to return. The following day I took Lita to Ascot. As we wandered through the crowd I was congratulated by all and sundry, on the election and on the job. The honeymoon was still continuing.

That weekend we went down to the country and I concentrated on my boxes and on sleeping. By the Monday, I had begun to feel that I had rejoined the human race. My first meeting was with Bryan Hayes and the head of the Policy Planning Unit (PPU). I vaguely remembered that this unit had been started by Patrick Jenkin when he first came to the Department of Industry. I asked the unit to take a radical look at the work of the Department to see what changes should take place. I was very keen to end sponsorship. This was the practice of the Department to shadow quite narrow sectors of industry or commerce. They wanted to ensure that ministers, and their civil servants, would know what went on. The reality was quite different: often quite junior civil servants would be given a sector for a three-year term, and then have to learn as much as they could about the business. This almost inevitably led them into the clutches of the relevant trade association and they ended up as a conduit for the industry to dun ministers for more money or more support. I thought there had to be another way.

The PPU had prepared a paper which was quite radical and advocated many changes. I knew because my secretary Margaret Bell was slipped a copy by a friend in the Department from the old days. Then I heard that it went to a committee of all the Deputy Secretaries, chaired by Brian Hayes, which promptly threw it out and asked them to start again. They did so, and I saw a copy of their second paper. Much less radical than before, but even that was thrown out. In the meantime, I had some quiet amusement asking my Private Secretary where the review had got to and was given a succession of excuses. Finally, the third paper passed the Permanent Secretary's committee and came to me. I threw it out as it was so bland as to be useless, and promptly dissolved the Policy Unit. Like the Central Policy Review Staff of old, it had outlasted its time and had become institutionalised. Once you relied on a consensus view, nothing would change.

240

I knew that I would have a much heavier work load and asked Willie Whitelaw for the best of our Whips. I was delighted when they gave me Maxwell Aitken, Lord Beaverbrook. He certainly had a very full year as my Lords Whip. The procedures are very different in the Lords, where the Whips perform all the functions of junior ministers in the Commons. Maxwell not only had to speak for DTI but he had to cover Employment and the Treasury when I was not there.

The new Lord Chancellor, Michael Havers, asked me to be one of his two introducers to the Lords. He had wanted a solicitor and I little thought when I gave up practice over thirty-two years before that the next time I would be wanted as a solicitor would be to introduce a Lord Chancellor into the Lords. The ceremony is very complicated and although the rehearsals were fine we took some short cuts on the day!

As soon as the Policy Planning Unit disappeared I decided that I would have to have, not a policy unit, but a unit to initiate change. I formed the euphemistically named 'Central Unit' and on Brian Hayes' suggestion put it under the command of Brian Hilton. That was a decision that I never regretted, and Peter Makeham soon joined the unit. Before long they were initiating suggestions for reorganisation, and the pace of change accelerated.

But long before this, at one of my early briefing meetings, I came across the Single European Act. We had been discussing Europe, and I, in company I suspect with the majority of Britons at the time, had paid little attention to what was happening in Europe. We had had to fight hard in Employment to prevent the reappearance of some unwelcome social legislation, and Kenneth Clarke had been brilliantly successful in transforming a negative, employment protection agenda in the community into a programme to introduce an enterprise culture.

This was different. The result of the Single European Act was that the veto could no longer save us from the consequences of changes in Europe. There were two main areas of change. First the social area; that was something over which we would have to work with other departments to prevent the worst of the practices of the seventies returning. The other was quite different. There was to be a single market in Europe in just five years' time! I asked around. None of my friends in industry or commerce had any idea what was going to happen in 1992. Expo or the Olympic games were often the only suggestions I got. Yet here we were, on the periphery of Europe, both physically and mentally, and yet standards and changes were being initiated that would transform business life in just a few years' time.

I asked who was the lead department; to my surprise I was told that we were. I told Brian that we needed to set up a special group to deal with 1992 and asked him to find me someone really good to head the unit. Before long he came to me and suggested Marianne Neville Rolfe. It was another of Brian's brilliant choices for, with Peter Loughead they would transform attitudes to Europe and to 1992. However, that was still in the future and I set them to work to find out the latest position and to plan a campaign to cover the negotiations.

I would meet with Kenneth Clarke from time to time. I found that almost by instinct we would arrive at the same position on each subject. In all our years together, not only did we not have a single row, but I can only think of one or two occasions that we did not see eye to eye on any subject. We were both determined to shake up the Department and set about a fundamental review. But for some time I was still searching for a new policy for the Department as a whole.

One day, during a Public Expenditure Survey meeting we were looking for ways to cut back and at the same time find some head-room for some extra expenditure. I suggested that we abolish the Regional Development Grant and Kenneth jumped at the idea. Our officials looked horrified. They told us that we could never do it. It had been a plank of regional policy for years. 'You will never get it through the House,' we were told.

The Regional Development Grant (RDG) was a flat rate grant that was paid as a percentage of qualifying industrial expenditure in an assisted or development area. Many friends of mine, indus-trialists all, had told me what a waste of public funds that repre-sented. A Chairman of one of our major companies told me that he regularly told a bright young executive to go down to DTI and compare their companies' expansion plans with the grants avail-able and see what he could pick up. Free money was the way he described it. I agreed that it was a waste of taxpayer's money. If we were to give money away then it should only be when the grant made the difference between the project proceeding or being can-celled. Automatic grants could never work that way – not that selective assistance was any better. We both hit the roof when we saw an application submitted by one of the largest companies in the country for over £1 million simply to move a plant less than three miles, just over the border into a development area. We made up our minds that this would change.

Early in July I instituted ministers' lunches, always on a Thursday after Cabinet. One of the problems of ministerial life was that we were all so busy. If we were not careful days and weeks could pass and we simply would not see one another. I knew the value of communications, of melding a group into a team. We would invite in all ministers, Lords and Commons Whips and our PPSs and Special Advisers. The food was never up to much at the start although Maxwell was given charge of our menu and in time it improved. It was quite the best way to improve communication between colleagues. We only had politicals (officials were not invited) and quite often all we had was the latest gossip around the House. But time after time I would learn something from those lunches that otherwise would have escaped me. After only a few weeks, the ministers in the Department were operating as a team.

On the first Thursday, Kenneth and I arranged to go over to Gwydr House, the London office of the Welsh Secretary. Peter Walker had somewhat surprisingly gone there after the election and we wanted to see him to tell him that we were thinking of a radical review of regional policy. Although we were, strictly speaking, the lead department for regional policy, the Welsh and the Scots had a considerable say in its administration and received a block grant from Whitehall which included the Regional Development Grant.

Gwydr House is a very pleasant, small building in Whitehall, next to Defence and opposite the Scottish Office. Peter Walker's office is probably one of the most agreeable in Whitehall, large and spacious with windows on three sides and an attractive outlook. We settled ourselves down and chatted for a few moments. Peter and I were hardly strangers for we had known each other for over twenty-five years. Peter's company handled all my insurances in my Eldonwall days.

We told him that we were having a good look at all our regional policies including the RDG. I said something about looking for new ways to improve the quality of businesses when Peter made a chance remark about how well the advisory services had worked in Agriculture. That set me thinking furiously. I sat there looking out of the window whilst Kenneth Clarke carried on chatting. That, I suddenly realised, is what I should be doing in the Department. I should concentrate on building up advisory services in design and marketing. That was the way to help the regions but also the rest of the country.

The meeting soon ended and I returned with my mind in a whirl. I cancelled my next meeting and it all began to fall into place. We should use consultants to spread best business practices. If we could devise a programme in which we would encourage smaller businesses, 500 employees was to be the limit, to use the services of consultants then we would bring back concepts like quality, design and marketing.

I called a meeting and asked Adrian Moorey and Howell to join us. I knew from my Employment days that the best way to reach a mass audience was to use television. This time I would have a far smaller mass market – probably less than 250,000 companies were my target, but the right use of television would get to them. I had already told Brian that I wanted to reach out and get closer to our customers. When I returned to the Department we had seven regional offices, the office for the whole of the South East being only a few hundred yards from 1 Victoria Street. We were to open up a further 28 outlets around the country over the next nine months. We quickly arranged to go out to tender for a marketing campaign and I arranged to see the companies to brief them early in August.

In the middle of the month Cranfield awarded me an Honorary Doctorate of Science. By chance, a few days later we happened to have a Cabinet sub-committee on Research and Development. At one point during the meeting, to make my point, I said to the Prime Minister that we were the only two scientists in Cabinet. She looked somewhat surprised at this hitherto hidden talent of mine and when I told her on what I based my scientific qualifications I got very short shrift.

The month gradually wound down. We carried on with our review of the programmes of the Department and the new pattern slowly and surely fell into shape. I wanted to change the name of the Department to give it a new image, but I thought that the Department of Enterprise would be a little much. I knew that I had to try to weld both sides of the Department closer together. There was a great difference in philosophy between the Trade people and the old Industry people. Brian Hayes had changed round many of the Deputy Secretaries in recent months to achieve the same result but I wanted to reach further down the Department. Robert Armstrong suggested the Department of Trade whilst I was keener on the Department of Commerce. The latter, I thought, combined both industry and trade.

The House rose and ministers went on holiday as quickly as they decently could. It had been a long time since Christmas, particularly for those going to new departments straight after the election. Before we went away I wanted to deal with our new brief for the advertising agencies. It went out on 28 July 1987. I could now go away. The agencies were to return their submissions by 4 September. It would be a busy August for them.

The brief was quite clear. We wished to show that the Department was a single entity, to promote its key activities to small, medium and large-sized businesses. It was important, the instructions went on, that the Department should be seen as a champion of wealth creation with the prime aim of encouraging people to create the wealth needed to meet the demands of modern society. It explained that in the past we had concentrated on purely financial support, but now we wanted to adopt a marketing approach to inform our audience about DTI and the services, advice and export help which we provide. We needed a readily identifiable departmental message. We were in the middle of a full review, policy priorities were being reassessed and a change of emphasis could be expected. To show how fundamental the changes were going to be, we asked for the approach to cover what the relaunched DTI should offer its customers. We were a government department, but we were also a service industry and we had customers – just like British trade and industry.

Lita and I were fortunate in having tickets for the *Ring* at Bayreuth. Opera is a passion of mine, and it was only in August that I could be certain about attending. We left on 1 August, taking the ferry and driving across France, Belgium and then into Germany. This year Lita had found a new hotel, a recommendation from an old friend. We arrived in the central square of a small town some 20 kilometres from Bayreuth. At first sight the hotel did not look very attractive. It was small, situated right on the square with traffic passing on both sides. I went in; it appeared deserted. I rang the bell and the proprietor arrived, but he spoke no English.

Eventually his wife arrived and things looked up. She spoke perfect English and she was very attractive; she showed us the room, which was not. It overlooked the rather noisy square and had no amenities, no telephone, not even a radio; and a bathroom from the twenties. A lorry thundered past – I asked to see another room. On the way out, walking down the stairs, she said, 'This is the best room in the house. I don't know why you are not satisfied. Herr Hitler used to have this very room for weeks at a time.'

My blood froze but we kept on walking. I have often wondered if she ever realised why we just paid up for our rooms and quietly left. We drove away and found another hotel.

Six days later we were back in London. I came into the office to see how the brief we had given all the advertising agencies had been received. I wanted to use advertising, both to sell the programmes and to spread the concept. Companies around the country, and this included the South East as well as the regions, should concentrate on design, quality systems, marketing, and all the other areas covered by the programme. If the commercials encouraged them to pay attention to these areas without coming to Government, well and good. What I wanted to do was nothing more than change attitudes.

When the usual departmental business was settled, I returned thankfully to my holiday. September soon came, and with it the 4th. I spent that day visiting the agencies who were quoting for our new programmes. All the presentations were good and I agonised which I would choose. The offices of WCRS were in Covent Garden and I called on them by appointment at 3.00 p.m. On the way in, I couldn't help noticing a rather attractive girl sitting and playing the cello just outside the entrance. I remembered thinking how much this whole area had come up over the last few years, when it had been left to the market and not the planners.

The presentation was excellent. WCRS had the right feel and had grasped the concept exactly. At the end, they showed a short commercial, which featured a busker taking a DTI consultancy, and as a result ending up conducting a symphony orchestra. I thanked them and left rather impressed. I got into my car and looked back. The single cellist had now become a quartet of attractive young ladies playing Schubert. The penny dropped. They got the contract!

Chapter 17
THE ENTERPRISE INITIATIVE

Once we had selected WCRS as the agency for the new programme we lost no time in inviting them in for a series of meetings. We had to let them into our thinking about the future direction of the Department. It was to be a more radical change than even I had hoped for at the beginning. By now, Kenneth and I had nearly agreed where we were going. Once again I was to find that we would meet separately with officials and invariably arrive at the same conclusion. If anything, Kenneth was the dry one whenever it came to our spending plans. The Central Unit was working overtime ranging across the Department, and all the time I was encouraging them to be more courageous, not less.

It was not all plain sailing. A radical revision of all the programmes of a Department are not taken lightly. Many of the decisions were market sensitive and I had to prevent leaks at all cost. Morale in the Department plummeted. Rumours abounded. All sorts of programmes, it was said, were for the chop. Whole sections of the Department were to be abolished. There was little that I could do, for until we had agreed the new programmes, and obtained collective agreement where this was necessary, nothing could be even hinted. We were planning on a White Paper, but that would not be out until after Christmas.

Negotiations had started with the Treasury on the next spending round. They heard with delight of our plans to abolish the Regional Development Grant but with barely concealed horror of my plans to bring the Department to the hundreds of thousands of medium and smaller firms through the use of television. There seemed to be two schools of thought in the Treasury – one that television was a frivolous medium and the other (Lord Spendmore was my name with them) that it would be too effective and the cost of my programmes would soar through the roof.

At the end of the first week we all met again for our ministers' lunch. Howell was there with all our colleagues. I left before the end as I had a meeting with Geoffrey Howe on our plans for export promotion. When I returned there was a queue of officials waiting for me, but Margaret Bell headed them off and followed me into my office.

'I have some bad news for you,' she said, 'Howell wants to leave and you simply have to let him go.' I was shattered until I found out the reason. He then came in to see me. He had put his name forward, in a rather casual way, for the job of Corporate Affairs Director on the Management board of the BBC. To his slight surprise they had called him in for a second interview and then offered him the job. He had to let them know within the hour. I agreed at once. It was a spectacular appointment, to go from being my Special Adviser to one of the top jobs in the BBC, but one that was very far-sighted of them. Howell's great talents would be sorely missed by me, but I was sure that he would do a great job for the Corporation. He did, and does so to this day.

Because his present job was political we agreed that he would leave almost immediately. He volunteered to come with me to the Party Conference, but second thoughts prevailed. I rang Tim Bell and once again he said that he had just the man. In a day or two Peter Luff came to see me. Within days he became my Special Adviser. Peter was very different from Howell. He was valuable to me in a different way. He was actually more political; he had been around for years and was on the candidates' list, looking for a constituency. He was able to help me with the politics of the job, particularly in maintaining contact with all parts of the party. His background was interesting. He had worked in Ted Heath's office and then with Peter Walker. He used to joke that he had come to me to dry out, but by now the differences between the wets and the drys, which seemed so important in the early years of the decade, had just about disappeared. Peter would have his baptism of fire when he come with me to the next Party Conference.

At the end of the second week of September we had arranged that all ministers would take a day off to meet to discuss the new shape of the Department. Alan Clark had invited us down to Saltwood Castle, his home in Kent. We all assembled for the day – ministers, PPSs, Whips and our Special Advisers. Although we were talking about decisions that were normally considered too sensitive for anyone outside a department, other than ministers, I thought that I should take a chance as I wanted to lay our ideas before as many people as possible. The reaction was all that I could have wished for.

Saltwood Castle provided a magnificent setting. Probably the oldest continuously inhabited house in England, it provided the right degree of isolation to enable us to concentrate on the rather drastic changes we were discussing. In the morning session we went through all the changes, hinting rather strongly that RDG was on the way out. As soon as I explained that we were planning a campaign along the lines of Action for Jobs, my colleagues became enthusiastic. The simplification of over fifty programmes into six went down well. We broke for lunch.

After lunch Alan asked us if we fancied some exercise. He then took us on a climb along the ramparts of the castle. The wall was very crumbly and at one point we were all stuck on a rather narrow ledge. For a few, rather anxious moments I thought it would be more than careless to lose my entire Department at a stroke! Particularly if it included me!

When we recovered and reassembled, I went through the outline of a White Paper that we would issue in a few months. It would contain a full review of the entire Department. Furthermore, I said that I was working on a simple set of objectives for the Department and these would form the basis of the White Paper. We all broke up in a good mood, and I knew that I now had my colleagues with us.

The objectives were another story. I had used objectives in Employment but they were too long and in the end were ignored. Keith Joseph had provided senior officials with a long reading list when he first arrived in the Department of Industry in 1979, but that would not suit my purpose. The fight for hearts and minds was long over – there was little or no debate today about the need for privatisation or even the importance of wealth creation in the economy. I was out to do something simpler, yet far more difficult – change the very attitudes of departmental officials in the way they dealt with everyday matters, and a reading list would simply not go far enough down the Department. Besides, I wanted to say something to those outside the Department.

When Brian Hayes heard that I was working on a set of objectives, he offered to write one for me. When it arrived it reminded me of the objectives that I had had back in Employment – they were about five pages long and covered every activity of the Department, but did not give the message that I was trying to convey. I sat down to shorten them and still convey an enterprise message. That took days, and only gradually it began to fall into shape. Somehow the shorter the document the longer and harder it is to write.

The following Friday I was due to go on a visit to Rover and Land Rover. I finished there at 3.30 p.m. and Norman Dodds drove me back from Coventry to Graffham. I had taken a portable computer with me in the car and by the time I arrived home I had finally finished the objectives. They now covered one side of a sheet of paper.

The Objectives of the Department of Trade & Industry.

The needs and demands of society can only be met by increasing prosperity. The prime objective of the Department is to assist this process throughout the economy and to champion all the people who make it happen, rather than just individual sectors, industries or companies.

We work with business to promote best practice and within Government to create a climate that stimulates enterprise and reduces red tape.

Business flourishes in a competitive and open economy and we aim to secure this both at home and abroad. We will continue to promote the growth of international trade and work towards a single market within the European Community.

We seek to
– produce a more competitive market by encouraging competition and tackling restrictive practices, cartels and monopolies;
– secure a more efficient market by improving the provision of information to business about new methods and opportunities;
– create a larger market by privatisation and deregulation
– increase confidence in the working of markets by achieving a fair level of protection for their individual consumer and investor.

We will encourage the transfer of technologies and cooperative research. The spread of management education and the growth of links between schools and the world of work.

Our objective will be to produce a climate which promotes enterprise and prosperity. In all our work we will take account of differing circumstances of the regions and of the Inner Cities to enable those who live there to help themselves.

As the party conference season was almost on us I decided to postpone the launch of the objectives until we came back from Blackpool. I asked for plans to be prepared to give a copy to each and every member of the Department, and to have them put up in the entrance hall of all our buildings. I also arranged to speak to all members of the Department, Assistant Secretary and above, on the day of the launch, as I wanted to try to allay fears that were gaining momentum

250

as the weeks wore on about the extent of the reorganisation.

Early in October I minuted the Prime Minister about the single market. I said that when we considered our strategy for Europe with colleagues on 1 October there was strong agreement that we would plan positively for a genuine single market in Europe. I undertook to launch the campaign, and the initial focus would be on a one-day national conference at Lancaster House for next March. I asked the Prime Minister to make the opening speech. She accepted and we set about planning our campaign which I wanted to announce in my Conference speech.

One day, Peter (for he had already started) came in to see me looking more than concerned. He had just received some of the advance literature for the Conference. It was smothered with Action for Employment, Action for the Environment, Action for Inner Cities and, it seemed, action for almost everything. I was horrified, for I knew that this would, in turn, make the Action for Jobs campaign run by the Department of Employment appear political. During the election I had made absolutely sure that Action for Jobs was never used during the campaign. We protested immediately to Central Office, but to no avail. Norman Tebbit did not want to know. For the sake of using the slogan in a minor way during a minor Conference (for it was after the election not before), we threw away one of the best known slogans and the logo of the opening door. Before October was out, the Central Office of Information had ruled that the Department of Employment campaign would have to stop.

But I soon had other preoccupations. First there was the Conference speech itself. This was a victory Conference and the atmosphere would be good. I was no longer in a Department in the heart of the storm, and I knew that my debate would attract less attention than before. I was quite wrong, for before long *I* was in the centre of a storm and not my department.

Stories had started a few weeks before, first in political gossip columns, but later more widely, that opposition was building up to my becoming Chairman of the Party. It was hard to put a finger on it, but from time to time friends of mine would come to me and tell me that a whispering campaign had started. It was not too difficult to find out who was making trouble, but that did not get me very far. On the very day that the Conference started Gordon Greig in the *Daily Mail* led in big type on the front page 'Row over new Tory Chairman'. The story said that the Prime Minister wanted me but Norman was against. He also identified Willie Whitelaw and John Wakeham as being against.

251

In politics, when an attack becomes very personal it is expressed as a matter of principle. The new 'principle' that emerged was that I could not have both DTI and the chairmanship at the same time. In addition, they went on, I was unelected, so what did I know about elections? That Lord Carrington was Chairman of the Party, Secretary of State for Defence and a hereditary peer all at the same time went unnoticed. Rab Butler held even more jobs at one time, but that was irrelevant.

The Conference went well. When I first appeared on the platform I received a great cheer. I had forgotten how often I had been on television during the election and how much better known I had now become. The employment debate, where I sat on the platform next to the new Employment team, was a great success.

Unemployment had continued to go down, and although the heat had gone out of the debate, the Party knew what a help that had been during the last election. Action for Jobs received many tributes but as I listened to them I wondered how long it would still be there. Norman Fowler was very kind about me, with his characteristic generosity.

My own debate went off without incident. I was now a more practised performer at party conferences, although I would never be anything other than average. My debate, on the Thursday, was not as packed as in past years but I did receive a good standing ovation. I announced that I was going to lead a campaign to make the business community aware about 1992. I said that I had written that day to a select number of business leaders to advise me and the Department on areas of concern to business in the negotiations.

Then I became unashamedly chauvinistic. I told the conference that 'the sick man of Europe was well again' and finished

'When King Charles was lead to the scaffold, he said: "Liberty and freedom consists in having of Government those things by which the people's life and goods may be most their own."

All of us, all of us in our creative party can be proud that, for a third time, the people have entrusted us with the duty to continue to give back to them the life and goods that are rightfully their own.

Our native spirit of invention and enterprise is at work again. The industries of Britain are profitable again. The people are free again. Great Britain is Great again.'

That was not the end of my speaking, for I had been asked to give the Centre for Policy Studies' autumn address that evening.

The Centre had asked Keith Joseph to introduce me. Keith was very amusing and far too prophetic for my liking. 'David has now become a proper politician,' was his theme. 'In the past,' he went on, 'he was far too popular with his colleagues. Now he has got on and now he has enemies.' Everyone laughed, save Peter and I.

My lecture, typically upbeat, was called 'Britain Resurgent: a return to a wealth creating economy'. In it I announced that I had arranged that future referrals to the Monopolies and Mergers Commission for newspapers would take two months, rather than three. Only a short time before I had ensured that future references to the MMC would be dealt with in three months instead of six. (I had achieved this by the simple expedient of asking the retiring Chairman to do it. Perhaps he was slightly demob happy, but he agreed on the spot. When the new Chairman arrived, he had to live with it!) I thought, in my innocence, that bidders would be less likely to agitate for a non-referral, since the delay would now be quite reasonable. That turned out to be as likely as any taxpayer being satisfied with the level of income taxes, merely because they were lower than they once were.

Rather embarrassingly, I had been given a very kind profile by James Naughtie in *The Guardian* on the Thursday. That was the last for a very long time, for on the Friday the papers started in earnest. By the weekend there were stories on the front page of most papers. It was not too difficult to detect whose fingerprints were all over the place. On Saturday, the *Daily Mail* was all in favour of my becoming Chairman in its editorial, but an inside story, shared by all the papers, had 'Tebbit sticks knife into Young on Tory top job'. Norman had told Robin Day on television that there could be a conflict of interest if I continued at DTI and was also chief party fundraiser. His memory must have slipped for that moment, since Alistair McAlpine was the Treasurer, and the Chairman rarely had anything to do with fundraising.

The other papers were equally divided but by the Sunday the knives were out. *The Mail on Sunday* told the world 'Young goes for Triple Crown'. Evidently I wanted to be Deputy Prime Minister as well. *The Sunday Times* had 'Ministers gang up to stop Young becoming Chairman', naming John Wakeham as well as Willie Whitelaw. I decided to just grin and bear it for there was little that I could do. Lita and I had taken the weekend off and we continued walking in the Lake District. As soon as I had got over the Sunday papers we went for another long and cleansing walk over the fells.

Monday saw me back at DTI in time for lunch. The papers were still obsessed with the succession to the Chairmanship of the Party.

Although *The Times* came out strongly in my support, Anthony Bevins in *The Independent* again had the campaign against me being led by Norman Tebbit and supported by Willie Whitelaw and John Wakeham. I decided to go and see Willie and find out what he really thought. In the meantime, I had far more important matters to concentrate on.

That afternoon I spoke to senior officials in the Department again in the canteen. I said that we had come a long way since my arrival in June. The review was nearly ready an would be launched at the end of the year. In the meantime I was now circulating the objectives of the Department and the review would be based on them. I told them that for far too long we had been concerned with failure, with industrial disasters.

> 'I have been very fortunate in coming back to the Department when the climate of industry is completely changed.
>
> 'We now have very successful, thriving firms. Our job is therefore quite different. We have a contribution to keep industry moving forward and to offer a signpost for opportunities in new technologies.
>
> 'The economy is different. Industry is different. So our aims must be different.'

I could tell that little I said brought any great comfort to my officials. Those in the know, in fact only the members of the Central Unit, were quite relaxed but all the others were concerned with the future of their own part of the Department. My talk did accomplish something. *The Times* lead with a four column story detailing my talk with the Department. When I did launch the objectives on the following day, the coverage was not nearly as extensive. At least they were back to my work in the Department, and not about the succession to the Chairmanship. In fact the main comment in the press was that now I would become Chairman, although I would have to surrender some of my powers in the Department. This was something I was determined not to do. I had seen how Paul Channon had had to give up his authority in some City matters as a result of his membership of the Guinness family, and I was not going to follow suit. In terms of my personal priorities I had no doubts. I was now obsessed with the reorganisation of DTI and could think of little else than how best to accomplish it. If the Prime Minister asked me to become Chairman I would, but the job would only become important in two years' time. For the time being my priorities lay here.

Straight after my addressing the Department, WCRS came in to see me with the fruits of their labours. They took my decision not to rename the Department, but to call it the Department for Enterprise, very seriously. Their presentation focused on the Enterprise Initiative and Robin Wight sat there as we were going through the storyboard of a blockbuster commercial introducing the campaign, contributing a tremendous 'Woosh' as we came to the blue streak. They had done their homework well, for they showed us a mock up of a booklet that described all our programmes, now rationalised into specific schemes for design, export, advanced manufacturing technology, quality standards and marketing. They went further, and showed how we could introduce collaborative research and even our schools/industry links into the booklet.

I approved the programme and agreed a tight timetable with them. They would present creative work by the beginning of November, we would agree it by 9 November, finish the artwork by 14 December, and then complete the commercial ready for the launch in the week commencing 18 January.

The following day I called in to see Willie. He had no quarrel with my becoming Chairman but he said I could not hold both jobs at the same time. He told me that, if asked, that is how he would advise the Prime Minister. My reminders about Peter Carrington were to no avail. He told me that times had changed. I did tell him that I thought that my place was at DTI, now that I had started on my review.

I put all this behind me, for I was off on my fourth trade mission to China. In order to leave after Cabinet on the Thursday we flew to Frankfurt and changed planes to Beijing. We all thought the flight rather bumpy at the beginning. Whilst we were flying, the hurricane struck Southern England and devastated whole areas, including my precious Graffham.

I arrived in Beijing on the Friday, just at the start of the 13th Party Congress. I had a long meeting with Zhao Ziang on the Monday morning. During the course of the meeting he told me that when we finished, he was to open the Congress. They were about to rewrite socialism, he told me, to a socialism based on the market. I wondered when I heard this how much would actually be left of socialism at the rate that everything was changing in China.

Once we had left Beijing on the Tuesday morning we were cut off from all news. I always took a powerful short-wave radio with me and all the time we were in Shaanxi province I would dash back to my room to hear the latest news bulletin. The stock markets of the whole world seemed to have collapsed on the Monday. All the BBC would tell us was that the market had dropped 200 points, or risen 120 points without telling us what level it had actually reached. Here I was, with responsibility for the conduct of the markets, and totally out of reach. We decided that if I cut my trip short people would really worry, so I had to wait until we reached Tokyo to find out where we were. I did hear one reference to the Chairmanship and that was a rather ominous reference to a smear.

During my visits to the provinces we visited Xian and saw the terracotta warriors. The sheer scale of the excavations was amazing. It was far larger than anything I had seen previously and they were sensibly keeping large areas for future generations to excavate. On a more serious note our trade prospects in China were improving. There was no doubt that by now I had become well known in China, almost achieving the status of 'old friend'.

When I came back I found that matters had taken a rather nasty turn. During the Party Conference I had been told once or twice that the word being put out was against my origins rather than my policies. I dismissed it out of hand, for I knew Norman as well as anyone and that was the very last thing that he would either say or countenance. That did not necessarily apply to others, for over the weekend I was away, the papers reported 'a crude political smear' over a long-standing acquaintance between Gerald Ronson (who had just been arrested in the Guinness case) and me. If the opposition was prepared to descend to those levels, I felt that I had nothing to fear.

There was a far more serious problem. During my time in China I had thought through my position and I was quite certain that DTI was more important to me, at least for the next two years. I could only reorganise the Department if I had full authority and although all the papers were reporting my victory in the Chairmanship race, I had already made up my mind to withdraw. I thought that I knew where my duty lay. I was convinced that the changes that I had dreamed about since 1979 in the Department of Industry could only come about if I was there in full charge. When that was done, then I could turn my attention to other matters. The only real effect the opposition had over their long campaign was to ensure that, in future, the Chairman could no longer hold a full departmental appointment as well.

On the Tuesday I started to hear of interviews that friends of mine had given to ITN and BBC in preparation for programmes on the Friday when the announcement was due. I then heard confirmation that I would have to surrender authority over mergers, and perhaps all City matters, to Kenneth. On the Wednesday afternoon

I asked Peter Luff to let it be known that I no longer considered myself available. A few phone calls and the job was done.

The Prime Minister was furious, it was said. Quite right, so I thought, for I had not consulted her. The papers read far more into my decision. They saw it as a victory for the old guard against the new. They also said that my relationship with the Prime Minister would be permanently soured. When I read that on the Friday morning, I made up my mind on the spot. I waited until it was 7.30 a.m. and telephoned the Prime Minister. She was suitably icy and told me in no uncertain terms that I should have consulted her first. However, when I put the phone down the ice was broken.

That was not where it all ended. The poison that had been spread about during this rather unsavoury period affected my standing in the Party. From then on I would always read about my unbridled ambition, extending on more than one occasion to the Leadership of the Lords itself. I could not help smiling when I read that one, for I still did not know my way around the House and my knowledge of the procedures and the people were rudimentary to say the least. I was, and remain to this day, ambitious, but not in the way my critics implied.

After all the excitement, it was back into the Department and on with the changes. I met with Brian Hayes and a number of my senior people and agreed that a new Advisory Services division should be created, and that the Department should adopt a more horizontal structure. I wanted to get rid of sponsorship since I was convinced, on good evidence from my friends in industry and commerce, that our officials who would spend three years with a particular industry before moving on would rapidly become the creature of the respective Trade Association. The last thing we needed were our people acting as a conduit for more claims on tax-payers' money. In a slightly wicked moment, I suggested in an interview that our officials should stop being taken out for lunch by all the associations.

I confirmed the basic concept of one national advisory scheme, with different grant levels for the regions. By bringing together all the miscellaneous other programmes we ran we could have some £78 million for the first year, £124 million and £150 million for the next two years. This would include promotion costs, but I was convinced that promotion was part of the programme; for if as a result of watching the commercials, smaller businessmen decided to take consultancy advice without our subsidy, that was even better. We then agreed an upper limit for firms with 500 employees, innovation grants of 50 per cent to firms with fewer than twenty-five

257

employees, higher grants for the regions. Once these details were settled, we got down to making the programme work. I remembered my own time in building up a small business and decided that we would insist on a first business audit before any applicant would be approved. We would need to recruit about 500 senior industrialists, to be called Enterprise Councellors, and I wrote to the top fifty firms in the country seeking candidates. We set up an in-depth monitoring of the scheme to assess the effectiveness of the Enterprise Councellors and of the scheme.

We agreed that DTI should adopt a recognised house style, including coordinated advertising. We were now getting nearer to the launch and I authorised Brian Hayes to discuss the changes with Under Secretaries and above, and I agreed to speak to the Regional Directors.

In the middle of the month I went back to Consett. The last time I had been there was just after the closure of the Steel Mill when the place was full of doom and gloom. The difference between then and now told in microcosm the tale of the last decade. Where there had once been one major employer, and that had closed, now there were over one hundred and forty small and growing businesses, a great tribute to the Derwentside Industrial Development Agency. One of these new employers would figure prominently in our commercial for the Enterprise Initiative. Another, one that I had come along to visit, manufactured over 10 per cent of the nappies used in the country. During my visit I was being shown around the monster machines engaged in producing disposable nappies by the mile by the Chief Executive. On the way round, he was telling me about a new super efficient machine they had just installed. As we got near to it, I could see out of the corner of my eye something go wrong and a stream of absorbent material go shooting up to the roof. Without breaking either his sentence or his stride, my host steered me away from the scene and I never did get to see his latest marvel.

Just as remarkable as the changed employment scene was the change in attitude of everyone that I met there. This really had become a 'can do' town, and they all knew that never again would they be faced with mass unemployment by the closure of just one employer. I returned to London feeling that much of what we had done was really worth while.

The following week Wolff Olins came in with the new headed paper and the logo of DTI, which were both approved. The White Paper was now taking shape. We had decided that we would amplify the 239 words of the objectives and the White Paper, '*DTI, the Department for Enterprise*', would bring together all our changes and explain them against the objectives. We would once again have a 'pop version', and I started a series of weekly meetings with my senior officials to check up on progress against a critical path I prepared for the launch. By 11 December we had the revised pop version for approval, the press advertising and the details of the launchings around the country. On the 16th I made a film in my office which would be used to introduced the White Paper to our officials. By the 17th we were ready to sign off on the White Paper and the draft statement for the House. Then such details as agreeing the voice for the commercials and the arrangements for the presentation to the Department and the recruiting of the Enterprise Counsellors were finally agreed. All was ready for the big launch before Christmas and we could go away in good heart.

The changes went so much to the heart of the work of the Department that I was determined that all 12,500 of our officials would hear about them at the same time. The earliest that could be was the moment I got to my feet in the Lords. At 3.30 p.m., on the day before the launch, I spoke to some 250 briefers, generally between Principal and Under Secretary grade back in the canteen at 1 Victoria Street. I explained the changes we were about to make. The relief when the news was finally out was apparent to all. Of course, the changes that went beyond organisational ones were kept for the House on the following day.

The next day came and with it the launch of the new Department. The moment I got to my feet in the Lords over two hundred and fifty meetings started, all around the country, taking all my officials in small groups through the changes. After a lead in by the briefer, a short video would be played including the new 80-second video that launched the Enterprise Initiative and the new logo. This was the commercial that talked about a new force behind British business – 'it's the Enterprise Initiative from the DTI.' It showed three case studies from companies that had been helped to grow by the use of consultants subsidised by DTI. We would then cover the changes to policies, to services and the new approach of the Department. Then they would go into more detail about the local effects.

Whilst all this was going on, I was on my feet in the Lords making my statement. I pointed out that the review was conducted in the light of the objectives published last October. That in an economy of over £400 billion, the main role of the DTI with its budget of £1 billion must be to influence attitudes. I said that the DTI would be a catalyst for enterprise, innovation and change. Contrary to my officials' fears, the news of the abolition of the Regional Development Grant was taken calmly. In fact, apart from one or two predictable opponents in our House, there was hardly any opposition. The changes we made to innovation, taking away single company grants and concentrating our resources to encourage Universities and industry to collaborate, the simplification of all our schemes, was accepted, even by our opponents. In the Commons there was a knee jerk reaction from Tony Blair and Donald Dewar. Their initial opposition to the abolition of Regional Development Grants contained more light than heat and little more was made of it. Surprisingly, Norman Tebbit came out against it, although that opposition also died away.

Even the press conference afterwards went well. I watched the *Seven O'clock News*. There in the first interval was our first Enterprise Initiative commercial. The papers next day were full of it. It made extensive coverage on the front pages of all the heavies. There was something there for all. Some concentrated on the schools/ industry links. We were going to ensure that all schoolchildren would have at least two weeks in industry or commerce before they left school. Furthermore, we were going to give 10 per cent of teachers each year experience of industry. I was determined to change the attitude of some teachers, once graphically described to me by Sam Toy of Ford. He was walking along the line in Dagenham when he saw a party of primary school children with their teacher ahead of him. Just as he drew level he heard the teacher say, 'See class, see what will happen to you if you don't work at your lessons.'

Other papers were attracted by the boost given to competition policy. The Tebbit rules, that mergers would be judged on competition grounds, were restated and the increased authority to the Director General of the Office of Fair Trading went down well, as did the promise of a Restrictive Trade Practices Green Paper in the future. The abolition of the Regional Development Grant was criticised in some quarters, but mainly because they thought that we were moving over to selective assistance. We were not, just leaving the existing selective scheme in place.

There was still a great deal to be done. Overnight the new signs went up on all DTI buildings. The new headed notepaper came into use and any member of the public telephoning the Department could not fail to notice the customer care training that I had insisted should be taken by over two hundred officials who dealt directly with the public. At 9.00 a.m. I was at the Barbican cinema to brief those from the CBI, the Institute of Directors, the Association of British Chambers of Commerce, the Institute of Marketing, the Design Council and the clearing banks. They would all be engaged in spreading the word about the Enterprise Initiative. Meanwhile, around the country, in Newcastle, Manchester, Birmingham, Leeds, Nottingham, Bristol and Cardiff, Francis Maude, Robert Atkins, John Butcher and the Regional Directors – with Peter Walker in Wales – would be meeting to brief the local contractors, those who would be managing the programme.

In the first week after the launch we had 9,700 enquiries, in the second 7,600, in the third 7,900. By the beginning of the programme proper, in April, we had applications for nearly 100,000 copies of the booklet and sufficient applications approved to keep to our target of 1,000 consultancies a month. Long before that, we had recruited our 500 Enterprise Councellors.

In February, the COI told us that we would have to go out to tender (which could include WCRS) for the new single market campaign. They recommended a short list. The brief went out on 10 February to be returned in two and a half weeks.

The brief said it all. 'The DTI wishes to appoint an agency to advise on and develop paid advertising support for a major campaign to ensure that the UK public and British businesses are aware of and prepare themselves for the completion of the single market in the European Community by the end of 1992.'

The campaign was to use the phrase 'Europe – Open for Business' and a special logo linking with the Department's current Enterprise Initiative campaign. A brochure on the single market was to be mailed, in mid-March, to some 130,000 businesses working with a telephone hot line. Our major launch conference at Lancaster House on 18 April would be followed by a series of twenty single market breakfasts around the country.

In the meantime, WCRS, who had been very anxious to get the work, had recorded three radio commercials for the single market campaign. They were only a qualified success. They were an effort to introduce humour, but occasionally the humour backfired and after a while we dropped them.

To everyone's surprise WCRS were not the winner. The best by a long way was D'Arcy Masius Benton Bowles (DMB&B), with a campaign that used television to let successful individuals sell the idea of the single market. They produced a dummy commercial using Bruce Oldfield, the dress designer. What I liked about their concept was that they were selling success. The Enterprise Initiative was about selling successful companies, this time it was about successful individuals.

Immediately after they were awarded the contract we met with them. I agreed that we would aim to have some six to eight people to participate in the commercials. I approached Alan Sugar, Richard

261

Rogers, John Harvey Jones, John Egan and Richard Branson. They all agreed immediately to my call. Richard Branson and Alan Sugar rewrote their scripts to their own liking. As they were both supreme marketeers, I accepted some of their changes.

The advertising campaign would use the logo and the DTI blue 'whoosh' of the Enterprise Initiative. They remade the mock advert with Bruce Oldfield for the programme.

We had to get formal approval for the programme from the Treasury. Of course, none of this was in our original spending round. The Treasury were not keen and after some difficulty I got grudging acceptance to the initial costs of the campaign (that is some £5 million). We decided to include Sophie Mirman of the Sock Shop, and on a second campaign from the second or third week in June into mid-July. I also asked the agency to prepare the commercials so they could be cut down to ten or twenty second clips.

John Harvey Jones sounded like a history professor. He said, 'If this sounds like a history lesson, I make no apologies. Because history is in the making. By the end of 1992 this country will be a key member of Europe's single market. Trade, as ever, leading the way. Trade has dominated British life for centuries. Trade inspired the great explorers of Elizabeth I's time, and fuelled the growth of industry under Victoria. Today exports represent almost a third of our national income.

'Now trade is also the key to British success in the Single Market. At ICI we started planning for 1992 in 1972. From then on, we only ever looked at Europe as an entity, not as individual markets. Now everyone in business needs to know how the coming changes will affect them. There is a phone line to ring to start you thinking about trading with Athens or Copenhagen as well as with Worthing or Aberdeen.

'Make no mistake. Europe is open for business.'

Later that month, in announcing the start of the 1992 campaign I said, 'Last autumn only 15 per cent were aware of the significance of 1992. My aim is to get the figure to more than 90 per cent by the end of the year.'

We started on 18 March with our single market campaign brochure being mailed to over 135,000 businesses. Our Lancaster House conference opened on 18 April, attended by 200 top businessmen. I met the Prime Minister and before we went in I showed her the new Spearhead database. This was a database which any member of the public could dial up to give details, continuously updated, of all single-market rules and regulations. At my insistence, it contained the names and telephone numbers of civil servants across all Whitehall for further information.

The Prime Minister spoke to a packed house, this time not using a teleprompter. After her speech she spent a few minutes with Jacques Delors and left. Jacques Delors and I spoke before the interval. We were both due to use a teleprompter. By chance, I noticed that Delors did not use it so I took a draft of my speech with me. When I got to the podium I saw with horror that the teleprompter was on the blink and useless. I used my rough typed copy. When I saw the recording afterwards it looked as if nothing untoward had happened.

When I said goodbye to Jacques Delors I told him that we would be negotiating seriously on 1992. I said, 'There are just two fundamental pre-conditions,' and he looked at me with great attention. I said, 'First, of course, all cars should drive on the left and, secondly, English should be the common language.' He looked startled for a moment, until he remembered the English sense of humour.

After the coffee interval the conference continued. Peter Hobday was the presenter and the penellists were Lynda Chalker, Sir David Scholey, Peter Bonfield and Sir John Hoskyns. After lunch we repeated the conference using video recordings for peers, MPs and other politicians. We showed highlights of the morning's speeches. I introduced the TV advertisements, the campaign video and excerpts from the '*1992 – What's That*' video and then we had a question and answer session. We had absolutely tremendous coverage on all radio and television and it could not have been a better launch. Afterwards, my people estimated that the coverage would have cost over £1.7 million if we had had to pay for it.

The campaign then started in earnest and seemed to catch the imagination of the nation. We took the message around the country through a series of ministerially-led single market breakfasts at twenty major centres. Each time, there was extensive coverage on local radio and television. At first the media were dismissive, in the traditional way they greet any new innovation. I was told that Sir David English, the Editor of the *Daily Mail*, was hostile to the whole concept, so I gave him lunch. By the time we had finished he was such an enthusiast for the Single Market that he continually criticised the Government for not going fast enough! Within a few weeks the mood of all the papers changed and we seemed to have caught the tide of public opinion. Soon it seemed that every programme on television was explaining what was going to happen. *News at Ten* gave seven minutes every night for an entire week. We could not even calculate the real value of that.

My target, which had seemed so difficult at the beginning of the year, was achieved with ease. Later the National Audit Office were to look at the campaign. They found that the first phase, of attaining 90 per cent awareness within nine months was achieved in four! Conversion of awareness into further action was happening; the CBI found that 70 per cent of the firms surveyed were taking some form of action and a later, rather bigger survey by my department found that for firms of over 250 employees that figure was correct. The CBI, in May 1989, arrived at a broadly similar figure. I received my due reward at the end of the year. *Private Eye* pondered over the matter and at Christmas, made me, Lord Suit, the 1988 Bore of the Year for my single market campaign. I could have asked for nothing more.

All this worked wonders for my Department. For a time we were no longer the 'Department of Disasters', always in trouble. Now we had a positive image, and were out there actually doing things and what is more, knew what we had to do. Each April the Department would advertise for a few places for new entrants in the London area. We normally we would get twenty or so applications – this April we received over 1,200! Such is the power, not of advertising, but of a positive image. If only DTI was simply concerned with making things happen! Alas, it is also concerned with stopping things, for it is also the Department of Regulation. That is a whole different story.

Chapter 18
THE RIGOURS OF REGULATION

I was quite at home with the Industry side of the Department. I had been away five years but little had really changed. I was far from comfortable with the Trade side. First, I suffered from culture shock. All the instincts of the Industry people were in favour of protection. I used to enjoy arguing with them. Not so with Trade. Here they were for competition with a vengeance. I sometimes found that, now, I was the protectionist! But Trade was not just about trading between nations, which I came to enjoy, but about regulation.

At the beginning I spent little time on pure trade matters. Alan Clark was my Minister for Trade and had been in the post when we arrived. I knew him well from our Employment days together, and I had every confidence in him. Somewhere ahead of us was the Uruguay meeting of GATT, the next negotiating round of the General Agreement on Tariffs and Trade. This was monumentally boring but undeniably important. Happily, my input could be left until some time the next year. I agreed to undertake Trade visits but my priorities were other areas, at least for the first year.

Francis Maude had drawn the short straw and had responsibility for most of the regulatory matters, particularly the City of London. Merger decisions would be mine, and mine alone, as a result of the way the law operated. I would receive the advice of the Director General of Fair Trading and then make up my mind. Indeed, this was the only time during my whole period in Government that I had any personal power. I consulted none of my colleagues, indeed only listened to them in the presence of my civil servants. When I had made up my mind I announced it. That way the blame could be all mine.

When I arrived, all was not well in the City. The Financial Services Act had gone through both houses before the election in a very different financial environment. The Guinness case had been in all the headlines during the passage of the Bill and as a result of

Commons pressure, the legislation ended up far more regulatory than had first been intended. Based on self-regulation, it was supposed to be a flexible, lightly-regulated system administered by the SIB, the Securities & Investments Board, under whom were a series of self-regulating organisations. Each SRO would be established for a different section of the financial services industry, with their own board, including practitioners, to ensure that the systems would be workable. All fine in theory; but it did not work out that way.

The trouble started when the SIB issued the draft rules. These first astounded, then infuriated, vocal sections of the City.

There were reasons for the complexity of the rules, partly stemming from the legal liability faced by practitioners but partly, I suspected, from the over-involvement of the legal profession.

I would have meeting after meeting with delegations from interested parties from the industry who told me that the end of the world was nigh, that the City would become a desert. Just when I would become too depressed, I would meet with American bankers in London, who would tell me that what we were contemplating was nothing compared with what they had to put up with at home.

The City was one of those grey areas in Government. The Treasury had long had responsibility for the banks, which they supervised through the Bank of England. We had responsibility for financial services. The difficulty was that financial services companies were now acting as bankers and the banks, who now often owned the old merchant banks and stockbrokers as well, had started to act as financial services companies.

Whether matters were as bad as our critics would have or not, something obviously had to be done. By chance the term of the Chairman came to an end and a new one would have an opportunity to make a fresh start. Sir Kenneth Berrill had been a very distinguished first Chairman, but it would have been very difficult, if not impossible, for him to simplify the new system. As a compromise during the passage of the Bill, it had been agreed that the responsibility for the appointment of the Chairman of the SIB would be shared with the Governor of the Bank of England. Naturally, both our sets of officials had their favourite candidate. In the end, I met with Robin Leigh-Pemberton and agreed with him to appoint David Walker, who up to then had been part of the bank, and knew the City well. Within a few days of his appointment, the complaints began to die down. He reworked the rules based on general principles, and although there are still some critics, the new system has been accepted.

It is ironic that although I came into Government to be the great deregulator, my legacy will include a vastly increased system of regulations. The more a Government professes to be non-interventionist, the more it has to intervene. This marks the difference between a *laissez faire* system and open markets. Open markets are controlled markets, with all the controls that are necessary to create a competitive economy. A free-for-all would inevitably lead to the growth of monopolies. My job was to ensure the growth of competition. This was invariably unpopular with the managements of companies, for the real beneficiary would be, not them, but the ultimate consumer.

We have had the structure of the Monopolies and Mergers Commission in place since the early sixties. For many years the system was operated on a fairly haphazard basis, but Norman Tebbit, during his period of office, announced that in future competition would, in the main, be the overriding basis for judging mergers. I was to find that the definition of competition, and the market in which such competition would be judged, would cause almost as much confusion in the minds of practitioners as had existed before.

The period after the election turned out to be a comparatively quiet time for bids and mergers. Then British Airways bid for British Caledonian, and that woke everyone up. I knew BCal of old, since Stuart had been an outside Director for many years, and I knew Sir Adam Thomson, the Chairman, almost as well as I knew John King (Lord King of Wartnaby) of British Airways. All bids which involve more than 25 per cent of the market or £30 million are looked at first by the Director General of Fair Trading, Sir Gordon Borrie. I had little to do until I received his advice on whether or not to refer the bid. But everyone else also offered me very good, but invariably contradictory, advice. The papers were full, day after day, either for or against the merger. One of the independent airlines even took a series of full page advertisements in the papers consisting of a letter to me, again offering good advice. I replied on the radio, saying that it would have saved them some money if only they posted the letter, but they should really direct their efforts to Sir Gordon Borrie.

July came and I went away with Lita for a short break to Bayreuth. Whilst I was away I heard that the advice was in, and we returned to London. The advice was unequivocal. I should refer the merger to the MMC. I was only in London for a day and a half, and that was pretty packed, briefing all the advertising agencies who were busy competing for our new programme. I decided on a novel course of action.

The usual practice in all merger matters is to announce the decision at 9 o'clock in the morning, before the market opens. There had been so much public discussion that I wanted to be sure that it was presented in the right way. I wanted to tell the parties myself, and let them digest the news, before they saw the press. Under the present system, they might first learn of my decision from a phone call from a journalist, and an incautious word might really set the fur flying. My Department was slightly horrified at my proposal. It had never happened, and that was reason enough. The existing practice was to let the decision speak for itself. I knew that that was part of the reason why the Department was always in trouble. If you let your political opponents have the first word (and in mergers our opponents were as much on our side of the House as theirs, although our people would vary from deal to deal and theirs would be consistently against), it is very difficult to get the advantage back.

We let it be known that I had sent for both parties at 5 o'clock.

I came back from the last meeting with the agencies to find a crowd of press and television reporters in the forecourt outside the offices. At 5 o'clock precisely, John King and Adam Thomson were shown into my room. I told them of my decision to refer. At this Adam Thomson looked far more cheerful, until I went on to say that the MMC had been asked to report back in the new time-scale, in just three months. Then John King brightened up. We spent a few more minutes chatting and they went downstairs and met the press. Their comments were now far more restrained than before, and all the heat went out of the debate almost overnight.

Now a new element entered the equation. It had been argued that the European Commission had no place in merger policy. It was thought, up to the early summer, that Article 85 and 86 of the Treaty of Rome did not give the Commission jurisdiction in these matters. A recent decision of the European Court of Justice found otherwise. We heard that Peter Sutherland, the Competition Commissioner in Brussels, had decided that this merger of two airlines had implications across the Community, not just the United Kingdom. In these circumstances he would wish to examine the case, but he would leave it until I had decided.

I received the decision of the MMC a day or two before the end of the period, in November. We followed the new procedure, and I invited John King and Adam Thomson in to see me at 9 o'clock on Wednesday morning, 11 November. That was as good as inviting the press, and they were all waiting outside the office and I gave them a cheery wave, but nothing more, when I arrived in the morning. Adam Thomson and John King came into my office on the dot of 9.00 a.m. I told them that the Monopolies and Mergers Commission

had found that the merger did not operate against the public interest
and the merger would be allowed, on certain conditions.

The actual decision was not an effective one, not because of the
merits of the case, but in the manner it was given. In giving their
evidence, BA had offered certain concessions, and those concessions had been accepted by the MMC and were contained in their
report and recommendations. The difficulty was that they found
that the merger did not operate against the public interest if certain
conditions were met. I had to let it through, without being able to
put any enforceable conditions on my decision. If the MMC had
said that it was against the public interest, but if certain things were
done, it would be all right, then I could apply legally enforceable
conditions. However, all was well, for I told John King that, if he
did not carry out his concessions in full, he would run the risk of a
full monopolies reference. In many ways that was the most strin-
gent penalty I had – for a full reference would often tie up senior
management for well over a year.

The merger went through, although there was another flurry of
publicity when Peter Sutherland decided in due course to extract
further concessions from BA relating to European flights. As a
result of this case, it became clear that some of our sovereignty on
mergers had transferred to Brussels, and gradually we began to
consider the proper relationship between domestic and European
mergers.

The lessons of this bid were not lost on us. We plugged the gap
shown up by the BA/BCal merger. In the following March we issued
a Blue Paper (a discussion document) on merger control. In future,
the parties would be able to give undertakings to divest to the Secretary of State which would be statutorily enforceable. This would
mean that where a fairly simple set of changes would remove any
detriment to competition, we would be able to save the parties a refer-
nce to the MMC. We also introduced a new formal, but voluntary,
procedure for pre-notifying mergers. If companies followed the new
procedure they would generally get clearance within four weeks.

Europe loomed large on the take-over front during 1988. I had
already started on our 1992 campaign, and one result was that all the
commentators wanted to know how the changing scene in Europe
would affect merger policy. The last stance that I wanted to take was
a protectionist one, although there was a strong movement within the
CBI to increase protection for existing boards from takeovers. I
thought that this was no more than special pleading – Chairmen and
boards of existing companies wanting to protect their jobs. I little
thought that I would be put to the test so completely or so quickly.

Tuesday 12 April was a fine spring day. That evening we had been invited to the state banquet for the King of Norway. It was to be held at Windsor, and would be the last banquet there for at least six years, as it was closing for rewiring. The day started with breakfast with Geoffrey Howe at 1 Carlton Gardens (we were still discussing my plans for export help), and then into 1 Victoria Street for 'morning prayers' with my ministers. That had hardly finished when my Private Office brought me in a note. Jacob Suchard, the Swiss confectionary group, had gone into the market early that morning and acquired a 14.9 per cent stake in Rowntrees in a dawn raid. The first shot in the Chocolate War of 1988 had been fired.

There had been rumblings for some time. General Cinema Corporation, a US Company operating in cinema ownership and soft drinks, had acquired 8.5 per cent of the shares in Cadbury Schweppes plc some fifteen months before. They had raised their holding to 18.2 per cent the previous November. No one knew what their intentions were, but the board of Cadbury feared the worst.

Their intentions were to remain unknown for a little longer. In the meantime an outside observer would have formed the impression that chocolate was a strategic raw material. The supporters of Rowntrees went into action and the popular press saw the issue in very clear terms – our Smarties were in peril.

Exactly two weeks later there were two, almost simultaneous developments. Nestlé, the Swiss international food group, announced a £2.1 billion takeover bid for Rowntrees. That did put the fat in the fire, and in all the fuss people hardly noticed that General Cinema announced that it should no longer be regarded as a 'passive investor' in Cadbury Schweppes.

Now campaigns started in earnest. A 'Save Kit Kat' campaign swung into action. Television showed interviews with workers in York fearful for their jobs. Early day motions from both parties were set down and attracted many signatures. The temperature heightened when in early May I referred the holding of the Kuwait Investment office in BP to the Monopolies and Mergers Commission. That was for quite another reason, but the supporters of Rowntrees were quick to latch on to any reason to support a referral. That day, Suchard went into the market and bought more shares taking its stake up to 21 per cent. I knew the issue was really heating up when Michael Heseltine jumped in with both feet, and wrote me an open letter. He said, 'it's like playing Snakes and Ladders with a competitor who habitually goes down the snakes and up the ladders'. All very picturesque, but what he meant was that if Rowntrees could not buy Nestlé, as they had shares that the Board

270

could refuse to register if owned by a hostile shareholder, then why should Nestlé be allowed to buy Rowntrees?

If only all issues were as simple as that. The position was that there was nothing in Swiss law that made takeovers impossible, but companies with the consent of their shareholders could make it virtually impossible. That was exactly the same in British law, and some of our largest companies were in a similar position. Trust House Forte had been trying for years to take over the Savoy, and could not even when they owned over 70 per cent of the non-voting shares. Even THF had their voting shares held in a trust, and it was thought that they were immune from a bid. But there was a much more fundamental point than that. At this time we were the second largest overseas investor in the world, the largest if you considered only equity. If we led the way by becoming protective, then we could expect retaliation on a massive scale.

In the meantime, Suchard continued to increase their holding to 29.9 per cent, but had still not made a bid. Nestlé had gone into the market and the two Swiss companies held between them over 40 per cent of the shares in Rowntree. Gordon Borrie was considering all the bids, and until he reported to me there was little I could do. Of course, there was no end of advice, generally proffered to me when it should have been offered to Gordon Borrie. I decided, on advice, not to refer the holding of General Cinema in Cadbury and then sat back to await the advice on both holdings in Rowntrees.

The next day MPs arrived back at Westminster to find boxes of Rowntrees Quality Street waiting for them. Over eighty had by now put their names down on an Early Day Motion. Labour's spokesman, Tony Blair, was talking, rather hysterically I thought, about tens of thousand of jobs being at stake. A great deal was being made of our new status in Europe, as if that would change effective competition at home.

Sir Gordon Borrie's report came in. There were no competition grounds worth considering. Nestlé and Rowntree combined were still smaller than Cadbury Schweppes. There were no real grounds on reciprocity. I decided not to refer the bid. There was an immediate burst of outrage. In the House all the predictable things were said. The Opposition claimed that I had put thousands of jobs at risk. I replied, as I usually did, that no Government could ever give a guarantee on jobs, only customers could. In the Commons, Kenneth was immersed in a similar stream of old arguments.

The television news that evening was full of pictures of workers in York about to be made jobless in the event of a takeover. The next day the leader in the *Daily Telegraph* was headed 'Courageous decision', and that worried me greatly. In the language of *Yes, Minister*, a courageous decision is a foolhardy one; but in fact I was relieved to find that the leader writer was very much in favour, as were all the serious press. I had argued the previous day that in a period of massive investment overseas we should be the last country to forbid inward investment, and that argument seemed to have been accepted.

From then on the story figured prominently in the financial pages of the papers. In the end Nestlé won, and Suchard retired hurt nursing a considerable profit. In years to come, Nestlé was to put their world headquarters for chocolate in York. None of the dire events predicted by all the opponents of the bid came to pass, and even Mr Dixon, the head of Rowntrees, ended up on the Nestlé board. The decision had sent a strong clear signal to all British companies. We were not going to protect them from an overseas bid. That was their job, and to do that they had better make sure that they keep the shareholders happy. Of course, if there were special grounds, then that would be different.

The 'special grounds' had led me to refer the holding of nearly 23 per cent by the Kuwait Investment Office in BP. The KIO had been very welcome investors after the sale of the Government's holding in BP had gone very seriously wrong after the stock market crash of the previous October. They had then held some 17 per cent, but despite repeated messages to the contrary, they had continued to buy more and more shares until they had reached their present holding. The KIO was not a separate entity, they were part of the Government of Kuwait, and Kuwait was a leading member of OPEC. If there was one thing that the British Government did not stand for, it was cartels. This time there was considerable criticism of my decision, often by many in the City who, I suspected, either did much business with the KIO or who wanted to.

Then, almost out of the blue, I became immersed in another situation, but this time one of far greater difficulty and complexity. Barlow Clowes first came to the Department's attention in 1975/6 when they were told by the Department that they did not require a licence to act as investment advisors. That was probably wrong advice, but if they had applied they would, according to the practice of the time based upon 1939 legislation, have received it. In any event, the Department did receive an auditor's report from Spicer and Pegler in July 1985 verifying clients' funds at the end of 1984 as evidenced by the books and records of Barlow Clowes.

From then onwards, there was a long tale of intermittent contact by the Department and occasional unofficial warnings about the conduct of the business. By 1987 suspicions were seriously aroused, but the Department had precious few powers, save that of refusing a licence, which would probably have brought everything down. The receipt of information from the Stock Exchange enabled Francis Maude to appoint Investigators and their report eventually came in the following April. By then the facts were clear and new powers became available under the Financial Services Act. On the very first day, 23 May (by chance the very day that Gordon Borrie reported to me on Rowntrees), the SIB, operating through powers delegated by me, served a notice on the company prohibiting it from carrying on business. Shortly after that, the company was wound up.

I do not want to go into details, for it is still sub judice, but there developed a tremendous political row over the Department's handling of the events of the last thirteen years. It started with the only note of comedy in the whole affair. Soon after the notice had been served, a Member of Parliament telephoned Francis Maude's office demanding to know why we were bullying a perfectly respectable constituent of his. A few hours later, he found out the full ramifications of the affair and from that moment onwards led a vociferous campaign against his constituent, and the Government.

For the facts were heartrending. Over 13,000 individuals, mainly unsophisticated retirees, had invested their nest eggs with the company on the promise of 'gilt' edged investments yielding above normal rates of interest. Then it came to light that there was a Gibraltar-based associate company who had never advertised in this country (save once in a special edition of *The Times*, who were leading the campaign against the Department), and were thus unknown to the Department.

Substantial funds had been transferred there, often without the knowledge or consent of the investor. Every night I would have in my boxes up to two hundred letters from MPs or ordinary investors, and the tales they told were pitiful. Many had cashed in their houses and pensions, invested all in Barlow Clowes, and gone to live in Spain. Teachers, nurses, public servants of all description, were caught. I was told, quietly, that the company had on at least one occasion gone into the DHSS and lectured their retiring civil servants on ways to invest their nest eggs. There were intermediaries, agents, who had recommended this investment, some of whom also immediately folded. One or two of the respectable intermediaries did refund their clients' investments in due course.

Every day more and more cases came to light, and the figures grew and grew. One day, at one of our ministerial lunches the whole

273

topic was the reaction of the Commons. I had no idea that so much heat was being engendered by this matter, which was very much constituency based. I made arrangements to meet as many of our backbenchers as possible for drinks in my room. Some were sympathetic with our point of view, but many were frankly hostile. For the first time I began to realise what a disadvantage I suffered from by my exclusion from the Commons.

The reason for our tardiness was not difficult to understand, but almost impossible to get anyone to accept in the heat of the moment. If the Government simply paid out for losses on a voluntary basis, even if there was failure on their part, then there would be no end to their liabilities. It went even further than that. In the end bad money would drive out good. Why invest with a prudent concern that pays a market rate of interest if you can invest with impunity with an imprudent concern that pays more and know that at the end of the day, should all fail, your benevolent Government will pay you back? Nowhere was that more evident than in the United States, where guarantees for the Savings & Loans movement ended up costing the Federal Government over $400 billion. The only practical answer was to let them sue us, and if we were found liable by the Courts, then we could pay knowing that the decision was ring-fenced. The other alternative was the Ombudsman, the Parliamentary Commissioner for Administration.

I had to do something, for the pressure became more and more intense. In the second week in June, I decided that we would hold an internal inquiry, which would be published, to bring out the facts. The Department closed ranks about the whole affair, and implied that they were not at fault. Our opponents, needless to say, took the opposite view and many on our back benches with constituency interests were also pressing us strongly.

I announced in the House that I would appoint an independent person of standing to investigate and report to me as soon as possible on the Department's handling of the matter. Sir Godfray Le Quesne QC, the recently retired Chairman of the MMC, accepted the task. Then the affair subsided, but we still had the time bomb ticking away as Godfray carried out his review.

This seemed to be the season for the return of old horrors. I had been in the Department for over a year and I had still not come across the affair of Lonrho and the House of Fraser. This had started almost as long ago as Barlow Clowes. Back in 1975, the Fayeds had been on the board of Lonrho and held over nine million shares in the company. The following year they sold their shares and left the board. Then in 1977, Lonrho increased their shareholding in House of Fraser. Lonrho subsequently increased their shareholding to 19 per cent, but were prevented from bidding for the company by the MMC. In November 1984, the Fayeds acquired the whole of Lonrho's shareholding in House of Fraser, and in the following March made a full bid for the company. Their bid was allowed, and the undertakings by Lonrho in relation to the Fraser shares were released, but in the event the Fayeds already had control.

Since then, Tiny Rowland had been waging an unceasing campaign to win the company. This had culminated in Paul Channon deciding, in April 1987, to appoint inspectors under the Companies Act. That report was due and came and was delivered to me on 23 July. In typewritten form, it appeared about a yard thick. I sighed, for I would have to read every word. In accordance with our usual practice, I sent it down to the Serious Fraud Office, who would be the prosecuting authorities, should that prove necessary. I wanted to publish the report after the next Party Conference in October, and I asked the SFO to let us have their views by the end of September.

In the meantime, another overseas bid hit the headlines. This time it was not to be chocolates but bread. Goodman Fielder Wattie, an Australasian company, put in a bid for Rank Hovis McDougall plc. Once again, cries of 'foul' and 'rape' rent the airwaves and the columns of our daily newspapers. Once again I was put under pressure to refer and once again Gordon Borrie settled down to listen to both parties. I was due to leave for Australia and New Zealand on a trade mission, and the advice from Gordon Borrie arrived just before I was due to leave.

This time he advised me to refer, not because of competition reasons, but because he thought that the bid was too highly geared. My view was simple. The market should decide such matters, not ministers. If the banks were prepared to lend the money, it was all right. If they felt the risk was too great, then the transaction would not go ahead in any event. On the other hand, the advice of the Director General had been ignored only nine times out of over 2,000 cases since 1979, and only three times since Norman Tebbit laid down the new rules. I decided to follow Gordon Borrie's advice, not least because that way there would be an opportunity for the MMC to rule on leverage. Then we could finally decide whether or not it should be a factor. I announced the referral on the very day I got on the plane to Australia. That alone ensured me plenty of publicity during my trip, even if it was the sort of publicity I would rather have avoided!

Within a fortnight Pat Goodman had abandoned the bid. I had a drink with him during my time in New Zealand. He told me that his financial commitments did not carry him over the referral period. I wondered, to myself, about the advice that allows a company to make a bid for one of the two main bread producers in the land without taking into account the possibility of the three month delay before the MMC. There and then I decided that I would have to do something extra to ensure that more people understood the way that merger control worked.

My visit over, we got on the plane for the 24-hour flight back to London. My Private Office, reluctant as ever to let me waste a minute, had sent out the House of Fraser report to the High Commissioner's Office in Wellington. As we got to the aircraft steps and made our farewells, the bulky packages were handed to me. As soon as the plane took off, I opened the first parcel. I finished the last page of the last package with a great sigh of relief just as the plane touched down at Heathrow. Waiting for me at the airport were the inevitable boxes. The first one I opened contained the Godfray Le Quesne report on Barlow Clowes!

The report was a full recital of the facts. I took advice but it got us little further. There was no legal liability on the Government. There was nothing that we could do without being sued (and then only if the courts did decide that there was a liability on the Government, and that was thought unlikely) or follow the decision of the Parliamentary Commissioner for Administration, the Ombudsman. There was so much interest in the report that I knew that I could not publish it until the Commons returned, so I put it away for the time being.

Near the bottom of the second box waiting for me at Heathrow was a letter from Tiny Rowland. He asked for an opportunity to make representations to me before I made my decision. The Serious Fraud Office were still working away, although I expected their reply before the end of the month. The report was away at the printers and could be ready in a few days. I agreed to see him and he came in on 16 September. I met him in the conference room on the eighth floor of Victoria Street, flanked by Gerald Hosker, my principal solicitor, Mr Mallinson from our Investigation Division and Neil Thornton, my Private Secretary who made a record of the meeting. They turned up six strong, led by John Beveridge QC who was Counsel for Lonrho and who sat himself down opposite me. He had two solicitors from Stephenson Harwood sitting on his left, whilst on his right were two Directors of Lonrho, Mr Spicer and Mr

Dunlop. Sitting on the far end of the table, huddled in his overcoat despite the mildness of the day, sat the silent, brooding figure of Tiny Rowland.

I opened the meeting, after introducing my officials, by saying that I had received the inspector's report and I was studying it. I wished to publish it as soon as possible. When that happened, they would have an opportunity to make representations to Gordon Borrie who would, in turn, advise me. With that advice I would be in a position to consider what I should do about the report. I could not discuss the report until then.

Mr Beveridge asked me whether I meant that the decision to publish the report had been taken in principle and the only question outstanding was when. I agreed, and when asked whether it was more likely to be days, weeks, months or years I replied that I would publish as soon as I was in a position to do so, but I had in mind weeks rather than years.

They all relaxed visibly after I finished and Mr Beveridge said that my assurance covered much that they wanted to say. He understood that many people were affected and therefore the consideration of the report could take some time. He hoped that we would be able to move quickly to publication, although he understood that the actual decision on the report would understandably be slower. Their sense of urgency was concerned with the possibility of a reference to the MMC. My power to do so expired within six months of receiving the report, and already two months had expired. If I decided not to refer, they would want to challenge my decision in the courts. They must have enough time for this to be done. He then went on to recite all Mr Rowland's achievements in building up Lonrho, the events of the past few years relating to House of Fraser, and in passing said that Lonrho had only known the Fayeds slightly before the bid. At that point, I could not restrain my sense of mischief and gently pointed out, 'Surely Mohammed Fayed had been on the Lonrho board.'

He glossed over that and went on to make a number of further points, ending up saying that the appropriate response was not prosecution but a reference. I said that I had listened to all that had been said, and the meeting broke up. At that point, Tiny Rowland, who had been entirely silent throughout, could not contain himself. He looked straight at me and asked why the Government was prejudiced against his company. He was never invited to Government functions when Africans were visiting London. It was shameful, he went on, that on a recent visit Geoffrey Howe should not have been received by President Neyerere of Tanzania. He would expect to, as a matter of course, on his visits there. There was no real answer to that, so I bid them farewell.

The next day I heard from the Serious Fraud Office. Their inquiries would take far longer than they had originally anticipated and there was no prospect of being able to say for some time whether or not there would be a prosecution. I only wished that they had told me that before my meeting with Lonrho, who would no doubt accuse me of bad faith. However, there was nothing to be done.

Having met one party, I offered a meeting to the Fayeds. The two brothers turned up on 28 September accompanied this time by their silk, Mr David Oliver QC, two solicitors from Herbert Smith, their own House of Fraser legal adviser and Sir Peter Hordern MP, who was one of our senior backbenchers. Their principle complaint was the scope of the investigations, saying that it had been broadened way beyond the terms of reference. I agreed during the meeting to give them three working days' notice of my decision to publish, to enable them to go to court if they so wished.

The day after, I issued a press notice confirming that the inspector's report had been passed to the SFO for consideration and that they had said that further time would be required. In reply to questions, I said that publication was off until we heard from them.

After the Party Conference the Commons came back. At the first opportunity I went down to the Lords to make the statement on Barlow Clowes. Tony Newton (for by now Kenneth Clarke had left me and become Secretary of State for Health), was to repeat it in the Commons. I thought that there was one thing that I could do and, when I came to the House to make the statement, I said that I had that day sent the report down to the Ombudsman. That was very unusual, but in all the heat of the day, it was totally overlooked. After the statement, I appeared before the Backbench Trade and Industry Committee. All my ministers turned up, together with Peter Luff. I had appeared many times before this Backbench Committee, and I was used to an attendance of about a dozen. This time the Committee room was packed, with at least ninety there.

I opened with a short statement. The first question was hostile, and it went straight downhill from then on. The general line was that the Government should pay. I was given a very stormy ride, but there was nothing that I could do that would satisfy them, for I could not agree that we should recompense all the investors for their losses, despite all the sympathy I felt for them. When the meeting was over I found the lobby waiting outside, like vultures circling the kill. I avoided them, but my critics did not. The press the next day was full of the roasting I had been given.

It was a salutary lesson in the ephemeral nature of political reputations. On the Thursday, I had attracted banner headlines in the *Daily Mail*, and most other papers, for my action in reducing gas prices for the consumer. I was the hero of the hour. One day later, 'Tory Fury Erupts Over Young' was the equally black headline in the same paper. Later I had both framed and hung in my office with the legend '24 hours is a long time . . .'. Nevertheless, the whole episode did me further harm in my standing in the party. Because I was remote, tucked away in the Lords, it was often difficult for me to gauge the strength and depth of feeling amongst our own back-bench colleagues. Many had rarely met me, although they were familiar with the rest of the Cabinet, if only from seeing them in their Division lobbies night after night. There was always the thought, with some, that I had had too easy a passage to the Cabinet, and I would be told from time to time that I continued to have one or two rather hyperactive enemies.

In the meantime, the SFO, working away on the House of Fraser report, had failed to keep to their deadline. They had asked for a further extension, and rather ominously, were unable to say when they thought they would be finished. They would not let me publish until they had decided whether or not to prosecute. Of course, if they were to prosecute then the publication would be delayed until after the case was decided.

I had been working on a speech to set out, in definitive terms, exactly where merger policy lay. I wanted to define competition in the market, so all would understand. The Stock Exchange held a conference at the QEII Centre on 27 October. I laboured long and hard into the night to produce a speech, in simple and straight-forward language, that showed how the market would vary, sometimes a local market, other times the United Kingdom, or Europe, or even the entire world. I said that the principle is that the customer is king, and in each and every case, it is the effect on the customer that is the test. If the merger would lead to loss of choice and higher prices for the UK customer (and that customer could be an industrial company), it would probably be referred.

I thought the policy simple, but few agreed. I had the book printed and sent out to over ten thousand companies up and down the land. I went further, and published and distributed thousands of copies of two coloured booklets, one on the mechanics of competition policy and the other on investigations. Despite all this, not only were the press still confused, but a television programme was still able to report, a month or two later, that nineteen out of twenty City people could not foretell merger policy and the decisions of the OFT and the MMC. I gave up at that point, but the unworthy thought came to me that if all the merchant bankers admitted that they knew what would happen it might cause them, from time to time, to discourage clients from bidding. No, that could never be.

In the meantime I was still waiting for the SFO on the House of Fraser report. Time was passing and I only had until 22 January before my power to refer to the MMC would expire. I had promised Lonrho that I would decide in good time and Gordon Borrie, who had been working away on the report, wrote to me on 22 November. His advice was clear and unequivocal. I should not refer. I barely had time to read it when I was told that Stephenson Harwood, Lonrho's solicitors, knew that the advice was in and were asking for one further meeting before I took my decision. I was reluctant, for all parties had had many opportunities to make numerous points, but in the end I agreed to see them later that day. They came in at 4 o'clock.

This time there was a far larger crowd. In addition to my previous supporters I included Hans Liesner, my Deputy Secretary responsible for competition in the Department as well as an additional lawyer and Andrea MacLean, my Press Officer. They fielded a far larger team as well. Their silk, John Beveridge, brought along his Junior Counsel as well as three solicitors and there were six directors present – Tiny Rowland as well as Messrs Spicer and Dunlop as before – but now Sir Edward du Cann, their Chairman, and with him two further directors, Sir Peter Youens and Mr Robinson.

I started by saying that Gordon Borrie had seen a copy of the report and had been considering the question of a reference to the MMC. Interested parties had all had an opportunity to make representations to him, but this morning Lonrho, through their solicitors, had requested a meeting to make representations based on new facts in advance of my decision. I was there merely to listen.

Mr Beveridge said that there were no new facts and proceeded to make a number of points. I was once again sitting opposite him, and unusually for me, had made full notes of all that he said. When he finished he asked me if I understood the points he had been making. I immediately, and to the slight amazement of my officials, repeated each of the five points he had just made. I said that I was open minded on the question of a reference, would reflect on the Director General's advice, would consider all relevant matters, including what I had heard this afternoon, and make a speedy decision. Then the directors entered the fray. Edward du Cann said that there was intense public interest in this affair and they were receiving 1,000 requests a day for *A Hero from Zero*, their publication about the Fayeds. Tiny Rowland said that over 40,000 copies had been sent out, with French and Arabic editions to be published soon. He expected to distribute 100,000 copies by the end of the year.

He went on to say that I had given him a clear undertaking at our last meeting that the report would be published within weeks, rather than months. I replied that I had not known at the time that the SFO would want further time, and clearly I could not publish when prosecutions were under consideration or injunctions outstanding. Neil Thornton, my Private Secretary, got out his notes of the last meeting and said that my exact words were that 'I would publish as soon as I was in a position to do so.' Tiny Rowland said that their notes did not include that remark, and went on to point out that during the course of the inspectors' report they had spent £2.5 million in legal fees, and the total costs to Lonrho of pursuing the House of Fraser was getting close to £20 million. I wondered, but to myself, whether the shareholders would consider this a good investment, and politely thanked them all for coming in. I said that I would now consider my position.

The following afternoon I made my decision and it was announced at 9 a.m. on the day after. The press notice said that after considering representations made to me, the advice of the Director General, and the findings of the inspectors' report I had concluded that a reference to the MMC would not be appropriate. However, it went on, it may be appropriate in due course for other steps to be taken in the light of the inspectors' report. That, I thought, when the notice was issued, was the end of the matter. How very wrong I was!

Meanwhile there were other problems. About a month before the MMC had reported to me on the holding of BP shares by the Kuwait Investment Office. They had recommended that the KIO bring down their holding in BP to 9.9 per cent within twelve months. I had taken the precaution of asking Sir Dennis Walters, one of our back benchers with close connection with the Kuwaitis, to come and see me at 9 o'clock on the morning that the decision was announced. I asked him to tell the Kuwaitis that I wanted to see an amicable settlement of the affair. They were to deal with Gordon Borrie to settle the details. Since then I had kept in touch with Dennis Walters, but little progress had been made. From time to time there were ominous warnings about the effect this might have on our other commercial links with Kuwait, but although much was written and said, little happened.

It became evident after a while that there would be no movement as long as the Kuwaitis thought they had to negotiate with the Office of

281

Fair Trading. The concept of a truly independent agency is foreign in many areas of the world, and they, no doubt, considered that they should be dealing with me direct. After some weeks of stalemate I obtained my colleagues' agreement to my conducting the negotiations. In early December there was a breakthrough. I received a message that Shaikh Ali Khalifa, their Oil Minister, was in London. I suggested that we meet and after some negotiations, we agreed that he would call on me at 11.00 a.m. on Friday 9 December. As it happened, we were in the middle of very difficult negotiations on the European Airbus, and I had a series of separate meetings with Jeffrey Sterling early and Professor Roland Smith later. The one other appointment I had, at 10.30 a.m., was with Peter Walters, the Chairman of BP.

Peter Walters was very concerned about the position. He thought that there was a chance that the KIO could sell their entire holding to an American Oil company. If that did happen, then BP would be 'in play'. Whatever political problems I had had up to now would be as nothing compared to the problems I would have then. I told him that I was concerned with the position, and that as he knew the KIO were asking for a longer period to sell their shares, but I would only do so if they agreed to a phased disposal, and not to one buyer.

In order to reduce the chance of any leaks, I had arranged that Shaikh Ali come to the back door of our Victoria Street offices, and be brought up by a back staircase straight to my office. I did not want him recognised, and stories start to run. Peter Walters was still with me as the clock ticked towards the hour. The last thing I wanted to happen was for them to meet. On the hour my Private Office intervened with a pretend phone call, and Peter took his leave. The very moment the door closed on him the other door opened and in walked Shaikh Ali Khalifa.

I took to him at once and we established an immediate rapport. We spent about an hour and a half together, at the end of which we had agreed a deal. If I gave them more time to dispose of their shares, as an act of faith, they would sell the surplus, some 14.3 per cent, back to BP within two or three months. He said that he would invite Peter Walters to Kuwait that weekend to settle the price. As soon as he left I picked up the phone to Peter. Never trust a politician, I started and told him of our meeting. He met with Ali Khalifa that afternoon and agreed outline terms. There were still a number of false starts to come but in the end I gave the KIO three years to sell their shares and sat back, rather nervously, for Shaikh Ali to deliver. Ali Khalifa had promised me that the sale would be agreed on Christmas day. On holiday I spent many an anxious hour

282

waiting for the message. It came through just in the New Year. All was agreed, and a few weeks later BP had acquired the balance of the shares.

At Cabinet in the New Year Geoffrey Howe paid me a handsome compliment about the outcome. It takes one semite to deal with another, I thought to myself.

My officials had told me that Lonrho had brought proceedings for judicial review against me for my decisions, both not to publish the report and not to refer back to the MMC. I was told not to worry about the case, but I noticed that as it went on they became less confident. In the event we lost in a spectacular manner. Using language which may have had a particular legal meaning but a much wider meaning outside the law, the Division Court said that I acted 'irrationally'. The court, without ever having read the report, decided that I should have published it and again, without having the advantage of reading the report, said that I should have referred to the MMC. Who, I wondered to myself, was behaving irrationally? Needless to say, the press made much of the result, and we put in an appeal. The consequences of the decision for government, of judges second guessing ministers and overruling them, would have great constitutional consequences if it were not overturned.

The appeal was heard in January and the decision came out on the 20th. It was total victory for us. Leave was given to appeal to the Lords, who faced the unusual step of sitting over the weekend. By agreement between the parties the clock was stopped at one minute to midnight before the expiry of the six months so the Appeal could be heard in the usual way.

I started to become the subject of Tiny Rowland's glossy publications. During the seventies, John Sunley, of Bernard Sunley, had been a client and a golfing friend of mine. I had lost touch with him at the end of the seventies, and he had written to me out of the blue about a year before telling me that he was developing a golf course at Lake Nona in Florida. He had asked the former secretary of the R&A, the last captain of the Ryder Cup and a few others to become honorary members. Would I also become an honorary member? At the time, golf was the last thing on my mind and I replied saying that I would be delighted to accept but I had played little golf for years and I had no idea when I would be able to visit the club. I had never been to Lake Nona, but according to this glossy publication of Lonrho's, Sunley had been connected with the Fayeds in the past. The offer and acceptance of the honorary membership was some sort of inducement to me not to publish and not to refer. I treated the whole accusation with the utter contempt it deserved

283

and merely looked at the expensively printed publication and wondered again what the shareholders thought!

Before the appeal could be heard there was an even more bizarre development. The day of the Annual General Meeting of Lonrho, the *Observer* published a special mid-week edition, the first since Suez. It contained a number of extracts from the report. Edward du Cann wrote to me to tell me that they had the report and delivered the letter by hand during the morning. We applied and obtained an immediate injunction. We demanded and received the report back. In due course the Lords were to conduct proceedings for contempt, but the real issue for me was finally decided when the Lords, with Lord Keith of Kinkel presiding, found for me on both points. 'No fault could be found with my decision making process' and the history showed 'a scrupulous anxiety on the part of the DTI to act fairly'. As far as the reference decision was concerned Lord Keith said, 'I find it impossible to say that it was irrational to decide not to launch the MMC on an enquiry that would cover ground already investigated by the inspectors, and which is being further investigated by the SFO and the Director of Public Prosecutions.'

I was rational again. In the end the prosecuting authorities decided, as I always maintained, that there was no basis to launch a prosecution and my successor published the report nearly a year later. Is this the end of the matter? I am not taking bets.

Chapter 19
ROVER'S RETURN

It was late on Saturday night, 11 June 1987. Brian Hayes had gone and left behind all his briefing papers. I had settled down to study them. At that time I had few clear objectives for my new Department. I was still suffering from the culture shock of leaving Employment and would suffer for many weeks to come. In a strange way I was rather upset by my promotion as it meant that I would not be able to put into effect all the plans we had made to tackle unemployment and restore enterprise.

Then I came to the section dealing with the car industry. I still remembered the great difficulties that Keith had experienced and the long meetings we had had with Michael Edwardes. I knew how important that industry had been to the West Midlands and how they had suffered during the long decline of the car industry. I made up my mind that I would see what I could do, not just to privatise our nationalised car industry but to persuade the Japanese or Koreans to come here. After all, they might have the ownership of the companies but we would own all the wealth creation processes here in the UK. If I could persuade not just Nissan but the other companies to come then that alone would revive all our component suppliers.

When I allocated duties in the Department I had kept the Rover Group for myself. Within a few days of my return to the Department I called my officials in for a meeting. One of my first comments to the press on entering my new office was that we would privatise Rover and British Steel during the life of this Parliament. I had gone further with the Prime Minister and told her that it was my ambition to dispose of all DTI's Nationalised Industries by Christmas 1988.

Of course BL had changed considerably since I was last in the Department. Jaguar had been floated off in August 1984. Over the following few years further parts of Rover Group – Trucks, Bus, Unipart and Freight Rover had gone. All I was left with were the two main operating businesses – Austin Rover and Land Rover. Michael Edwardes had long since gone and now Graham Day was the chief executive.

I had a not very cheerful first meeting with my officials. The figures alone, approved by Barings as well as the Treasury, showed that at best it would cost us some £750 million for debt write-off and rationalisation. I had been convinced for years that Sir Lewis Carroll had been Second Permanent Secretary at the Treasury. It would have taken the author of *Alice in Wonderland* to have devised the rules relating to the public sector. BL was a public company with only 0.2 per cent of shares still in outside hands. The company was totally bankrupt and had been so for years. The only way it had been able to continue trading was because of the Varley-Marshall undertakings. These undertakings, given in Parliament, meant that the Government stood behind all the debts of the company. I was told that they now approached £1.6 billion. These liabilities would not be part of the Public Sector Borrowing Requirement until they were called in! The normal rules relating to nationalised industries hardly applied. Even worse they were now the Varley-Marshall-Joseph undertakings since they had been reconfirmed by Keith during my time with him.

The options before us were few. I could see that my officials had little confidence in any of them. There was no doubt of Ford's continuing interest in the company but I could not see where that would lead us. There had been such an outcry only eighteen months before when it became common knowledge that talks with Ford and General Motors were in progress that I doubted that we could ever revive them. Indeed assurances had been given to the House that talks with Ford would not be revived.

Our discussions with General Motors foundered when Ministers decided that Land Rover could not be included in any sale. It is difficult now to recall the hysteria that the proposed sale to GM had raised. 'The jewel in the crown' was how many regarded it and there was a very active 'Keep Land Rover British' campaign. When we told GM that we would have to withdraw the Land Rover part of the package they withdrew. When my predecessor announced the ending of the talks with GM he informed the House of the Government's determination to retain a measure of real UK control over Land Rover. After that other ways had to be found to dispose of the remainder of the package – the merger of Leyland Trucks and Freight Rover with DAF and the management buyout of Unipart and Leyland Bus.

It was even worse with Rover. When the news of the talks with

Ford broke the resulting controversy devastated sales. In one month market share plummeted from 18.4 per cent to 15.8 per cent. That amounted to annual sales of £250 million or about 40,000 cars. The reasons were simple.

Cars are sold through a well motivated dealer network. They can only sell to customers who think the car has a future. The level of second-hand prices are vitally important when new cars are bought, especially for fleet purchases. If buyers thought that there was even a chance that the range would be discontinued then prices would slump. So that when the talks became public many of the dealers went into a state bordering on panic. They knew that if the company was sold to Ford their livelihood would be at risk. Some had bailed out before even waiting to learn of the results of the talks. We could not afford for that to happen again, I was told.

There was one further complication. Today Rover was dependent on their relationship with Honda. Their collaboration on a new medium car, the AR8, was essential to Rover's future. As a result of Ford, Honda had cooled. Before I arrived the Department had heard that they had little wish to be associated with 'a shaky company'. I did want Honda to come here and if Rover went to another car company we would lose Honda.

Graham Day had a rather complicated scheme that involved a placing of the shares with institutions within eighteen months followed by a full placing in '93 or '94. That seemed a rather long shot to me but I agreed to meet Graham to discuss it further. I had one other idea.

I knew Sir John Egan of Jaguar well. We would meet from time to time during my Employment days and on one occasion at dinner he told me of his fears that his company would be vulnerable to a bid with the expiry of the golden share at the end of 1990. I had an idea that I ran past my colleagues and obtained their agreement. I then invited him to come and see me.

John told me that he was working on a scheme to build up a series of blocking holdings which would make him safe when the golden share expired. I was sceptical and told him so. I then offered him a alternative. You buy Land Rover. You share many of the same dealers. As Range Rover is concerned you are in the same part of the market. 'If you do this,' I said to John, 'I will find a way to put a golden share on Land Rover that might well protect you until the mid-nineties.' I knew that this would satisfy the undertakings we had given Parliament and John went away promising to think my suggestion over. I gave him until the end of September.

A few days later I took Graham Day to dinner. I knew Graham

slightly from his days at British Shipbuilders and I got on with him from the first. He was a Canadian who had settled over here and had spent much time in recent years in the nationalised industry sector. We both knew what the objective was – to return Austin Rover to the private sector. Over dinner I agreed that we would go along with his idea of a flotation provided that he supplied me with a series of check points to cover our progress over the next eighteen months. If he failed to make any one check point then we would then consider the question of trade sale.

The summer soon passed and in September I visited Land Rover at Solihull and Austin Rover at Longbridge. I was very impressed with the new small Range Rover being developed at Solihull and even more with the performance of the Range Rover I drove over the jungle trail, the test track at Solihull. I was so impressed that a few months later I actually bought one for myself!

Then before the end of September two developments occurred. Alan Clark, my Minister for Trade, went to the Frankfurt Motor Show. There Dr Hahn, the President of Volkswagen Audi Group, made a point of meeting him and indicated that he might well be interested in purchasing both AR and Land Rover.

Before I could really absorb the news, John Egan telephoned me. He could not take up my suggestion for a merger with Land Rover. He wanted to concentrate on developing Jaguar and thought that adding Land Rover would be too much of a distraction. I was very sorry. Although I would see John from time to time when he would tell me of his plans to keep his independence I doubt if he had any more confidence in them than did I! A little over two years later Jaguar became a wholly owned subsidiary of Ford.

There is a remarkably developed grapevine in the car industry and Graham very quickly heard about VW and came in to see me. I told him to meet them for the climate had changed in the last year, although I was uncertain whether we could include Land Rover. Graham thought that VW would not be interested just with Austin Rover although he thought that Ford might. VW was thought to regard the inclusion of Land Rover as a precondition. Their people had indicated that they expected the Government to deal with the accumulated debt, restructuring costs and forward financing on the scale envisaged in the corporate Plan.

Our work on the VW option seemed to indicate cost between three quarters to £1 billion although I doubted that VW could even carry through such a purchase. Their local State government owned 20 per cent of their shares and the combination of political and trade union pressures had already limited the transfer of Polo production to Spain. There seemed to be no other option, as my colleagues felt that we were bound by the terms of our undertakings to Parliament not to reopen talks with Ford.

In October Graham's privatisation plan turned out to be a great disappointment. It failed to contain any of our agreed check points. The more we studied the plan the less we thought that it would work. Our impressions were confirmed when the 1988 Corporate Plan was received. It required about £1 billion reinvested during the five-year plan period and the profits forecast was just too fragile to support any kind of flotation. Then, just when the prospects appeared the darkest there was a startling development.

Professor Roland Smith, the new Chairman of British Aerospace had mentioned to Graham Day who passed it on to Brian Hayes in November that he could be interested in Land Rover. That was interesting and I put it to the back of my mind just in case we could do anything with Rover alone. As I was about to leave the office for my Christmas break my Private Secretary gave me a message. Roland Smith had spoken to Brian again. Now he thought that he could be interested in the whole of the group but he would not be sure until some time in February. What a marvellous Christmas present, I thought. I did not put too much store on it.

Roland Smith is an interesting man. An academic, but an academic with a difference. He was still a visiting professor at Manchester Business School but over the last few years had spent less and less time lecturing and more and more putting his lecturing into practice. We did have two people in common. He knew Isaac Wolfson well from the old days and maintained links with Leonard Wolfson and the Great Universal Stores people. The other was – Tiny Rowland. Roland Smith had been Chairman of Harrods and House of Fraser during Lonrho's assault on the company and had also been there when the companies were taken over by the Fayeds.

When we came back from our break little had changed. We had a meeting fixed with Graham Day on 3 February. He was desperately working on methods to revise the profit forecasts upwards. We could fully integrate Land Rover and Austin Rover and save overheads of many millions a year but then never be able to separate the companies. We could increase car prices but this depended on the market. The test remained – would the institutions buy the plan?

Two days before our meeting Graham Day came to see Brian Hayes. He told him that he had been talking to Roland Smith. They were now interested in the whole group. As soon as Brian told me I telephoned Roland Smith who confirmed his interest.

The next day Nigel Lawson, Kenneth Clarke and I met with the

Prime Minister in her study at No. 10. Graham Day arrived a few minutes later but only after we had all agreed that the present Corporate Plan would not do. The need for £1 billion over the planning period seemed insuperable. Graham was questioned closely on the interest of BAe. He was adamant that they were interested. I was duly authorised to determine by the end of the month whether this was a realistic route to privatisation. Until then nothing was decided on the Corporate Plan which was neither accepted nor rejected.

Graham was very keen that we buy out the remaining shareholders. Although they only held some 0.2 per cent of the shares they were the original shareholders when the company was originally taken into public ownership in the mid-seventies. They still had considerable rights under both the Takeover Panel and company law. They had proved a thorn in the side of the company for many years. It was a quite unrealistic situation. The shares still in circulation were traded on the stock exchange and varied from time to time but the price was about 70p. As there were over 5.5 billion shares in existence that would value the company at about £4 billion. In fact its real value was a negative one for the company was insolvent. In the end we decided to leave the outside shareholders for the time being.

I returned to my office and telephoned Roland Smith. I was very concerned about the decision that we had just taken. Both BAe and Rover were both listed companies and I was responsible for the conduct of the Stock Exchange. We had to avoid making a false market in either shares. When I spoke to Roland he was adamant. He would not start negotiations until he had cleared the position with Ray Lygo, his Chief Executive, who was on a tour of the Far East and did not even know of the matter. It would just have to wait until his return on 20 February. I did get a promise that he would then decide within a week whether or not to proceed. Barings advised us that no announcement was yet required under the takeover code. We agreed a contingency statement with BAe in case the shares moved and we had to make a premature announcement.

Graham Day came in to see me at the end of the week. He told me that BAe were almost certain to insist on a period of exclusivity for any negotiations. Even if they did not he was concerned about the effect any negotiations would have on the existence of the company. He was sure that they simply could not survive another outcry like that which followed the disclosure of the Ford discussions.

My officials then took legal advice, and discussed the position with Barings. Although a competitive procedure had obvious advantages, in this case the risks of the collapse of the business and thus triggering the Varley-Marshall undertakings were such that I should grant exclusivity, I was advised, provided that it was for a reasonably short period. There were no real difficulties with Article 85 of the Treaty of Rome or the Takeover Panel.

For the next two weeks I would hold meetings with a tight group of officials on 'Florentine'. Why the code name Florentine was chosen I never did find out but we did keep all knowledge of the proposal secure. Ray Lygo returned as arranged on the 20th and on the 24th I received a letter from Roland Smith.

Roland had a very long shopping list. His offer was conditional on exclusivity and then to our providing appropriate warranties, representations and indemnities. He wanted us to liquidate all of Rover Group's borrowing and liabilities and to provide adequate working capital over the next few years. As if that was not enough he wanted continuity in the Honda relationship and in Graham Day's services. They should have commercial freedom to develop the business and still be eligible for any generic support for the motor industry.

Jeremy Godfrey, one of my Private Secretaries, brought in the letter with a broad smile. I read it and agreed with his assessment. Hidden in his letter was the makings of a deal although if you were to cost out the terms of his letter in full it would come to around £1 billion. I was sure that it was merely an opening gambit. Now all we had to do was to find out what they would really settle for.

The next day was Cabinet and I arranged to see the Prime Minister and the Chancellor of the Exchequer in the afternoon. Whilst Cabinet was being held my officials were holding a meeting with BAe. It appeared that they were looking for a cash injection of £750 million and full warranties. Barings were asked to draw up a counter proposal, and suggested a different formula.

When I met with the Prime Minister and Nigel Lawson I took them both through all the calculations. I also told them that my officials had advised me that the Barings offer might be a good place to start, but that we would probably be forced to settle for a very substantial contribution. I went on to say that I had decided that we should offer no warranties. 'If it is to go, then let it be a clean break.' I was given authority to negotiate on an exclusive basis and to agree a contribution up to £500 million. We also discussed ways of preventing a subsale of Land Rover, or any of the other subsidiaries. The Prime Minister looked very pleased, but rather sceptical, at the thought that this sale might actually take place.

The Friday was fully taken up with a conference on the City that I was hosting with the Governor of the Bank of England. Apparent over-regulation of the City had become a political issue and the conference was designed to see where we could relax regulation with safety. It was ironic that I, who claimed to be the great deregulator, inherited and would probably leave behind me a vast system of over-regulation. Despite the urgencies of Rover, I could not cancel the conference without arousing suspicions.

Up to now not one word of the impending sale had leaked out. I could not believe our luck would last. I arranged that I would meet with Roland Smith and his team on the Sunday evening in my office. The Saturday was my birthday and I spent it very pleasantly with my family. The Sunday was taken up finishing my boxes, and after tea I drove in through dark empty streets to the office. The prize of disposing of Rover Group as a whole to a politically acceptable purchaser seemed too good to be true. I left my car at the back entrance where no one would notice it and went up to my office carrying my boxes. My officials came in at 5.30 p.m., an hour before Roland Smith was due. My ambition was to reach a stage in the negotiations so that a statement could be made on the following Tuesday.

Roland came in, accompanied by Ray Lygo and Bernard Friend, his finance director. After all the pleasantries, Roland took out an A4 writing pad that I could see was covered with notes.

'You must forgive me,' he started off, 'but I am only an old academic' and proceeded to give me a lecture about BAe. From that moment onwards I would always call him 'the Professor' and would tease him about being 'only an academic'. His lecture ran that BAe was now the greatest manufacturing company in the UK. How there could be no better home for Rover. They simply could not afford to jeopardise BAe by overpaying for Rover. My heart sank at this, and my suspicions were soon confirmed. All the good work that my officials had done on the previous Thursday was to no avail.

Roland certainly started high. He suggested that the Government should liquidate all the bank debt, buy out all outstanding leases and provide Rover with all their working capital for the whole of 1988. My officials added up the bill and slipped a note to my Private Secretary who passed it on to me with a wry smile. It came to a cash contribution of £850 million!

The negotiations then started in earnest. After about an hour I got him down somewhat but there he stuck. On the other issues I was more fortunate. Roland Smith agreed that they would have to

292

buy out the minorities, that they could not resell the businesses for a specified period, that they would waive any tax losses over £1 billion. I was also adamant that we would grant no warranties and that was also accepted although in the weeks to come they tried continually to get me to change. Eventually I said that I would go back to my colleagues and at that we parted and arranged to meet the following day.

I then went over to No. 10 and met with the Prime Minister, Nigel and other colleagues. I told them that we had ended without agreement and with a substantial amount between us. Even then I had considerably exceeded the authority given me at our last meeting. I explained that we might well get a better offer from another car manufacturer who might want to buy out Rover's market share and who would be able to utilise the £1.6 billion tax losses in full. Not only would that add to our costs, but there would be considerable dislocation with the thousand distributors and the many component suppliers. There went undertakings given to Parliament. In the end I was authorised to grant a period of exclusivity until 1 May and to continue negotiations. I went away knowing that we had a sale in our sights.

The following morning I was up early and in Broadcasting House for the *Today* programme at 7.15. I was due to leave shortly for Japan. I had launched an Opportunity Japan Campaign, and I had a full morning of interviews on the radio and television. All the time I was giving interviews I could not help thinking that if they could read my mind they would have one of the biggest business stories of the year! Otherwise I was worrying about the forthcoming meeting and how I would handle it.

All the businessmen coming with me to Japan were due in at 10.30 with a press briefing at 11.30. As chance would have it, Roland Smith was coming to Japan with me and it escaped attention that he arrived some fifteen minutes early and that neither of us came into the briefing until it was half way over. When our meeting was over and we came into the Japan briefing, I suspect that we were both uncharacteristically quiet.

During the morning I had decided that my meeting with Roland Smith should be private and without officials. That broke the logjam. We both compromised and I could see that we were close enough to give negotiations a good chance of succeeding. I agreed to the exclusively period and we exchanged letters later that day and I telephoned Graham Day to tell him.

Barings remained unhappy with the idea of the exclusivity period, and wrote again to me suggesting some form of limited tender. I had little doubt that some form of limited tender could produce more for the company but on the other hand so could an asset strip. What we were after was not necessarily the best price but the best solution, and the best interests of both the company and the workforce dictated the exclusivity route.

At 5.30 I went again to No. 10 and went through the end position with the Prime Minister and the Chancellor. By chance, Cabinet was on Tuesday that week and that would give me an opportunity to tell all our colleagues prior to making a statement in the House. I returned to my office to give Max Hastings, the editor of the *Daily Telegraph*, a drink. I just hoped that he would not be too upset, as I did not hint that anything was in the air.

The next morning Cabinet was at 10.30 and when the Prime Minister called me I told them the news. I was greatly comforted by the looks of sheer surprise on the faces of my colleagues. The secret had been kept. Some rather doubted the ability of BAe to carry off the acquisition, whilst others thought that in time Rover might sink Aerospace! We had a slight hitch during the morning because BAe did not want to suspend their shares, but after the announcement went up on the annunciator at the House, both shares were suspended. Even then only some of the analysts guessed the true situation.

The statement in the House went off smoothly enough but the press conference back at DTI was a riot. If there is anything that the media hates, it is to be caught out, and no one had any inkling that this might happen. I only just stopped the news programme on television reporting that BAe would be buying the company for over £5 billion! All the journalist had done was to multiply the share price by the number of shares in existence. That might work for normal companies, but not Rover.

The questions, and the interviews on television, were often hostile, not to Government for a change, but to BAe. The next day's press was not too helpful. *The Times* reported that BAe market-makers said the move was 'unbelievable', 'bizarre', 'confusing' and 'very bad news for the company,' and the City was stunned. Hamish Macrae started off his column in the *Guardian*, 'This is madness.' *The Independent* reported that it was widely believed in the City that Rover's problems can only get worse in the short term. The Lex column in the *Financial Times* said that 'from the viewpoint of Rover and the Government the deal has everything . . . for BAe's stunned shareholders the benefits look a good deal more arcane.'

The sale received support from only two sources. The *Daily Telegraph* was firmly in favour and so were the strikers on the picket line at Land Rover. All the time I was negotiating the sale, the Land Rover workers were on strike. The effect on the share price was only to be expected. Suspended at 354p the shares plunged 41p before recovering to 329p. Roland had to get his lecture kit out again, and make the round of the institutions. He was very successful and before too long City opinion had changed. At his request I refrained from emphasising the advantages to the Government in the sale. There was real and understandable concern that the board would not be able to take the institutional shareholders with them.

It is the politician's prerogative to use hindsight to the full but the media is not totally immune from it. In time to come, many managed to convince themselves that Rover was the jewel in the crown of British industry. It is a pity that they did not bother to research their own comments at the time.

As soon as the announcement was made we did have other approaches. Mr Nat Puri, a constituent of Kenneth Clarke's, had approached us earlier through his company Melton Medes to buy Land Rover. As it was an enquiry about a subsidiary, we had referred him to Graham Day. This time he enquired about the whole group. I doubted if his company would have been large enough to relieve the Government from the Varley-Marshall undertakings, but in any event nothing could be done until the 1 May. We also heard from some old friends, the Chairman of Ford Europe, and Dr Hahn of VW. They all received a similar reply. The new enquiry was from Lonrho, who said that they were acting for a major car manufacturer. When I enquired who, they replied Toyota. That was an intriguing reply, for Rover were tied up with Honda and I could not imagine Japanese companies behaving in that way. I never did find out, for we could not follow up the enquiry in any event until May, but I rather doubted that it would have led anywhere. We were to deal with Toyota, but this was not the time. Besides, I had great hopes of getting them here as car manufacturers in their own right.

We quickly put BAe and Rover together. As I insisted that there should be no warranties, I agreed that there should be full disclosure. There was much ground to cover and both parties set to work. I added Graham Day to our party to Japan and he was able to introduce Roland Smith to Honda. Before the end of my trip, I invited Mr Kume of Honda to the Embassy for a well-publicised visit when I assured him of the support of the Government for BAe. I gained the distinct impression that they would be much happier with BAe than any other purchaser.

Peter Sutherland was the Commissioner in charge of competition and state aids and I would need his consent, not to any sale, but for permission to write off the past losses in the Rover group. I had dealt on many occasions with him, and had begun to know him quite well. I had a high regard for his ability and character. He was Irish, a former Attorney General, and I thought quite outstanding in his grasp of both concept and detail in all the City and competition matters we had dealt with together.

I had telephoned him telling him of the announcement just before going to the House. Whilst I was in Japan my officials had met with DGIV, the directorate in the Commission that reported to Peter Sutherland, and had arranged for the appropriate notification to be given and the Procedure (as the Brussels process was known) opened. On 23 March I had the first of a long line of meetings with Peter Sutherland.

I knew that I would be in for a long and difficult negotiation and I was not to be surprised. I outlined the position as far as we had got. Peter said that he would like to be helpful, but he did not think that the case would be an easy one.

The next day I had another meeting with Roland Smith and discussed the basic terms and the way our arrangement would be restructured should the Commission make changes. Over the next weekend the lawyers worked overtime, as did my officials, and by Monday morning the Sale and Purchase agreements were ready for signing. I agreed that I would take them to the appropriate Cabinet sub-committee and make a statement in the House on Tuesday 29 March.

Peter Sutherland had an engagement in Dublin and we had agreed to meet at Manchester airport for a few minutes. Unfortunately, air traffic control problems kept him in Brussels but at the very last moment I was able to arrange an RAF plane to fly me to Brussels. There was a great deal of press interest in our meetings. I wished to keep the present state of negotiations as confidential as possible until I had at least made the statement. We arranged to meet, not at Balleymont, the great Commission building, but at the offices of the Director General of DGIV, which was in another part of Brussels. I used the military part of the airport and none of the press saw me either coming or going.

I told Peter that an announcement was imminent and I had now negotiated BAe down to a cash injection of £800 million less £150 million for the shares, a net consideration of £650 million. He was not very enthusiastic and stressed all the difficulties. I returned to London rather worried about the attitude of his officials. At least, I thought, the Procedure will open at the end of the month.

296

That evening was the first formal dinner of the Trollope Society. I was one of the very early members, as I had been an avid Trollope collector. Book collecting was one of the first casualties of my time in public life. In the middle of dinner I was given a message to return to my office as there were troubles with Rover. There were, but they were quickly settled on my return. Then about midnight, just as we were leaving the office, we heard that *The Independent* was going to run a story that the statement was going to be made. We made arrangements for the shares to be suspended, which they were but only at noon.

The following day I obtained approval for the agreements and the statement was duly made. The Procedure was duly opened and my officials began making a long series of journeys to Brussels. They made little progress and I met again with Sutherland on 26 May. The gap between us had increased. I could not even understand the basis of the calculations that the commission officials used. The officials had a further series of meetings. I met with Peter Sutherland for the fourth time on 7 June. The gap had widened, and it was becoming more and more obvious that we had the makings of a serious political problem on our hands. On my return to London I went to see the Prime Minister and she agreed to write to Jacques Delors and to raise the matter in the margins of the forthcoming Toronto Summit, should it still be necessary.

I quickly heard from President Delors and on 15 June I went again to Brussels and met with Delors, Arthur Cockfield, and finally held my fifth meeting with Peter Sutherland. Both President Delors and Commissioner Cockfield appeared to appreciate the adverse reaction that the banning of the sale would have on public opinion in the UK. It was perverse in a way. I was the foremost advocate of 1992 in the Government, and our campaign to rouse British business to the advantages and the dangers of the forthcoming single market was succeeding beyond our wildest dreams. Yet at the very same time this threatened to undo all our good work.

The meeting was bizarre. Sutherland's officials produced figures that bore no relationship to the real world. They took full value of land and property without taking into account the £550 million of redundancies necessary to achieve those values. I protested that we were selling a going concern, not undertaking an asset strip; to no avail. At the end of the meeting Peter Sutherland suggested that our officials do more work. When they met they did offer a way forward by suggesting that some of the debt write off we could give as regional aid, but the other proposed, mainly valuing tax benefits, we did not think would be attractive to BAe.

All this time I had been keeping BAe roughly aware of where we were. We had had one difficult meeting at the beginning of June. However, throughout this period they had learned a great deal more about the businesses. The strikes that had so plagued Land Rover had been settled, some of the other difficulties investigated, and the car market continued to expand. As a result, they were persuaded to accept a reduced write off, but not where we were with the Commission.

A long series of meetings took place throughout June and the Prime Minister did discuss the matter with Delors both at the Toronto Summit on the 19/20 June, and again at the European Council at Hanover at the end of June. We made little progress, although as a result of heroic work by my officials the gap did narrow. Eventually on 4 July I met Roland Smith.

The position was becoming desperate. Quite apart from an enormous political row that would have erupted should the Commission prevent the sale going through, we were less than four weeks from 1 August. That was the month car registrations changed and as a result it was by far the best in the year for car sales. If BAe were to withdraw, the consequences would be disastrous. Public and dealer confidence in the very existence of Rover Cars would slump. It would be far, far worse than 1986, and we would be faced with another, probably permanent, loss of market share. There was now a very real chance that the setback could undermine the existence of at least the Rover part of the company.

Roland came in accompanied by Ray Lygo and Bernard Friend. I told them that we were still £360 million apart but Sutherland would now be prepared to agree £150 million of other assistance, principally regional aid. Roland said that he could go no further than £100 million and I then pointed out that some £80 million would be painless to them. I then suggested that to help to bridge the gap I would be prepared to relax some of the restrictions placed on the use of tax losses and give a contribution towards their costs of buying out the minorities. That was still not enough and the suggestion arose of deferring the purchase price for a period. Roland went away and telephoned me later asking for greater flexibility for any on-sale within the five-year period. When I refused any further concessions, he agreed to my suggestions. Later on I obtained my colleagues approval to these terms.

The next day I was back to Brussels for my sixth meeting with Sutherland. I was aware that this was probably going to be the single most important meeting of my entire decade in Government. I took my team of officials most closely associated with all the

298

negotiations, Mike Cochlin and Catherine Bell, and with them Andrea MacLean of the press office and Jeremy Godfrey, my Private Secretary. I knew that the timing was such that there was only one more meeting of the Commission to approve this transaction before the end of the month. There were twenty-five days to the first of August. The Commission was on vacation for the whole of August but in any event Parliament rose on 29 July and it would be mid-October before it resumed. It was today or not at all.

I held a private meeting with Peter first and then called in our officials. It was a very difficult meeting, with Sutherland's officials proving far harder than even we had feared. They quickly clawed back on their earlier agreement to allow £150 million of regional aid and limited it to £78 million. After a long and painful argument, I was able to persuade the officials that we could have a further £29 million debt write off and the removal of some ring fencing on capital losses and allowances. As soon as we agreed I shook hands with Peter and hurried back to London. I was due in the Lords for the report stage of the Steel Bill. Later I met again with Roland and his team.

The reaction was not favourable. We could not agree on how much the tax changes were worth, and we parted without agreement. The next day they were back with a letter that set out their proposals. They wanted a deferment of the purchase price, help with buying out the remaining shareholders and threw in a demand that we look again at lifting the restrictions on the golden share. As far as that was concerned, I said that we were already looking at the position of Rolls Royce as well as BAe, and we would continue to do so but without reference to this transaction.

Roland began to push for a longer deferment of the purchase price. He was entitled to some deferment, for he was taking the Group 'as is' with no warranties and he was entitled to have some clarification about the tax position. He began to push for a period that would extend up to eighteen months. I asked for a definition of 'State Aids', and was told that it did not exist, but depended on the circumstances of each case. I thought about the deferment, and could not see how it could be defined as a State Aid. There were always two points of view so I warned Roland that a deferment of the purchase price for too long would run the risk of the Commission taking a different view. If so, there could be a clawback from the Commission, but the risk would have to be his. As far as help with the shareholders was concerned, I would have to speak to Sutherland.

Later on I telephoned Peter Sutherland. I described our proposal to assist BAe with buying out the remaining shareholders of Rover, and said that it was effectively a payment to the shareholders of Rover and would appear to be outside the rules. I did not ask for his formal approval, and he said that he would consider the matter. I asked Sir David Hannay, our Representative to the Commission, to repeat the message.

On 12 July I wrote a formal letter to Roland setting out the full variation of the terms including the deferment of the purchase price. I offered him a number of options, telling him that the longer he took the more chance the Commission might require some repayment. I also included the other terms we had agreed. By the end of the day I heard that their board had accepted.

Wednesday 13 July will be a day that will live long in my memory. It started quietly enough with a ministers' meeting in the Department. I then had a Cabinet sub-committee, followed by opening an Australian British Chamber seminar at the Inn on the Park. All through this my officials had been agreeing the wording of the statement I was to make in the Lords. Some were busy taking Kenneth Clarke through the position, so that he could repeat the statement in the Commons. Lita and I were due at No. 10 for a lunch the Prime Minister was giving for the President of Turkey.

By chance, Ray Lygo was also a guest at the lunch. After we had been introduced to the President we chatted briefly during the reception. I was in very good humour and was looking forward to the statement in the Lords. He was quieter and rather mysteriously referred to some difficulties that had arisen at the last moment. 'Nonsense,' said I, and we parted. A few moments later he came back to me and said that he had just rung his office. He thought that there were some real difficulties. Just then lunch was called.

We all filed in and received the Prime Minister and the President. Lunch was served and I forgot about the conversation. Just as they were about to serve me with the entrée, I was handed a note. Could I call my Private Office immediately? I slipped out of the lunch and afterwards Ray told me that when he saw me go, he also left. I hate to think what the President thought!

I called the office and heard one word 'Trouble'. Norman Dodds was waiting outside and at about a quarter to two I was back in my office. The news could hardly have been worse. BAe wanted to pull out. The wording of the Commission Procedure had been delivered that morning. Cookson, the Company Secretary to BAe, had objected to the Commission's ruling that they had to follow the five year corporate plan to the letter. They wanted the wording changed, and I could see their point. A five year plan is there for planning purposes only. No one could be expected to follow it to the letter. By now it was nearly two twenty and I had a statement to make in a few minutes. We could not cancel it, for an announcement had gone up on the Annunciator at the House at noon. We quickly drafted out a holding statement and rushed over to the Lords. If I was not so depressed, the expression on the faces of the Opposition would have been really comical. All I could say was that there had been a last minute hitch, and we would come back to the House. We were in such a muddle that Kenneth later told me that he sent his PPS to listen to me to make sure that he read out the correct one of the three statements on Rover he had been given!

I came out of the House and Roland was waiting. He was pale and looked a worried man. 'Let's get going,' I said, 'and see what we can do.' We both had Rover cars, but by chance his did not have a telephone, so we swapped cars to let him get on with making the necessary arrangements.

That evening I received a letter from Roland Smith setting out his Board's concerns. He asked for confirmation that there would be no obligation on them to repay any of the debt write off if they did not follow the corporate plan in full. There were some other requests, but this one was the only one that mattered. I met with my officials and none of us thought that there was any chance of persuading the Commission to change the wording. I had telephoned Peter Sutherland on returning from the House and he sounded worried and concerned about what had happened. He offered a meeting if it would help. I asked Sir David Hannay, our representative in Brussels, to meet with Sutherland on the following morning.

Jeffrey Sterling telephoned to offer his assistance and I asked him to spend time with Roland. He had been one of the four 'wise men' dealing with the reorganisation of Airbus and knew BAe well. He went over to them and spent many hours going through the position. I minuted my colleagues in rather pessimistic terms.

The next morning at Cabinet I was very cautious. I refused to get drawn on what would happen if it fell through, although Graham Day had dusted down his plan for a placing. He thought that the market had improved so much that this time it would work. I just hoped that we would not have to rely on it.

When I returned from Cabinet the position had improved. Peter Sutherland had leaned over backwards to the very limit of his position. David Hannay sent over a minute of his meeting which was rushed over to BAe. A combination of a full explanation of the language of the Procedure, explanations from Jeffrey Sterling, and I suspect considerable second thoughts, were sufficient to turn the trick. At 4 o'clock I received a letter from Roland. His Board was content and they would proceed.

We signed the Sale and Purchase agreements and I went down to the House later on to announce that the transaction would proceed. Everything else, the extraordinary general meeting of the companies, the agreement of the Varley-Marshall schedules – all went through like clockwork.

It was done!

Chapter 20
OPPORTUNITIES

As soon as we were back from the Party Conference in Blackpool in October 1987, Kenneth Clarke came to see me. Kenneth had the Industry side of the Department, which included both British Steel and British Shipbuilders. Although I knew of the immense difficulties of shipbuilding I knew little of the progress of steel. I had of course kept in close touch with Ian MacGregor during his time at BSC, but he had long since gone and the Chairman now was Sir Robert Scholey.

Kenneth came straight to the point. He thought that there was a window of opportunity to privatise BSC. The financial results were shaping up well and it would only require a short Bill to turn the Corporation into a plc. The trouble was the Queens Speech had no mention of steel in it, and we had a full year of legislation ahead. I doubted if our colleagues would volunteer to surrender any of their legislation time for our Bill. I told Kenneth that I would do all I could to get the Bill in, and I went to see Willie Whitelaw.

Willie knew exactly how difficult it would be to find time for a Bill, which, although neither long nor complicated, could be expected to raise a certain amount of heat from the Opposition. I offered to introduce the Bill in the Lords first, since we would have spare time there early in the season. Attractive as that thought was, it was felt that legislation of this nature should come through the Commons first. Besides, it was on Kenneth's side of the House. The Prime Minister was very supportive, particularly when I told her that after this Bill I had the ambition of privatising all my Department's nationalised industries by Christmas 1988.

Before long we had it agreed. We waited until the half year results were ready. Then, on 3 December I went down to the House. I drew attention to the half year profits of £190 million against the previous profits of £178 million for the full year. Now, I said, was the time for the corporation to return to a fully commercial environment. The one difficulty we had had for years with the

303

Scottish lobby was the position of Ravenscraig. Great credit was due to Kenneth for persuading Bob Scholey to go on the record and say that, subject to market conditions, the mill at Ravenscraig would be operating for at least the next seven years. They even said that, if for any reason after then, it was decided to close Ravenscraig they would consider, on a commercial basis, any wholly private sector offer. That effectively disarmed the Scottish Lobby.

I heard little more of steel for many months. Kenneth would come to me from time to time and tell me of progress. We suffered the crash of October 1987, which brought on the disaster of the sale of BP shares. The Government received all the proceeds of the sale but the underwriters had had to face losses running into tens of millions. This would be the first privatisation since BP.

The Bill made its way through the Commons and in May I launched it on its uneventful progress through the Lords. Kenneth would come and ask my advice from time to time, but the matter was left with him. The Bill received the Royal Assent on 29 July. By then Kenneth had left the Department and had gone, on much deserved promotion, to Health. Without Rover my workload was now much lighter, so when Tony Newton arrived I kept back steel privatisation, although he continued to look after the industry. I quickly brought myself up to date. I had met Bob Scholey the previous April, at the Cutler's Feast in Sheffield. I found him rock solid, my admiration for him growing the more I had to do with him.

From then onwards from time to time I would meet John Mogg and his team of officials who would worry away at the prospectus and all the myriad details of a major flotation. He would always come to me looking very worried, and I would tease him about being a great worrier. Gradually all his problems were solved. We published the pathfinder prospectus at the end of October. British Steel, (the Corporation disappeared with its new status as a plc), showed £270 million profit before tax for the half year to 1 October and was now forecasting £550 million for the full year. Then just as John Mogg started to relax I started to worry.

We had agreed to meet on the afternoon of Monday 21 November, to fix the price for the share offering. The usual form was that the advisers would meet and make recommendations and we would decide the issue price. As well as my own officials I would have Norman Lamont, the Financial Secretary of the Treasury, with me. All was set fair and as the days passed our expectations of the issue price was gradually increasing. 'Just you watch,' I warned our officials, 'how the bankers will find reasons to reduce the price at the very last minute. Just watch me ignore them,' I boasted.

On the Thursday afternoon before the price fixing, my Private Secretary came into my room, closed the door and sat himself down opposite me. I was in the middle of a big battle to save the new Challenger II tank for Vickers, and in the middle of a fight over the organisation of Airbus with the French and Germans, so when he told me that he had heard a whisper of what might turn out to be bad news, I naturally thought of those. The rumour he had heard I thought silly, then depressing, and then the relevance struck home.

I had a very nervous weekend indeed. On the Monday afternoon we all assembled in the large conference room on the eighth floor at Victoria Street. Norman Lamont and I sat ourselves down to listen to our advisers.

They started off with a rather bullish account of the market. They were aware that this was the first privatisation since BP and that the Government wanted a success with Water and Electricity to follow. So did I, I murmured to myself. Then they got down to details. The first price they mentioned was 125 pence. That was the cautious figure, they said. Then they spent a few minutes at 127. Then they went on to 130 and finally, with obvious pain, much hesitation and considerable warnings, they went up to 132. There was little doubt that they expected us to settle for 130 pence. Norman and I and our officials excused ourselves and went outside the room. We just nodded at each other. 'Good luck,' said Norman and we returned.

'Gentlemen,' I said, 'we have considered the position and our price is – 125 pence.' There was a look of considerable disbelief on the other side of the table, quickly followed by the suspicion that they had missed something, then just plain relief. The flotation would be easy. They left as quickly as politeness would dictate.

On the Wednesday we held the press conference. In a rather theatrical manner we disclosed the price. There was a gasp of disbelief. At questions the main line was that I had agreed a giveaway price to ensure the success of the issue. I said that this was an offer for Sydney, not Sid. I made the point, as strongly as I dared, that this was for sophisticated investors, not widows and orphans. Then I went back to an urgent meeting that Tiny Rowland had requested.

I scoured the papers the following day. Only one commentator voiced a suspicion that there might be other reasons, but in the main I was given a hard time for giving the shares away too cheaply.

On the Friday morning at 9 o'clock, I announced my decision not to refer the Fayed's purchase of the House of Fraser. I dealt with some press calls, met with the Japanese Ambassador and then drove down to Staines to open the new head office of Atlantic Computers. I was out on the M4 at 11.29 a.m. and telephoned the office. At 11.30 a.m. the trade figures were due to be released. Up to now the worst trade figure on record was a deficit of just over £1 billion. This time it was a deficit of £2.43 billion. In just one month! They kept me on an open line to find out how the market went when the news was released. The index, which stood at 1·1 points down, fell sharply away after the announcement. I continued to hold on to the telephone as we drove along and listened as the market continued to adjust to the news. The index stood at 18·8 down at noon. Just then I arrived at my destination. 'Good,' I said to the office. 'It will be right, I will speak to you later.' 'Hold on,' a voice said, 'interest rates have just gone up 1 per cent.'

By then I had arrived and I was soon pumping the flesh and opening the offices. All I could worry the whole time I went round was what the interest rate hike would do to the market. I do not know what my hosts thought, for my Private Secretary stayed on the telephone and brought me a note every few minutes. The market fell over forty points at one time, although it did recover a little at the close. By the end of the afternoon the underwriters had not given up hope and I started to relax. The next day the papers assumed that I did not give away the shares too cheaply.

In the end there was a last-minute rush and the shares were oversubscribed 2·3 times. They opened with a premium of half a penny. In time to come, the National Audit Office was to issue a report on the privatisation of British Steel. Unlike their report on Rover, this one the national press considered merited two paragraphs at most, with no mention of me. The reason was simple. This was the first privatisation in which the NAO had no criticisms at all! Not one, not even about the extent of the pre-sales advertising.

Advertising was always a sore point with some, and much was made of my different campaigns. Once the 1992 campaign had started, the amount of advertising the Department was undertaking started to attract a certain amount of political criticism. There were occasional snippets in the papers about the attack that Labour was going to launch.

Towards the end of April 1988, Lord Jay put down a question in the Lords about the amount of DTI expenditure in advertising and publicity over the previous three years. When I looked at the figures they did not appear too encouraging – this year's figures were still under discussion, but the year before we had spent £13.6 million, with only £4.3 million in '86/87. I could see this turning into a small political storm when I was saved at literally the last minute. I was about to leave for the House to answer the question, when I was given some figures that had just come in from COI. Ten years ago the Labour Government spend on advertising, uprated for media cost inflation, came to £58 million. Last year, excluding privatisation, we spent just £54 million!

I held this information back until the right moment and used it with great effect. From that day onwards, although the Opposition would still moan about the Government use of advertising, the heart had gone out of the argument. Excluding privatisation, which was a special case, all that was happening was that the Government was spending its money to better effect.

I had always maintained a keen interest in the technology side of the Department. Within a few weeks of my arriving at the Department the Telecom people had come to me and, in a meeting devoted to the shortcomings of telephone call boxes, told me about a new system that Ferranti were pioneering.

This system would use an unused portion of the spectrum, with a light weight telephone that would only work within 100 metres of a station. I thought the idea a little far-fetched. The crisis over telephone boxes were resolved when the new Chairman of British Telecom Iain Vallance, put his job on the line if 90 per cent were not working in six months. Needless to say, they were.

The problem receded still further when Mercury, the subsidiary of Cable & Wireless, came into the market, and I went to open their first call box. As their system did not use cash they were not vandalised and gradually more and more boxes became cashless. However, it was not the last I heard of the new system. My officials would come to me from time to time with reports of progress, made initially by Ferranti, but now other companies were getting into the act. Here was an area where we were world leaders, for the simple reason that no one else had even thought of it. I asked Bryan Carlsberg, the Director General of OFTEL, to look at it.

Bryan Carlsberg is a remarkable public servant. He single-handed has kept the spirit of competition alive in an industry that is dominated by BT. Thanks to him, we have seen the evolution of perhaps the most competitive environment for telecommunications in the world.[1] When I did hear from Bryan, he suggested that we open up the service to competition and I jumped at it.

I announced on 28 July 1988 plans for a new type of telephone service, not an alternative to call boxes, that we would call Telepoint. Applications for at least two and up to four operators would be invited against detailed criteria to be published later. BT and Mercury would have to convince Bryan Carlsberg of their case if they wished to offer Telepoint services.

We issued the criteria in September, and in October we had 11 applications. Our officials got to work. I met Bryan Carlsberg in December. We agreed the new radio spectrum for a third or even a fourth cellular operator. I wanted this new network to be digital, to make a quantum leap in technology. It would be possible to carve out some more spectrum for the existing cellular telephones if the Ministry of Defence would agree. They did. Bryan promised me advice on Telepoint before Christmas. After Bryan left, I said that I wanted to make a major announcement on telecommunications in the New Year. We would announce extra frequencies for existing cellular operators, the licensees for Telepoint, and the new frequencies [at 1.7–1.9 gigaHerz] for the new digital cellular operators. I asked our people to look into the possibility of a January announcement.

The announcement turned out to be probably as far reaching as any that I made during my time in Government. We announced the additional spectrum for the existing cellular telephones service that would serve to relieve congestion within the M25. We announced the successful consortia for Telepoint. That broke new ground, for among the consortia were included companies like French Telecom, Nynex and Philips. I hoped that other countries would follow suit in due course. The really exciting document that was to travel around the world and set new standards was the discussion document 'Phones on the move, Personal Communications in the 1990's.'

We outlined a vision of personal communication networks of the future, introducing a new expression, PCNs, into the

[1] In all of these discussions I was motivated by my previous experience in the Department of Industry in the early eighties. First, there was the change in BT as soon as Mercury was announced. Secondly, when we licensed two cellular operators the best expectations were 100,000 users by the end of the decade. Germany licensed one operator at about the same time. Germany has a more numerous, richer population. By the end of the decade Germany would have about 100,000 subscribers. We would have nearly a million. Germany then licensed a second operator. That is the power of competition.

vocabulary. Without being prescriptive we looked ahead to a time when communications might be free from the fixed link network and opened a vision of interlocking links of communications, some very local, some national, some global. We brought together paging, telepoint, cellular, radio and fixed link. To the immediate interest of most of the telecommunication companies in the world we asked whether there were any potential operators interested in advanced PCN networks at 1.7 to 2.3 GHz. We asked for comments on the way forward by the end of April.

The interest that this announcement aroused, both in the popular press but much more importantly from communication companies around the world, was all that we could have wished. In the end we had fifty-two responses. They disclosed an enormous range of ideas and gave a great headache to our people and OFTEL. I announced the number of replies and sat back to await the recommendations.

Bryan Carlsberg's advice was that I should announce that I should consider applications for at least two new public mobile systems. We would judge these applications on the basis of the innovative ideas produced, and he would again advise me when they were in. But Bryan's letter also contained a surprise. He noted that Mercury was at a disadvantage with BT in having Telepoint interests and radiopaging interests but no cellular business. The disadvantage came from the increased need for inter-working between fixed services and mobile services. At present, he noted, Cellnet (BT's cellular phone) clearly will not consider ordering fixed services from Mercury. 'This creates an imblance in the market and it is one that I could perhaps tackle directly. However, establishing rules to deal with the situation would be complicated and completing Mercury's portfolio is a better solution in the long term.'

To my surprise he strongly recommended that we go ahead and award a licence to Mercury. During our meeting he amplified his recommendations and we meet again later in the month. Following discussions with me, he proposed to make the award of a licence to Cable & Wireless subject to them putting together a satisfactory consortium and a good detailed proposal. I was happy to accept. We then said that we would consider a further one or two licensees and asked for detailed proposals.

I left office before the licences were granted. Seven detailed applications came in September and in December Eric Forth, who had remained in the Department after my departure, announced that the Mercury/Motorola/Telefonica consortium had been accepted together with two further consortia, one headed by British Aerospace (including French, American and Japanese partners) and the other headed by STC, including American and German operators. We now have a clear world lead in communications and the next decade promises well.

My concern with the car industry did not begin and end with Rover. I knew from earlier discussions that the Japanese car manufacturers were casting an eye on Europe. They had first concentrated their expansion on the United States, but as the European Community seemed increasingly serious about the creation of a single market, they wanted to be on the inside.

It was difficult to know where to start. It had taken the Department many years of patient negotiations, and a considerable amount of cash, to land Nissan. But that had been in the old days, in the early years of the decade when we still had an inhospitable climate for investment, at least for Japanese investment. The best way was to find out for myself, so I decided to go on a trade mission to Japan and left in the Spring of 1988.

It had all started in my first few weeks in the Department. The Trade people came to me and told me that they would like to launch an 'Opportunity Japan' campaign. At that time I had quite enough of campaigns. The Enterprise Initiative and the 1992 campaign were still to be launched and the last thing I needed was to announce yet another campaign. My heart sank when I found out that they were planning a series of breakfasts around the country. At first I sent them away in short order, but later I relented and asked more about the basis of the campaign. In their view, we were losing out in our exports to Japan because there had been so much publicity in the press about the closed nature of the Japanese market that our exporters had simply given up trying.

The Japanese were conscious of their great imbalance in exports and only recently Mr Takeshita, the Prime Minister, had made a speech saying that it was their patriotic duty to buy imported goods. The more I looked into it the more I became aware that there was something that we could usefully do. The message I had to get across was that Japan was open for the right exports – and their national obsession with quality did give some of our products, not all, a very good chance. The best way to launch the campaign would be to go there. I telephoned around and made up what turned out to be a powerful team of businessmen to accompany me.

The British Aerospace people were keen to get orders for their BAe 146 aircraft. I had helped them in China a year or two before,

310

and I saw no reason why we could not try again. Roland Smith quickly accepted my invitation, which became even more worthwhile after the talks on Rover had started, so I added Graham Day as an unofficial member of our party for a meeting with Honda. We were joined by Peter Cazalet of BP, Dick Giordano of BOC, David Alliance (now Sir David Alliance) of Coats Viyella, Anthony Tennant of Guinness, Terry Harrison of NEI, Francis Tombs (now Lord Tombs) of Rolls-Royce, Arthur Walsh of STC and finally Rocco Forte of THF. All were Chairman or Chief Executives of their companies, and all had an interest in increasing their trade with Japan.

The press conference was called to launch the campaign at the end of February. I announced my impending visit and the campaign itself, which was being headed by Michael Perry, a director of Unilever. During questions, I was asked what my target for judging the success of the campaign was. I gained no inspiration from a glance at my officials so I simply said, 'Double our exports.' How long? Another glance, 'In three years.' The journalists appeared satisfied, but my officials looked too shocked to protest.

The visit to Osaka and Tokyo went well as did the ministerial meetings. The BAe 146 that we brought with us performed splendidly. In fact, it was so quiet that on one occasion, at a demonstration take-off in Osaka, it was in the air and away before our hosts even realised it had taxied into position. But we landed no orders for the aircraft. I was able to make sufficient progress on the vexed problem of Scotch whisky (since completely solved), but not on the extra places on the Stock Exchange (that took a further two years). I went to visit one of the Nissan plants. I could not get over the speed of the production line, and the way the young workers literally attacked their work. There is a real difference between us, I thought. They also showed me their 1952 car, which was on display in their museum. It was an Austin A30, built under licence.

One evening my host, Mr Tamura, the Minister for International Trade and Industry (MITI) and my opposite number, gave me dinner at an excellent Japanese restaurant. Over dinner I talked about our holding trade talks later that year in the UK. I suggested that we both invite about ten of our leading industrialists, and we could sit down over a weekend and settle any outstanding problems. There was not a flicker of interest. 'We could hold it at St Andrews,' I continued. At that I had all eyes on me.

A few weeks later the Japanese Prime Minister was in London. We had been invited to a dinner being given in his honour at No. 10. When I arrived at the head of the line, the Prime Minister

311

introduced me to Mr Takeshita. 'Ah, Lord Young,' he said, 'you have been giving Mr Tamura a great deal of trouble.' At this, the Prime Minister looked most concerned, shot me a glance, and Mr Takeshita continued, 'So many of our industrialists want to come to St Andrews with him for the golf. He simply cannot decide!'

The weekend was fixed for July. I had hardly played since I first came into Cabinet, so I resolved that I would find some time to practise. That was another broken resolution. Before that, we had to get some times reserved on the Old Course. I remembered that Willie Whitelaw was a former Captain of the Club, and I resolved to ask him. Before I could use what influence I had, the problem was solved. One of the people on the Japan desk in the Department had a father-in-law who was Secretary of the club. We had our times.

The weekend itself was a great success. I heard a few days before we were due to meet that Mr Tamura had only taken up the game after my invitation. I suggested that we play as foursome partners, and the two businessmen we played against, one Japanese and one British, did their duty. With considerable effort on their part the day was saved, and they let us win. There was no doubt that the foundations were laid over that weekend for industrial cooperation between British and Japanese companies.

After the summer, I heard rumours that Toyota were considering manufacturing in Europe, with the possibility of an assembly plant in the UK and a joint venture engine plant in France. I wondered what I could do to make sure that they came here, when an opportunity was handed to me on a plate. The Nissan plant in Sunderland had doubled its production, and part of the new production was for export. They had invited me up to Sunderland on 1 October to drive the first Bluebird off the production line. A day or so before, I heard that the French were going to count these cars out of their Japanese-manufactured allocation, effectively banning them from entry into France. It was odd; only a few days before President Mitterrand had made a great speech about political union in Europe. Here, over two or three thousand cars, they were going to create difficulties.

The first car off the line was actually bound for France. My office telephoned, and as a precaution we asked them to change it for one due for the Netherlands. I flew up the night before to Leeds, and we started, appropriately enough, with an 'Opportunity Japan' breakfast, I then went to Sunderland and drove the first car off the line. I had written the day before to the Commission protesting at the French attitude, and asking the Commission to put it right. At the press conference I made a great song and dance about the right of Nissan to have its cars exported anywhere in the Community. 'Nissan is a Japanese-owned British company,' was the line I took, 'just as Ford is an American-owned British company.' I went right out on a limb, but I knew that our case was very strong indeed. Nissan had undertaken to source at least 80 per cent of parts in Europe, and were already just over 70 per cent. Who knew, or even enquired, what proportion of other cars manufactured in Europe was sourced locally? There was no actual agreement, but the cars were undoubtedly British under the general rules of the Community.

Later, when all the ceremonies were over, I went on a tour of the production line. I could have been back in Tokyo, for the line was going at the same speed as the Nissan plant in Japan – only this time the production workers almost running on the line were young Brits. I realised that it was all down to training, and achieving the right atmosphere at work. Here was a factory right in the heart of the most unionised part of the UK, with a one union agreement, and yet only about a quarter of the workforce had bothered to join the union. That told me a great deal about the quality of the management, and its desire to ensure that all who worked at the plant were on the same side.

The popular press took up the issue with great relish. All I said from then onwards was that it was up to the Commission to implement. Every now and then our cause would receive a great boost when a French Minister would make an anti-Japanese speech, along the lines that 'we must keep them out of Europe.'

My reward was not long in coming. Before the end of the month George Turnbull of Inchcapes (now Sir George Turnbull) had called on me and told me that he was working hard to persuade Toyota to establish their assembly plant over here. There was a chance that the engine plant could still come here.

I wanted to send a strong message that they would be welcome, and would ensure, from time to time, that the Nissan case would receive a boost in the press. I would refer to it, only in the depths of my office, as the Battle of Agincourt, Part II. I received a series of visits from the car manufacturers of France, asking me to keep the Japanese out. I would reply that my interests were the consumers of Europe, not the manufacturers. As the weeks passed the issue persisted. Then, at an Anglo-French summit the issue appeared settled, and the papers carried stories that President Mitterrand had agreed the issue with the Prime Minister.

The very next day I received a visit from Mr Numata of Toyota.

The Commission in Brussels were instituting a tight new regime for the car industry, which made it unlikely that grants would be allowed for the industry, other than those allowed for normal regional assistance. That helped us greatly, for we could then be judged simply on our merits. The only offer I made was that they could meet the Prime Minister, but only if we get both plants, I joked. Gradually our discussions firmed up, and in January I was able to announce, by way of a written question, that we were the lead country in Europe for Toyota. The French, ever mindful of our interests, again blocked the import of Sunderland Nissans, and that issue was not finally settled until the middle of April.

By then, I had seen both the President and the Chairman of Toyota, and they had had their call on the Prime Minister. On 18 April, the papers carried the story that the French Government had lifted the ban on the Sunderland Nissans. Later that day, I signed Heads of Agreement with the Chairman of Toyota which gave us 80 per cent local content in future. Then I went down to the House to announce that the race for the site was won by Derby. The first prize was 3,000 jobs. We even won the race for the engine plant, and another 1,000 or so jobs, for Wales. It costs us nothing in subsidies from central Government, not one penny, but we did offer something that our competitors did not. A warm welcome. At all times we welcomed their investment as something that would benefit us, and not be a threat.

In the meantime we were keeping abreast of the developments between Rover and Honda, which were developing well. The Opportunity Japan campaign gathered momentum and was even taken up by MITI in Japan, where they ran an Opportunity Japan campaign to persuade Japanese stores to buy British! The time had come for another visit to Japan, and in May I returned.

Virgin Airlines were about to inaugurate their service to Tokyo, so I travelled out with Richard Branson, three bands, two fashion shows, and part of the band of the Royal Marines. It was not a restful journey! I did not feel much better when I was met by Sir John Whitehead, our Ambassador, off the flight. He showed me no mercy, for he immediately took me to a Cable & Wireless reception where I had to speak.

The visit went well, with three main gains. First, I could see an end to the dispute about seats on the Tokyo Stock Exchange. Secondly, our exports were running over 40 per cent up on last year. We were well on course to achieve the Opportunity Japan target. The main prize was the third.

I met with Mr Kume of Honda again. They were making good

314

progress with Rover, and had now firmly decided to enter into a share exchange with them. They were also considering adding an assembly plant to their engine plant in Swindon. I encouraged him as much as I could, and suggested that they announce their decision before the summer break.

On 13 July I was able to sign Heads of Agreement that again ensured 80 per cent local content. I went down to the House to announce the new assembly plant in Swindon as well as the new arrangement with Rover. I had long known when I was going to stand down from office, and it was with a great deal of pleasure that I could announce the final element of the grand design whilst I was still there. We had secured an investment of £1.8 billion from the three companies, creating some 16,000 to 17,000 jobs. Most of all, we could now see, at some time well before the end of the decade, that we would be making as many cars as we buy. We would save at least £10 billion each year on the balance of payments. Our component industry now had a chance to recover the ground lost over the last three decades. It was now up to them.

After we had privatised all the Department's nationalised industries (for Kenneth and Tony managed to sell off most of British Shipbuilders and close Sunderland), my workload diminished. In December, John MacGregor and I went on a very frustrating visit to Montreal for the GATT negotiations. We came back with nothing more useful than a cold. I told the Prime Minister at Christmas that I intended to spend much more time on the Trade side of the Department. I had been to Australia and New Zealand in the late summer of 1988, but apart from China and Japan I had not done much travelling. The Trade officials hardly needed any encouragement, and before long I found I had a very full schedule.

Early in February, I went to Davos to speak at the World Economic Forum. There I found myself promoted out of my class. I appeared at a plenary session with five prime ministers of the Community and the Chancellor of Austria. All were socialist, and all spoke in favour of the latest craze, the proposed Social Charter, which would bring back many of the excesses that we had known in the seventies. When it came to my turn I had some fun. I threw away my speech, and said that since I found myself here in the company of so many prime ministers I would promote myself to Prime Minister. I would take the sixth largest country in the Community – the unemployed. 'Today,' I said, 'the unemployed were increasing in every country, save the UK. Yet the policies they were advocating would increase it further.' I really enjoyed myself, but I suspect that they did not. I also said that . . .

315

'we were considered the bad Europeans. Yet look at the record. Of all the decisions of the European Court at the middle of last year we were in arrears with two, and they have now been put right. France was in arrears with five, Germany with nine and Italy – with twenty-eight.'

At that a laugh went up from most of the thousand people listening to us, but a definite hiss from the Italian section. Still, it was in good fun, even if there was a serious message. I was invited back for the following year.

The Soviet Trade Minister, Mr Kamentsev, came to London for a visit. I took to him straight away. He had spent much of his life at Murmansk in the fishing industry, and was hard working and active. He was instrumental in getting us a substantial contract for a UK food processing company on his return. I said that I might go to Moscow.

In February we went to India for the first time. We were received very well by Dinesh Singh, my opposite number, in Delhi. I was due to have a meeting with Rajhiv Gandhi and the High Commission and I went along to his offices. We were stopped at a barrier and asked to leave our car, walk through, and then travel the last hundred yards in an electric car. I had never seen security so tight anywhere in the world. I had a long and interesting talk with Rajiv Gandhi. We went down to Bombay, just missing a gigantic demonstration outside our offices, protesting about Salman Rushdie's book.

We were the largest investors in India but the opportunities for increasing trade were fairly limited. I tried very hard to encourage them to relax their inward investment policy. India had practised a closed economy for many years, and I believe that they paid a high price for it. They were still manufacturing a 1954 Morris Oxford in great quantities. It might be suitable for Indian conditions, but it certainly had no export potential. On the way back we stopped at Delhi again. On the last night, Dinesh Singh invited Lita and I for dinner. We spent a delightful evening; at one point I looked around the table. All the other guests were either maharajahs or maharanees or princes or princesses or their children. All were ministers in a socialist government.

To while away the long hours of travel, I started to ponder on what I would like to do next. I thought that my time was now up at DTI. It had become more and more a Department of Regulation, and that was not for me. There were no more industries to privatise, the new structure would soon be there, telecommunications were

OPPORTUNITIES

falling into place and there was little left for me to do. The employment scene was now under control and there was nothing for me there. The papers talked of me going to Defence, but I had not even done National Service. I knew nothing of the forces. I stopped thinking about the future.

When we came back to London I found that Mr Gorbachev was coming to London, and that Mr Kamentsev was coming back with him. I had not seen President Gorbachev since his first visit to London, in my first months in Cabinet. I would have a great deal to do during his visit, as was always the case with State trading nations. President Bush would follow him on a visit, and I would not be invited to a single function.

I took Mr Gorbachev up to the Case Communications plant and then back to a function I hosted at Lancaster House for him to meet a selected number of our businessmen. I introduced him and he then spoke for a few minutes and answered questions. During his speech, he said that twenty years before the shops were full but the people had no money. Today they all have money but the shops were empty. He greatly impressed all at the reception with his frankness. I signed some further contracts with Mr Kamentsev, and arranged to go to Moscow in July on a return visit. We all went up to Heathrow to see the Gorbachevs off. I was praying that the flight would not be late and as soon as he left, luckily on time, I dashed round the airport and joined my party for another visit to China.

This was to be my fifth visit to China. It had changed greatly in the four years since my first visit. This time we arrived on a Saturday afternoon. My first official function was at 8.00 a.m. on Sunday morning on the first tee of Beijing International Golf Club, in the valley of the Ming tombs. I was due to play with Zheng Tuobin, who in the last two and a half years had become a keen golfer. He played off a handicap of twenty, and later I was told that he claimed that he had played over 250 rounds of golf in that period. I think that in the last three years I had been lucky to play 6!

The visit went well, and we travelled extensively around China. On one occasion we were due to visit Yue Yang, where GEC had a power station contract. We were told that it was an eight-hour drive there, two hours at the power station, and then an eight-hour drive back to fit in our schedule. At that point I rebelled and in the end they told us that they could put an extra coach on a train that would leave at 10 o'clock at night and get there in under three hours. We had already spent the whole of that day travelling, but I agreed.

The train was, of course, rather late, and the journey took much longer than forecast. Approaching 4 o'clock in the morning, we were dozing in our carriage when we arrived at our destination. John Cooke, one of my senior civil servants, was with me, and we quickly woke ourselves up and climbed down from the train.

There drawn up on the platform was the Mayor, the Deputy Mayor, the head of the Planning Commission, and about twenty local dignitaries, television cameras and lights and a number of reporters. At 3.45 in the morning!

After I had greeted everybody, given a short statement to both television and newspapers, I was taken to my hotel. I thanked everybody for their hospitality and wearily started to go to bed. There was a knock on the door and a young girl came in with some tea. I thanked her and she left. A minute or two later, there was another knock and another girl entered bearing some snacks. I thanked her and she left. A moment or two later there was another knock. I looked at my watch and realised that we had to get up in two hours. I do not believe that whoever was outside the door understood English, but they certainly understood my meaning. I was disturbed no longer.

We came out through Canton and Hong Kong. Whilst we were in China, Hu Yabang had died and the first demonstrations started in Tiananmen Square. But no one could have foreseen the consequences. We flew back on the overnight flight from Hong Kong.

As the plane took off, the thought occurred to me that perhaps my job had been done and I should step down. I remembered Alan Clark, at a recent ministers' lunch, arguing that all political careers end in tears. I had to leave at that point for our Lords front bench meeting, but I remembered thinking 'that must not happen to me.' Then again, one of my civil servants, who had been with me from the early days in Cabinet, had said to me just recently that my job was done. 'Enterprise has become a bore,' was his comment. I laughed at him at the time, but now I was not too sure.

I settled down to sleep. By the time I was awake and the plane had landed, my mind was made up. I was just 57. There were plenty of years in me for at least one more challenge. I would have to go into purdah for a year or so after DTI, but if I stood down this summer, it would be best for the Prime Minister and for me.

I had another visit to Japan, an excellent but short visit to Kuwait, and a visit to the Soviet Union still to make, when I ran into real troubles.

The MMC had produced a report on beer. They showed that there was a monopoly caused by the vertical nature of the brewers' ownership of pubs. They had spent two and a half years on the report; my officials offered no further advice to me and I published the report saying that I was 'minded' to implement it. That was my first mistake. The popular press and the television featured it heavily.

A few days later John Elliot, of Elders, came to see me. He had bought Courage a year or two before. He told me that the report was flawed. Brewers would either sell the breweries or the pubs. The end result, he forecast, would be an increase in foreign beer. I listened to what I took to be special pleading, but I felt uneasy nevertheless.

Nothing happened for a few weeks, save the brewers started a campaign with posters and newspapers adverts. It rumbled on in the press, with Francis Maude having a few low-level meetings with the brewers. One day at our ministers' lunch, Eric Forth started to tell me about the strength of feeling around the Commons. He told me that he had never encountered such a uniformly hostile reaction to a government proposal. He told me to take it very seriously indeed, and with memories of Barlow Clowes, I did. I then found that I was in trouble in the Lords. A debate was put down where I found that every other speaker was hostile. Even a bishop!

I ran into more trouble with the backbench committee and again with the 1922 Committee. Too late I realised what had happened. It was nothing to do with public opinion, which was uniformly for the proposals. It had nothing to do with the merits, which were rarely discussed. It had everything to do with the brewers' support for constituency associations up and down the land. Eventually I had a meeting with the Chief Whips of both the Lords and the Commons. I was told quite firmly that they could not get my proposals through either House. I had to drop them.

For a moment or two, I harboured the unworthy thought that I should leave the solution to my successor. Then my conscience reasserted itself. I dropped the proposals, and suggested a compromise that the big brewers jumped at. They then realised the full implications, but by then it was too late. Within days the brewers put up the price of beer. No wonder they were not exactly popular with the public, but they need not have minded, for the public blamed me for the price increase. I had more unfavourable mail on this one issue than in my entire time in public life. It was not my happiest moment.

But before then I had my last official visit. We flew to Leningrad, Kiev and Moscow. Wherever we went, the first visit was to the Memorial that marked the losses of the last war. The cemetery in Leningrad that contains the nearly half million dead of the siege is an awesome and chilling place. Babi Yar, in Kiev, is remarkable for the absence of any religious description of the victims. They were not so fortunate in real life.

The visit went well, and our relations prospered. There was a great need for further investment, particularly in the food processing industries. On the Thursday night, Mr Kamentsev gave our party dinner in the Kremlin. I had got to know him quite well by now – after all this was our third series of visits in five months. When I came to reply I said, 'I, who have been neither elected nor confirmed, salute you.' We all thought it a great joke. Not the next day.

I had a series of meetings in Moscow culminating in a lunch we were giving for Mr Kamentsev and our businessmen in the Embassy. When I arrived there I was told that he was delayed, then would not be able to come. Our Ambassador, Sir Rodric Braithwaite took me aside. Kamentsev had failed to get a sufficient majority for his confirmation.

The next morning *Pravda* referred to the incident and merely said that the vote had been adjourned until the Monday. The vote on Friday had become a non-event. Alas, on the Monday he lost by a greater margin and had to retire.

I, in common with other ministers visiting the Soviet Union, had met with refuseniks in Kiev and Moscow. I wanted to go one step further, and visit the synagogue on the Saturday morning. My hosts promised every inducement not to by way of tours of the Kremlin. We accepted, but at 11.00 a.m. dropped out of the tours for an hour and went to the synagogue. The Braithwaites asked if they could accompany us. On the way out of the synagogue, a young man stopped me. In English, he asked me who I was. 'Just a Jew,' I said. 'No,' he insisted, 'you must be someone important.' 'I am not important,' I replied, 'but I am in the British Cabinet.'

'Ah,' he said, 'that accounts for it. There haven't been as many KGB at service for years!'

I arrived home and the next day I went to Chequers to tell the Prime Minister of my decision. She understood at once. I think that we both realised that I had reached the end of the help that I could give her in Cabinet. After all, I had come for just two years over ten years before.

Within a week or two the story had leaked out, and it became common knowledge that I was going back to private life. My last day was Monday 24 July. I knew that all my ministers were set. My last appointment was at 5 o'clock at Admiralty House. One of the most pleasant and prestigious chores of my job was to stand in on occasion for the presentation of honorary awards. On this occasion Anton Poot, the Chairman of Philips, was receiving an honorary CBE. The form is that all the people assemble, I wait outside, and on the hour I enter. All there rise, for at that moment I personate the Queen. The citation is then read out and I present the medal. I do not pin it on, merely present it. All went according to plan.

At 5.12 p.m. on Monday 24 July 1989, I ceased to personate the Queen. At 5.15 p.m., I ceased to be Secretary of State for Trade and Industry. The adventure was over.

Chapter 21
EPILOGUE

It is now nearly a year since I stood down from office. When I read what I have written, I find it curiously one-dimensional. Hardly mentioned are many of the stirring events of the decade – the Miners' Strike, the Falklands war, and many others. They passed me by, and are not for me to record. This is clearly not a history of the decade. Nor is it the tale of how I spent all my time. That would be of no interest to the general reader; but for the record I did spend many hundreds of hours over the years, in the Lords, either on my feet answering questions on subjects as a five-minute expert, opening or winding up debates, or just interminable hours in committee. It was not all boredom, for there were moments of pure farce.

On one occasion I was down to open an economic debate. I thought that this was an occasion of major importance, one on which the reputation of the Government could be made or lost, but I suspect that I was mistaken, for I have long ago forgotten both the occasion and the subject. I found my speech in my box the night before. It was wet and wimpish and I rejected it out of hand. It was now nearly midnight and there was nothing for it but to write a new one. I turned on my machine and finished wearily at four in the morning. The following day the speech went around the Department to ensure that the facts were correct and the policy in line with my previous decisions. Lunchtime came and all the comments were not in. I had a rushed sandwich, approved the final draft, and I went over to the House for questions with the speech to follow.

Then began the nightmare that we all dreaded. The third question had started and my speech had not turned up. I looked vainly and furiously at the box but none of the officials were mine and they looked blankly back at me. I hissed to my colleagues, 'Drag out the answers,' and they responded magnificently. My Whip found me an earlier draft, and I tried vainly to remember all the alterations. The fourth question came, was dragged out but eventually died. There was no further delaying for the Debate was called and with it me. Out of the corner of my eye I saw my Whip rushing to me with a document. I stood up and said, 'My Lords, the subject of our debate this afternoon. . . .' and reached over and smoothly took the proferred speech and turned to the first paragraph. Luckily for me it was the speech and the pages were in order!

More useful, I suspect, were the hours I spent just walking through the lobbies. Early on I discovered my real value. Once, within a few days of arriving, I dashed in to vote with only a few seconds to spare. I saw Bertie Denham, our Chief Whip. 'Which way do I go?' I cried out to Bertie. 'That way to resign,' was his answer pointing to the Opposition lobby. I took the hint!

Unrecorded are the literally hundreds of party functions, lunches, dinners or just receptions which so filled my life over these years. Government and politics are entwined, and I was no more insulated from it than my other colleagues. Indeed, having no constituency to guard, I found that my conscience persuaded me to accept more invitations than the average.

What is also left out is Europe. There are few more important changes to come in our lifetimes, and in the lives of our children. Here I was a mere foot-soldier. I took part in some skirmishes, assisted Kenneth Clarke and Francis Maude in great endeavours to keep the cause of enterprise in Europe alive. There has developed a fashion among our commentators in the press and television to assume that we are feet-dragging in Europe, that the Germans and the French are automatically right and Margaret Thatcher and the British Government are insular and automatically wrong. Partly it is a matter of style. The Latins, and here Chancellor Kohl is a Latin, have a habit of keeping their gaze fixed firmly on the horizon and building castles in the air. That is why President Mitterrand could make a great speech announcing the coming of the United States of Europe with France in the vanguard, and the next day block two thousand Sunderland Nissan cars. That was simply below the horizon. The British, on the other hand, keep their gaze firmly on their feet and look carefully where they are going. They never gaze up at the horizon. We look into every aspect of every piece of legislation before it is agreed – and then put it into effect even if we disagree with it. There are others in Europe that agree everything and do nothing. Somehow we need to have more of a Latin outlook, and they certainly need more of ours.

Many are the bids and battles that remain unrecorded. The Minorco bid for Consgold, and the ultimate Hanson victory and many, many more. The battles fought and won for the new tank, the new pavilion at Expo '92, the battle fought and drawn for the new broadcasting regime, the battles lost without number. What general in his dotage recounts days of disaster? What I have tried to do is to give a flavour of what the decisions and the difficulties are all about. To feel the width.

Some of my errors came back to haunt me whilst I was still in office. One, that in retrospect pleased me greatly, came about in a curious way. In early November 1988, Neil Thornton, my then Private Secretary, came in to see me with a peculiarly diffident air.

'Excuse me, Secretary of State,' he said, in the manner which I had long ago learned was regarded within the service as the approved manner to impart bad news to your master, 'Excuse me, Secretary of State, but I have had the Treasury on the telephone.' 'Well,' I said sharply, knowing that few calls were ever really welcome from the Treasury. He continued unperturbed, 'They would like to know whether you would be prepared to allow the commitment for matching funds for the Prince's Youth Business Trust to be capped at £40 million.'

For the moment I wondered what on earth that had to do with me. Then I remembered. If the capacity to blush was still with me, I would have. It went back some years, when Sir David Rowe-Ham was the Lord Mayor of London and I was still Employment Secretary. I wanted to help the Prince's Youth Business Trust and had met with the Trustees once or twice in my office. The PYBT did sterling work, helping young people, often in the inner cities, to start their own business through a series of loans and grants. I offered to match everything raised in their Appeal up to £3 million. David Rowe-Ham had adopted PYBT as his Charity during his mayoral year and had given a lunch at the Mansion House. After he had spoken I was asked to say a few words, and in a fairly impromptu, lighthearted way, I said, 'Don't worry, Lord Mayor, whatever you raise we will double,' meaning my commitment up to £3 million. I had left promptly to go to the House.

When I returned to my office an hour or two later there was a letter waiting for me from the Lord Mayor. It merely thanked me for my offer to double all that they raised. I smiled, thought it a bit crafty, and got on to other matters. I heard no more, for the appeal faded. Now they had actively relaunched the appeal and were seeking £40 million to celebrate the Prince of Wales' 40th birthday! They expected a matching £40 million from Government. Thanks to my loosely worded reply they were given it! It certainly taught me to be more than careful how I express myself, but I was delighted with the outcome.

Another row developed when the National Audit Office reported

325

on the sale of Rover. They decided, with a magnificent display of hindsight, that it was worth more than it was sold for, despite the fact that I had pushed British Aerospace to the very brink. It was as nothing to the Auditor General that the House had firmly instructed me not to sell to Ford, even if they, or anyone else, had come forward. It was of no account to him that a sale to another car manufacturer would have put in jeopardy the 200,000 jobs bound up in Rover. If my job was simply to get the highest price, then I could have closed the business down and sold off the assets. That might have pleased the National Audit Office but it would not do for me. I wanted to re-establish the car industry in Britain.

Gordon Brown, the Shadow Trade & Industry spokesman, in a shameless display of sanctimonious indignation, accused me of all manner of tax and other inducements. All he succeeded in doing, and I write this before I have heard what Leon Brittan will do, will probably ensure that BAe will have to repay some money to the Government. A strange way to help the British car industry, but Mr Brown has a great deal to learn. At least he will have pleased the officials in the European Commission, who were always convinced that I got too good a deal out of Peter Sutherland, and could not wait to get their own back. From what has been leaking from Brussels over the last few weeks, they will succeed.

The reality is quite different. Respectable academic research has now woken up to the fact that by the end of the decade the car producing nations of Europe will be Germany and the United Kingdom. From all recent developments, I believe that we could well be up to 2.75 million cars a year, and apart from making all the cars we buy, we could be net exporters of over 500,000! The only independent British car company will be – Rover. In years to come, it will be seen that we laid the foundations for the rebirth of the UK manufacturing industry during the eighties.

I re-read Trollope's *The Prime Minister* last summer. The Duke of Omnium, when Prime Minister, was sorely troubled by the brewers. I take comfort that I was merely the latest in a distinguished line, although I take even greater comfort from the Chairman of Grand Metropolitan, Alan Shepherd, who said, at his last Annual General Meeting that 'David Young has caused more change in the brewing industry than any politician for a hundred years.' The Duke will rest easy after that.

Now the concerns of the nineties now appear so different from the seventies. That is the measure of our success. The need for enterprise, for small firms, for self employment, the simple acceptance of the necessity to create wealth before we spend it, has become

generally accepted. The battle against unemployment now has a
curiously dated air, as if, after forty-four consecutive months of
decline to one of the lowest rates in Europe, it is no longer of
importance. It is, for we forget it at our peril.

The beliefs that motivated Margaret Thatcher and Keith Joseph
in the Centre for Policy Studies in the mid-seventies have done
much more than infect the British Government. I have spent time in
Eastern Europe during the last few months. There the words
'Margaret Thatcher' and 'Privatisation' dominate all conversation.
The need for a market economy, the retreat from socialism and the
command economy, is complete. I recall that it took Mohammed
thirty years to dominate most of the then known world. It seems to
have taken us a mere dozen!

But there are some aspects of my exciting decade worth recording. Firstly, how little company from outside Government I had. I
came into Government because I simply did not know that it was
not done! Many of my American friends would spend time in
academia, then commerce and then Government. I assumed that it
was natural for us. It is not.

I can think of a few from the world of business who came into
Government. They came as part time civil servants. Lord Rayner
and Sir Jeffrey Sterling are amongst distinguished businessmen
who have given generously of their time. Sir Bryan Nicholson, my
successor at the MSC and now the Chairman of the Post Office,
came in on a full time basis. One or two others have come in to head
agencies for a greater or lesser period. Some civil servants go out on
secondment for a year or two to industry. One of my former Private
Secretaries is out for two years and will soon be back. They gain
valuable experience. Then it is rarely used. I remember meeting, in
the early eighties, an Assistant Secretary who had just returned
from spending two years with 3i's, gaining valuable experience on
funding small firms. He would have been invaluable in the Small
Firms division in the old Department of Industry. Instead he
returned to his former Department, not Industry, to a job light
years away from his new-found knowledge and experience.

There are a few others. The numbers are slowly increasing. I
helped to launch a scheme called The Bridge (and paid for the
advertising costs out of my budget!) that encourages short term
secondment between the private and public sectors across all of
Whitehall. I hope it prospers. But there is not the two-way traffic that
exists in France or the United States between commerce and industry
on the one hand and the Civil Service on the other. Where are the very
best of civil servants who leave and go into industry in their early

forties, as the French do as a matter of course? How many in our great companies have the faintest idea how Government really works? One or two, not more. How many in the Civil Service come in from academia? Hardly any. Some have left completely, dissatisfied with career prospects. Some, from the old CPRS, are today distinguished Heads of Colleges. There are very few late entrants into the Civil Service, and no way of coming in for a few years as part of a normal career development. We practise a doctrine of separation of experience that appears absolute. Then we wonder why it is that Government has an imperfect understanding of the needs of commerce and industry – or even an enterprise society.

But that two-way traffic appears a veritable flood compared to the political arena. I passed over that great divide in September 1984, for I was the first since the forties to go overnight from the Civil Service into the Cabinet. Arthur Cockfield (Lord Cockfield), another outsider, had just left, on his way to the Commission in Brussels. Only about once a decade does someone come from outside into Cabinet. There are others, like Lord Bellwin, who came in as a non-Cabinet Minister from a distinguished career in local government. But how very few we are!

The French, the Americans, many of the other nations in Europe take a different view. There, a Minister cannot be a member of their legislative assembly. If they are, then they have to resign before taking up their post. The Cabinet, all Ministers, are open to all members of society. They have a full choice of all the talents. We have a closed shop. We say, that as a general rule, all our ministers, irrespective of party, must come from a small sample of some 600 who get elected to the Commons. They all have to serve a long apprenticeship, either as lobby fodder or as a Whip, or both, before they become Junior Ministers. By the time they are given charge of a department they have become part of a world apart. It does not help the understanding of all the processes of society. It is little wonder that all too many ministers for decades past have believed that they can communicate Government policy merely by making a speech in the House.

Yet there are great obstacles to more coming in from outside, even if they come in, like me, through the Lords. Within our House there is a class system, not obvious to the eye, but crucial in practice. Any peer who was once a member of the Commons, even in decades past, has the full run of all the facilities of the Commons, the bars, the tea and smoking rooms, where all the members congregate. You can spend all day, every day there, if you like. Even more, you can eat there, or buy or be bought the occasional drink. You have the chance to be seen, to mingle, to be approachable. If, like me, you were never in the Commons, then all that is denied. It is curious that lobby journalists, the press, should have full access to areas of the Commons where some Cabinet ministers cannot go.

Why is this so important? It is bad enough to come in from the outside, to take a job that is thought to belong to the preserve of the Commons. It is worse to be catapulted there overnight, even if it did take me five years. But these are not insurmountable problems, and with goodwill can be overcome, at least initially. Where the problem arises is with the steady erosion of goodwill over time caused by remoteness. I have little doubt that when problems, arise as arise they will, the mere fact that you cannot meet the cause of your difficulty, you cannot beard your colleague in the lobby one evening, begins to raise the suspicions of remoteness. What, they think to themselves, can he know of problems in the ivory fastness of the Lords?

It even applies to the lobby. I would meet the members of the lobby at party conferences and at the occasional lunch. They are to a man (or woman) strangers. Never are they seen at the Lords, which in any event are covered by different correspondents. When they have a story, and the Commons late at night is a fertile ground for stories, they cannot come up to me and get an immediate denial, or a different slant. Besides, there are some stories too good for checking. So in it goes, and another cause for friction arises.

I have some suggestions, offered with little optimism of acceptance, for what closed shop abolishes itself voluntarily? My suggestions are offered in increasing order of difficulty and utility.

First, just allow Lords ministers to have the run of the Commons, if only whilst they are ministers. We could extend this to the Opposition Front Bench, to whom exactly the same considerations apply. I raised this once when invited down to our Whips in the Commons for a late night drink in their room. All agreed that it was nonsense, but few thought that anything would change. I, for one, might have been more aware of impending storms in Barlow Clowes or with the brewers, had this been possible. It would involve no constitutional reform, cost no money, require only a modicum of change, yet produce real dividends over the years.

Next, go one further. Why not allow all Lords ministers to appear in the Commons at First Order Questions? This is the occasion, once every three weeks or so, when the entire department appears to answer questions about the workings of their department. Then the Lords ministers would be able to feel part of the team, and the House would feel that they were part of the Department. That would involve a constitutional change that presumably would require legislation. On the other hand, it is not so outrageous. I appeared many times over the last few years to answer questions from our own and opposition members of the Commons before different Commons select committees. The principle is already broken – why not the practice?

Both those changes would be worthwhile, yet something more is required if there is to be a real sea-change in practice. I offer my last suggestion secure in the knowledge that it will be rejected by all in the Commons. Nevertheless, it would allow a real chance to bring in, for short periods, outsiders to play a part in the political process and then depart.

It is a simple suggestion. Allow the Prime Minister of the day the right to bring in one or two unelected outsiders into Cabinet who would be allowed full membership of the Commons during their period of office. They might be members of the Lords as a convenient constitutional peg, but they would operate in the Commons. It would offer the chance of a radical improvement in the political process without ending democracy in the country at large.

Now that my time in the mainstream of political life in the country is over, do I have any regrets? Yes, but only as a result of my own inadequacies. I would have liked to have seen vocational and technical education more firmly reestablished in the country. That might well come, with over two million pupils taking TVEI courses this year alone, but we really cannot afford to wait.

Will Europe be Bonapartist and restrictive, or will it be entrepreneurial and open? That question is yet to be decided, and requires a far more thoughtful answer than the passionate cohorts of pro-Europeans ever give. There are many lessons that we have learned painfully during the last decade that have yet to be learned by many of our partners in Europe. We can learn much from them. What we have to do is respect our differences of culture, not seek to cover them up. What the Community will not be, is unified, although we might surprise ourselves by the extent of monetary union that we will come to embrace. I hope that we will be well on the way to Margaret Thatcher's concept at Bruges of a Europe reaching from Lisbon to Warsaw.

It was a great adventure. I embarked upon it in the spirit of giving something back, but when all is said and done, I gained greatly from the experience. I made many, many friends in the Civil Service, friends whom the conventions will not allow me to credit as I would wish in my narrative. I made many, many friends in the political world and I suspect, since I am but human, left behind some who were not entirely sad to see me go. Such is life.

Out there, just over the horizon, is the next great adventure. During my last days in office I was asked when was my best time. 'That's easy,' I replied, 'Next year.'

Graffham
April 1990

Index

Ackland, Anthony 130
Aitken, Maxwell (Lord Beaverbrook) 241, 243
Aitkin, Jonathan 82
Alison, Michael 92, 98, 104, 208
Alliance, David 311
Anderson, Bruce 160
Archer, Jeffrey 160-1, 230
Armstrong, Sir Robert 118, 120, 123, 244
Atkins, Robert 133-4, 146, 149, 183, 208, 238, 261
Attenborough, David 203

Baker, Ken (TUC) 79
Baker, Kenneth 35, 157, 195, 199, 211, 215-16
    at Department of Industry 49-50, 56, 58, 60, 64, 104
Baldry, Tony 193
Barber, Martin 30-1
Baring Brothers 290-1, 294
Barlow Clowes failure 272-4, 276, 278-9, 328
Barlow, Sir William 40
Barnes, Sir Kenneth 68
Barnett, Lord 182-3
Beckett, Terry 92
Bell, Catherine 299
Bell, Margaret 39, 41-2, 72-3, 118, 138-9, 240
Bell, Tim 99-100, 143, 191, 200, 209-10, 214-29, 234, 248
Bellwin, Lord 327
Benn, Tony 239
Berrill, Sir Kenneth 266
Berwin, Stanley 11
Beveridge, John QC 276-7, 280
Beveridge, Lord 127-9
Bevin, Ernest 153
Bevins, Anthony 254
Biffen, John 142

Birt, John 213
Blackwell, Norman 199, 212-13, 218, 227, 229
Blair, Tony 260, 271
Blunkett, David 87, 206
Boaden, Roger 196
Bonfield, Peter 263
Borrie, Sir Gordon 267, 271-7, 280-1
Bottomley, Peter 154
Bowe, Collette 41, 189
Braithwaite, Sir Roderick 320
Branson, Richard 262, 314
Braude, Max 22-3
brewers/beer controversy 318-19, 328, 329
British Aerospace, privatisation of 45
British Airways/British Caledonian merger 267-9
British Steel Corporation 42-4, 47, 54-5, 64-6, 303-4
    see also privatisation
British Telecom, privatisation of 51-2, 57
Brittan, Leon 86, 93, 131-2, 165-70, 325
Britto, Keith 209, 218-19
Broakes, Nigel 120, 132
Brown, Gordon 325
Bruce, Brendan 261
Bruce, Malcolm 227
Brunel, I.K. 26
Bush, George and Barbara 189
Butcher, John 238, 261
Butler, Rab 252
Butler, Robin 117

Cable & Wireless privatisation 45, 51-2, 60, 70
Callaghan, James 32, 115
Carey, Sir Peter 36-8, 64, 67-8, 72
car industry 45, 176, 285-302, 310-15, 325-6
Carlsberg, Bryan 307-10
Carnegy, Elizabeth 76, 79, 86, 98, 125

Carr, Peter 142
Carrington, Lord 252, 255
Cazalet, Peter 311
Chairmanship controversy (Conservative Party) 251–7
Chalker, Lynda 263
Channon, Paul 202, 254
Chope, Chris 219
Churchill, Winston 153
Clark, Alan 154–5, 238, 248–9, 265, 288, 318
Clarke, Kenneth 151, 155, 157, 164, 170, 186, 189, 211, 227, 278
  at Department of Trade and Industry 235, 237–43, 247, 300–4, 315, 323
Cochlin, Mike 299
Cockfield, Arthur 117–19, 297, 327
Cole, John 214
Cooke, John 318
Cotton, Bill 230

Dawe, Roger 193, 195, 234
Day, Graham 286–95, 301, 311
Day, Robin 130–1, 230
Dearing, Ron 56
Delors, Jacques 263, 297–8
Denham, Lord 121, 323
deregulation 141–4, 146–50
  see also privatisation
Dewar, David 260
Dimbleby, Jonathan 178, 230
Dobbs, Michael 215, 217
Dodds, Norman 118, 169, 203, 224
Donovan, Terry 227
Du Cann, Sir Edward 280–1, 284
Dworkin, Paul 184, 196

East, Barry 15, 20
Eccles, Jack 53, 69
Edwardes, Michael 56, 285–6
Edwards, Nicholas 193
Egan, Sir John 287–8
Egan, Richard 262
Elkin, Sonia 76, 98
Elliott, John 319
employment creation 153–90, 195
  'Action for Jobs' 175–82, 185, 187–9, 193, 195, 251–2
  Job Clubs 155, 159, 170, 174, 198
  Jobstart 163–5, 170–2
  New Workers Scheme 174
  Restart 174–5, 182–7, 191, 198
    see also Manpower Services Commission; unemployment
English, Sir David 263

English Industrial Estates Corporation 44–5, 50, 53
Enterprise Initiative (DTI) 255, 257–62

Fayed (El) brothers 274–8, 289, 306
Feldman, Sir Basil 161
Financial Services Act 265–6
Foot, Michael 17, 101
Forte, Charles 262
Forte, Rocco 311
Forth, Eric 309–10, 319
Fowler, Norman 127–8, 195, 212–13, 239–40, 252
Friend, Bernard 292, 298
Frost, David 226

Gaddafi, Colonel 176
Gandhi, Rajiv 316
Giordano, Dick 133, 311
Godfrey, Jeremy 291, 299
Golding, John 81–2
Goodman, Eleanor 117
Goodman, Geoffrey 68
Goodman, Pat 275–6
Gorbachev, Mikhail 131–2, 317
Gowrie, Grey 117, 119, 121, 141, 146
Grade, Michael 203, 208
Graham, Ken 78, 98, 101, 103
Great Universal Stores 9–12, 63–4
Green, Dr Malcolm 98
Green, Michael 181, 184, 192
Greenwood, Tony 30
Greig, Gordon 251
Griffiths, Brian 203
Grimond, Joe 193

Hahn, Dr 288, 295
Hailsham, Lord 157
Hall, John 198
Hamilton, Sir James 60
Hancock, David 112–13, 118
Hanna, Vincent 228
Hannay, Sir David 300–2
Harris, Robin 194, 203–4
Harrison, Terry 311
Hart, David 208
Hastings, Max 294
Hattersley, Roy 186
Hauge, Gabe 19–20
Havers, Sir Michael 241
Hayes, Sir Brian 235–42, 244, 249, 257–8, 285, 289–90
Heath, Edward 15, 28, 76
Helmore, Roy 76, 79

Heseltine, Michael 50-1, 59, 167-70, 219, 270-1
Hill, Jonathan 227, 229
Hilton, Brian 241
Hinton, Graham 261
Hirst, Gerry 13
Hobday, Peter 263
Hodge, John 153
Holland, Geoffrey 67, 69, 73, 75, 78-81, 90, 94, 158, 181, 195
Horden, Sir Peter 278
Hosker, Gerald 276
Hoskyns, John 58, 263
House of Fraser takeover 274-81, 306
Howard, George 105
Howe, Elspeth 131-2
Howe, Geoffrey 42, 65-6, 131-2, 145, 157, 161, 199-200, 205, 283
Howell, Ralph 127
Hurd, Douglas 117, 119, 199-200
Hu Yaobang 180

Ingham, Bernard 123, 134, 143, 147

James, Howell 143, 147-8, 166-7, 178-9, 205, 212-17, 221, 234, 247-8
Janner, Barnett 68-9
Janner, Greville 68-9, 196
Jay, Lord 307
Jay, Peter 91
Jay, Tony 226-7
Jefferson, George 56
Jenkin, Patrick 57-9, 64-5, 67-9, 71-2, 143, 240
Jenkins, Hugh 31, 45
Jenkins, Roy 203-4
Jones, John Harvey 262
Joseph, Dr Joe 183
Joseph, Keith 28-30, 32, 192, 253, 326
   at Department of Education 60-1, 89-90, 93-4, 109-10
   at Department of Industry 35-46, 51, 55-8, 285

Kahn, Hermann 1-2
Kamentsev, Minister 316-17, 320
Keith, Lord 284
Keys, Bill 78-9, 106
Khalifa, Shaikh Ali 282-3
King, John 133, 267-9
King, Tom 106, 109, 134, 143, 146, 149-50, 154, 161
Kinnock, Neil 94, 185, 209-10, 212, 220
Kohl, Chancellor Helmut 324
Kume, Mr 295, 314-15

Kuwait Investment Office and BP 270, 272, 281-3

Lamont, Norman 58, 134, 304-5
Lasko, Roger 84
Lavender, Gerry 55, 58
Lawson, Nigel 124, 161, 164, 173, 186, 199-200
   and 1987 election 209, 211, 214, 217
   and sale of Rover Group 290-3
Lawton, Alistair 98
Lee, John 202
Leigh Pemberton, Robin 266
Le Quesne, Sir Godfray QC 274, 276
Lewis, Leigh 119-20, 127, 138, 143, 155, 193
Leyard, Richard 218
Li, David 130, 229
Liesner, Hans 44, 280
Linguard, Robin 120, 122-3
Li Peng 136, 180
Livingstone, Ken 233
Lloyd Webber, Andrew 212
Longdon, Wilson 98-9
Lonrho and House of Fraser takeover 274-81, 283-4, 306
Loughead, Peter 242
Luff, Peter 248, 251, 257
Lygo, Ray 290-2, 298, 300
Lyons, Terence 76

McAlpine, Alistair 125, 207, 220, 223-5, 230, 253
MacGregor, Ian 54- 6, 64-6, 100, 120
MacGregor, John 53, 61, 84, 157, 164-5, 194-5, 315
MacLean, Andrea 280, 299
McLoughlin, Patrick 177-8
Macrae, Hamish 294
Makeham, Peter 234, 241
Mallinson, Mr 276
Manpower Services Commission (MSC) 56, 61, 66-116, 123-90, 195-6
   and colleges of further education 107-11
   Community Enterprise Programme/ Community Programme 76, 81, 87-8, 91, 100, 103-5, 109-12, 158, 174, 198
   Enterprise Allowance Scheme 83-4, 99-100, 111, 130, 161, 173-4, 198
   Information Technology Centres (ITECs) 104
   Loans Guarantee Scheme 174
   Skillcentres/Jobcentres 74, 85-6, 91, 105-7, 111, 193
   Technical and Vocational Educational

Initiative (TVEI) 89–97, 110, 329
  Youth Opportunities Programme (YOP)
    60, 66, 75, 85, 97, 99–102
  Youth Task Group 66–7, 75, 80–1
  Youth Training Scheme (YTS) 67, 80–1,
    84–113, 116, 123, 134–6, 141, 146,
    174–5, 195
  see also employment creation;
    unemployment
Manufacturers Hanover Trust 17, 19–20,
  32, 35
Marsh, Richard 15
Mathias, Peter 26
Maude, Francis 238, 261, 265, 273, 319, 323
Maxwell, Barbara 230
Meacher, Molly 194
Mirman, Sophie 262
Mitchell, David 40, 53
Mitterrand, François 312–14, 324
Mogg, John 304
Monkhouse, Bob 226
Monopolies and Mergers Commission 253,
  265–84, 318–19
Moody, Ken 73
Moorey, Adrian 68, 159–60, 167, 178–81,
  189, 236
Morrison, Peter 56, 66, 84, 101, 104–7, 124,
  196–7, 206
Moynihan, Colin 218
Müller, Anne 39
Mundella, A.J. 153
Murray, Len 76, 78

Naughtie, James 253
Newton, Tony 278, 304
Nicholson, Bryan 110, 158, 326
Norgrove, David 223, 233, 235
Numata, Mr 313–14

O'Brien, Sir Richard 61, 67–8, 71, 73, 77–8
Oldfield, Bruce 261–2
Olins, Wolff 258
Oliver, David QC 278
Oppenheim, Sally 214
Organisation for Rehabilitation through
  Training (ORT) 22–3, 29, 31–2, 56,
  60, 67, 90
Orr-Ewing, Hamish 98, 113

Pardoe, John 203
Parkinson, Cecil 101, 106
Payne, Norman 98
Pender, Tony 44, 50
Pike, Alan 112
Ponsonby, Lord 144

Poot, Anton 321
Powell, Charles 228
Prescott, John 158, 184–7, 205, 207, 217,
  227, 233
Price, David 88
Prince's Youth Business Trust 324–5
Prior, Jim 46, 56, 63, 85, 117, 134, 154
privatisation 39–40, 45–6, 49, 61, 285, 303,
  307, 315, 326
  British Aerospace 45
  British Telecom 51–2, 57
  British Steel Corporation 303–6
  Cable & Wireless 45, 51–2, 60, 70
  Rover Group 176, 285–302, 325–6
  see also deregulation
Profumo, John 174
Puri, Nat 295

Quinlan, Michael 112–13, 151, 158, 203, 206
Quinton, John 84

Rae, Alex 53, 72–3, 82
Raison, Timothy 30
Rayner, Lord 156, 326
Reagan, Ronald 141, 166, 176
Reay, Peter 87
Redhead, Brian 236–7
Reece, Gordon 224–7
Regional Development Grant (RDG) 242–3,
  247, 249, 259–60
Ridley, Nicholas 124, 132, 146
Rifkind, Malcolm 170
Robin, Steve 209, 211–12, 223
Rodgers, Bill 213
Rolfe, Marianne Neville 242
Ronson, Gerald 256
Rosser, Sir Melvyn 76, 83
Rossi, Hugh 30
Rover Group privatisation 176, 285–302,
  325–6
Rowe-Ham, Sir David 324–5
Rowland, Tiny 275–7, 280–1, 283, 289, 306
Rowntree takeover 270–2

Saatchi & Saatchi 99, 220–7
Savile, Jimmy 194–5
Scanlon, Lord 71
Scargill, Arthur 100
Scholey, Sir David 263
Scholey, Sir Robert 303–4
Seifert, Col 16
Sharkey, John 215, 220–5, 227
Sharp, Eric 51, 133, 138, 238
Shephard, Giles 183
Shepherd, Alan 329

Sherbourne, Stephen 196, 203, 208–10, 219, 225, 228
Sherman, Alfred 30
Sinclair, Clive 50, 64
Sinclair, Jeremy 225
Singh, Dinesh 316
Single European Act (EC) 241–2, 251, 310
  marketing campaign 261–4, 297, 307
Smith, Cyril 101
Smith, John 203
Smith, Professor Roland 282, 289 302, 311
Snow, C.P. 28
Snow, Jon 230
Soames, Christopher 144
Soames, Sally 207
Social Charter (EC) 241, 315
Somerville, Julia 230
Sterling, Jeffrey 15–16, 29, 71, 236, 282, 301–2, 326
Stingl, Dr 108
Story, Professor 218
Stradling, Don 76
Strathclyde, Lord 178
Strathcona, Lord 46
Stubbs, John 120
Sugar, Alan 262
Sullivan, John 203
Sunley, John 283
Surr, Jeremy 87, 88
Sutherland, Peter 268–9, 296–302, 325

Takeshita, Prime Minister 310, 312
Tamura, Minister 311–12
Tarbuck, Jimmy 226
Taylor, Harry 19–20
Taylor, Robert 199
Tebbit, Margaret 124–5, 131
Tebbit, Norman 49, 56, 124–5, 131, 150, 182
  as Chairman of the Conservative Party 161, 164, 184–5, 195, 251–4, 260
  at Department of Employment 57–8, 61, 66–8, 80, 84, 87, 91–3, 98, 101–4, 154
  at Department of Trade and Industry 106, 124, 267
  and 1987 election 199–203, 210–13, 215, 221–9, 234
Teff, Sol 7
telecommunications 307–10, 316–17
Tennant, Anthony 311
Thatcher, Carol 208–10
Thatcher, Denis 200, 209–10, 215, 219
Thatcher, Margaret 28–9, 31–2, 65–6, 81, 133, 136, 192–3, 207, 262, 326
  in Cabinet 121, 124, 197

Thatcher, Margaret (contd)
  and deregulation 141–2
  and Lord Young 111–12, 115–17, 123, 131, 160–2, 167, 192, 195–8, 233–4, 257, 303, 320
  and 1987 election 207–31
  and Norman Tebitt 182, 191–2, 201
  and privatisation 65–6, 290–3, 297–8
  and Strategy Group 199–203
  and unemployment 93, 97, 100–1, 115, 122, 135–6, 148–51, 160, 181, 186–7, 239–40
  Westland 'affair' 169–70
Thomas, Harvey 160–1, 207
Thomas, Lord 125
Thomson, Sir Adam 92, 267–8
Thorton, Neil 276, 281, 324
Thwaites, Roy 76, 79, 86
Tien, Vice Premier 146
Tombs, Francis 311
tourism 143–4, 146–50
Town & City Properties Ltd 14–16, 20–1
Toy, Sam 260
trade missions
  China 130, 133–4, 136–9, 165–6, 255–6, 317–18
  India 316
  Japan 69–70; 'Opportunity Japan' 293, 295, 310–15, 318
  Russia 31 9–20
Trenchard, Lord 44, 49
Trippier, David 202
Tucker, Clive 195
Turnbull, George 313
Turner, John 195, 198, 202–3, 234
Twyman, Paul 143–4

unemployment 40, 53–4, 56, 59–61, 64, 67, 75, 91, 104, 108–9, 112–13, 141–3, 146–51, 156–90
  black economy 105–6, 158–9, 170–2
  long-term unemployed 75–6, 81, 84–8, 91, 104, 157–63, 170–5
  reversal of trend 185–7, 191, 194–6, 205, 239, 326
  youth 123, 130, 134–5, 146, 188
  see also employment creation; MSC

Vallence, Iain 307
Vere, David 116
Villers, Charles 43, 54

Wakeham, John 125, 199–202, 210–11, 220, 251, 253–4
Walker, David 266

Walker, Harold 101
Walker, Peter 243, 261
Walker, Tim 238
Wall, Christine 196
Walmsley, Jeffrey 36
Walsh, Arthur 311
Walters, Sir Dennis 281
Walters, Peter 243, 261
Weinstock, Arnold 133–4
West, David 113
Westland 'affair' 167, 169–71
Westwood, Barry 82
Wheatcroft, Anne 184, 196
Wheeler, John 208
Whitehead, Sir John 314
Whitelaw, Celia 199, 201
Whitelaw, William 118–19, 195, 199–202,
    216, 220, 251–5, 303
Wicks, Nigel 235
Wight, Robin 255
Williams, Shirley 17, 23–4, 101

Willis, Norman 196
Wolfson, David 31, 39, 58, 208, 222, 225,
    227
Wolfson, Isaac 9–11
Wolfson, Leonard and Ruth 9, 11–12, 122
Woolhouse, John 96–7
Worsthorne, Peregrine 199
Wright, Alan 82

Yankalovich (Young), Rehosh 3–5
Youens, Sir Peter 280
Young, Jimmy 233
Young, Lita 9, 17, 89, 201, 225–6, 235, 245
Young, Shirley 230
Young, Stuart 6, 8, 12, 14, 92, 117, 180–3,
    267
    and the BBC 91, 105, 122
Younger, George 170

Zhao Ziang 136, 141, 145–6, 255
Zheng Tuobin 317